"WELL WRITTEN AND THOROUGHLY RESEARCHED . . .

[*Ripcord*] evokes admiration for American and North Vietnamese infantry soldiers engaged in intense fighting and contempt for what passed for American higher military and political leadership. . . . This is powerful stuff. How did it happen? Why the thirty-year wait to get the whole story? . . . U.S. soldiers knew what to do. They fought and died. But American senior commanders were indecisive, even petty. They were torn between doing what was necessary to win the battle—commit more combat strength—and an awareness that a bloodbath like that on Hamburger Hill [a few miles away and a year earlier] was unacceptable in 1970. . . . This reviewer thinks Nolan got it right and tells it well."

—Dr. Henry G. Gole, Colonel, USA (Ret.)
A combat infantryman in Korea and Vietnam
U.S. Army War College Parameters

"Astoundingly, the battle at Ripcord went virtually unreported at the time; thus this book ranks not just as another saga of the war, but as a real and original contribution to military history."

—Donald Kirk
Author of *Tell It to the Dead*

"Gripping . . . Meticulously researched . . . Deliberately kept out of the news at the time . . . the battle for Ripcord is finally told here. It is well worth reading as a searing narrative of soldiers and small units in battle . . . and as a microcosm of America's last painful year in Vietnam."

—Lt. Gen. John H. Cushman, USA (Ret.)
U.S. Naval Institute Proceedings

Also by Keith W. Nolan
(published by Presidio Press)

INTO CAMBODIA
DEATH VALLEY
THE MAGNIFICENT BASTARDS

RIPCORD

SCREAMING EAGLES UNDER SIEGE, VIETNAM 1970

KEITH W. NOLAN

PRESIDIO PRESS

BALLANTINE BOOKS • NEW YORK

A Presidio Press Book
Published by The Random House Publishing Group

Published in the United States by Presidio Press, an imprint of The Random House Publishing Group, a division of Random House, Inc., New York, and simultaneously in Canada by Random House of Canada Limited, Toronto. Originally published by Presidio Press, an imprint of The Random House Publishing Group, a division of Random House, Inc., in 2000.

ISBN 978-0-89141-809-2

Map on page xv by Aegis Consulting Group

Printed in the United States of America

www.presidiopress.com

First Mass Market Edition: June 2003

For my wife, Kelly, and our daughter, Anna Britt

Contents

Glossary

AA antiaircraft fire
ADC assistant division commander
AIT advanced individual training
AK-47 standard communist 7.62mm automatic rifle; a version with a folding metal stock was known as an AK-50
AO area of operations
ARA aerial rocket artillery
Arc Light bombing mission by B-52 Stratofortresses
arty artillery
ARVN Army of the Republic of Vietnam
ASP ammunition supply point
blivet rubberized bag used for transporting and storing fuel and water
CA combat assault
C&C command-and-control helicopter
CAR15 shortened, all-metal version of the M16 5.56mm automatic rifle
C4 plastic explosives
CG commanding general
Chinook nickname for the CH-47 transport helicopter
CO commanding officer
Cobra nickname for the AH-1G helicopter gunship
CP command post
CS tear gas

DEROS date eligible for return from overseas
DISCOM Division Support Command
div arty division artillery
DMZ demilitarized zone
DOW died of wounds
EOD explosive ordnance disposal
E1 pay grade for recruit private
E2 pay grade for private
E3 pay grade for private first class
E4 pay grade for corporal or specialist fourth class
E5 pay grade for sergeant or specialist fifth class
E6 pay grade for staff sergeant or specialist sixth class
E7 pay grade for sergeant first class
E8 pay grade for first sergeant or master sergeant
E9 pay grade for sergeant major or command sergeant major
FA field artillery
FAC forward air controller
FDC fire direction center
FO forward observer
FSB fire-support base
G1 personnel officer at division or corps level
G2 intelligence officer at division or corps level
G3 operations officer at division or corps level
G4 logistics officer at division or corps level
HE high explosive
HHC Headquarters & Headquarters Company
Huey nickname for the UH-1 helicopter
Intruder nickname for the A-4 all-weather jet fighter-bomber
JP4 aviation fuel
KIA killed in action
klick kilometer
LAW light antitank weapon
LNO liaison officer
LOH light observation helicopter
LP listening post
LRRP long-range reconnaissance patrol
LZ landing zone
MA mechanical ambush

MACV Military Assistance Command Vietnam
MG machine gun
MIA missing in action
M16 standard U.S. 5.56mm automatic rifle
M60 standard U.S. 7.62mm light machine gun
M79 standard U.S. 40mm grenade launcher
M203 M16 rifle modified with 40mm grenade launcher under barrel
NCO noncommissioned officer (pay grades E4 to E9)
NDP night defensive position
NVA North Vietnamese Army
OCS Officer Candidate School at Fort Benning, Georgia
OP observation post
ops operations
Phantom nickname for the F-4 jet fighter-bomber
PIO public information office
POL petroleum-oil-lubricant
PRC25 standard infantry radio
PSP pierced steel planking
R&R rest-and-recreation leave
REMF rear-echelon motherfucker
RIF reconnaissance in force
ROTC Reserve Officer Training Corps
RPG rocket-propelled grenade
RPD standard communist 7.62mm machine gun
RTO radiotelephone operator
shake 'n bake nickname for graduates of the Noncommissioned Officer Candidate School at Fort Benning, Georgia
S1 personnel officer at battalion or brigade level
S2 intelligence officer at battalion or brigade level
S3 operations officer at battalion or brigade level
S4 logistics officer at battalion or brigade level
SOI signal operating instructions
SSI special signal intercept
TOC tactical operations center
USAF United States Air Force
USARV United States Army Vietnam
USMA United States Military Academy at West Point, New York

VC Viet Cong
WIA wounded in action
WP white phosphorus
XO executive officer

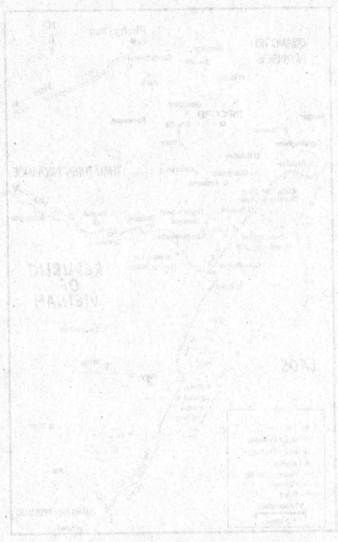

(For a detailed map of hill country around Firebase Ripcord, see page 242.)

RIPCORD

Introduction

Firebase Ripcord was originally established by the 2d of the 506th, a line infantry battalion commanded by Lt. Col. Andre C. Lucas, to support an offensive into an enemy base area overlooking the A Shau Valley of Thua Thien Province, Republic of Vietnam. Occupying the denuded crest of a ridge, the firebase was a whitish brown hump amid jungle-covered mountains. East of the firebase, the mountains descend to foothills, also jungled, beyond which, barely visible from Ripcord, sandy plains meet the South China Sea. To the west, the green peaks push successively skyward; along the far horizon stretch the great mountain ranges that originate in central China and dominate the entire frontier between Vietnam and Laos.

Dependent on helicopters for logistical support, Ripcord was less than twenty-five kilometers, a fifteen-minute flight, southwest of Camp Evans, the rear area of Lucas's battalion and its parent command, the 3d Brigade, 101st Airborne Division (Airmobile). Ripcord was nevertheless deep enough in the mountains, closer to Laos than its own support base, that the heavier of the two howitzer batteries on site could fire southwest into the enemy-controlled A Shau Valley. More to the point, both batteries could range on the supply installations on Co Pung Mountain, a major terrain feature immediately northeast of the valley and nine kilometers south of Ripcord. Those supply installations and the two North Vietnamese regiments that protected them were the objective of the planned offensive. Fighter-bombers utilized a navigational beacon positioned on the firebase to further soften up the area with air strikes, as did—flying too high to be seen or heard—B-52 Stratofortresses of the U. S. Air Force's Strategic Air Command.

No more than a bare hilltop when first established, Ripcord was two and a half months later a heavily bunkered bastion standing ready to provide artillery coverage for the opening of three firebases directly in the objective area. It was at that time, on the eve of the allied offensive, that the enemy struck at the intruders in their mountains. Mortar crews began shelling Ripcord early one morning, and small teams of enemy infantry engaged those units that choppered in to silence the mortars. Resupply helicopters came under heavy antiaircraft fire; two were downed. In a terrible finale to that first day of surprises, a sapper force penetrated the perimeter of a company bivouacked for the night on a strategic peak two and a half kilometers southwest of Ripcord and demolished the unit from the inside out. The sappers themselves also suffered heavy losses.

Thus began the battle for Firebase Ripcord. Colonel Benjamin L. Harrison, the brigade commander, was given operational control of the division reserve, a full battalion, but it was not enough. The enemy had prepared the battlefield too well. Moving down trails hidden under the canopy, several North Vietnamese battalions—the exact number remains unclear—had slipped bit by bit into the hills around Ripcord during the quiet days before the storm. Advance parties had prepared extensive bunker complexes for them, all superbly camouflaged, and laid in supplies. They had also dug firing pits for 60mm and 82mm mortars, as well as enough .51-caliber machine-gun positions to ensure that helicopters approaching the firebase could be tracked from any direction.

Despite constant patrolling by Lucas's battalion to cut the infiltration routes to the heavily populated lowlands, the buildup had gone mostly unnoticed, there being too few troops and too much ground to be covered. Most significantly, the North Vietnamese had been able to fortify a dominant hill only a kilometer west of Ripcord. Once the battle was joined, the enemy shelled Ripcord from that vantage point, their log-reinforced bunkers withstanding the artillery fire and air strikes called down in return. Lucas pushed a reconnaissance team, then one company, then two, up the blasted hillside. The bunkers, almost impossible to see amid the debris of bomb-smashed trees, were connected by tunnels, allowing the enemy to reinforce those that were knocked out, and none of the assaults made much progress. Those mortar crews on the hill were forced to take cover, but the shelling continued unabated from the numerous other positions around Ripcord.

The enemy matched each escalation of the action. Colonel Harrison had deployed the reserve battalion, Lt. Col. Otis W. Livingston's 2-501st Infantry, on a ridgeline running southeast from the peak that had been overrun by the sappers. By day seven, the reserve battalion had accumulated so many casualties that Livingston was ordered to march out of the area to clear the way for the B-52s.

The bombing did not shake the enemy's grip. Meanwhile, on the twelfth day of the battle, Colonel Harrison sent Livingston to reinforce the assaults on the fortified hill west of Ripcord. Whereas Lucas had attacked from the east and north, Livingston was to go up the western slope. The 2d of the 501st never reached its objective. Instead, the reserve battalion became bogged down in a bunker complex that sat hidden in the jungle, blocking the western approach to the hill. Division had committed major fire-support resources to the battle, but what was needed was another infantry brigade; as decisions were made about how next to proceed, the Co Pung offensive was reluctantly postponed. The enemy, therefore, was achieving his goal, denying the allies access to an important logistical site and an approach into the even more valuable A Shau Valley.

Even the best-laid plans tended to come to ruin in connection with the A Shau. It is a natural sanctuary. Running northwest-southeast between two mountain ranges at the western edge of Vietnam, the valley, some thirty-five kilometers long and a few hundred meters to four kilometers wide—the fifteen kilometers extending northwest like a fissure from the heart of the valley are the most narrow—could hardly have been farther removed from the allied bases along the coast. The valley is at certain points only three kilometers from Laos. Several branches of the Ho Chi Minh Trail, the thousand-veined infiltration corridor from North to South Vietnam by way of Laos, snaked easily into the A Shau.

The area is isolated not only by geography but by the weather. For much of the year, fog and thunderstorms conceal the mile-high, wind-buffeted mountains to either side of the valley. The A Shau, a place from the beginning of time, was originally inhabited by Montagnard tribes, which hunted with crossbows and practiced slash-and-burn farming. These primitive hill peoples were victimized during the early years of the war by the Viet Cong (VC), who forced them to serve as porters and guides for guerrilla units carving out bases across the border with Laos—those who objected were summarily executed—and the Army of the Republic of Vietnam (ARVN), which, fearing the Montagnards might succumb to communist indoctrination, proceeded to burn their villages and crops, slaughter their livestock, herd the people into squalid refugee camps, and treat the handful of souls who could not be torn from their ancestral lands as enemies to be shot on sight.

After the hill tribes were removed, the 5th Special Forces Group established a border surveillance camp midway up the A Shau Valley in March 1963. The camp occupied the site of an abandoned Montagnard village called Ta Bat. A month later a second camp was built at the southeast end where the village of A Shau, from which the valley draws its name, once stood. Each outpost, part of a chain all along the border, was home to a Special Forces A-team and several companies of troops, primarily Montagnards, who had been recruited into the Civilian Irregular Defense Group (CIDG) by the Green Berets. The interdiction patrols they ran from the outpost chain rarely encountered VC, neither catching the guerrillas when they slipped into the mountains to attack government-controlled towns and villages in the lowlands nor when they returned to Laos.

It was better not to catch the enemy. Defeated routinely in engagements big and small, the CIDG troops and the unmotivated, poorly led ARVN had proven themselves no match for the Viet Cong. To complete what the VC had begun, Hanoi began infiltrating not only supplies and reinforcements but entire North Vietnamese Army (NVA) regiments down the Ho Chi Minh Trail. The first such regiment crossed into the south in December 1964. To tip the scales back again, President Lyndon B. Johnson ordered the Marines to land at Da Nang on March 8, 1965. More units soon followed, and when the buildup was complete, two Marine and seven army divisions, backed up by what was then the greatest concentration of firepower in the history of warfare, would be fighting in South Vietnam.

Commanded by Gen. William C. Westmoreland, the confident and aggressive force did not know defeat. It found its spirit in the battle of the Ia Drang Valley—the first major clash between the U. S. Army and the North Vietnamese—which saw a battalion from the 1st Cavalry Division (Airmobile) utterly destroy the NVA regiment that was attempting to destroy it during three savage days on the Cambodian border in November 1965.

The old war of advisors and indigenous troops continued on the border with Laos. In May 1965, a third border surveillance camp was established five kilometers northwest of Ta Bat at another abandoned village, A Luoi, where the A Shau Valley narrows to a fissure. After quietly surrounding Ta Bat and A Luoi, the enemy hit both outposts with mortar and ground attacks in December 1965. Both were evacuated, leaving the stronger Camp A Shau to stand alone in the valley. The enemy made the triangle-shaped outpost their next objective, and on March 10, 1966, after two days of mortar bombardments and human-wave attacks, they took it. The communists paid a real butcher's bill, piling up bodies in the barbed wire as the Green Berets kept up the fire of their CIDG troops and called in air strikes almost on top of themselves. The enemy victory was nevertheless so complete that the A Shau became the stuff of legend; stories were told, all true, of the enemy swarming in over their dead, of CIDG troops joining the communists once the perimeter had been breached, of other CIDG troops trampling the wounded and fighting among themselves for places on the evacuation helicopters, forcing those advisors who were still alive to open fire on the hysterical mob. After that, no other combat zone in the country chilled the blood quite like the A Shau Valley.

No new border camps were built in the valley, and it wasn't until April 1967 that Project Delta reconnaissance teams slipped back into the A Shau; they reported that enemy infiltration, unchecked as it was, had increased dramatically. There was little to be done about it, however, as the U. S. Marines, who had responsibility for all of I Corps—the five northernmost provinces of South Vietnam, including Thua Thien—were more than fully occupied combating the guerrillas in the coastal villages and blocking conventional NVA thrusts across the demilitarized zone (DMZ) between North and South Vietnam.

The allies basically ignored the A Shau for two years, and in that time, subjected only to infrequent bombing and long-range artillery fire, the enemy transformed the area into a giant logistical base. Thousands of engineer troops, equipped with some few Soviet bulldozers but mostly laboring like coolies, widened the existing network of Montagnard footpaths to accommodate bicycles and supply carts, and the main trails were upgraded to handle trucks. Night reconnaissance flights sometimes spotted enemy convoys, headlights glowing, as they rolled down roads not yet concealed by tying together the tops of the trees along either side. Mountain caves were used to store the material being transported across the border. To safeguard the supply depots, the enemy expanded and interconnected the fighting positions on the high ground. The place became an invisible fortress, the most elaborate and well-defended enemy staging and supply area in all of South Vietnam.

General Westmoreland was not oblivious to what was happening in the A Shau Valley. The theater commander, believing that the populated areas around Saigon and along the coast had been pacified by his search-and-destroy operations, was, in fact, preparing to end the war by pushing into border strongholds such as the A Shau when the communist Tet Offensive broke across the length and breadth of South Vietnam three hours before dawn on January 31, 1968.

The enemy hit every major town and city that morning. The heaviest fighting took place in Hue, capital of Thua Thien Province, which was seized by a division's worth of VC and NVA. The retaking of Hue by three Marine battalions and most of the 1st ARVN Infantry Division bogged down in a house-to-house battle that left major portions of the old and beautiful city in a shambles before the communist flag was finally hauled down on February 24.

The occupation of Hue had been a reign of terror. Aided by local sympathizers, political cadres rounded up whoever they could find with any connection to the government—students, teachers, bureaucrats, businessmen, foreign missionaries—and marched them into the countryside, where they were murdered and buried in mass graves. The communists thus disposed of three thousand potential enemies in what was the single worst atrocity of the Vietnam War.

The enemy units that took Hue had bivouacked in the A Shau, and five fresh NVA battalions had been able to slip in during the battle on the infiltration routes running northeast the thirty-five kilometers from the valley to Hue. Elements of the 1st Cavalry and 101st Airborne Divisions had to be deployed between Hue and the A Shau to cut the enemy supply lines. Heavy contact in the rural hamlets of the area continued into the first week of March 1968.

In terms of casualty ratios, Tet was an indisputable allied victory. It nonetheless exposed the extent to which the American people had been misled by officials who were themselves terribly disconnected from reality. Westmoreland's war of attrition had failed. The communists, rarely forced into battles from which they could not withdraw, were able always to replace their losses. It was the enemy, not Westmoreland, who controlled the rate of attrition on both sides. They had been able to strike everywhere during Tet, even downtown Saigon. Though the Viet Cong and North Vietnamese had been unable to hold what they grabbed for more than a few hours or days in the face of U. S. firepower—Hue was the tragic exception—the ferocity of their assaults turned the American public's perception of the war on its head. The enemy had not been pushed back to the borders. There was no light at the end of the tunnel. There was only the prospect of war without end against an enemy willing to sacrifice its young men by the hundreds of thousands—year after year, for as long as it took—until, like the French, the Americans were wearied unto death of the Vietnam War.

General Westmoreland, still confident, went on the offensive after Tet, focusing with a vengeance on the A Shau. The mission to destroy the key logistical base went to the 1st Cavalry Division, then headquartered at Camp Evans. The 1st Cav was widely regarded as the best division in Vietnam. It had performed magnificently from the Ia Drang to Bong Son to the An Lao, and after Hue it had conducted the relief of the besieged Marine garrison at Khe Sanh, in the northwestern corner of South Vietnam, with a fluid and graceful precision fully in keeping with its reputation. Following five solid days of air strikes and the devastating B-52 missions known as Arc Lights, the 1st Cav's lead two assault battalions landed in the northwest end of the valley on April 19, 1968. The offensive was code-named Operation Delaware. The first wave was unopposed, but subsequent lifts coming in through the low clouds, including CH-47 Chinooks with sling-loaded artillery pieces suspended underneath, were subjected to heavy .51-caliber and 37mm fire from the mountains. Ten helicopters were shot down, another twenty-three damaged. No previous operation had experienced such heavy antiaircraft fire, and Westmoreland hastily imposed a news blackout on Operation Delaware.

The enemy offered only token resistance once the cav started scouring the valley floor with two brigades and an attached regiment from the 1st ARVN Infantry Division; more ARVN and a brigade from the 101st were screening the mountains to the east. The raid, terminated after twenty-eight days, was declared a major success. In some regards it was. Pushing through ambushes and artillery fire from Laos, the 1st Cav discovered truck parks full of abandoned vehicles, captured mortars, flak guns, and tons of ammunition. In the only sustained engagement of the operation, the 1st Cav even knocked out a Soviet-made PT-76 tank while driving an enemy force from an area known as the Punchbowl, through which ran a sunken corduroy road. Under the area's canopy were a hospital, supply bunkers, and a regiment-sized headquarters from the 559th NVA Transportation Group.

For all that, the allies never really took control of the valley. The enemy's antiaircraft fire was too effective, the weather too bad. Combat engineers reopened the airstrip at A Luoi for supply planes, but it was washed out quickly. An air force C-130 cargo plane was shot down while parachuting supplies in, and even routine helicopter resupply missions became unnerving ordeals as pilots tried to find holes in the cloud cover without flying into the sides of mountains. One cav battalion that was weathered in on a ridge could neither be supplied nor evacuated and was finally forced to move on foot to a more tenable site. It took four days to move six kilometers. It was obvious at the end of the operation that more had been missed than found, and that the enemy would shortly be emerging from caves or slipping back in from Laos to reclaim the A Shau Valley.

The 1st Cav was soon thereafter dispatched to other hot spots, leaving the 101st—the Screaming Eagle division of Normandy and Bastogne fame—to shield Hue and pacify Thua Thien Province. The 101st established its base camps along Highway 1, which follows the coast all the way from Saigon to Hue to Hanoi and on into China. Camp Eagle, site of the division headquarters, was ten kilometers southeast of Hue, with the 1st Brigade in the adjacent Phu Bai Combat Base. The 2d Brigade was at Landing Zone (LZ) Sally, ten kilometers northwest of Hue. Another ten kilometers up the road, the 3d Brigade took over Camp Evans, which was nestled between the highway and the first ripple of foothills off the South China Sea.

The only two airmobile divisions in the war zone, the 1st Cav and the Screaming Eagles, were comparable in terms of unit pride and professionalism. Trained as an airborne shock force, the 101st was more hard-nosed, however, more willing to take casualties, which it proved as it pursued the enemy to the point of extinction through the rice paddies, sand dunes, and villages of the coastal plains. By the end of the year, the resident VC were a shadow of their former selves, and the NVA had been pushed back into the mountains, far from Hue.

For the 101st, the next step was to take the A Shau. The division had been there not once but twice before. In August 1968, Gen. Creighton W. Abrams, having replaced Westmoreland the month before as commander of Military Assistance Command Vietnam (MACV), had ordered the 101st to conduct a follow-up raid into the valley to catch the NVA as they returned to it in the wake of Operation Delaware. The raid was another ordeal of bad weather, heavy aircraft losses, and inconclusive firefights with a phantom foe, but no major caches were discovered as compensation.

What was needed to secure the valley was a permanent force. Given the hazards of aerial resupply, what was needed to sustain such a force was an all-weather road running into the A Shau from Camp Eagle. Such a road was built into the foothills. Before the engineers could push on into the mountains, the enemy had to be pushed out. Accordingly, the 2d Brigade, 101st Airborne Division, went into the A Shau on March 12, 1969. This time, the NVA stood and fought, but after pitched battle at places such as Bloody Ridge, the battered enemy quit the valley and withdrew to their Laotian sanctuaries. Having seriously disrupted enemy control of the area, the 2d Brigade, a little bruised itself, was lifted out on May 8.

To keep the pressure on, the 3d Brigade went in two days later, executing a massive air assault, Operation Apache Snow, to cut off the retreat of those enemy still in the valley. Instead of mopping up a demoralized foe, one battalion found that the 29th NVA Regiment had bunkered itself in on a jungled summit amid the mountains on the western side of the A Shau. The peak, marked as Hill 937 on topographical maps, its height indicated in meters above sea level, was known to the Vietnamese as Dong Ap Bia.

The troops who had to go through the meat grinder to take the position would rename it Hamburger Hill. Seven assaults, six of them unsuccessful, were launched up Dong Ap Bia from

May 11 through 20, 1969, resulting in 56 U. S. dead and more than 400 wounded, against an official NVA body count of 630. The political fallout from such heavy casualties would reshape the conduct of the entire ground war in Vietnam and profoundly influence the way in which the 101st Airborne responded to the action at Ripcord.

The military was made to understand after Dong Ap Bia that minimizing American casualties was more important than closing with the enemy if President Richard M. Nixon was to maintain public support long enough to implement Vietnamization, the policy by which U. S. units were to be gradually withdrawn and replaced by a better-trained, better-equipped ARVN. Ironically, like Tet, the other psychological disaster of the war, Hamburger Hill had been a tactical victory. That is not to say the battle had not been a mess. Helicopter gunships—sleek, murderous AH-1G Cobras—repeatedly strafed the battalion assaulting the hill. A sudden, blinding rainstorm turned the denuded slope to mud and halted one attack just as the troops were about to gain the crest. Worse, by the time the division appreciated the strength of the enemy defenses and committed the three additional battalions needed to take Hamburger Hill, the battalion that had started the fight—and, at the insistence of its hard-driving commander, would participate in the final assault—had been rendered combat ineffective.

Most battles, however, are messes, and on Dong Ap Bia the enemy had been found, fixed, and destroyed, however clumsily, however painfully. By the old rules, that would have been enough. There had been numerous battles before Hamburger Hill—battles not denounced on the floor of the U. S. Senate—in which units were badly hurt while seizing remote villages and mountains that were without value except that they were occupied by the NVA. Like Hamburger Hill, those objectives were also abandoned once taken, the premise of the attrition strategy being not to hold terrain but to kill the enemy whenever and wherever he was found until Hanoi had neither the manpower nor the will to replace its losses.

The Tet Offensive, however, had demonstrated the futility of the attrition strategy as applied to Vietnam. It was the American people, not the communists, who grew demoralized.

Sixteen months after Tet, they had no more stomach for the type of news footage coming from Hamburger Hill—the body bags and the grimacing, rain-lashed wounded—for it appeared to represent carnage without progress, sacrifice without meaning. It seemed that way to the troops, too, most of whom at that stage in the war were actually basic-issue draftees despite their assignment to an airborne division. Hamburger Hill could not have been taken without their raw courage, but during the battle they had talked to reporters about their senior commanders as if they considered them as much their enemy as the NVA. The same mood would prevail at Ripcord.

Except for sapper attacks on several firebases in the area, there was little further interference from the enemy after the battle on Dong Ap Bia as an all-weather airstrip was constructed and the road into the valley completed, allowing armored and self-propelled artillery units to drive in over the mountains. The permanent base that was to have dominated the valley floor was never built, however, because the 101st pulled out of the A Shau on August 12, 1969.

The military had run out of time. President Nixon's promised withdrawal of U. S. units had begun in July. The Screaming Eagles were forced to expand their area of operations (AO) into Quang Tri Province, which faced the DMZ, as of August—thus the exit from the A Shau—to take over for the departing 3d Marine Division.

Shortly thereafter, the 101st Airborne and the well-led 1st ARVN Infantry Division, with which the Screaming Eagles were teamed as part of Vietnamization, drew back to a line of firebases that could be reached by road in the foothills between the coast and the mountains as the northern monsoon began in mid-October 1969.

The enemy used the cover of the rainy season to reestablish their supply bases and lines of communication. The buildup, monitored after a fashion by air-cavalry flights and daring six-man long-range reconnaissance patrol (LRRP) teams, was most intensive around Co Pung Mountain, four kilometers northeast of the A Shau. Nicknamed the Warehouse Area for all the caches previously uncovered there, Co Pung was home to the quartermaster units supporting the 29th and 803d Regiments of the 324B NVA Division.

The weather dictated tactics. When the rains stopped, the enemy would begin moving into the lowlands. The 101st planned—perhaps too ambitiously, given the current political climate—to preempt the North Vietnamese by launching a major offensive with the 1st ARVN Infantry Division into the Warehouse Area. The attack, to begin after the monsoon, was code-named Operation Chicago Peak. To disrupt the enemy in the interim and establish the key firebase to support the offensive, Lieutenant Colonel Lucas's 2-506th Infantry was tasked to seize the ridge on which Ripcord would be built. Two air assaults were turned back with heavy casualties. The site was finally secured by ground attack on April 11, 1970.

There were more tough actions as more fire-support bases were opened on the fringes of the Warehouse Area under the auspices of Operation Texas Star. When the monsoon petered out in mid-May, however, and the sky was again full of scout ships and gunships, the North Vietnamese seemed to vanish. That they had not, that they had instead been avoiding contact—not difficult in those mountains—as they encircled Ripcord, began to come into focus only after the shelling of the firebase began on July 1, 1970.

Having seized the initiative, the enemy retained the initiative. The problem was that whereas the communists were willing to absorb whatever losses were required to achieve their goals, the U. S. Army was trying to fight a war, or, more precisely, keep the enemy at bay until the ARVN could stand on its own, without taking the kind of casualties that would further exacerbate the political divisions in the United States. The 101st Airborne in particular could not afford another Hamburger Hill. Colonel Harrison, the brigade commander, instinctively desired to meet force with overwhelming counterforce, but division headquarters proved reluctant to be drawn into the kind of bloody slugging match that would have been required to push the enemy out of their entrenchments around Ripcord. When the division reserve, like Lucas's battalion, became decisively engaged, no additional units were piled on, as would have been done without hesitation if the old rules had still applied.

The new rules made for a strange battle. When the attacks on the hill west of Ripcord failed, there was great hesitation about keeping them going, though that dominant terrain feature was vital to the security of Ripcord. Similarly, when a company from the reserve battalion did secure—on the twelfth day of the battle—another fortified hill that afforded the enemy a direct line of fire into Ripcord from the southeast, then suffered heavy casualties while repelling five successive night attacks, it was not replaced with a fresh company when lifted out to recuperate. The NVA reclaimed the hill even as the battered company moved toward its extraction LZ. Few troops see their sacrifices so quickly thrown away.

The troops on the firebase were already living an underground existence because of the incoming fire when, on the seventeenth day, the enemy brought up powerful 120mm mortars to shell Ripcord. On the eighteenth day, a resupply Chinook took a burst of antiaircraft fire in its fuel tank while hovering over Ripcord with a sling load of artillery shells. The helicopter crashed straight down into the ammunition storage area of one of the howitzer batteries, and the cataclysmic explosions that followed literally blew the top off the hill, completely destroying the battery in the process.

Crisis piled upon crisis. On the twentieth day, a company attached to Lucas from the 1-506th Infantry was inserted on a ridge east of Ripcord. The company was immediately engaged in yet another hidden bunker complex. As if to confirm that the NVA were everywhere, one of Lucas's own companies, commanded by Captain Hawkins, discovered that same afternoon a land line running along a trail in a narrow valley only two kilometers south of the firebase. Tapping into the line, the company interpreter found himself eavesdropping on conversations between an enemy division headquarters and one of its subordinate units.

On the twenty-first day, the 1-506th company—surrounded, under mortar fire and ground attack—was forced to leave its dead behind as it straggled to another hill for extraction. Hawkins's company, meanwhile, was ambushing and killing numerous enemy soldiers who moved through the area of the wiretap with the confidence of an occupying army. An annotated map found on one of the bodies spoke to an upcoming assault on Ripcord. The best available intelligence indicated that there were at least six battalions massed around the firebase, mostly from the 6th and 803d NVA Regiments. The location of the 29th NVA Regiment was unknown.

Before Ripcord could become an American Dien Bien Phu, the 101st Airborne Division did what the U. S. Army did not do in Vietnam: It backed away from a major engagement, ordering the evacuation and destruction by air strikes of Firebase Ripcord.

The decision to withdraw was made on the twenty-second day. Hawkins's company was hit by an NVA battalion while moving to an extraction site that afternoon. Fighting with the desperate courage of men who knew they had to save themselves or die, Hawkins and his badly outnumbered grunts somehow pushed the enemy back.

On the twenty-third day, an armada of gunships and fighter-bombers attempted, unsuccessfully, to suppress the enemy mortar and antiaircraft positions as Chinooks lifted the remaining howitzers off Ripcord. Next, in an amazing display of airmanship, UH-1 Hueys darted in between mortar salvos to evacuate the troops five at a time. Lucas, standing in the open as he coordinated the evacuation, became one of the last casualties of the battle when a 120mm mortar round landed at his feet. The final act was the extraction soon thereafter of Hawkins's decimated company.

Evacuation had seemed the only realistic option, given the political situation. It was galling nonetheless to leave the enemy in possession of the battlefield. As if wishing Ripcord down the memory hole, the 101st—which had banned reporters from the base during the latter stages of the battle—had not a word to say in the magazine it published for its troops in Vietnam about a fight that had been more costly for the division than even Hamburger Hill.

There had been few reporters on hand to turn away. The big story that summer was not an obscure action in the hinterlands but the invasion of Cambodia. For its part, the command in Saigon had downplayed Ripcord, referring only to light action in the mountains west of Hue. After the evacuation, an event of obvious news value, the command prepared a memorandum for the press. It naturally emphasized enemy casualties, but instead of acknowledging that the NVA had simply made it too costly to maintain Ripcord, given the restrictions on U. S. casualties, it explained away the evacuation as a redeployment of forces to attack the rear areas of the very regiments that had encircled the firebase. The evacuation was accurately described in contemporary news accounts as a retreat, the memorandum an attempted cover-up. But, because the fighting was already over, it was basically a one-day story. There was no follow-up to see if the enemy bases were actually attacked as promised, no analysis or detailed description of what had been a remarkable victory for the North Vietnamese Army.

The enemy victory was total. With Ripcord evacuated, the keystone to the summer offensive had been removed. Instead of a big push, Operation Chicago Peak when finally launched was merely a quick ARVN raid with gunship support but no ground support from the 101st Airborne. Division was hesitant after losing so many troops at Ripcord to lose any more, and no Screaming Eagles ventured onto Co Pung Mountain. The logistical bases there went mostly undisturbed. Meanwhile, in early August, the enemy, including the missing 29th NVA Regiment, opened a new front against Firebase O'Reilly, an isolated position north of Ripcord from which U. S. forces had also withdrawn when they turned it over to the ARVN. Relying on lavish air support from the 101st and the U. S. Air Force, the South Vietnamese did battle with the NVA battalions around O'Reilly, which was being heavily shelled, until the approach of the monsoon threatened to cut off the mountaintop base from helicopter resupply. It was prudently abandoned on October 7, 1970, as the 101st Airborne and the 1st ARVN Infantry Divisions again retired to their cordon of firebases in the foothills.

Ripcord was the last big battle that the American infantry fought in Vietnam. It marked the end of an era. As the withdrawals continued, battalion commanders, acting upon the unspoken wishes of their superiors, crossed known enemy strongholds off their maps, and the troops basically went through the motions on patrol, none wanting to be the last man killed in a war that was not going to be won. Contact was infrequent, with most casualties the result of accidents, booby traps, and small, quick enemy ambushes.

However unmotivated, the grunts were still good soldiers in comparison to the mass of support troops in the rear. Discipline, dry-rotting since around the middle of 1968—the big problems were drugs, racial tension, the hatred between draftees and lifers—had completely fallen apart in the rear by 1970–71. There was spawned the hideous fragging phenomenon in which unit leaders who tried to maintain order were killed or wounded with fragmentation grenades rolled into their quarters at night by their own troops.

Even as the war wound down, the Screaming Eagles struck one last time into the A Shau Valley. That final, uncontested raid was designed to keep the NVA from slipping into the lowlands while allied units massed in the Khe Sanh area for the infamous Laotian incursion of February–March 1971. Though the invasion was an ARVN show—advisors were not even permitted to accompany their counterparts across the border—elements of the 101st Airborne secured forward support bases to facilitate the push, and divisional aviation units were among those flying into Laos itself to provide lift, medevac, and gunship support to the South Vietnamese.

The enemy counterattacked with such ferocity that despite the able performance of some few units, most notably the 1st ARVN Infantry Division, the invasion ended in a rout with the dead and wounded abandoned and terrified ARVN soldiers clinging to the skids of evacuation helicopters. Vietnamization had failed.

The situation was hopeless. As unable as his predecessors to find a solution, Nixon wanted to at least push the communists back far enough—thus the invasions of Cambodia and Laos—to provide a face-saving interval between the final departure of U. S. combat units and the inevitable fall of Saigon. The last full division, the 101st, pulled out in March 1972; a battalion previously detached to a support command for base defense followed in July. The last two infantry battalions still in-country at that point, one from the 196th Light Infantry Brigade, the other the 1st Cav, stood down in August, officially ending the American ground war in Vietnam. Those aviation units still supporting the ARVN were withdrawn in March 1973 following the signing of peace accords in Paris, clearing the way for a conventional invasion of South Vietnam by the NVA. Saigon surrendered on April 30, 1975.

What happened at Ripcord bears recording to fill a gap in the historical record and, more fundamentally, to honor the soldiers who fought there. Unable to fathom why they were not being supported by the full weight of combat power available up the chain of command, the troops, responding to good leadership at the platoon and company level, nevertheless held their own against a tough and aggressive foe. There were moments of stunning courage, and as the men who did their best at Ripcord won a personal victory inside a larger defeat, the circumstances of that defeat—the indecision, the restraints, the limited effort against the enemy's total commitment—make Ripcord something of a tragic metaphor for the entire Vietnam War.

PART ONE

A Bad Beginning

Those sappers were good. They were inside the perimeter before anyone knew it, and they knew exactly what to hit.

—Pfc. Gerald A. Cafferty
Company C, 2d Battalion, 506th Infantry
101st Airborne Division

CHAPTER 1

Incoming

The first mortar salvo landed during the usual morning routines on the firebase. Lieutenant Colonel Andre Lucas was still inside his tactical operations center—the TOC—probably with a cup of coffee and the first cigarette of the day in hand as he checked the latest intelligence readouts from division. The ops center, encased in adjoining steel shipping containers known as conexes, each about the size of a small office, was entrenched directly below the top of the hill on the eastern side of Firebase Ripcord.

Major Herbert E. Koenigsbauer, the battalion operations officer, was crossing the small helicopter pad leveled off in front of the TOC. Responsible for base security, Koenigsbauer made the rounds first thing every morning, checking the police call, inspecting the defensive wire, generally touching base with the commanders of the two howitzer batteries on the hill and the infantry company manning the fighting positions around the perimeter.

Koenigsbauer hadn't gone thirty feet that morning when, without warning—the enemy mortar crew was too far away to be heard as it fired, and the whistling descent of the salvo was lost amid the high winds that slapped almost constantly across the firebase—he saw the first round of that first salvo hit the corner of the partially submerged TOC where a tall, two-wheeled aircraft fire extinguisher was parked in case of crashes on the helipad. Even though the command bunker's radio antennas were offset so as not to mark its exact location, the enemy had studied the firebase with binoculars well enough from the surrounding high ground to determine the location of the TOC. The big red fire extinguisher must have stood out as the perfect aiming point.

Koenigsbauer dashed back around the blast wall that protected the entranceway to the operations center as the rest of the salvo came crashing in behind him. Those first five 82mm rounds, which hit at 7:03 A.M. on July 1, 1970, according to the battalion log, barely dented the hard-packed helipad. Ears were ringing inside the command bunker, but it too had been damaged only superficially. Amid the excited exclamations of the staff officers and radiomen on duty, Lucas made an appreciative comment about all the hard work that had gone into the construction of the heavily sandbagged TOC. The battalion commander also wryly observed that if the enemy could hit the TOC with his first round, he undoubtedly had already pinpointed all the other important targets on Ripcord.

Moments later, Capt. Rembert G. Rollison, commanding D/2-506th, the company securing the perimeter, reported by radio that the base was taking automatic-weapons fire and RPGs—hard-hitting rocket-propelled grenades—from a rocky hill only seven hundred meters to the east. The hill, part of the same jungled ridgeline as the hilltop occupied by Ripcord, was separated from the firebase by a shallow draw. Rollison's grunts, surprised that the enemy would engage them in broad daylight but otherwise unintimidated by the fire, rushed to their fighting positions and excitedly returned fire with M16s, M79 grenade launchers, M60 machine guns, and a heavy, tripod-mounted .50-caliber machine gun.

There was a second infantry element on the base, SSgt. Paul E. Burkey's 3d Platoon, C/2-506th. Though the timing now seemed ironic, the platoon had been lifted up the day before in accordance with a new policy that afforded the line platoons an overnight stay on Ripcord on a rotating basis to rest, resupply, and treat the various skin diseases picked up from operating in the jungle.

In short order, the 105mm howitzers of Capt. David F.

Rich's B/2-319th and the 155s of Capt. Gordon A. Baxendale's A/2-11th Field Artillery (FA), working from preplotted grids of likely enemy firing positions around the firebase, were booming in answer to the NVA. Ripcord's perimeter was a figure eight in shape; the 105s occupied the top of the higher, wider southeast half of the hill, whereas the 155 battery was set up on a narrow lower tier that rose to a bouldered knoll at the northwest end of Firebase Ripcord.

The enemy drew immensely more fire than he delivered. In addition to the howitzers, the 81mm mortar platoon from E/2-506th, the battalion support company, was pumping out rounds from its gun pits below the TOC. Air support also began to converge over Ripcord as the incoming fire was reported from battalion to brigade to division. Less than fifteen minutes into the action, a Pink Team arrived from the 2-17th Cav, the division's air cavalry squadron. Pink Teams consisted of an OH-6A light observation helicopter (LOH) from the White Platoon of its troop and a Cobra gunship from the Red Platoon. Having been alerted to a mortar on what was from Ripcord the back side of Hill 805, the bouldered peak of which was two kilometers (klicks) southeast of the firebase, the scout ship buzzed down to identify the target and mark it with smoke grenades for the fast-moving Cobra.

The mortar position had been called in by Capt. Thomas T. Hewitt, commanding officer (CO) of C/2-506th, which, except for the platoon on the firebase, was in position atop Hill 902, a prominent terrain feature two and a half klicks southwest of Ripcord. At 7:28 A.M., a two-round salvo wounded one of Rich's cannoneers—the first casualty of the battle—and Hewitt quickly alerted the TOC of another firing position, this one on the back side of a knoll less than a kilometer from the firebase. The mortar was situated as if on an invisible line drawn directly between 902 and Ripcord.

The Pink Team was followed by a fire team of rocket-laden Cobras from the 4-77th Aerial Rocket Artillery (ARA). The division's ARA battalion was responsible for knocking out entrenched targets such as dug-in mortars, whereas minigun-equipped Cobras from the 2-17th Cav usually responded to reports of enemy troops in the open. Moments later, the low-flying LOH from the Pink Team reported a suspected mortar position in a draw one klick southwest of 805 and two klicks southeast of Ripcord. The scout ship banked away sharply, with ice green tracers snapping past from Hill 805.

There was by then an air force forward air controller (FAC) above the battlefield in a little O-1 Bird Dog. The FAC reported a fourth mortar position on a small knoll at the northern base of Hill 902. The FAC, meanwhile, marked targets with white phosphorus (WP) rockets. At the forty-five-minute mark, F-4 Phantom fighter-bombers began laying bombs and napalm canisters (snake 'n nape) on 805 and, given the sniper fire, that part of the ridgeline running southeast from Ripcord toward Hill 805. It was quite a show, and some of the troops on Ripcord broke out their cameras as the jets flashed past in the valley below. The tactical air strikes—tac air, for short—were right on the money, but the Phantoms had no sooner pulled up than the mortar crew under the bombs defiantly lobbed a few more rounds toward Ripcord. Later, two LOHs from a 2-17th Cav White Team went down for another look, only to draw more automatic fire from Hill 805.

It was an old story. The allies had the firepower, but the terrain favored the enemy, who remained mostly unseen under the jungle canopy as they alternated their fire from numerous locations. The key terrain features around Hill 927, atop which Ripcord was built, include Hill 805, situated across a sharp draw from the southeast end of the firebase ridgeline at four o'clock—as viewed from above, with the firebase at the center of the clock—and Hill 1000, a kilometer away at nine o'clock on the same ridge. A small, unnumbered knoll sits between Hill 927 and Hill 1000. The ridge descends behind Hill 1000, then turns southwest and climbs to the top of Hill 1298—Coc Muen Mountain—which dominates the area and is three kilometers from Ripcord at eight o'clock. A major ridgeline descends to the southeast from Coc Muen, with Hill 902 situated along it between six and seven o'clock.

Lieutenant Colonel Lucas was stretched too thinly to occupy all the high ground and before the battle had no reason to be tied down in so defensive a posture. On the morning of July 1, Company D was on Ripcord while A/2-506th secured Firebase

O'Reilly, a mutually supporting U. S.–ARVN position seven kilometers northwest on Hill 542. Most of Company C was bivouacked atop Hill 902. Intelligence had earlier predicted the incursion of an NVA battalion in the hills between Ripcord and O'Reilly, and Lucas's remaining maneuver elements—a team from the Reconnaissance Platoon of E/2-506th, B/2-506th, and D/2-501st, which had recently been placed under Lucas's operational control from the division reserve—were deployed to meet that threat.

The enemy concentrated his intermittent fire on Captain Rich's battery on the highest part of Ripcord. First Lieutenant Tore D. Hewlett, the executive officer (XO), and Sfc. Frank J. Rankins, the firing chief, were hit, as were a dozen cannoneers as they loaded and fired the 105s. Though most of the injuries were minor, three men from B/2-319th FA did require helicopter evacuation. Rich, a highly experienced artilleryman, strode among his gun crews under the shelling, keeping their spirits up. As artillery officers were trained to do, he rushed into the smoke of each explosion to inspect the crater and determine where the round had been fired from based on the angle of its impact. The battery commander was twice peppered with shrapnel in the process, but his crater analysis, in coordination with data from the base's countermortar radar, allowed for the placement of extremely accurate fire on the enemy around the firebase. In the first three and a half hours of the shelling, after which it petered out, the enemy managed to put only about thirty rounds in the air, half of which overshot Ripcord.

Captain Hewitt helped adjust the arty from his vantage point atop Hill 902. The gunships and jets also continued to make their runs. It took time, however, to work over each identified enemy position in its turn, and Hewitt's troops, while waiting, put several M60s into action, firing at the mortar directly between their hill and the firebase, and another on the facing slope of Coc Muen, though both were just beyond the weapon's effective range of eleven hundred meters. More realistically, they also targeted the mortar at the northwest base of their hill. The crew down there was popping an occasional round through a small hole in the canopy marked by the smoke ring that would puff through it with each thump of the mortar tube. Some men on that side of the perimeter readied a number of LAWs—single-shot, over-the-shoulder light antitank weapons usually used to blow open bunkers. The first one, aimed skyward to give it a little extra range, arced down into the jungle. It fell short, but the next rocket hit the mark, an expert shot. Though there were no secondary explosions to confirm a direct hit, the mortar ceased firing. The grunts would later come to regret the accuracy of that LAW.

CHAPTER 2

Rube's Roost

The shelling was not heavy. The response of gunships, tac air, and counterbattery fire had been standard, as was Lucas's present decision to assault B/2-506th by helicopter onto Hill 805 to silence the mortar firing from behind its peak. "I flew over the area, checking in with Lucas and asking if he needed anything," Colonel Harrison, the brigade commander, later wrote. "I was both surprised and very interested in the increase in enemy activity, but did not conclude that something big was about to happen. Lucas and I did not discuss the situation in those kind of terms."

For more than a week, Company B, commanded by Capt. William J. Williams, had been working through a massive bunker complex built by an advance party to shelter the NVA battalion thought to be moving into the area to the north. There had been numerous fleeting contacts with an enemy not yet ready to fight. When given the mission to take Hill 805, Williams was bivouacked atop Hill 797 four klicks northwest of Ripcord with his 1st and 2d Platoons. The 3d Platoon—Bravo Three—was on an adjacent ridgeline. A small landing zone had previously been cleared amid the trees on Hill 797 with chain saws and plastic explosives, and as Bravo One and Two formed themselves into helo teams, Williams instructed Bravo Three to move as quickly as possible to the LZ to join the tail end of the attack. Everything was happening fast. In fact, air assaults, known officially as combat assaults, or CAs, though requiring close coordination between the lift, gunship, and fire-support elements, were everyday affairs in the airmobile 101st Airborne Division.

Most assaults encountered no enemy. That morning, however, gunships could be seen wheeling and diving in the distance, and smoke belched from some of the far hills. "You could tell by the look on Captain Williams's face that we were going to get into it," recalled SSgt. Thomas E. "Rube" Rubsam, the draftee platoon leader of Bravo Two. "Our hill was high enough that we could watch them prep 805 with artillery as we waited for the helicopters."

The troops were not anxious to go into battle under Captain Williams. That he operated aggressively at a time when the grunts had reason to be anything but, and that he was balding, bespectacled, and uncharismatic, was enough for him to be sized up as a ticket-punching staff officer looking for a promotion. First Lieutenant Stephen C. Wallace of Bravo Three chalked up the ill feelings to the fact that "Captain Williams was all business, and like most career officers tended to place the mission before the men."

Looks could be deceiving. Horn-rimmed glasses aside, Bill Williams was a pugnacious, highly experienced combat officer. He had been commissioned through the Reserve Officer Training Corps (ROTC) program at Colorado State University in 1963 and had pulled a 1966–67 tour with the 5th Special Forces. Whatever the troops thought, one of Williams's squad leaders found him to be "very professional, very smart." Another noted with approval that Williams "enforced noise and light discipline, and was very strict about digging in." Platoon leader Rubsam was of the opinion that "Captain Williams saved a lot of lives in Company B because he simply would not allow us to relax and get slack no matter how quiet the situation. He made sure that things were done right, but he still gave us platoon leaders a lot of authority to make our own decisions. He was an excellent company commander."

Lieutenant Wallace was their best platoon leader, but as he was still en route to the landing zone, Williams told Sergeant

Rubsam, two months in-country, to lead the assault on Hill 805 with Bravo Two. To keep an eye on his most ineffective platoon leader, Williams would go in on the second wave with well-meaning but in-over-his-head 1st Lt. Joe Delgado—a pseudonym—of Bravo One.

Landing one at a time, Hueys from the 158th Aviation Battalion, the division's lift element, began picking up 2d Platoon, B/2-506th, at 10:26 A.M. The lift ships, known as slicks, could carry six to eight combat-loaded troops each. It was a quick flight to the objective, too quick for the infantrymen sitting at the open doors in a state of gut-tightening anticipation, and a rough one too, given the turbulent mountain winds. The assault was to be made into an LZ two hundred meters west and ten meters below the little bouldered peak of Hill 805, with the line of Hueys swinging first into a high and wide orbit to make room for a last bomb run by the Phantoms.

Following the air strike, the slicks started their descent. A pair of Cobras streaked in ahead of them, punching off rockets until the last possible moment to keep the enemy down. Undeterred, the NVA opened fire as soon as the gunships peeled off. Unable to risk a landing, the lead Huey merely slowed to a hover some three to four feet above the LZ. Sergeant Rubsam, his heart pounding, jumped from the skid, landing hard under his rucksack. The helicopter roared away as Rubsam's troops scrambled into the old foxholes around the landing zone and immediately began laying down suppressive fire to cover the approach of the next Huey.

Informed that the landing zone was hot, Captain Williams gave the troops on his slick an enthusiastic thumbs-up, as if to say, let's go, the game is on. Williams was marked as a unit leader by the radio telephone operators (RTOs) disembarking with him. Rubsam, looking back over his shoulder between M16 bursts, was shocked to see spurts of dust kicking up all around the captain and his command group as they dashed off the open LZ.

As his slick made its approach, Sgt. Robert L. Judd of Bravo One saw a muzzle flash and caught a quick glimpse of somebody among the boulders on top of Hill 805. "He was firing at us as we went by and the door gunner was firing back at him," recalled Judd; when the Huey slid into its hover, "we unassed it as fast as we could. . . ."

As best as could be determined amid the noise and confusion, there was one enemy soldier with an AK-47 atop the hill and two or three others firing from the jungle below the western side of the landing zone. Rubsam was facing uphill. One of his machine gunners, Specialist Fourth Class Dempsey—"a gung-ho Alabama guy"—was in position on the other side of the perimeter when shot in the back and gravely injured by the enemy soldier atop the hill. "That LZ was horrible in that the enemy could fire right down on it from 805. We were like fish in a barrel," noted Williams. "I was so frustrated that just to piss off that little son of a bitch on top of the hill, I jumped up on a log and screamed at the top of my lungs a phrase we had all memorized during my first tour about Ho Chi Minh having relations with his mother. After I yelled it, I looked down and there was one of the troops looking up at me with an expression that said you have got to be the craziest, dumbest bastard I've ever seen. He was probably right. It wasn't a very smart thing to do."

When all of Bravo One got on the ground, Sergeant Rubsam's platoon, having dropped rucks and spread out on line, started its attack up the side of the hill. The whole thing was unfolding like a live-fire exercise, which amazed Rubsam, in his first big action, because he'd always assumed that their training was so much "horseshit." The only discordant note was a man named Foster who, stunned into inaction or at least trying to appear so, was sitting on the slope below the landing zone, looking away from the action, his rifle between his knees. He was mumbling to himself, something like, "What am I doing here? What the hell am I doing here?"

Rubsam jerked Foster up by his collar, spun him roughly toward the hill, and snapped, "Son, they're up *there!*"

Rubsam was leery that Foster might someday settle the argument with an accidental discharge in his back. "I always kept an eye on Foster because I'd had a few other run-ins with him when he wouldn't do his job," recalled Rubsam. The problem wasn't just that Foster was a nonhacker but that the

Jamaican-born GI with the thick accent was into Black Power. He struck a hostile pose. In fact, using one of the movement's derisive nicknames for whites, he had written KILL RABBITS on his helmet cover over his Magic Marker drawing of a black hand plunging a knife into a white rabbit. It was a pretty bold proclamation, thought Rubsam, given that in combat you wanted all the friends you could get.

Racial conflict, rampant in the support bases, was mostly absent in the line units. "Everybody suffered equally," noted Lieutenant Wallace. From that simple truth there developed a camaraderie in which every man could depend on every other man. Given the times, though, Rubsam's platoon was divided into two white squads and a third—under Sgt. Clarence "C. C." Clark, a black Regular Army noncommissioned officer (NCO)—whose members were all black and Latino GIs. "Clark had six or seven years in and was very capable," said Rubsam. "He did an excellent job with his guys. They were as good as anybody."

All except the sullen Private Foster, who, as it turned out, never fired his weapon in anger, either at Rubsam or the NVA. "He'd just hide when we were under fire, and I realized he wasn't a threat to anybody," noted Rubsam. "He was just baggage. I finally told the company commander and he was reassigned to the rear a month or so after Ripcord. He just went away. He was one of those guys that don't work out in the infantry. We had white ones, too."

The attack pressed on. Rubsam was more excited than scared as he squeezed off bursts. He was so pumped up, in fact, that it barely registered when the AK-47 cracked again from up above, and he was hit once in the arm—the bullet punched through his left biceps, missing the bone, a clean wound—and again in the face by a fragment from a shattered bullet or piece of rock as more rounds splattered the boulder to which he had instinctively headed for cover. Feeling no pain, Rubsam didn't realize he'd been shot until the platoon medic, a good friend, told him that he was bleeding.

The medic relieved Rubsam of his M16 before getting a bandage around his arm. Rubsam had no intention of being jerked to the sideline. He took his rifle back, but moments later

Captain Williams got him on the horn and told him to hold in place. Bravo Three was finally on its way, and the company commander wanted Wallace to lead the attack instead of the wounded Rubsam.

Though disappointed, Rubsam didn't miss much, because the two shark-bodied Cobras working the hill—each had rocket pods under stubby wings, and a nose turret with an automatic cannon and a six-barreled minigun capable of firing up to four thousand rounds a minute—nailed the NVA who was holding them up shortly before the arrival of Bravo Three. Unable to hit the enemy soldier when he was down behind the boulders, the pilots finally decided to trick him out of his cover. The first gunship made a dry run past the hill. Realizing he wasn't taking fire, the NVA, a brave man, rose up, trying against all odds to shoot down a Cobra with an AK-47. The second gunship was already diving in, however, with rockets flying and the minigun and grenade launcher blazing. There was a ferocious ripple of explosions and much smoke and dust; afterward nothing moved and not another shot was fired from Hill 805.

Moving as a platoon in the jungle was bad. Moving as a company was even worse. The enemy usually heard you coming and had the option of slipping away or setting up an ambush for the point team. Lieutenant Wallace instead broke down his platoon into six-man tiger teams, fighting the war like the enemy fought it. When moving as a unit, Wallace's well-trained troops operated with an alertness not seen in the average platoon, threading slowly, cautiously, almost noiselessly through the jungle. The platoon leader was so adamant about using hand signals and speaking in whispers when it was necessary to speak at all, even on the radio, that Lucas had jokingly tagged him as Whispering Wallace. "As far as we were concerned, that nickname was a badge of honor," said Pfc. Rodger D. "Chip" Collins, a rifleman in Bravo Three.

"I may have taken it to the extreme, but I believed in being quiet in the woods," said Wallace, a country boy from South Carolina. "You always took risks, but being smart minimized those risks."

Like most infantry lieutenants, Wallace, a college dropout who signed up for Officer Candidate School (OCS) at Fort Benning, Georgia—he also volunteered for jump school, pathfinder school, and special warfare school—spent his first six months in Vietnam leading a rifle platoon, after which he was automatically rotated to staff desk in the rear. Unlike most lieutenants, he soon asked for another platoon. He had no career intentions, but he had come to do a job and thought it was "absolutely insane to pull lieutenants out of the field as soon as they figured out what was going on."

That's how Wallace got Bravo Three. Shortly to be revered by his troops as one of the few lieutenants who could keep them alive, he had at first been resented as a hard-ass. "It was my platoon and they were going to do what I said," recalled Wallace. "I demanded discipline. You'd be surprised how guys who consider themselves combat veterans will make noise and get sloppy, but they were a pretty good group, typical American boys, and if you held their feet to the fire, they'd do what they were supposed to do."

That first morning of the battle, however, the platoon broke all its rules as it moved in noisy haste to the pickup zone atop Hill 797. In case of trouble, Lieutenant Wallace took a position in the column just behind his point team. Hill 797 was "terribly steep, one of the worst hills I remember climbing," said Wallace; given the speed of the march and the suffocating summer heat, "we were really huffing and puffing with the loads we were carrying."

It was rough, but because the rest of the company was in trouble and needed help, "there was a lot of cooperation during the trek up the mountain," wrote Chip Collins. He passed along the way a number of guys near physical and emotional exhaustion, including a sweat-soaked machine gunner fading under the load of his twenty-five-pound M60. "I went up to the top," noted Collins, "dumped my ruck, and went back for him and the gun."

Bravo Three was shuttled one ship at a time from the mountaintop to the LZ below Hill 805 between 12:14 and 12:20 P.M. Rubsam and Dempsey were evacuated aboard the platoon's slicks. There was no fire from the 805 at that point thanks to the Cobras. Collins thought the fight was over, and Captain Williams, seeing the unhurried trooper, barked at him: "Get your ass down."

Private Collins did so just as the NVA downhill to the west opened up again with AK-47s. "The company was in such a tight little area that we were all packed on top of each other," recalled Collins. "It was so crowded I almost shot somebody who popped his head up in front of me when I was trying to return fire."

Williams told Wallace to take the hill, and, dropping rucks, Bravo Three started into the thick vegetation between the landing zone and the bald, bomb-blasted top of 805. "We had to climb over and around and through stuff, and we were all bogged down," said Collins, whose turn it was to walk point. The tension was terrific as the lead troops leapfrogged across the steep, open ground directly below the top of the hill. If anyone was still in position up there, the grunts knew that he'd get one of them with his first burst. He'd get one before the guy knew what hit him. There wasn't anything to do but hope you weren't the one; it was a matter, recounted Collins, of "hiding behind a tree stump or whatever, and then climbing and scuffling to the next little place of cover. There wasn't any fire, but many of us, me included, just threw up when we reached the top from the heat and the anxiety and the physical exertion."

Bravo Three cautiously checked the top of the hill. Spotting a small bunker under a boulder, Collins pitched a grenade through one of its two entrance holes, and after the muffled blast another trooper pulled out a dead enemy soldier. The first confirmed kill of the battle was credited to the gunships. "Not that I cared one way or the other," recalled Collins. "Our platoon wasn't into body counts."

The top of Hill 805, from which the ocean could be seen in the far distance, looked like a castle for all the boulders. Williams placed his command post (CP) among the rocks with Bravo One and Two. There being little room remaining, Bravo Three established a separate night defensive position (NDP) back down on the LZ.

After digging in and setting up claymore mines and trip

flares, each platoon sent out a three-man listening post (LP) to monitor the most likely avenues of enemy approach to the NDPs.

The taking of the hill might have been only a skirmish, but, given the generally low tempo of action in the area, it was a big deal to Bravo Company. Williams christened the hill Rube's Roost, in honor of Rubsam, and affixed to the remains of a blasted tree the Irish flag that he flew over his CP whenever they were on Ripcord.

As tallied in the battalion log, the dead enemy soldier's bunker contained clothes, medical supplies, some marijuana, a fifty-pound sack of rice, grenades, ammo, satchel charges—and an RPG launcher with ten rockets. "The only thing I can figure is that the launcher was jammed," said Williams, "because we were coming into a one-ship LZ, and all that guy had to do to screw that whole operation up was blow up the second or third ship in the middle of the LZ. Nobody else could have landed, and those people already on the ground would have been stuck because that North Vietnamese was in a position where one or two people could hold back an army."

The man's AK was missing, however, perhaps blown to bits, perhaps carried off by a second unseen NVA. It didn't matter. The one kill was satisfying enough. "After weeks and weeks of getting plinked at and never seeing the sons of bitches, it was good to finally get one and see what they really looked like," recalled Williams. "We looked at this guy as kind of a trophy," noted Sgt. Thomas P. "Phil" Tolson of Bravo One. "We propped him up next to his bunker. He had a towel in the bunker. We put the towel over his shoulder and a cigarette in his mouth, and posed for pictures with him like we were old buddies at the beach."

At least one mortar salvo had previously been reported coming from a ridgeline with three small peaks, known informally as Triple Hill, a kilometer north of Hill 1000. As Company B dug in, an air strike went in on the ridge, and a FAC who went down for a look reported the mortar destroyed and an enemy soldier killed.

The lull in the incoming ended an hour and a half later, at 1:35 P.M., when a single mortar round hit Ripcord. Fifteen minutes later, a 75mm recoilless rifle opened up from Triple Hill. Several rounds missed the firebase, but at least five others didn't. "You could see where the recoilless rifle was firing from, and you could see the smoke trails zipping toward Ripcord," said Judd. Second Lieutenant Aaron Andrasson, the artillery forward observer (FO) attached to Company B, was known for his speed in adjusting fire. "He called in one marker round," noted Judd, "then adjusted and fired for effect—and got secondary explosions. We let out a cheer."

Lucas requested a resupply of mortar and artillery ammunition, and toward late afternoon Chinooks from the 159th Aviation Battalion began arriving. Coming in groups of two and three, the big CH-47s, twenty-five in all, replaced the thousand-plus rounds that had been fired before sundown. Guided by a pathfinder, each Chinook hovered over the main logistical pad in its turn and placed its sling load of ammunition on the ground before banking away. The operation came under heavy fire. When the escorting gunships rolled in on one muzzle flash, others would wink from other hillsides. At 3:50 P.M. a Chinook from B/159th took enough hits as it unhooked its load that it was forced to shut down on Ripcord.

Concurrent with the resupply effort, an aerorifle platoon from the 2-17th Cav went into a hot LZ on Triple Hill. The mortar and recoilless rifle that had apparently been destroyed there were nowhere to be found, and the enemy who had fired on the helicopters bringing the platoon also vanished as the cavalry troops called in gunships and secured the top of the ridge. Before being lifted out the next day, the platoon discovered bunkers all over the hill, as well as trails heavily tracked with fresh sandal prints.

Other enemy, meanwhile, mortared the firebase to try to destroy the downed Chinook. At 7:21 P.M. another CH-47, this one from A/159th, was shot down on the log pad—ominously, the fire came from a heavy .51-caliber machine gun—but, hastily repaired by its crew, was able to depart for the nearest lowland firebase, where it could be worked on in safety. One grunt on the perimeter watched as Lucas "walked to the edge of the hill, trying to see where the fire was coming from even as his staff officers tried to pull him back into the TOC."

The machine gun was firing from a knoll a klick down the slope on the southeastern side of Ripcord. Captain Rich of B/2-319th FA had one of his 105s rolled forward to fire down on the knoll. The .51 was in a cave. When helicopters approached, the crew would push it to the front of the cave, "and then when the artillery zeroed in on them, they'd just wheel it back inside," explained Judd, watching from 805. "The fast-movers came in," he said, referring to the jets, "and napalmed the whole area, and we thought, boy, nothing can be alive down there—but after the air strike, the little bastards wheeled that gun back up to the opening and popped off a few more rounds just to let us know they were still there."

It was assumed that, having inflicted some damage, the enemy would pull back during the night. At best, he might hang on for a few days, then melt away as the allied response intensified. The major concern as the sun went down was that the enemy would follow up the shelling with a sapper attack on the firebase. "We did not anticipate the all-out enemy offensive that was about to take place, or actually was taking place," stated Koenigsbauer.

The action sputtered on after dark. The 105s and 155s fired methodically around the firebase to deter the possible sapper attack. A U. S. Air Force flareship orbited overhead for a time, lighting up the hills.

A trip flare went off on the knoll between Ripcord and Hill 1000. The mortar platoon put a salvo on the spot. The 81s shifted their fire when Company D reported limbs breaking about seventy-five meters down from their perimeter positions on the southern slope of the firebase. "When the flares went up, you could see NVA moving around outside the wire," noted a grunt from Company C, watching the action from 902. "They were really getting bold."

The ground attack, when it came an hour and a half before midnight, was launched not against the firebase but Company B atop Hill 805. Forced to work their way in close because of the thick vegetation, several enemy soldiers opened fire with

AK-47s while another fired RPGs at the boulders shielding Bravo's CP. "It's a very colorful thing seeing an RPG fly over your position," recalled Williams. When fired, rocket-propelled grenades "make a coke-can-pull-top sound," noted another officer, "then leave a streaking sparkler trail as they 'whoosh' toward their target. It isn't hard to pinpoint where they're coming from at night."

Williams was gratified that though it went against their instinct, the troops, as trained, responded only with frags and M79s, because a muzzle flash would identify their position for the next RPG. When the shooting started, a new guy out on LP immediately darted back to the NDP. He thought he was supposed to. When his squad leader asked him what he was doing—listening posts pull back only on order—he resolutely dashed back out through the fire to rejoin the two men he had inadvertently left behind.

While the mortar platoon put up illumination rounds from the firebase, Lieutenant Wallace, down on the LZ with Bravo Three, moved into a position from which he could zap the enemy RPG gunner with a LAW. Wallace fired the rocket himself, concerned that an overly excited trooper might forget about the weapon's backblast and hurt somebody. Wallace sent the rocket flaming toward the enemy, then quickly moved away before he drew fire—an unnecessary precaution, he noted, because "after I fired the LAW at the guy with the RPG launcher, he shut up right quick."

CHAPTER 3

Stay Alert, Stay Alive

Earlier, as night had approached, Captain Hewitt reportedly requested permission to move Company C off Hill 902, the unit having compromised its position by firing at the enemy mortar sites with machine guns and LAWs. "I was monitoring the radio, and Hewitt was emphatic about getting off that mountain," stated Sp4 Gary A. Steele, an RTO in Charlie Two. "We knew we were going to get our ass kicked, but the colonel told us to stay put." As Hewitt had supposedly feared, Company C, minus its detached platoon, was hit hard during the night. Casualties were heavy; Hewitt was among those killed. Steele blamed Lucas. Major Koenigsbauer, however, would have no memory in later years of Hewitt wanting to move to a new NDP. If he had, Lucas would have indeed refused the request, said Koenigsbauer: "Pulling off that hill wouldn't have made any sense. It was key terrain. The counter-mortar radar on the firebase was good, but we needed eyes out there, too, and from Hill 902, Hewitt and his FO could observe enemy firing positions and report back to us the effectiveness of our counterbattery fire."

Whatever the advantages, leaving the company on the hill involved a calculated risk. Units rarely spent two nights in the same location, on the assumption that the enemy needed at least one night to reconnoiter a position before attacking it. For Lucas to leave Hewitt in place implies that the battalion commander thought an attack on Company C much less likely than the resumption—come daylight—of the shelling of Ripcord. Though Hewitt might have argued that he could regain the high ground from his new position at first light, Lucas apparently did not want to gamble that the NVA wouldn't occupy the strategic peak during the night. In any event, if Hewitt did argue with Lucas, if accounts to that effect did not generate after the fact to explain away the heavy casualties, what remains baffling is how indifferently Company C set up for its second night atop Hill 902. Enemy sappers, supported by regular infantry, were able to creep close enough to the perimeter to identify not only the company commander's location—Hewitt had picked the wrong night to string up a hammock for the whole world to see—but also the uncamouflaged platoon CP and M60 positions on the side of the perimeter through which they planned to strike. Those positions were all eliminated in the first few seconds of the attack, allowing the enemy to dart inside the NDP.

Such is a best-case scenario. Many survivors became convinced as they tried to figure out what happened the next morning that at least some of the sappers—stripped to dark shorts, blackened from head to toe with charcoal, their folding-stock AK-50s slung tightly against their backs so their arms were free to feel ahead of them in the dark—had slipped with catlike stealth between men dozing in two foxholes and were already inside the lines when the shooting started. However the sappers got in, the men scrambling to return fire were stunned to realize that not only did they have NVA to their front but that more shadowy figures were behind them, throwing satchel charges down at their foxholes from the vicinity of the company CP.

Had the enemy mortared Hill 902, Colonel Harrison noted that moving would have proved the wiser course of action after all. "But against a sapper-infantry attack," he wrote, the troops "were on terrain that should have favored them." The brigade commander blamed Hewitt for "not preparing good defensive positions with an adequate number of claymore mines and trip flares, etc."

Because Company C had been as loose as a unit in a quiet area, the melee in the flare-lit night was a madhouse of terror and confusion. "We did not know until reports came in the next morning from the relief force that the company had failed to dig in and otherwise prepare appropriate positions," said Koenigsbauer. "I have a hard time with that. Should I have gotten on the radio and gone through the steps of establishing a night defensive position with Hewitt? Maybe, but he had been in command long enough that he should have known. If the company had been dug in and alert, that night would have ended much differently than it did, and Hewitt wouldn't have paid for his complacency with his life."

It is true that Hewitt basically killed himself. It is also true that he might have proved at least an adequate commander had he had more time to get his feet on the ground. As it was, Hewitt didn't last long enough to do anything but compare unfavorably to his predecessor, Capt. Isabelino Vazquez-Rodriguez. "Captain Vazquez was the ultimate soldier," said one sergeant, speaking for the entire company. A native of Puerto Rico, the bantam-sized Vazquez was a veteran of the Korean War and had pulled several tours in Vietnam as a senior Special Forces NCO—he limped a bit from an old leg wound—before receiving a temporary commission and orders to the Screaming Eagles. His combat experience was awe inspiring. "The colonel and the battalion staff didn't know shit compared to that man," said 1st Lt. James H. Campbell of Charlie Two. Vazquez, unsmiling, black eyed, was a hard man to work for. Campbell, himself the subject of several "ass-chewings" as he got his act together as a platoon leader, noted that the captain was "incredibly severe and had the fiercest temper of any human being I have ever met in my life. He had zero tolerance for error. Vazquez lived and breathed war. He had been on the ground fighting the enemy for years. He didn't think about going home. He thought about terrain, tactics, routes of travel, avenues of approach, fire support, and the readiness of his troops twenty-four hours a day. He didn't seem human. He seemed immortal."

The six-month rule also applied to company commanders. To make room for Captain Hewitt, Vazquez was wastefully reassigned to a staff position—battalion supply officer—when his time was up. The original intent of the rule had been to spread around as much combat experience as possible in the officer corps in what was expected to be a quick war. The practice had since been institutionalized to serve the needs of career officers who required a combat command to remain professionally competitive. The constant rotation of officers from platoon leaders to brigade commanders might have benefited individual careers, but it cast an amateurish quality over the war effort as a whole and resulted in needless casualties.

Compared to the flinty Vazquez, Hewitt, a twenty-five-year-old family man from Topeka, Kansas, with ROTC bars, came across as an eager kid, especially when he showed up with a shotgun and a hot little .38 in a shoulder holster, which the troops dismissed as affectations. That he had served as an ARVN advisor before extending his tour to get a company did not impress the troops either.

Captain Hewitt looked like a high-school basketball player with his crew cut and thick glasses. "Hewitt was a good guy," said Pfc. Gerald A. Cafferty, the senior company medic, "but he just didn't have it as far as experience, and he didn't get the chance to learn what he needed to know before we got hit by the sappers."

Lucas had passed the company guidon to Hewitt during a week-long battalion stand-down at Camp Evans. When it ended on June 15, the battalion, having been brought up with replacements to what was considered full strength during the withdrawals—ninety men per company instead of the usual seventy-five—launched a combat assault to relieve the 1-506th Infantry, which had temporarily been given responsibility of the Ripcord AO.[1]

Captain Hewitt and Company C landed on the ridgeline running southeast from Hill 902 to replace a 1-506th company that lifted out aboard the same Hueys. Lieutenant Campbell went in on the first chopper with his point man, radioman, and best machine-gun team. Knowing that the rest of the company would not be far behind, they immediately started down the trail that ran along the spine of the ridge. Campbell took the slack position behind his point man. Moving quickly, the two had gone only 150 meters when they crested a small rise and were surprised to find themselves face-to-face with two equally startled North Vietnamese.

The enemy soldiers had been trailing the 1-506th company and had been in the process of rigging a claymore when they heard the Hueys. Unable to see that the lift ships were not only taking out their quarry but bringing in a fresh company, they began dismantling their ambush. "They were standing in the middle of the trail, and, suddenly, we were right there on top of 'em," recounted Lieutenant Campbell, a tough, bluff doctor's son who'd put aside his plans for law school and joined up to see what he was made of after four beer-blasted years at Louisiana State University. "The closest gook was rolling the claymore in his hands, wrapping the detonating wires back around it. When he saw us, he just looked at the AK-47 he had leaning up against a tree. He knew he was screwed. He didn't have anyplace to go. We killed him and his buddy just like that. We just shot the shit out of 'em. . . ."

True to form, Sp4 Layne Hammons charged forward and laid down a sheet of M60 fire as Campbell and the point man hit the dirt and from their bandoliers tore fresh magazines for their M16s. Campbell was still reloading when he noticed a third NVA off to one side of the trail. "I came up shooting, but he disappeared into the brush," said Campbell. "The three of us kept firing because we didn't know what we had, but nothing else developed so we grabbed our stuff and dragged the two bodies back to the LZ."

The move continued, each platoon branching off along a separate route before establishing separate night defensive positions. The routine continued for the next four days as the company worked its way downhill from the landing zone to the southeastern tip of the ridge, a distance of about two kilometers. Captain Vazquez had always preached that however slow and exhausting, in such circumstances it is wiser to cut a cross-country route than risk ambush by walking trails. "Vazquez possessed a particular blend of caution and aggressiveness," noted Chuck Hawkins, who served as a platoon leader under Vazquez before making captain himself. "He knew when and how to fight, and when and how not to."

Though it meant courting contact on the enemy's terms,

Captain Hewitt ran the mountain trails in headlong pursuit of the NVA. The unsettling change in tactics wasn't the only thing that had the troops spooked. The heavily jungled ridge was dotted with "freshly dug, heavily fortified, well camouflaged bunkers," wrote Pfc. Michael Womack, a new guy in Charlie One. Additionally, Womack's squad found an inch-thick cable "snaking its way through the jungle attached to trees about four and a half feet off the ground with light blue-green glass insulators. I wanted to cut the line but the other guys wouldn't let me. They told me the enemy would send people to find out why it wasn't working and they might run into us. I thought that was what we were there for."

Upon reaching the end of the ridge, Company C was picked up late on the fifth day of the mission and assaulted back into its original LZ, the idea being to push uphill this time to the top of Hill 902. The sweep was to begin after a squad from Charlie One returned to the bivouac it had occupied the first night in the area and retrieved two claymore mines concealed in the brush along the trail running through the NDP. It had been hoped that the claymores, utilizing fishing line as trip wires, would blow away any enemy soldiers who came to forage the site for the rations and ammunition that undisciplined troops were known to discard to lighten their loads. When deployed by U. S. forces, such booby traps were euphemistically referred to as mechanical ambushes (MAs).

The squad from Charlie One set up for the night with Lieutenant Campbell and Charlie Two. As the squad got organized the next morning, June 21, Campbell requested some 81mm fire along the intended route "to shake the gooks up." The mortar section leader on Ripcord, apparently unconcerned because it wasn't a contact mission, said it would be a while before he could get any rounds out. "It was real early, and he gave me some bullshit about having to reset the base plates on his mortars, which would then require additional adjustments," recalled Campbell. "What he was probably doing was screwin' around, eating breakfast or something."

The patrol moved out. Following the trail, it took the four-man point team an hour to reach the first MA. The enemy had moved it, however, and the North Vietnamese crouching in the spiderhole to which a detonating wire had been run, and from which he could observe the trail, presently squeezed the firing handle, setting off the claymore. The man quickly slipped away into the jungle, having successfully wounded the three troopers behind the point. None were killed, because they were not in the actual kill zone of the claymore, having halted to the side of the forward-pointing mine to let the rest of the patrol catch up with them. That's when the stunning explosion suddenly blew them off their feet. The point man, unaware that the explosion had been command detonated, rushed back to his wounded buddies, frantically apologizing because he thought he had blundered into a trip wire.

Lucas landed before the medevac did. "Lieutenant, as long as you've been out here, you should have known better than this," the colonel snapped at Campbell. "Why didn't you prep the area?"

Campbell tried to explain that he had called for fire but had been told that he couldn't get a mission anytime soon. Lucas squinted suspiciously. "Well, you call up there and see if you can get a fire mission," Campbell said hotly. "If you use your own call sign, hell, yeah, they're gonna fire, but use mine and see what they do."

Lucas made the call. Getting the same static as Campbell, he threw the radio handset to the ground in an uncharacteristic display of anger, snatched it back up—"I want the mortar platoon sergeant up at the helipad by the TOC when I get back," he said—then stalked to his Huey. Lucas was a cultured, normally reserved West Pointer on his second combat tour, forceful in a quiet sort of way and considered by his superiors and peers to be one of the most professional and effective battalion commanders in the division. He gave the impression to some of his more junior subordinates, however, that the war was a professional contest for him, his troops pieces on a game board. Campbell was fuming as Lucas departed. "It wasn't a major event," he said later, "but Lucas chewed me out in front of my men, then just left without another word when he found out what really happened. I know colonels don't apologize, but for my sake he should have said something like, 'I'm going to jack that crew up, lieutenant. This won't happen again.'"

The wounded being brought down the trail at that time included new guy Mike Womack, with four steel pellets and a chunk of the claymore fuse in his legs. It was a torturous trip. The poncho litter into which Womack had been loaded quickly came apart, dumping him on the ground. The litter was put back together, but as they continued, one of the guys carrying it bumped a nest of red ants, which showered upon Womack in a biting and stinging frenzy. "They set the litter down and broke out the GI insect repellent and gave me a good dousing," Womack later wrote. "The next thing I knew, I was on fire. I had wounds in the back of both thighs that no one was aware of and the repellent was burning like hell." Mercifully, the platoon medic administered morphine. Moving on, the litter team encountered a tree that had fallen across the trail, with U. S. Air Force cluster bombs hanging from it. Unable to bypass the obstacle because of the thick jungle, the litter team had to lift Womack over it, which they did without disturbing any of the bombs, at which point the litter gave way for a second painful crash. Womack thanked God when they finally reached the LZ and he was loaded aboard a medevac Huey. The crew chief stuck a business card in his pocket: "Congratulations. You have been successfully dusted off by Captain John Doe, 326th Medical Battalion, 101st Airborne Division."

The day after the ambush, Charlie One, with which Hewitt's command group was then moving, humped to the top of Hill 902. Lieutenant Campbell was supposed to link up with Hewitt that evening, so as dusk approached Charlie Two jumped on a trail cutting up the mountain from the southwest. Campbell and his point man, Sp4 Thomas C. Manbeck, were extremely cautious as they approached the crest; they were concerned about getting fired on by Charlie One. "As we approached the perimeter, we kept asking for radio acknowledgment that the security covering the trail knew we were coming in," wrote Campbell. Acknowledgment was received, but there was, in fact, no security to worry about. Hewitt had deployed Charlie One in a half circle on the eastern side of the bald mountaintop but had left the western side open, knowing that Charlie Two would shortly take up positions there. "There might have been a couple guys sitting and watching the western half," recalled Campbell, "but it wasn't the way it ought to have been."

It got worse. Though it was already getting dark, a man in the center of the perimeter was boiling a cup of coffee field style: Cut holes in a C-ration tin, light a heat tab inside it, and place a larger fruit can full of water and instant coffee over the intense flame.

Lieutenant Campbell kicked the cans over in an incredulous rage. "You stupid shit," he growled at the startled trooper. "You know better than to light a fire after dark in a goddamn perimeter."

"L. T., I was just cooking a cup of coffee for the captain."

Campbell realized that Captain Hewitt was sitting right next to the man he was berating. "Captain, come here a minute," Campbell said, leading Hewitt away from the CP. Campbell's six months of combat time were actually over, but Lucas had left him in the field an extra month to ease the transition from Vazquez to Hewitt. "Look, I don't want to act like I'm trying to run the company," the veteran platoon leader said to Hewitt when they were out of earshot of the command group, "but we've got to get some things straight out here. First thing is, nobody lights fires out here at night. Nobody lights a cigarette. You just don't do that. We're out in the mountains and the gooks can see that fire from anywhere."

Hewitt nodded, and Campbell went on, questioning the new commander about why there was no security on the west side of the perimeter. Explained Hewitt, "I knew you were coming in."

"I think we got to be a little tighter than that, Captain."

Campbell next asked Hewitt if he'd deployed a three-man LP to cover the trail where it ran into the NDP from the southeast. Hewitt responded in the negative. "You gotta get LPs out to cover the trails unless you're working in small groups," Campbell replied. "Men don't like to go on LP or ambush, but they understand the need for it, and they'll do it if you make 'em."

Hewitt thanked Campbell for his advice. "It wasn't an adversarial conversation, which I was worried about," Campbell recalled. "Hewitt was a real nice fella." Perhaps to justify himself, Hewitt described how his ARVN unit had operated in the lowlands of III Corps, and Campbell got the impression that Hewitt had been fighting VC, not NVA, and that he'd picked up some bad habits from the South Vietnamese: "The ARVN went out in battalion size, toting chickens and ducks with them, and they had cooking fires at night. They thought security was a matter of numbers."

Campbell, scheduled to leave in a day or two for R&R, after which he was to be reassigned to the rear, sat down that night with his platoon sergeant, Sgt. Thomas H. Herndon—good soldier, good friend—who would be taking over Charlie Two until a new lieutenant arrived. "Sarge, this is something different," Campbell said of the increasing enemy activity. "This thing is changing. You've got to keep everyone's shit together out here. . . ."

As the sappers were to prove, the company did not keep itself together. "In a firefight, they were hellacious soldiers," Campbell said of the draftee infantrymen in Charlie Company. "They'd do whatever you told 'em to do, every damn one of 'em. But there's no sorrier bastard in the world, soldiering-wise, than a U. S. soldier who's not scared, and that's the never-ending problem of being a commander—trying to keep the men combat ready when they decide there's nothing to worry about and get complacent."

What Captain Hewitt needed were some old pro Regular Army NCOs. He had none. There simply weren't enough left at that stage in the war. Absent Campbell, two of Hewitt's platoon leaders and almost all his platoon sergeants and squad leaders were products of the Noncommissioned Officer Candidate School (NCOCS) at Fort Benning, which made sergeants of those who showed leadership potential in basic and advanced individual training (AIT). Honor grads were promoted to staff sergeant. The whole process, from recruit to NCO, took eight months. Though bright and motivated, these instant sergeants, known as shake 'n bakes, lacked the experience that normally went with so many stripes. Given that they were the same age as their troops and were often draftees themselves, they tended to be more buddies than taskmasters.

The contacts continued. On June 24, Company C was at the southeastern end of the ridge again when Hewitt reported that he had fifty NVA in the open, moving up the slope of a partially denuded mountain thirteen hundred meters to the south. The result was a feeding frenzy—mortars, arty, gunships, tac air—but when the company swept the mountainside, there was not a single body, weapon, or piece of equipment to be found amid the craters.

On June 27, Charlie One opened fire on two enemy soldiers whose line of retreat inadvertently led them directly toward Charlie Two. Herndon popped a claymore on them at twenty-five meters, and the platoon opened fire, killing both NVA. As part of a new program to help morale, Charlie One was lifted up to Ripcord the next day for an overnight vacation, complete with a barbecue over sawed-off oil drums. Hewitt and Charlie Two went in the day after that. "It was pay day, and we had a poker game going inside a bunker," recalled Sgt. Jerry D. Moyer, a squad leader bumped up to serve as platoon sergeant of Charlie Two. "Captain Hewitt was in the game. I wasn't. They were playing for forty and fifty dollar pots, high stakes for me. Hewitt was doing real good, talking about 'this is my car payment . . . this is my house payment. . . .' It's kind of ironic that he got killed right after raking in all that cash."

Before Hewitt helicoptered back out with Charlie Two, Lucas attached to his command group Company D's FO, an artillery lieutenant with little to do while his company secured Ripcord. Prior to that, Hewitt's forward observer had been an artillery sergeant. Linking up with Charlie One, Hewitt and Charlie Two returned late that afternoon to the top of Hill 902. Charlie Three, meanwhile, was lifted up for its turn on Ripcord. When the shelling began the next morning, Hewitt and the FO helped direct the counterbattery fire while a handful of troops opened up with M60s and LAWs. In response, the NVA planned a sapper attack on Hill 902. Radio conversations to that effect were monitored by a special signal-intercept (SSI) team in an underground, sandbag-covered conex only a hundred feet from the TOC on FSB Ripcord. It should have been simple enough to pass that information to Lucas. However, for security reasons, SSI teams were under strict orders to bypass their host units and forward their raw data directly to division headquarters, which would decide what to send back down the chain of command to the line battalions. In this case, division prepared an intelligence warning, but for reasons never explained the alert hit a snag and did not reach Lucas until after the attack on Hill 902. At that point, it only added insult to injury.[2]

With an overconfidence born of inexperience, Hewitt deployed no listening posts that second night on Hill 902. Nor did he insist that everyone dig in and camouflage their positions. The company commander himself slung a hammock between two naked trees to one side of an LZ that had been cleared near the top of the mountain before air strikes removed most of the rest of the vegetation around the upper slopes. "Everybody was too casual, too relaxed," recalled Cafferty, the senior medic, who, along with Sgt. Jack H. Dreher, senior radioman, had dug in near Hewitt. Another member of the command group, Sp4 Robert C. Smoker, an ex-rifleman now in charge of resupply, was supposed to share their hole, but "we were kind of clumped together, which didn't make sense to me, so I wound up digging a hole off by myself."

As before, Charlie One, down to about fifteen men, was on the eastern side of the hill and Charlie Two on the western side with twenty-five troops. The perimeter was a ring of three-man positions, thirteen in all. "Some guys did dig foxholes, but most didn't," said Sergeant Moyer. "We weren't very far apart. We had about ten yards between positions, and the whole perimeter was about the size of a softball diamond with the captain at the pitcher's mound."

Actually, most of those troops who dug foxholes simply scooped out the shallow, half-eroded ones left over from whatever unit had established the first NDP atop Hill 902 years before. "There was no fresh dirt on that hill," contended Sergeant Burkey, whose platoon, Charlie Three, flew in the next morning as the relief force. Burkey was appalled that the company had used the original foxholes "just like every other bunch of idiots that ever went up there. They should have moved off the hilltop a bit and dug a new perimeter. Vazquez made sure you understood that you never go near a foxhole that's already been dug because the enemy knows right where it's at. Vazquez would have come from the rear and kicked me in the ass if he had found us setting up in old foxholes."

Instead of digging in, Sergeants Herndon and Moyer, and Gary Steele, the platoon radioman, had made a little poncho hootch. Two feet high, the shelter provided relief from the sun during the day and some warmth during the cool of the night. A grenade tossed atop it, however, would take out the entire platoon command group, and it was a bad example. Other easy-to-spot poncho hootches dotted the mountaintop. "I thought putting up a pup-tent was really stupid," said Sp4 Stephen L. Manthei, a survivor of ten months in the bush with Charlie One. "I spoke to 'em about it, but they outranked me, and nothing was done. You looked up the hill and the CP was sticking out like a sore thumb, too. It was ridiculous to set up like that after we had ticked off the enemy by firing down at them that morning."

According to Manthei, neither he nor Bob Tarbuck and Don Holthausen, who were in position with him on the south side of the hill, shared the general no-sweat attitude. "We dug our holes deep as we were expecting totally to get messed with," said Manthei. One man was supposed to be awake at all times at each position, and when Manthei took his first watch after dark, "it was a beautiful night, starlit, with some mortar and artillery shows you could see off in the distance. We pulled our guard shifts with a little more intensity than usual that night—at least at our position."

Having probed the firebase and another company that night, good diversions both, the enemy didn't strike their primary target until almost four in the morning. It was the textbook hour for a night assault, a time when bleary-eyed guards, convincing themselves that nothing was going to happen in the two hours remaining before dawn, were most likely to nod off. "It was really quiet on the hill, almost an eerie quiet," remembered Manthei, awakened for another turn on watch shortly before the attack started. The first indication of trouble was the whispered report of an alert guard who had seen movement in front of his position. Manthei put a hand on Tarbuck and Holthausen and silently indicated that they should get in their holes. The perimeter guard on the radio was instructed to open fire, and that's when "all hell broke loose," said Manthei. "I saw an RPG flash across the hill into the command post, and the radio went dead from that position. The explosion knocked me backwards against the inside of my foxhole, and then in the next instant numerous grenades and satchel charges started going off, gunfire erupted from everywhere, and there was a lot of hollering and screaming in the dark, both by us and the Vietnamese. . . ."

CHAPTER 4

Hell Night

Sergeant Herndon nudged Jerry Moyer awake for his turn on guard shortly before the attack began. "What in the hell, how come you're waking me up now?" Moyer whispered harshly after checking the luminescent face of his watch. "It's fifteen minutes early."

"I don't know," Herndon whispered back. "All I know is Steele woke me up, and I did my hour and twenty minutes."

"Okay, we'll straighten this out come daylight. We'll find out what went wrong," Moyer said angrily. Either the platoon leader or the radioman had not pulled an entire guard shift.

Moyer scooted down to a fallen tree about ten feet in front of their poncho hootch. No sooner had the acting platoon sergeant gotten into position behind the tree—with weapon, ammunition, grenades, and the detonators to their claymores within easy reach—than he heard something moving on the side of the hill. You don't cry wolf with the first brush snap, he thought. It was most likely a monkey or a wild pig, but the noise definitely put his ears on alert.

The rustling continued, and Moyer finally contacted Sergeant Dreher, who was on radio watch up at the company CP. "We've got serious movement out here. Wake the captain up, and see what he wants to do. I think we need to go to fifty percent alert till daylight."

"Roger, wait one," Dreher replied. He returned to the radio a moment later: "Yeah, start waking people up. . . ."

Moyer had not been the only one reporting movement. Private First Class Michael K. Mueller, an assistant machine gunner, was on guard two holes down to Moyer's left—the gunner himself and the team's ammo bearer were sleeping against a log just behind Mueller—when he heard something about twenty-five meters down from his foxhole where the scrubby brush below the denuded top of the mountain merged back into thick jungle. Next—and at this Mueller's chest squeezed tight—he saw an enemy soldier, a black silhouette against a dark gray background, crouch down for a moment, then slip off into the shadows. Mueller got Dreher on the horn and was told, "The next time you see that guy—fire 'im up."

Mueller dropped the handset and began spraying the bushes with his M16. It was too late; the enemy was already in position. As soon as Mueller cut loose, a rocket-propelled grenade shrieked out of the dark and slammed into the company CP. Satchel charges began exploding. Hearing someone blow a claymore, Mueller snatched up the detonator to his own, but when he squeezed down on it, nothing happened. The sappers had apparently cut the wire snaking downhill from the detonator to the mine itself.

It was 3:46 A.M. on July 2, 1970. Captain Hewitt, found sprawled in the tangle of his shredded hammock after the battle, missing one arm and both legs, was killed by that first RPG. The newly attached FO lieutenant was temporarily shell-shocked by the same blast.

In the command group foxhole, only about six feet down from the captain's hammock, Dreher was wounded by the rocket that took out Hewitt, as was Doc Cafferty, who'd been sleeping on his air mattress just above the hole. Peppered all over with little fragments, his left arm sliced open from elbow to wrist, Cafferty slid down into the foxhole, grabbing his M16 and an ammo bandolier along the way. "I was so fucking scared I didn't even know I was injured," he recalled. "My medical bag was gone. My rucksack was gone. Everything was gone. We didn't know what had happened to the Old Man, but he was obviously dead because he never got in the foxhole. Total confusion. There were explosions going off everywhere. It was like waking up on the Fourth of July."

Dreher whispered frantically into his radio handset, calling for illumination and gunships. "I was just hiding in the corner," recounted Cafferty, "and all of a sudden something fell against my back—and it was a fuckin' satchel charge." The sappers were using one-pound blocks of C4 plastic explosives, which produced terrific, head-ringing blasts and, if packed with enough scrap metal, could tear an arm or a leg into bloody ribbons. The satchel charge thrown into the command group foxhole wedged between Cafferty's rear end and the wall of the foxhole as he knelt there. Said Cafferty, "I said to myself, this is it, I'm gone. I'm going to blow all over Dreher—he won't get hurt because it's behind my back—but the thing never went off. The blasting cap didn't work, which was very common, thank God."

When the first rocket crashed in, Moyer was crawling back to wake up Sergeant Herndon and Gary Steele. They rolled out from under their poncho hootch at the sound of the blast, and Herndon stood up on one side and Steele got to his knees on the other, reaching for his M16. Steele immediately spotted someone with a floppy bush hat standing at the top of the hill, aiming down at them with a rocket launcher over his shoulder. Steele was stunned that a sapper could appear behind them so suddenly. The apparition convinced him that the sappers must have already been inside the perimeter when the shooting started. Steele threw his rifle to his shoulder. He thought he had the man atop the hill dead to rights, but as groggy as he was he had forgotten to flip off the safety, and when he pulled the trigger nothing happened. An instant later, he saw the quick jet of flame that was the backblast of the RPG.

The rocket exploded just behind the poncho hootch. Steele, sent flying by the blast, lay where he landed, stunned, hoping the enemy would think him dead. He could feel warm blood leaking from his ears and mouth and rectum, such was the concussive force of the explosion, and he was having trouble breathing. He would later learn that a big chunk of shrapnel had punched through his back, cracking several ribs, one of which punctured his left lung.

Sergeant Herndon was in even worse shape. The sappers atop the hill heaved a satchel charge down at where they could hear him screaming. It wounded not only Herndon but splattered Steele in his legs and rear end with more shrapnel, painfully flipping him over.

The first illumination round, fired by the mortar platoon on the firebase, popped overhead, trailing thick white smoke as it descended under its parachute. The enemy took cover, but when the flare burned out and the hilltop was again swallowed in darkness, another satchel charge came sailing toward Herndon. It landed on the left side of Steele—*boom!*—rupturing his eardrum. Another flare, another pause in the enemy fire. The flare blinked out. More satchel charges exploded. *Boom! Boom! Boom!*

Herndon's sobs were drawing most of the satchel charges, and Moyer hissed loudly to his buddy, "Shut up, Tom. Shut up."

Sergeant Moyer was back at his log, helmet hastily slapped on. Holding his fire so as not to give away his own position with a muzzle flash, he instead chucked frag grenades down the slope, not comprehending that the enemy soldiers throwing the satchel charges were actually inside the perimeter.

Each time Herndon screamed, Pfc. Richard J. Conrardy, the new platoon medic who had dived behind Moyer's log, muttered that he should try to go get the sergeant. "No, no, hold up," Moyer barked at him, "just hold up a minute—wait till this dies down."

Finally, Conrardy, a tall, skinny, nineteen-year-old conscientious objector from Wright, Kansas, blurted, "I've got to go get him."

Rising to his knees, Doc Conrardy was shot before he could make his move. He pitched backward against Moyer, who knew that the medic was dead as soon as he hit him; the kid was just a lifeless weight. Moyer, however, couldn't make sense of the fact that the shot that killed Conrardy had come from the top of the hill. Another satchel charge exploded moments later, abruptly snuffing out Herndon's screams. The acting platoon leader was dead. For having tried to get to Herndon, Conrardy was posthumously awarded the Silver Star.

Sergeant Lee N. Lenz was dug in with a machine-gun team between Herndon and Mueller to cover the trail that entered the perimeter from the southwest. The position was taken out with a satchel charge in the first moments of the attack. Though it is likely that some sappers had already infiltrated the perimeter, most probably darted in behind the satchel charge that eliminated that key M60. Lenz scrambled uphill for cover. His machine gunner, Sp4 Roger D. Sumrall of Hattiesburg, Mississippi, had been killed by the satchel charge and would be affectionately remembered by Campbell as a "tough, stocky bastard and a good soldier."

All that was later found of Sumrall's assistant gunner, Pfc. Stephen J. Harber—he was another good soldier, a quiet, blond-headed draftee with a wife back home in Minnesota—was a jungle boot with a foot inside and one of his dog tags secured to the laces. Harber apparently survived the explosion that killed Sumrall, only to be blown to bits moments later by an RPG. After the illumination rounds started, Steve Manthei saw someone who looked like Harber try to dash up the hill. "There was a hell of an explosion at that moment," recounted Manthei, "and he was gone. He was blown away. There were pieces of human everywhere. It was terrible. Harber had a lucky dollar bill that he carried with him all the time, and right after the explosion a ripped half of that dollar bill floated down next to my foxhole. I still have it. . . ."

Gary Steele crawled back to their blasted poncho hootch for his M16, only to find that the weapon had been damaged beyond use. Luckily, the grenades he had laid out were still there, but he was so rattled that after pulling the pins he threw the first two up where he had seen the RPG gunner without thinking to remove the safety clips on the spoons. Oh, you dumb son of a bitch, he thought; now they're gonna take them clips off and throw 'em back.

There were intense moments of automatic fire and explosions in the intervals between illumination rounds, lulls when new flares popped. "You just can't imagine how many satchel charges went off. I want to say hundreds," noted Moyer. "There was a little AK fire, but not much. Not as much as we were firing our M16s."

The enemy infantry supporting the sapper attack could be heard down on the slope, and Moyer, like many others, thought they were the ones throwing the satchel charges. C'mon, give me a target, give me something to do here, he thought during one lull as the flares cast weird, shifting shadows through the naked trees. At that moment he heard a satchel charge land behind him. It rolled down against his boot. He crawled over his log like a shot and braced for the explosion. "It never did go off," he recalled. "I scooted back to my position, but it still hadn't registered that we had been overrun. I couldn't comprehend that they were behind me. You know, they don't get behind you. That just didn't happen."

When Mike Mueller opened fire, his team leader, Sergeant Mendez, snapped awake and jumped into the foxhole with him, as did their ammo bearer, a kid nicknamed Shaky. Mendez got behind the M60, ready to open fire and expose the position of this key weapon only when the enemy rushed in behind their satchel charges. Mueller fired single shots down the slope, not realizing until he happened to glance back and saw figures flitting against the night sky at the crest of the hill that sappers had already breached the perimeter. Before Mueller could swing his M16 around, he saw a satchel charge rolling down the hill at them. He pulled his head down. The first explosion was quickly followed by more—*boom, boom, boom!*—then the fourth or fifth satchel charge bounced into the hole, and Mendez, Mueller, and Shaky scrambled out in a heartbeat, going face first into the dirt below their position. *Boom!*

They piled back in. Mueller, having lost his web gear and ammo bandoliers, had only the single magazine in his M16. There was no time to fire, because another satchel charge fell in with them. They dove out of the foxhole again—*boom!*—then jumped back in. The first flare burst overhead at that moment, exposing two sappers in black pajamas who were crouched behind a log above them, methodically flipping satchel charges at their foxhole. Another one rolled in. Mueller dove uphill, lost his footing, and slid back down the steep slope so that his left leg was across the top of the foxhole when the satchel charge at the bottom detonated. Mueller skidded into the hole, his knee a bloody mess, then popped up and frantically cut loose on the sappers with what was left of the magazine in his M16.

Many things were happening at the same time. Dreher and Doc Cafferty were still in their foxhole when a close friend of the medic's, Sp4 Robert P. Radcliffe, and a man Cafferty didn't recognize in the dark—it was Sergeant Lenz—clambered in with them, desperate for cover. The foxhole was no refuge. "There's too many people in here," Cafferty said. "They know this is the goddamn CP. We're all going to get killed with one grenade. I'm outta here."

With that, Cafferty started crawling away, unaware that almost as soon as he exited the foxhole an RPG exploded at its edge. Dreher survived the blast. Lenz and Radcliffe were decapitated.

Doc Cafferty shimmied over a fallen tree to his right, numbly noticing that his left forearm was sliced open. "I didn't care," he recalled. "I could still function, and that's all that mattered."

Seeing the artillery recon sergeant in a foxhole, Doc Cafferty "just fell in on top of him because I didn't know where else to go. I was scared shitless." It was tight quarters in the little hole, and Cafferty was in an awkward crouch, half in and half out, when "I got hit in the helmet with a goddamn grenade. It bounced off and was laying there in front of my face. It was a U. S. baseball grenade. I might have been able to reach it, but I just froze. I said to myself, that's it, I'm gone. I thought of my mother and my fiancée. . . ."

The grenade never exploded. Cafferty made a point to examine it after the battle and saw that, though the pin was missing, the spoon was still held down by a safety clip. He assumed a sapper had scooped up the U. S. grenade and thrown it without knowing he needed to do more than just pull the pin. Actually, the grenade was probably one of the two that Gary Steele had heaved uphill in such haste that he forgot to remove the safeties. If Steele had removed them, he would have killed Cafferty and never known about it.

Cafferty suddenly realized that the artillery lieutenant was huddled at the bottom of the foxhole under the recon sergeant. "I swore I was going to kill that guy someday," said Cafferty. The FO was the ranking man on that hill after Captain Hewitt, but instead of taking command, "all he did was hide in his foxhole all night," noted Cafferty. "I guess I really can't blame him for being scared because we all were, but, Jesus, he should have did something."[1]

Furious with the lieutenant, Doc Cafferty jumped from the foxhole. He spotted a sapper and shouldered his M16. "I finally got my shit together and started shooting. I finally got some balls. . . ."

The sapper was standing about thirty feet away, ready to throw another satchel charge down at them. Bullshit, Cafferty thought as he squeezed off his entire magazine, putting most of eighteen rounds into the North Vietnamese. Fuck you.

The sapper went down like a spastic marionette. Jerry Cafferty—a wisecracking, extremely dedicated draftee-medic from an Irish neighborhood in West Haven, Connecticut—saw only then that another sapper was beside the first, and he frantically grabbed a fresh magazine from the bandolier across his chest. The magazine jammed in his weapon. Cafferty had no way of knowing until he inspected the magazine in the morning that it had already stopped a bullet for him. He'd been pumping adrenaline so furiously as he shot the first sapper that he hadn't realized that the second one had been blasting back at him with his AK. Cafferty hadn't felt a thing when a round hit the magazine in question, which was over the center of his chest, mangling the magazine so that it was useless in his M16.

Feeling insanely exposed as he struggled to clear the jam, Cafferty finally popped the malfunctioning magazine back out, thumped another one in, and resumed fire. He cut down the second sapper, along with several more who materialized out of the light and shadows. "I can still picture those guys lined up," Cafferty, awarded the Silver Star, would haltingly recall, still rattled, still haunted. "I just shot. I put it on semiautomatic, and just started firing 'em up as fast as I could. If they stopped shooting, I figured I got 'em. I was scared to death. I had no idea why I was there in that country, but somebody had to do something. Everybody else on that side of the hill was dead or fucked up. There weren't a lot of other guys firing, and I figured I was already dead. I should have been killed by that satchel charge. I should have been killed by that grenade. I had already said my prayers and said good-bye to my girlfriend and my mother and father. I was gone. I didn't have anything to lose. . . ."

Bob Smoker was in his foxhole when he heard something and, turning, saw the silhouette of someone standing about ten feet uphill from him. The man didn't notice Smoker. By his size, he was obviously Vietnamese, and Smoker's first thought was that he was one of the NVA defectors attached to the company as a Kit Carson scout; but then it hit him that Hewitt, not trusting the scouts, had left all of them on Ripcord. The sapper was so close that Smoker didn't have to sight in but merely raise his M16 quietly and slowly in the silhouette's direction. He squeezed the trigger once. The sapper dropped like a stone, shot in the forehead. Other unseen sappers began whispering urgently to one another. Smoker lobbed two grenades in their direction. He didn't know if the frags killed the sappers or sent them scuttling for cover, but there was no more chatter.

Mike Mueller saw Shaky scramble down the hill after the third satchel charge landed in their hole. Mendez also disappeared in the chaos. Mueller might have been alone, but at that point he found his two missing ammunition bandoliers, which gave him a total of fourteen magazines. He also grabbed his web gear, to which several grenades were attached. Finally able to fight back, he began spraying the log shielding the two sappers who'd been throwing the satchel charges down at his foxhole. He crouched to change magazines, then popped back up to fire another burst—and realized that one of the sappers had popped up himself with his AK.

Mueller could hear shots cracking past his head, then what felt like a baseball bat caught him in his left shoulder, and he dropped back in his hole, stunned and numb. The two sappers, thinking him badly wounded, started down the hill to finish him off. Suddenly enraged as he realized that this was for real, that these bastards meant to kill him, Mueller was about to pull the trigger of his M16 when Mendez sprang up directly in front of him from a hole in which he'd been hiding, screaming at Mueller as he tried to get away from the sappers, "Don't shoot, don't shoot."

Mendez dove to the left, leaving the enemy in full view again, but after almost shooting his team leader in the back, Mueller was too rattled to do anything but duck back down. Luckily, the sappers had also been unnerved by the commotion, and they scrambled back behind their log. They heaved a satchel charge toward Mendez, then charged down the hill again, one of them slung with bags of satchel charges, the other armed with a folding-stock AK-50.

Mike Mueller, a naive, dependable, Billy Budd type with a stammer that would put a smile on your face, had grown up on his stepfather's homestead in Alaska. To win the Silver Star, Mueller had leveled his M16 at the onrushing sappers and, remembering his training, raised his left index finger at the end of the barrel to give him something to guide on, because it was too dark to use the front sights. Mueller dropped the sapper with the AK-50, then nailed the one with the satchel charges in turn. The second sapper fell out of sight, screaming horribly, and Mueller burned off a couple more magazines, trying to shut him up. Able to take the keening no more, Mueller finally exited his foxhole to finish the man off. He was shot almost immediately in his left leg—again, it felt like a hard-swung baseball bat—by an enemy soldier who spotted him in the flare light. Mueller retreated back to his hole, and Mendez crawled in with him. The bullet hole in Mueller's upper thigh was the size of a quarter; when the shock wore off, his entire leg throbbed so badly he could barely move. The round had shattered the compass in his pocket, scoring his leg with little bits of metal, then ricocheted like a hot poker through the muscle from the ball joint of his hip to a point about six inches above his knee. He was bleeding badly.

The private battles continued. When Steve Manthei of Charlie One, in position with Tarbuck and Holthausen, heard something moving in the undergrowth below them, he blew their claymore. The movement stopped. Most of the NVA were on Charlie Two's side of the hill, but they did hit the position occupied by Sgt. Daniel Smith, Charlie One's platoon sergeant, on the left flank of Charlie Two. Specialist Fourth Class Robert W. Zoller was killed, and Smith and the third man in the position were wounded.

Smith, terrified, kept screaming to Manthei for help. No way, Manthei thought, hoping that Smith didn't think him a chickenshit for not rushing headlong to his aid. There was no way to get over there without getting killed, though. If the sappers didn't blow you away, your own guys would in the confusion.

Instead, Manthei, Tarbuck, and Holthausen lobbed grenades out in front of Smith's position to keep the enemy at bay. Meanwhile, things were starting to quiet down, most of the sappers having been killed during the first thirty intense minutes of battle, when the Cobras finally made it to Hill 902. To mark the NVA infantrymen supporting the attack, Manthei threw one hand flare directly down the hill to the south and another as far as he could to the southwest, then got on the radio to the gunships: "Dump everything you got in a straight line from one flare to the other."

As the gunships made their passes, the fight on the hill dribbled away to an occasional explosion, an occasional shout. Sergeant Moyer, who hadn't actually seen a single enemy soldier, was still prone behind his log. He didn't hear the satchel charge that landed next to him. As he discovered in the morning, his rucksack had absorbed most of the blast, but he still caught a lot of shrapnel in his buttocks, and the explosion sent him tumbling down the hill. He instinctively kept a grip on his M16. After he could think straight again through the roaring in his ears, he realized that he was lying on his stomach among some tree limbs about fifteen feet from the cover of his log. His legs didn't feel right, and as he reached back to slap them awake he saw that the seat of his trousers was on fire. He frantically swatted out the little flickering flames, thinking not of being burned but being spotted by the sappers.

Moyer's heart was pounding. He had lost his helmet, he didn't have his ammo bandoliers, he didn't have any grenades.

He remembered, though, that he had thumped a fresh magazine in his rifle just before the explosion. He tried to decide if he should crawl back to his log. The problem was that Layne Hammons's gun team occupied the next position to the right of the log. Moyer became convinced that if he moved, Hammons would shoot him full of holes in a case of mistaken identification. The hell with it, Moyer thought, feeling secure enough where he was. I'm just gonna wait here till daylight and see what happens.

What happened was that another flare popped overhead, catching an NVA in green fatigues as he moved up the slope in a half crouch—his AK-47 at the ready—directly in front of Moyer. The man was about twenty feet away. Moyer instantly cut loose on semiautomatic—*pop-pop-pop-pop-pop-pop-pop*—and the enemy soldier jerked backward four times as at least four rounds hit him. You've got to stop shootin', you fool, Moyer suddenly thought, you ain't got no more bullets. He ceased firing. Everything was quiet. The NVA was nowhere to be seen. Moyer desperately wondered how many rounds he had left. He touched the dust cover of his weapon. It was closed, meaning there was a round in the chamber. Good enough. He wasn't about to remove the magazine and check how many more rounds it contained, afraid that the noise would reveal him to any other enemy soldiers slinking along the slope. He stayed low. It would be morning soon enough.

In the hushed stillness that had fallen over the hill, Gary Steele could hear Vietnamese voices about twenty feet up from where he lay next to his smashed poncho hootch. The sappers were talking loudly, as if they owned the hill. I guess they think they won the war and we're all dead, Steele mused bitterly. Though in considerable pain from his wounds, he pulled the pin on a grenade, removed the safety clip, and crawled toward the sappers, afraid that if he didn't take care of them, they would eventually take care of him. They were squatting together, apparently planning their next move. Steele quietly pulled the spoon off the frag, let the grenade cook off—one, two, three—then tossed it into the group and scrambled back down the hill as fast as he could manage.

Steele lay low again until twilight, when he spotted three fellow survivors in a position down the line to his right as the sky began to turn a neon gray. No fire had come from that foxhole during the night, and Steele had assumed the three men there to be casualties. They were not. They were simply cherries—replacements too scared and confused to start blasting away in the dark.

When Steele saw them in the first hazy light of the morning, he called to them, "I'm wounded. I'm comin' over."

Not sure which side held the hill but expecting the worst, Steele pulled the pin on his last grenade and kept his hand wrapped around the spoon as he started crawling toward the foxhole. He was determined that if any sappers jumped him along the way, they'd be in for a big surprise when they rolled his body over.

To get to the foxhole, Steele had to get past a fallen tree. There wasn't enough room to crawl under it, so he backed up, got on his haunches, and dove over it. As he did so, a shot cracked out from behind. Instead of hitting the meat of Steele's buttocks, which would have been a bad but not permanently disabling wound, the round went straight up his anus, destroying his whole rectum.

It felt to Steele as though someone with a pointy-toed boot had kicked him for all he was worth right in his anus. The pain was so intense for one terrible second that he was surprised he didn't drop his grenade and blow himself up, but then everything went numb and he crawled on, furious that the cherries weren't laying down some cover fire. Another round cracked out, grazing his right knee.

Steele finally reached the foxhole, but it wasn't much of a hole, and for Steele to pull himself in, one of the cherries had to get behind some other piece of cover. The petrified kid did so only reluctantly. Steele held up his frag, meaning to get rid of it, but he was fading at that point and instead slipped and let the spoon fly off. One of the new guys snatched the grenade and heaved it down the hill. Steele asked for a cigarette, then lay back in the hole, feeling relieved, almost safe. The last thing he remembered before passing out was turning to the cherries and saying, "I quit."

* * *

It is impossible to know if any sappers escaped the perimeter before dawn. Four of them were definitely still inside at daybreak. They tried to slip out the way they had come but, having waited too long, were silhouetted against the twilight skyline as they started down from the top of the hill. Mike Mueller, rising up from his foxhole, squared the sights of his M16 on the head of the first sapper, then emptied the rest of the magazine on the next one in line, leaving them both sprawled dead on the hillside. The other two darted behind some debris, and Mueller lobbed two frags in that direction. The enemy soldiers did not reappear. They were found later where the grenades had gotten them, one of them sprawled atop an RPG launcher that was pointed toward Mueller's position.

CHAPTER 5

Picking Up the Pieces

The silence just before twilight was so total that Sergeant Moyer wondered whether he was the only man left alive on the hill, although he knew that was impossible. When it got light enough, he made eye contact with Layne Hammons. Moyer held up two fingers and pointed to his front. Hammons's assistant gunner, Chuck Damron, pulled the pins on two frags and, moving down to Moyer, scanned the jungle with hard eyes as he asked in a hard whisper, "Whatcha got?"

"The last dink I seen was right there," Moyer answered, gesturing to the spot where he had blasted the now-missing NVA.

Damron threw his grenades, then stayed with Moyer until the relief force began landing. Moyer checked how many rounds he had left—he had to know—and discovered that in addition to the one in the chamber he had only one more in the magazine. He turned loose of his M16 as Damron helped him up the hill. They passed the bodies of numerous half-naked, charcoal-streaked sappers along the way, and a dumbfounded Moyer realized for the first time that the enemy had been inside the perimeter with them.

The top of the mountain had been secured shortly before the arrival of the relief force by Doc Cafferty, who, hearing shouts and screams from wounded men on Charlie Two's side of the hill, did what had to be done to get to them. The senior medic rounded up two guys from a nearby foxhole—they looked scared to death, and he had the impression they'd played turtle during the whole fight—and, barking at one to get on his right, the other his left to cover him, he nervously started up the hill, not trusting that his wide-eyed companions wouldn't freeze if they ran into trouble. One of the wounded men screeching in pain was the sapper with the bags of satchel charges who had been cut down earlier by Mike Mueller. There was a single shot in the morning stillness that abruptly silenced the enemy soldier, then Mueller heard Cafferty shout, "Currahee."

The old regimental motto served as a catchall password in situations where friend could not be distinguished from foe. Mueller gave the obscene counterresponse with his distinctive stutter: "C-c-currahee, m-m-mother-f-f-fucker."

"Alaska, is that you?" Cafferty shouted, hearing the stutter.

Mueller called back that it was, and Cafferty shouted, "Get up here and help me clear this hill."

"I'm w-w-wounded."

"We all are, man. Get up here."

Cafferty and Mueller walked the entire hilltop at that point, methodically shooting each sprawled-out NVA in the back of his head. "To this day I regret having to do that," Cafferty would recall sadly, "but what was I going to do? I didn't want to walk by one who wasn't really dead and have him shoot me in the back."

Bob Smoker threw unexploded satchel charges off the hill. There were dozens of the one-pound blocks, and it didn't register with Smoker in the heat of the moment that any one of them could have exploded in his hands. Meanwhile, in the absence of anyone else able or willing to take over, Doc Cafferty realized that he was the de facto commander of Charlie Company. Frantic to get to the wounded, he first had to reestablish the perimeter. He spread out the survivors to fill the empty foxholes, then, grabbing what few battle dressings he saw lying around in the debris, he started doing what he could for the wounded, bandaging those he had bandages for and organizing litter teams to get them up to the LZ.

Gary Steele dimly realized that six troopers were carrying him up the hill in a poncho. Cafferty hit him with morphine—

the pain miraculously ebbed away—and slapped the biggest dressing he had over Steele's split-open anus, then told a new guy to stay with Steele and keep him talking, to make sure he didn't go into shock.

"Where you from?" the cherry babbled encouragingly. "Hang in there. . . . You're doing great. . . . You're going home, man."

Steele knew what the cherry was doing. He had done it himself for other wounded men in other firefights. He wasn't listening. Instead, he asked about the guys who had been at his position.

"Sergeant Moyer's doin' good," the cherry said.

"Where's Tom?" Steele knew that Tom Herndon was dead but wanted to see him one last time before he was medevacked.

"Tom's fine," the new guy lied. "He's over there, he's okay—"

"Bullshit. How many pieces is he in?"

Nearby, other troops were stacking up the dead sappers. "How many did we get?" Steele asked angrily. "A lot," the cherry said. The body count was fifteen, not including the numerous blood trails leading down the hill. Against that, Company C had one man, Steve Harber, who was missing in action (MIA), seven killed in action (KIA), and six officially wounded in action (WIA).

Cafferty found Dreher, the senior radioman, sitting deaf, wounded, and dazed after having coordinated illum and supporting fires while dodging satchel charges. Captain Hewitt was nearby in a mangled clump, both legs and one arm blown off, his remaining limb hanging on by a few strands of muscle. Seething at the stupidity of the captain's death, sickened and saddened by the waste, the senior medic wrapped Hewitt's remains in a poncho.

Moving on, Cafferty also policed up Lenz and his good buddy Bob Radcliffe, whom he was stunned to find in the foxhole he had vacated during the fight. They had no heads—a piece of skull the size of a cupped hand was flopped down on one's back—and their upper bodies were red and black mush, cauterized by the heat of the RPG that killed them. Sergeant

Lenz was identified by the cutoffs he had worn during the recent battalion stand-down when the company was trucked down for an afternoon at Eagle Beach, the division's R&R center on the South China Sea. He was still wearing the cutoffs under his fatigue trousers.

"It was the worst thing we'd ever seen," said Manthei of the scene on the hilltop. "I remember this one black kid, he lost it. He grabbed a machine gun and poured about three hundred rounds into some dead gooks that were piled up on the south side of the hill. We all consoled him, and told him it don't mean nothin', you gotta move on, that we were gonna get all our boys and get the hell outta there."

Captain Lieb and Sergeant Burkey's platoon, Charlie Three, had departed Ripcord under mortar fire and were inserted into the LZ on 902 under ground fire. Burkey's people urgently fanned out across the hilltop, securing it, shocked at the devastation that had been wrought upon their buddies from the other platoons. "Some of the survivors had that thousand-yard stare," said Sgt. Frank Bort, a squad leader in Charlie Three. "They were devastated."

For all that, when Burkey tried to medevac his buddy Cafferty, whose left arm hung limp and bloody, the medic shot back, "No way, I'm not leavin' this hill till all my men are out of here."

Cafferty placed Hewitt's remains inside one of the Hueys. When Steve Harber's foot-filled jungle boot was found, part of Charlie Three pushed down the mountain, trying to find the rest of his body. There was no sign of the missing man. During the search, Sgt. Rodney G. Moore saw someone's brains splattered against a tree. "I didn't know if it was from an American or a Vietnamese," he recalled, adding that "everyone was uptight because we knew the North Vietnamese had the hill zeroed in, and the longer we stayed there the more likely it was we were going to get mortared."

Captain Lieb called in tac air when the mortaring began. Red smoke was popped, a warning to the pilots, as the Hueys landed for the KIAs and WIAs. The wounded included several guys who claimed to be deaf, so desperate were they to get to the rear. After the casualties were evacuated, what was left of

Charlie One and Two was shuttled to Ripcord. Lieb and Charlie Three were lifted out shortly before noon. Rodney Moore was the last man on the last Huey. The enemy mortar was thumping again. The slick came to a hover several feet off the ground, and the four guys with Moore immediately hauled themselves aboard, knowing that the pilot had no time to linger. Moore, terrified that he might be left behind, jumped toward the skid with a surge of adrenaline and hit the metal with one foot just as the pilot started to lift off. Having turned as he pushed himself up, he landed on his rear in the center of the cabin so that he was looking out the door as a mortar round exploded an instant later off to one side of the landing zone. Several more rounds landed on top of the smoky hill as the helicopter banked away.

PART TWO

What Came Before

We told division from the beginning that if we went into that damn firebase without sufficient forces, they were going to attack.

—Maj. Robert A. "Tex" Turner
S3 Operations Officer
3d Brigade, 101st Airborne Division

CHAPTER 6

Two Strikes and a Walk

Lieutenant Colonel Lucas had been in command only eight days when the 2d of the 506th launched its first assault on Ripcord. At that time, the battalion was operating from Camp Evans, as it had been since the northern monsoon had forced the entire division out of the mountains five months earlier. The winter had been dispiriting for the Currahees. Three of their line companies, washed by cold rains under low, leaden skies, had worked the foothills, seeing little of the enemy, their casualties the result of booby traps and hit-and-run ambushes. Working on a rotating basis, the fourth line company secured a muddy brown circle in a sea of elephant grass called Firebase Jack.

After such routines, a major offensive deep into the mountains was a matter of high drama. "We felt that we had a very important mission," said Major Koenigsbauer, the battalion operations officer. "The 1st ARVN Infantry Division was one of the best units the South Vietnamese had, and not only Lucas and I, but also the ARVN officers with whom we coordinated, were eager to go."

Two months before the end of the monsoon, the weather was still marginal. The assault was postponed several times until there was a break in the rains on March 12, 1970. Lucas and Koenigsbauer rode in the command-and-control (C&C) ship of the 158th Aviation Battalion, which was committed in full for the CA, while at higher altitudes the brigade and division commanders observed the assault from their own C&C Hueys. The plan was to open a firebase atop Hill 902. To secure the area, Capt. Carmelito Arkangel and B/2-506th landed at the southeastern end of the ridge running down from the peak. Shortly thereafter, two ARVN companies were inserted on a ridge running north from Coc Muen Mountain. One of the LZs was mortared, but after a brief firefight the ARVN reported the capture of an AK-47 and a body count of two NVA.

The supporting forces in place, Capt. Albert P. Burkhart's A/2-506th approached Hill 902 in a line of Hueys. The objective was hazy with smoke. There had been a ten-minute artillery prep, then Cobras from the 4-77th ARA had unleashed several "rocket ripples," starting with 2.75-inch high-explosive (HE) warheads and finishing with "nails"—rockets packed with dartlike flechettes, which were meant to detonate any booby traps on the LZ. The flechette rockets exploded with a distinctive burst of red smoke, which signaled that the last pass was being made. The Hueys started in, but at that point the plan went awry. "For security reasons, brigade had not permitted us to conduct a good aerial reconnaissance of 902," said Koenigsbauer, the concern being that a LOH buzzing around the mountaintop would tip their hand. The vegetation was denser than had been estimated, and the lift ships could find no place to land. "The only way the troops could get in was to jump off the skids," noted Koenigsbauer; the Hueys could hover only so low, "and there would have been numerous injuries as the troops crashed down into shattered trees and broken-off stalks of bamboo."

Lucas conferred on a secure net with Col. William J. Bradley, then the brigade commander, and the decision was made to divert A/2-506th to Hill 927, the site of an old firebase originally opened by the 1st Cav in 1968 and renamed Ripcord when used by the Screaming Eagles in 1969. Hill 927, the flattened upper half of which was still bald and covered in spots with runway matting, was an easy place to land a helicopter, but it had not been selected as the primary LZ because it was dominated by nearby Hill 1000. The alternate landing zone was prepped only with ARA, "in part because there were no obstacles," explained Koenigsbauer, "but mostly because we needed to get the troops on the ground and get the operation rolling."

Captain Burkhart, in his first big action after two months in command, had gotten on the ground with one platoon when the next slick in line came under heavy automatic-weapons and mortar fire from Hill 1000. "There were Cobra gunships flying all over the hill and the tension was rising," read the journal of Sp4 Frank W. Marshall, an M79 grenadier on that first Huey to take fire. "We were all very quiet, just looking at each other in fear, knowing that something was about to happen. As our helicopter was landing, a red smoke grenade was thrown and right then we knew it was a hot LZ. The door gunners were yelling to get off fast and stay low. . . ."

Lucas and Koenigsbauer brought in arty and guns, orchestrating the fire support so that a corridor remained open for the lift ships bearing in with the rest of A/2-506th. One of the slicks took hits and crash-landed atop the firebase when the enemy began firing from the upper slopes of the mountain itself. Several infantrymen were shot and badly wounded as they bounded for cover. The Cobras spotted one of the hillside positions but hesitated to fire, given its proximity to the top of Ripcord. Burkhart sent a platoon to do the job. "We dropped our rucksacks and just grabbed our weapons and ammunition and started down the hill, taking cover as we could," wrote Frank Marshall. The brand-new platoon leader, 2d Lt. Dudley Davis, was killed by an RPG. Davis's radioman was medevacked over his protests that the scratch behind his ear wasn't serious, only to die en route to the evac hospital, a small piece of shrapnel in his brain. Marshall realized he had shrugged off his ammo vest along with his rucksack. "I had to run back up the hill while my squad covered for me, then back down," he wrote. "I was never so scared as bullets were flying all around me. When we found the enemy position, I kept firing grenades at the position. . . . Between my grenades and the . . . gunships, we knocked out the position. . . ."

With tac air coming in, a Chinook was able to extract the downed Huey. The lull ended at dusk with another barrage. Everyone expected a ground attack, and the company's field first sergeant, a two-war Regular Army E7, "cracked on us," noted 2d Lt. James P. Noll, one of the platoon leaders in Company A. "Just went to hell. Started crying. We had to send him out. We never saw him again." The night passed without incident, the company surrounded by a wall of artillery fire. In the morning, Burkhart moved down the ridge to the rocky knoll east of Hill 927. There he stayed for most of three days until the decision was made to lift Company A to the vicinity of Company B so the mortar positions around Ripcord could be saturated with fire without endangering friendly troops. Noll was running a local security patrol when "we were told to turn around and run back up to the LZ. Turned out they were going to B-52 the place. They didn't tell us. We were the last to find out. I was on the last chopper out of there, and, literally, as we were departing, here came the bombs. . . ."

Major General John M. Wright, the division commander, ordered another attack on Ripcord. "Obviously, the initial set-back did not mean the end of the summer offensive," explained Koenigsbauer. Hill 927 was redesignated the primary LZ. Like the first assault, the second one was repeatedly postponed by the rains. In the interim, all available artillery was brought to bear, including 8-inch and 175mm fire from corps; when the weather permitted, tac air hit known or suspected mortar positions within range of Ripcord. "That told the enemy we were coming back," noted Koenigsbauer, "but we didn't have any choice. It was critical that we take the hill, and to take the hill we had to suppress the firing positions around it."

When Captain Arkangel's six months were up on March 26, Bill Williams took over Company B, flying out to its NDP on the ridge below Hill 902. As Williams disembarked from the slick, a poncho-wrapped body was loaded aboard; the dead soldier, a point man, had been shot in the back of the head on patrol as he turned to alert his slack man that he thought he'd seen something up ahead.

Chip Collins, a rugged kid who'd joined up to escape the poverty of his Virginia coal-mining roots, was also assigned to Company B at that time, one of several replacements packed aboard a log bird at Camp Evans. The veterans ignored the new guys. Morale had shriveled in the cold rain. To Collins the grunts looked "like men gone two steps back toward ape. They stank. They were bearded. Their fatigues were dirty and ragged. They ate with their hands, hunched over, wolfing down the food. They were quiet, speaking little, signing with their hands to communicate. They had fear written on their faces."

Originally assigned to Bravo One, Collins spent that first night in position with two battle-rattled GIs, one of whom, taking advantage of the army's cynical policy of getting draftee grunts to sign over three more years in exchange for immediate reassignment off the line, "was plotting a way to get to the rear so he could re-up to get out of the field."

Collins was detailed to an observation post (OP) the next day. The other two guys were digging in when "an NVA in pith helmet and khakis almost walked on top of us." Collins was on guard with an M16, but "I was so cherry that I hadn't even locked and loaded. The delay in my response permitted that NVA to fight another day."

The observation post became a listening post at sunset. The night was frightful. "The rain beat down unmercifully," Collins would later write. Wraiths heard but not seen probed the perimeter, "and we were repeatedly told [by radio] not to fire unless engaged first. Should we have been 'engaged' and attempted to come in with the enemy close at our heels we would likely have been killed from fire along our own perimeter. In close bush, being on LP really meant you were an expendable first alert for the main force."

On Easter Sunday, March 31, Bravo One followed a scout-dog team along the spine of the ridge right into two or three enemy soldiers who, concealed in spiderholes in the dense underbrush, held their fire until the dog team was about twenty feet from the muzzles of their AK-47s. Three men were killed in the sudden fusillade, including the dog handler—along with his scout dog—and the platoon leader, alert, hard-charging but green 1st Lt. Harry E. Hayes, United States Military Academy (USMA) Class of 1968.

Bravo Three linked up with Bravo One and, passing through, firing as it advanced, discovered two blood trails leading off the ridge. The wounded and dead were carried to a landing zone, but the medevac had to break off its approach in the face of more enemy fire. "Air strikes went on all around us," wrote Collins, who half-expected the bomb fragments slashing past "to take off our heads." After the enemy was silenced and the casualties were evacuated, Collins wondered what he had gotten himself into. "The trails we were walking on were practically four-lane highways and we kept going back over the same ones every day. Was someone stupid? You be the judge."

The big guns from corps were good, but howitzers were better. They were more accurate and could be adjusted faster. Accordingly, on March 29, after Colonel Bradley had personally inspected the site with a ten-man security team, C/2-506th combat-assaulted onto Hill 316, seven klicks northeast and well within 105 range of Ripcord. Lucas's mortar platoon and a howitzer battery, Captain Rich's B/2-319th Field Artillery, went in next. The position was dubbed Firebase Gladiator. The weather had broken. The assault was on. With Companies A and B positioned southeast of Ripcord, Lucas deployed his last company, D/2-506th, to the northeast on March 30.

Lucas selected Company B for the second assault onto Ripcord, which commenced late on the morning of April 1, 1970. Captain Williams had gotten on the ground with two platoons and a three-man pathfinder team headed by 1st Lt. Michael D. Anderson—the elite, all-volunteer pathfinders were essentially combat air-traffic controllers—when, fifteen minutes into the operation, there was a single explosion on the mountaintop. In the pause that followed, Williams reckoned that a rocket from the gunship prep had cooked off late, but then more mortar shells began raining in behind that first registration round. "They had been waiting for us," recalled Williams. "The fire was coming from every direction. The enemy knew every spot on that hill, and they walked rounds all over the place. It was like being in the middle of a huge bull's eye."

One platoon leader was seriously wounded. Captain Williams and another platoon leader, SSgt. Terry W. Ratcliff, were running together, checking positions, making sure that everyone was either digging in or returning fire on the NVA. "I turned right for some reason," recounted Williams. "Ratcliff didn't, and he was hit just that quick." Making it to a shallow depression, Chip Collins was shocked to see soft-spoken, bush-savvy Ratcliff, one of the few veterans who had been encouraging rather than disdainful when dealing with the new guys, lay sprawled in the open like a rag doll. "A widening pool of blood flowed out from under him," Collins wrote. "Raw-boned Doc Kellogg scrambled over, felt for a pulse, shook his head at us, then gently laid Terry's helmet across his face. . . ."

Major Laurence J. Law, the battalion executive officer, had landed with a jump CP. Along with the pathfinders, Law's group, which included advance parties from the engineer platoon and artillery battery that were to have been lifted onto the hill, set up against one of the man-high boulders on the upper half of Ripcord. While Anderson kept the lift ships coming in, door gunners blazing, Law coordinated the medevacs. The lift ships were also used to evacuate casualties. "As the troops were bouncing off, we'd madly try to throw the wounded on the same slicks," noted Anderson, who was peppered with shrapnel in his legs and arms in the process. Three badly wounded men were rushed aboard one medevac, which was splattered with mortar shrapnel and came crashing back down as soon as it started to lift off. Through it all, battalion, brigade, and division commander—stacked up overhead in their command ships—were bringing in gunships, arty, and tac air, everything they had and plenty of it. It wasn't enough. "The NVA had pre-plotted firing positions all around the hill, and as quick as we hit one they moved to another," noted a frustrated Koenigsbauer. "For all the firepower available to us, we could not suppress the mortar fire."

Captain Williams dashed over to Law to give him a quick situation report and had just taken off again when he was knocked to the ground by the concussion of a mortar round that slammed into the boulder sheltering the CP. Getting up, Williams saw that 2d Lt. William P. Wall, his FO, had been killed instantly by the blast. One of Anderson's pathfinders was also sprawled dead against the boulder, and the other was badly wounded in the leg. Anderson used Wall's belt for a tourniquet. "Major Law came stumbling out of the smoke and dust with blood coming out of his mouth," said Williams. Law had big holes in his back, and "he had that thousand-yard stare you get when you're in shock," noted Williams. "I got ahold of him and sat him down, and he mumbled something about getting the mortars, and I of course agreed with him, and then we got the medics and got him out of there."

The battalion communications officer, 1st Lt. John E. Darling, USMA '68, took command of the CP and, with Williams, moved the radios and surviving RTOs into a shell crater. People from brigade and division, meanwhile, kept breaking in on Williams's company frequency, asking questions, demanding updates, and giving orders such as: "I want you to get out and get those mortars."

"Which one do you want me to get?" Williams barked, utterly exasperated. "I got 'em at three hundred and sixty degrees."

Lucas began insulating Williams from all the advice from above at that point, letting Williams, Anderson, and Darling organize the suppressive fire and medevacs without further interference. To disrupt the enemy mortars, Lucas inserted Captain Rollison and D/2-506th northeast of Ripcord. To put help within Company B's reach, Lucas inserted Captain Burkhart and A/2-506th back onto the rocky hill east of Ripcord. The company was shelled, but a Cobra swinging over to assist spotted the mortars in the open on Hill 805 and expended its entire load, getting multiple secondaries.

To further reinforce Bravo Company, Lucas dispatched the battalion reconnaissance platoon under 1st Lt. John W. Wilson from Camp Evans. Wilson, a veteran of five months in-country, had taken command of the recon platoon only the day before. He did not know his troops and they did not know him. The enemy mortared the mountaintop with a renewed fury at the approach of recon's lift ships, preventing any from landing or even hovering despite repeated attempts. At best, a few pilots were able to glide over the landing zone low enough for some of the troopers to leap to the ground. In that way, Wilson and ten of his men made it into position with the grunts. Low on fuel, the slicks finally had to turn back with the other half of the platoon still on board.

The mortar fire petered out at dusk. Captain Williams, having suffered too many casualties to hold the hill—seven dead, twenty-one wounded—was instructed to link up with Company A. At that time, all the casualties had been evacuated except two KIAs. The bodies had no sooner been thrown aboard a Huey that reluctantly landed than the mortar fire started again, and the door gunners shoved the bodies right back out to lighten the slick for a quick takeoff. A trooper from the artillery advance party who had helped load the bodies fell back into his foxhole only to have a mortar round land directly on his chest. The explosion blew his flak jacket open and left the man gasping, lungs exposed, the nose cone of the shell stuck in his chest, for the horrible minute it took him to die.

Williams ordered the bodies wrapped in ponchos and concealed under old sandbags in an ammo-crate bunker near the command group's boulder. They would have to be recovered later. Abandoned weapons were piled by the downed medevac and blown up with plastic explosives. "We were low on water," wrote Chip Collins. "I felt like hell rifling through a dead man's ruck for food and water." Before moving out, Williams had a Cobra zip over to investigate a fire burning on one of the hills to the west. Williams watched as tracers came up from the hill and the gunship took evasive action, then swung around and fired the area up, killing and wounding numerous ARVN. It is unclear if a trigger-happy South Vietnamese had brought the wrath down on his unit, or if it had been an enemy position that had fired on the Cobra and the ARVN had simply been too close to the NVA. Williams, meanwhile, got on the horn with the CO of Company A "and asked him to send up a team to meet us as we came down the ridge and guide us into his perimeter so we wouldn't get shot up by friendlies. He refused."

Lieutenant Wilson's troops led Company B's seven-hundred-meter march east to the hill occupied by Company A. "Everybody was scared shitless, but it was a disciplined move," said Sp4 John A. Schnarr, a recon RTO. The troops, each hanging onto the rucksack of the man in front, moved in rhythm with the illum being fired for the column from Gladiator, stopping when the eerie light sifted through the trees, moving another few meters in the dark interval before the next illumination round popped overhead.[1]

The ordeal was not over. Thunderstorms rolled in the next morning, preventing the planned extraction of Company B. When the rain let up, Wilson's recon troops, cloaked by a misty fog, slipped up onto Ripcord, unearthed the poncho-wrapped dead, and carried them down to a platoon from Company A waiting in the saddle below Ripcord. Lucas—taking a risk that was either bold or divorced from reality—immediately ordered Wilson back onto Ripcord. Wilson was to secure the LZ with five of his men, then dispatch the other five to Hill 1000 to pinpoint the mortar positions there for counter-battery fire. The five-man patrol never made it, halted by several AK-47s and an RPD light machine gun while moving up the hillock between Ripcord and Hill 1000. The recon troops took cover, but firing back into the fog served only to reveal their positions to an NVA with an RPG. In the ensuing explosions, Schnarr was peppered with shrapnel in his back and buttocks, and their slack man caught a red-hot fragment the size of a butcher knife in his thigh, with an end sticking out either side.

The hillside went quiet. No one moved. When someone did, the enemy sent a quick RPD burst his way. Wilson presently arrived with his five men, having just weathered a mortar attack on Ripcord. "As the lieutenant came up from behind, he radioed us to break contact," said Schnarr. "We just kind of scooted out of there, and, fortunately, the gooks didn't fire at us or follow us."

The wounded were not evacuated. The area was totally socked in. Recon had run out of daylight anyway and, forming a tight circle, spent an unnerving night on the hillock. Before rejoining the grunt companies the next morning, Lieutenant Wilson first had to recover the signal operating instructions (SOI) booklet that had fallen out of his pocket on Ripcord sometime the day before. Wilson's men argued against going back for the sake of a codebook, "but Wilson didn't want to start off his command by reporting that he had lost his SOI and forcing the whole division to change codes," noted Schnarr. "He insisted that a small group of us were going back up with him. We didn't want to, but we followed orders."

Moving quietly through the fog, the point man approached an old perimeter bunker. It was occupied by two sleeping enemy soldiers. Lieutenant Wilson rushed up, shot them both with his silencer-equipped M16, then shouted to the rest of the patrol, "I got 'em, I got 'em." Other NVA on the hill opened up with AKs. Wilson and the point man started back down, but an RPG landed directly in front of them. Wilson was blown off his feet. The point man dragged him to where the rest of the recon troops were waiting, and a medic went to work—the platoon leader had a sucking chest wound and a serious head injury—while Schnarr called for a medevac and a fire mission on Ripcord. The hilltop was obscured by fog, but the artillery rounds rumbling through the sky sounded as though they were on target. Shortly thereafter, a medevac pilot who'd volunteered to brave the low clouds in an attempt to save a life arrived on station. "He got through, but we couldn't spot him through the fog, and he couldn't spot us," said Schnarr. "We could hear him and were trying to direct him by sound, but there was just no visibility. He loitered as long as he could, but finally said he was running low on fuel and had to turn back. Wilson was lying there, semi-conscious, semi-coherent, trying to hang on, but when I got off the radio and told the guys that the medevac was heading back, he kind of let out a final breath and moan and died right there. He just couldn't hold on anymore."

The recon troops pushed through the jungle at the base of the hill, desperate to link up with the line companies on the other side of Ripcord. Their slack man, his badly injured leg swelled and stiff, limped along with an arm thrown over a buddy's shoulder. They also brought out Lieutenant Wilson. A litter hastily fashioned for him from ponchos and two sturdy branches kept coming undone, so they finally hefted Wilson's body onto the back of a trooper named Neal Whittler, lashed the dead man's hands together to help keep him in position, and kept moving.

Recon didn't reach Company A's perimeter until nightfall on April 3. The grunts had been buried in a cloud bank on the rocky hill for two days, the body bags in their perimeter putting out a bad smell and worse vibes. "It was a spooky, ghostly time," recalled Lieutenant Anderson. "We couldn't see thirty feet in the daytime, and less at night. The enemy knew where we were, and we knew that they knew. Tensions were very high. We were almost out of food and water, so there was a lot of sharing, cutting bamboo, and drinking the water out of the stalks, making one LRRP ration last for two days, that sort of stuff."

The weather cooled enough the next morning, April 4, that the clouds sank below the top of the hills, and a medevac finally got in for the wounded recon troops. The log bird that landed next came under mortar fire as Wilson's body was loaded aboard, along with the three remaining KIAs from the April Fools' Day Assault.

The weather turned foul again before Captain Williams and Company B, which had moved off the rocky hill the day before and linked up that afternoon with Company D at the northern base of the ridge, could also be resupplied. The air force tried to parachute in cases of C-rations, but the bundles were lost in the fog. Captain Rollison had his troops share what rations they had with Company B.

Williams told one of his sergeants to coordinate with the NCOs in Company D about setting up the NDP. "No, bullshit," said Rollison, a steady, second-tour pro. "You guys are dead on your feet. Just get some rest. We'll handle the security tonight."

"Rollison was the exact opposite of the captain in Company A," reflected Williams. "Delta Company was a good bunch. They took us in and gave us a chance to regroup. We owed them. There was always a special bond after that between Bravo and Delta Company."

It was clear enough again on April 5 for an element from the 2-17th Cav to CA onto Ripcord to recover the medevac shot down during the April Fools' Day Assault. The Huey was checked for booby traps and rigged for extraction amid incoming mortar fire, which wounded two men. The element departed under automatic-weapons fire. The Chinook under which the Huey was sling-loaded ran low of fuel on the way back to base and was forced to punch its load. The Huey was destroyed on impact.

The situation had again been stalemated by the monsoon. During the interlude, Brig. Gen. John J. Hennessey, the assistant division commander for operations, flew in for a conference with Bradley and his staff at Camp Evans. It was understood, recalled Bradley, that there would be a third assault—as many as would be necessary, in fact—so that when the dry season began, Ripcord would be ready to support the offensive into the Warehouse Area. "It wasn't just our brigade, the entire division and the ARVN were committed to interdicting the NVA supply routes deep in the mountains," Bradley noted. To begin that process, "Ripcord, literally, was where you had to go. That being said, it was a matter of how to best take and defend the objective. We needed the tools to do the job, and I emphasized during the meeting that the farther out you went, the more risky it became, and the more troop strength you had to have."

Though Bradley had three maneuver battalions on paper, only Lucas's was actually available for offensive operations. The 1-506th was tied down defending Evans and the firebase cordon in the foothills, and the 3d of the 187th Rakkasans were totally committed to the pacification campaign in the coastal villages, as they had been since the battalion was destroyed on Hamburger Hill in 1969.

Hennessey promised that Lt. Col. Bobby F. Brashears's 2d of the 501st Geronimo Battalion would be committed to the taking of Ripcord. "That was the division's swing battalion, meaning it was always ready to respond to wherever it was needed most," noted Colonel Bradley. "It was a very alert, very tough outfit."

Major Turner, the brigade operations officer, recalled that Bradley's basic message to Hennessey was that division should go to Ripcord in strength or not go at all. Bradley knew of what he spoke. "Colonel Bradley was a cool, calm, thoughtful commander, and a real firebreather when it came to going after the enemy," said Turner. Bradley had been twice wounded as a mechanized infantry sergeant during the push across France in World War II. Selected to attend West Point after the war—he was USMA '51—Bradley had led a platoon and a company in the Korean War, commanded a battalion from the 82d Airborne in the Dominican Republic expedition of '65, and was presently regarded as the best brigade commander in the 101st. "Bradley's was the most nimble brigade we had," stated Lt. Col. Charles W. Dyke, the division G3, "the one that would react the quickest and with the surest hand."

Returning to the Ripcord question, Turner noted that "we'd gotten our ass kicked out of there twice, and if we went back in with what we had, we were going to get our ass kicked again." The terrain so overwhelmingly favored the enemy as to make irrelevant the attachment of the division reserve to Bradley. "It was going to take more than just a couple of battalions," said Turner, a young West Pointer on his second combat tour in Vietnam. "If we went back in, the enemy was going to respond in force, and then it would take a couple of brigades to hold the damn place."

It was unlikely that such a force would be piled on when it was needed—not in the era of Vietnamization. "We didn't mind getting in a fight in the One-O-First, but we had to be very careful about casualties," noted Lieutenant Colonel Dyke, a veteran of thirty-three months with the 101st in Vietnam, 1965–66 and 1968–70. "The big anti-casualty push started after the so-called Hamburger Hill action," explained Dyke. "I was the division personnel officer at that time, and was present when General Abrams flew up to Camp Eagle and told General Melvin Zais, then the division commander, 'Goddamnit, Mel, find a better way to do it.'" From that point on, Dyke continued, "both of the division ADCs and myself, first as G1 and subsequently as G3, were always on the phone with our parent command, XXIV Corps, and sometimes even with USARV [United States Army Vietnam] down in Long Binh, explaining in detail why a particular company in a particular battalion had lost two or three people the night before. We were under great pressure to hold the casualties down. That was well understood in the division."

Precisely because the restriction on casualties was well understood, recalled Turner, a certain reluctance to return to Ripcord was expressed, albeit obliquely, during the briefing for General Hennessey. First, the brigade intelligence officer, Maj. William G. Keoho, a mono-tonal, fireplug-shaped Hawaiian—"one hell of a stud, and a good S2," noted Turner—provided a lengthy analysis of the enemy situation in the brigade area and the mountains to the west. The unmistakable message, as Turner later paraphrased it, was that "the NVA were moving into the A Shau in droves from Laos, and that if we didn't go out there in force, Ripcord was eventually going to become an untenable position."

Next, Turner went to the map to outline options. "If you want a general to pick a particular course of action, you make it your first recommendation," he mused. The first three recommendations presented by Turner were variations on the theme that the brigade hold onto its existing firebases and, taking advantage of the division's airmobile assets, hit the North Vietnamese as they tried to infiltrate through the foothills to the lowlands. At the end of his supply lines, the enemy was at his most vulnerable in the foothills. The last recommendation was to reoccupy Ripcord. Division was determined to strike into the enemy's vitals. "When we finished briefing Hennessey," recalled Turner, "all he said was, 'Well, you're going back to Ripcord.' "

Brigade's preferred course of action was modeled on the standing operations order written by Dyke and approved by General Wright in December 1969 when the 101st was regrouping after the withdrawal of the 3d Marine Division from Quang Tri Province. At that time, Dyke had divided the newly expanded Screaming Eagles AO into three sectors. The heavily populated lowlands of Thua Thien Province became the protected zone. Within it, units assigned to pacification ran civic action programs for the villagers and joint combat operations with the local militia forces. The NVA had been pushed completely out of the area. There were still Viet Cong remnants, but, given the division's close coordination with the militia, said Dyke, "we were able to respond very quickly if there was an attack on a village, or if a school was being burned down, or if a government official had been kidnapped or assassinated. We also provided medical support after such terrorist incidents."

The foothills—or piedmont, as the region was identified on military maps—constituted the primary zone of engagement. "That was where we preferred to do battle," noted Dyke. In the foothills, the insertion and extraction of troops, like the use of gunships and tac air, was unhampered by the vagaries of the monsoon, the weather being almost always flyable below the mountains.

The reconnaissance zone stretched west from the firebase cordon to Laos and northwest all the way to the DMZ. It encompassed the mountains of Thua Thien Province and all of Quang Tri except for a system of strongpoints in the lowlands held by the 1st Brigade, 5th Infantry Division (Mechanized). The reconnaissance zone was monitored by brigade recon teams, the division LRRPs, and the 2-17th Cavalry. In the event of an enemy buildup, a U. S.–ARVN operation, multibattalion in size though limited in duration, might be mounted. More frequently, a 105 battery, an infantry company attached to provide security, would launch what was known as an artillery raid. "You get a good, sunny day, you hook up the howitzers, and you head out to an old firebase," explained Dyke. "You shoot up the place, then come back in either that same day or within a couple days depending on enemy capabilities in the area. We made sure that we didn't give the North Vietnamese enough time to gather enough forces to overwhelm those positions. We also had to play bet-your-ass with the weather so that we didn't get people hung out there beyond our reach. I was a pretty cautious guy on that, and watched those positions very carefully."

Division seemed to be throwing caution to the wind with Operation Chicago Peak. There is always a case to be made about taking the fight to the enemy, and Wright eventually gave Bradley a battalion from another brigade, freeing up the 1-506th for the push into the mountains. Nevertheless, the idea of another assault on zeroed-in Ripcord seemed a bit mad. "It was as if there was a personal vendetta between the 803d NVA Regiment and our division staff," said Capt. Philip L. Michaud, a career officer with the 2-319th FA. "They couldn't face up to the fact that the Screaming Eagles had been denied access to the area, so we were attacking again just so we could say we took a place on the map called Ripcord."

Sergeant Burkey of C/2-506th thought the division was possessed of "what I call the Hamburger Hill Syndrome—the going back after something over and over, the senseless loss of people for no fucking good reason. Hamburger Hill was probably the most shameful thing the 101st ever did. Ripcord was more of the same."

Specialist Fourth Class Richard R. Blythe, a former combat infantryman in the Big Red One assigned as assistant to the 2-506th chaplain, wrote home on the eve of the third attack that "for an unimportant far away hill [Ripcord] seems to me to be a hell of a place to die. To save face and for the morale of this battalion I'm not so sure that we don't have to go back to the place where we were knocked off of. I only hope they do it right this time."

It has been speculated that division was determined to open a firebase in such a contested area to draw the enemy to it like ants to sugar, the idea being that it would be less costly to destroy the NVA with firepower as they gathered around Ripcord than to dig them out of their elaborate bunker complexes on Co Pung Mountain. It was a valid tactic in theory. Given what actually transpired, though, Dyke perhaps had no other choice but to state that such a firebase-as-bait scheme "was never the plan at Ripcord."[2]

Lieutenant Hawkins, acting commander of C/2-506th—Vazquez was on R&R—choppered into Company A's NDP from Gladiator on April 5, having been relieved there by a unit from the Geronimo Battalion. Lucas had previously moved a jump TOC to Gladiator. Captain Leroy "Lee" Fox, the battalion chaplain, was thus on hand to visit the troops the night before. "I don't think there was a man in Charlie Company who didn't go and get the blessing from the chaplain," recalled a squad leader, "and at the same time drop what he hoped wasn't his last letter in the mail bag sitting there."

The stranded troops from the engineer and artillery advance parties went out on Company C's slicks. In preparation for the third assault, Lucas fanned out his companies to find and destroy the enemy mortar positions. Company A, badly shaken from the top down, balked and did not get moving until volunteers had been organized to lead the way. Two platoons from Company C, meanwhile, walked into a bunker complex on the knoll between Ripcord and Hill 1000 on April 6. Pinned down with two dead, eight wounded, and a flipped-out platoon leader—the other platoon leader, 1st Lt. Robert "Gypsy" Wallace, took charge of the fight—the grunts finally had to dig in where they were as night fell. Hawkins, having moved up with the rest of the company by then, carefully walked artillery in on the North Vietnamese. When Hawkins medevacked his casualties the next morning, the landing zone came under fire from more enemy soldiers atop Ripcord.

Hawkins reported to Lucas shortly thereafter that he could hear hand-cranked generators used for Morse code in the jungle to his south as well as up on Ripcord. The enemy was definitely well equipped. Rollison's company, sweeping toward Hill 805 that same morning, killed a lone NVA; the man had thrown a grenade, run, and was cut down. He had an AK-47, three magazines, three grenades, web gear and pack, an extra uniform, and a new rain poncho. He also had a pen, paper, a map, and documents that identified him as leader of a seven-man squad that packed two rocket-propelled grenade launchers. Enemy morale was high; as recorded in the battalion journal, one of the dead man's notes, when translated, turned out to be a "letter to [his] wife stating NVA winning in the south[.]"

The division reserve was committed during a break in the bad weather that afternoon. Captain Christopher C. Straub and D/2-501st landed under fire on Hill 902. After securing the landing zone, Straub dispatched 1st Lt. Terry A. Palm's platoon, Delta One, on a RIF, or reconnaissance in force, along the ridge leading up Coc Muen Mountain. The platoon followed a trail into an unoccupied base camp. Palm had no sooner deployed security than an M60 gunner cut down the point man of an NVA squad walking unawares back into camp. "[W]e stuck a 101 airborne patch in the hole in the back of his head and started chasing the rest," Palm wrote in a letter home. "We followed them for 6 hours through a fresh company[-sized] NVA base camp. My people wanted to stop but I told them I wasn't quitting until we had swept the entire ridgeline."

Reaching a knoll, Palm, sensing trouble, signaled his men to get down, which saved some lives because the enemy detonated a claymore a moment later and "rained satchel charges all over us," the lieutenant's letter continued. Most of the NVA "opened up on me, personally. They had seen me talking on the radio and knew I was the leader." An RPG exploded six feet away, and Palm took light shrapnel in his shoulder. All the while his platoon was literally shooting the jungle flat. "[A] gook dashed out of the bushes and we fired him up good," Palm wrote. The enemy began to pull back. Palm organized an on-line assault, but Straub, on the radio, prudently ordered a withdrawal. "With M-16s and M-60 machine guns red hot and blazing fire 2–3 feet out of the barrels, we pulled back to an NDP position with all weapons, [and] packs . . . we took 13 minor wounded. One man may lose his sight, however. . . . When we went forward the next morning, we found another dead gook and many blood trails leading away, and 2nd Platoon killed one of the wounded ones down the hill. There still are many gooks here, so I expect more contact. Don't worry, there's not a gook alive I wouldn't tangle with after I've seen what this platoon can do."

For the Currahees, the area remained jinxed. On April 8, one of Rollison's platoons discovered a bunker complex at the southeast base of Ripcord and, spotting movement, popped smoke to mark its location before the Cobra from a Pink Team supporting Company D rolled in hot. Unable to see anything but treetops, the pilot fired his rockets based on directions given him from the smoke. The smoke, however, had not actually emerged over the friendlies as it slowly sifted its way up through the jungle canopy, the result being that the platoon calling in the Cobra took one KIA and fourteen WIA.

Over the next two days, there were more quick contacts, more finds—Company D walked into a deserted enemy bivouac with uniforms hanging on a clothesline—and through it all, arty, tac air, and ARA continued to work over likely enemy mortar sites.

Resistance faded. With friendly units spread all over the high ground, watching for enemy mortars, it was time to take Ripcord. Lucas selected Hawkins and Company C, positioned halfway up the southern slope of the mountain, to make a ground attack, supported by Company D. Hawkins moved his people into position in the dark, and the assault began with a quick artillery prep at first light on April 11. There was no enemy fire as the troops advanced up the open slope, then into the interior of the firebase. After the position was checked for booby traps—there were none—Lieutenant Anderson of the pathfinders was inserted with a team to control the lifting in of supplies and equipment. The troops on the mountaintop held their collective breath when the first Chinook hovered over the landing zone with a sling-loaded engineer bulldozer. No mortar rounds dropped in, however. The enemy did not contest the third attack in any way. Anderson had actually been expecting trouble. For that reason, "I had wanted to go back," he recalled. "I had started the fight. By God, I was going to finish it. I had my pick of other pathfinders who wanted to go as well. We all had unfinished business on that hill. We set up our base of operations next to the same boulder where we had previously taken casualties, partly out of bravado, but mostly because it was the best spot on the firebase with the best visibility. . . ."

CHAPTER 7

Dinks in the Wire

Major Sidney Davis, the new battalion executive officer, choppered out as soon as Ripcord was secured to set up a jump CP. Gruff and thickset, he reminded Hawkins, meeting him for the first time, of Ernest Borgnine. Hawkins would write that Davis, on his second tour, "knew what combat was all about," and that "if he liked you, then he loved you. If you got on his shit list, watch out."

Not yet appreciating Davis's temperament, Hawkins got on the major's list that first afternoon on Ripcord. Hawkins was busy getting his company positioned and dug in when Davis called him over and told him in an amiable way that he wanted a roll of concertina wire around the firebase by last light. Wire and engineer stakes had been brought in but no gloves or sledgehammers. "When we get the proper tools, we'll get it in," the cocky Hawkins replied, starting to leave before Davis could reply. "Lieutenant," the XO barked. Hawkins turned back around. Davis was livid. "You get that wire in now," he thundered. "Have your men wrap their hands in sandbags, and use rocks and the flat side of ax heads, but you get that damned wire up before nightfall or I'll have your bars."

Davis's anger was more than justified. "There are enemy all around this hill who would love the chance to come in and hit us when our defenses are down," the major growled at Hawkins. "You get that wire in pronto. Do you understand me?"

Hawkins did. Wrapping his hands in sandbags, he joined his men and laid wire "until my hands and arms bled and dusk approached," he later wrote. "That night, Ripcord had a single belt of staked-in concertina all the way around it, and a second belt had been started. That was the last time Davis ever chewed me out."

The weather turned sour again, preventing the insertion of the battalion's attached 105 battery for five days. Meanwhile, the mortar platoon shelled itself while registering close-in targets—two men were wounded—and one of Hawkins's grunts was killed while digging a foxhole when his shovel hit a rusty grenade buried along with other unused ordnance by the last unit to occupy Ripcord.

It was a dreary, if busy, time. Lucas asked Captain Fox, battalion chaplain, about the morale of the troops during one of the colonel's quick trips to Camp Evans. "The Chaplain let him have it," chaplain's assistant Rick Blythe wrote in a letter home. "Fox told Lucas exactly what the morale of the troops was," Blythe would later recall. "Basically, it was lousy." Hoping to bolster spirits, Lucas dispatched his popular chaplain to Ripcord. Expecting the worst, Fox came up with a shoulder-holstered pistol and an M16. He also strapped a Randall fighting knife to his leg. "He's ready for bear," wrote Blythe. "A real combat Chaplain." The wind-buffeted flight to Ripcord was unnerving, the base itself frightful, all alone high up in rugged mountains. "The fog has rolled in," wrote Blythe. "Virtually no air traffic before noon of each day." Blythe's next letter read: "Still digging and filling sandbags at Ripcord. Some incoming and lots of outgoing. Thank goodness someone had cigarettes so I could put the filters in my ears. Guard duty on the perimeter in the rain. We made sure there was some outgoing."

Captain Vazquez, back from leave, took charge of the construction of the firebase perimeter. Vazquez did not model Ripcord after the division's other firebases but after the border outposts he had helped build during his tours with the Special Forces. The average firebase had big sandbag-and-timber bunkers that stood out like road signs. In some cases, conex shipping containers were used, firing slits having been cut out with an acetylene torch. "There be no sandbagged bunkers on this firebase," Vazquez informed his platoon leaders in his harsh Puerto Rican accent. "That is the way the Army does it, but when you see a sandbagged bunker, you're looking at a death trap. On my firebase, we have fighting positions—we don't have no sandbags stacked up so the gooks know where to shoot."

Instead of bunkers, Vazquez had his men dig L-shaped fighting positions amid the tree stumps around the perimeter. Each was home to a three-man fire team. The fighting leg, a grenade sump at one end, allowed the whole team to stand shoulder to shoulder and fire down into the wire. At night, two men could stretch out on air mattresses in the sleeping leg while the third member of the team took his turn outside on guard. The fighting leg was open. The sleeping leg was covered by sandbags and runway matting—PSP, officially, for pierced steel planking—to absorb mortar fire. The sandbags and runway matting were, in turn, covered with earth so as to blend into the bald hillside. "When we ran security patrols around Ripcord," noted Lieutenant Campbell of Charlie Two, "you couldn't see a single fighting position when you looked back up the hill. Nothing was above ground level."

The defensive wire wasn't by the book, either. "Lieutenant Campbell, there be no gook get through my wire," Vazquez said, putting the platoon leader in charge of the wire-laying detail. "Every other unit pulled out two spools of concertina side by side like a pair of slinkies," said Campbell, "threw a third spool on top, and said they had wire out there. Bullshit." Vazquez required multiple rings of the triple-stacked concertina, all of it tightly secured so a sapper couldn't wiggle between the loops, with additional concertina mashed into the folds of the earth underneath and held down with crisscrossing strands of barbed wire. It was an old Special Forces trick. The beauty of it, noted a squad leader, was "if sappers blew holes in the wire on top with bangalore torpedoes, the concertina underneath, being really resilient, would pop back up, so they would've just created another barrier for themselves."

In addition to the massive amounts of concertina, Vazquez also requisitioned hog-wire fencing. Each section consisted of metal rods in a metal frame the size of a door. "You never saw it on conventional firebases," noted Campbell. "To stand up, it had to be anchored in a trench, but digging in that rocky, uneven ground was murder. We were laying wire and clearing fields of fire from morning till night for a month," Campbell continued. "Vazquez was merciless. There were no breaks to get out of the sun because the base had to be made defensible before the enemy could mass for an attack. The troops were just brutalized. I had men come up to me, saying, 'L. T., I'm begging you, let me go out on the RIF today.'"

When finished, the briar patch of wire ringing the firebase was fifty meters wide. Two trails leading downhill through it were closed at night with wire barriers. "It would've taken the NVA thirty minutes to get through all that stuff with bolt cutters in broad daylight," Campbell asserted. With wry bravado, the troops began to refer to the seemingly invulnerable firebase as Cheeseburger Hill.

Vazquez and his lieutenants took turns scanning the slopes at night with a starlight scope. The wire was studded with hundreds upon hundreds of trip flares and claymores, the detonating wires of the mines carefully covered with dirt. Each fighting position had in front of it a fifty-five-gallon drum of thickened fuel known as phougas. The phougas barrels could be ignited by firing the claymore behind each, which splashed burning fuel into the wire. Vazquez came up with another use for the thickened fuel. "Vazquez had us take the metal canisters that mortar and artillery rounds were delivered in, and bury them in the ground a little ways, upside down," noted Campbell. "The bottom of each would hold an inch or two of thickened fuel. After burying it, you tied a trip flare to a stick so that it pointed down at the canister, then ran the trip wire back to your fighting position. If you got hit at night, you pulled the wire and the trip flare would ignite the fuel, providing illumination which lasted a lot longer than flares or illumination rounds. You know, we wanted off that damn firebase before we all dropped dead from exhaustion," concluded Campbell, "but, man, I'd of given my left nut if the gooks would have hit the place while we were there. I believe we would have handed them their ass."

Lucas had his operations center built on the eastern slope, near the top of the hill. The engineers bulldozed a trench a hundred feet long and four feet deep into which four steel conexes were placed. Two sat side by side at one end to be used as the TOC. Two more were at the other end—one for the battalion aid station, the other an ARVN CP. Steps led up from the TOC to the helipad that was leveled off in front of it, which, being used by Lucas and visitors from brigade and division, was called the VIP pad. The roof was layered with sandbags and runway matting. Ammo boxes, filled with earth and held in place with engineer stakes, protected the exposed front and sides of the conexes. The ammo boxes were in turn reinforced with an outer wall of sandbags, which neatly joined the sandbagged roof. "We worked around the clock on the bunker, myself as a major filling sandbags alongside our RTOs," said Koenigsbauer. "When we were finally finished, we had a TOC that we thought would stand up to anything—and which, in fact, did when the time came."

The mortar section and the infantry company CP were dug in below the VIP pad. Captain Rich's B/2-319th FA was positioned on top of the base, along with a small countermortar radar and a pair of 106mm recoilless rifles from E/2-506th. The base had two distinct levels. The 105s occupied the upper or southeastern tier, which was about the size of a football field. The 105's ammunition supply point (ASP) was at the far end of the plateau, adjacent to the base supply conexes and the main logistical pad, where sling loads of beans, bullets, and bandages were daily delivered by Chinook.

The saddle between the southeastern tier and the lower and smaller northwestern tier was originally occupied by an ARVN 105 battery, which supported the South Vietnamese regiment operating near Coc Muen Mountain. When the South Vietnamese redeployed to FSB O'Reilly in late May, the ARVN CP was converted to a communications center, and the ARVN 105s were replaced by the 155 howitzers of Captain Baxendale's A/2-11th Field Artillery.

The saddle rose to a gentle hump. The elephant-sized boulder atop it, a dominant landmark on the firebase, was nicknamed Impact Rock because of the splatter of white shrapnel scars it bore from one of the previous occupations of Ripcord. A secondary log pad was established on the lower tier, as was a POL (petroleum-oil-lubricant) pad with sandbagged blivets of JP4 aviation fuel for emergency helicopter refueling. Attached from corps, a four-barreled M55 .50-caliber machine-gun antiaircraft system known as a Quad-50 was positioned inside a sandbagged parapet adjacent to Impact Rock.

General Hennessey inspected Ripcord, walking down beyond the wire with Lucas and Vazquez to get a look at the hill from the enemy point of view. Hennessey, thinking he had found a blind spot, pointed out a gully to Campbell, who was laying wire with his troops. "You can't see it," Campbell said, "but there's a claymore covering that gully. It's right behind and tied to that empty sandbag lying there." When Hennessey asked Hawkins to see his best fighting position, Hawkins led the general's entourage to a fire-team leader known as Buffalo in charge of what had been dubbed The Electric Bunker. "The name was apt," Hawkins wrote. "Not only was it wired to about twenty claymore mines, the detonators to which Buffalo could finger without looking, but it also had three phougas barrels. Additionally, and the brass weren't exposed to this, the bunker drew electrical power from the firebase generators to light the interior. I didn't have it that good in my own shelter."

Those units operating around the firebase continued to make heavy contact as the monsoon petered out. First Lieutenant James W. Kwiecien was assigned to A/2-501st at that time. He boarded a resupply slick at Evans with several grunts returning to the field and was flown out to join his new company on the ridge running southeast from Hill 902. He didn't make it. The Huey was flying low level down a valley toward the company headquarters and the platoon it was with when a rocket-propelled grenade suddenly exploded beneath the helicopter—Kwiecien could feel shrapnel thud into the metal floorboard under his feet—and the pilot poured on the power to get out of the area. Losing fuel, the Huey made an emergency landing on

Granite, the reserve battalion's new mountaintop firebase nine klicks east of Ripcord, and passengers and crew realized how lucky they'd been when they gathered to inspect the sieve of holes ripped in the underside of the Huey.

Unable to sleep that night, Kwiecien listened to the outgoing artillery and ruefully recalled that his biggest concern upon arriving in-country a week earlier had been that, with the war winding down, he might not earn a CIB, the coveted Combat Infantryman Badge.

Jim Kwiecien, age twenty-three, product of working-class Chicago and a Catholic education from grade school through college, had been considering a military career since signing up for ROTC at Loyola University. Whether he stayed in or not—eventually he would decide not to—he took duty and patriotism seriously. He was, in sum, a true believer who had volunteered for Vietnam, though he considered the war a lost cause, because "I felt that I had to put my body where my mouth was."

Kwiecien need not have worried about the withdrawals. There was still plenty of war left where he was going. The new lieutenant had no sooner joined the company headquarters the day after his first aborted attempt and met Capt. James E. Mitchell, the steady, confidence-inspiring CO of Company A, than the outfit's separated platoons CA'd into a little hole-in-the-jungle LZ from which they could support B/2-501st. Company B had of late been ambushing and killing NVA at a trail intersection on a hill situated along the ridge three klicks down from the top of 902. "We moved off the LZ and I spent my first night in the field," wrote Kwiecien. "The next morning, the sounds of a not-so-distant firefight awoke us. Bravo Company was getting hit on their hill. We saddled up and moved to join them." The enemy, repelled, left two bodies; Company B lost one dead, twelve wounded. "When we arrived," Kwiecien continued, "their commanding officer was standing there, wearing a ranger patrol hat, bringing in air strikes on a knoll a few hundred meters from the hill. The jets would roll in, drop their ordnance, and, in return, there would be the sound of a single AK-47. The enemy soldier shooting at the jets popped a green smoke grenade, an effort to confuse the pilots about who was where in the jungle."

Bravo Company moved down the ridge to the east, leaving Captain Mitchell's outfit, known infamously as Hard Luck Alpha, in possession of the hill. Events soon confirmed the nickname. During the company's second day in position, April 18, it was mortared, then toward dusk one of its platoons, Alpha Two, was ambushed crossing a gorge on the southern slope of the ridge. Two men were killed, two wounded. Mitchell sent Kwiecien to take over Alpha Two from its acting platoon leader—a shake 'n bake E6 who normally served as platoon sergeant—as it set up on a subhill below the main company NDP. "One of the KIAs was well-liked, a family man, and his death really did a job on the platoon. The men were seriously rattled," wrote Kwiecien, who had hoped to rely on his platoon sergeant until he got his bearings. The young E6, however, had greeted him with, "I'm glad you're here, sir. I'm an 11C, mortars—I don't know anything about this infantry stuff."

Kwiecien was not sure how much he knew himself. "I'm flat-out jealous of the platoon leaders who fought in our other wars," he would reflect. "They had a chance to get to know their men and train with them before they went into combat. We lieutenants in Vietnam, on the other hand, just got plunked down in the jungle, green as the vegetation around us, and were told to lead. . . ."

Captain Mitchell took the company down the side of the ridge the next day, April 19; the point platoon, Alpha One, came under fire from a bunker complex east of the ambush site, losing one KIA and five WIA. For Kwiecien, whose platoon was second in line, the day had already been ordeal enough. "I was in good shape," he noted, "but nothing could prepare you for humping a ruck that weighed almost as much as you did up and down mountains as rugged as the Rockies in 110-degree heat with 90 percent humidity. . . ."

At Mitchell's direction, Lieutenant Kwiecien moved his platoon forward along a trail as automatic-weapons fire reverberated under the canopy. Kwiecien was coming down the trail himself when an unseen NVA took three quick shots at him from the trees to his left. "Within a second or two, I located the source of fire, asked myself why someone was trying to kill me since I had never done anything to him," Kwiecien wrote of his baptism by fire as an infantryman, "answered myself that I was out there trying to kill him so he had a right to try to kill me, dropped to one knee, and returned fire. The shooting from that direction stopped."

Shortly thereafter, the platoon radioman took a round through his cheek, splattering Kwiecien across the face and chest with blood and gobs of flesh. The contact began late in the day. By the time Alpha Three moved up to help Alpha One and Two pull back—the ARA called in had not silenced the enemy—it was getting dark. "We couldn't fully break contact," wrote Kwiecien, "but the fighting did taper off as our elements moved back from the bunkers. When night fell, we were in a horrible position to defend and would have been in serious trouble had they decided to come after us. The medevacs came in by the light of the strobes we used to mark our position. It was surreal, like an imagined scene from hell. . . ."

The action continued two more days. There were more casualties, more close calls, including an incident in which a short 105mm WP shell landed within fifteen feet of where Kwiecien was conferring with his squad leaders. "The shell was defective," he noted with relief. "It just split and burned without actually bursting the way it should have. If it had, we would have been fried. . . ."

The bunker complex was not secured until the air force hit it with Daisy Cutters, devastating 15,000-pound bombs normally used to blast landing zones out of the rain forest, on April 21. What had been lush jungle now resembled the surface of the moon. Blood was splattered against some of the shattered tree trunks. "It was a real emotional event to finally take the bunker complex," wrote Lieutenant Kwiecien. There was a flip side to the elation of victory. "At some point during the battle, I realized that there was no way I was going to survive my tour. You simply could not go through this day after day without getting seriously hurt or killed. . . ."

Hard Luck Alpha returned to the top of its hill. As if in payback for the destruction of the bunker complex, the enemy hit the NDP that night. The attack began three and a half hours after midnight on April 23. There was a ferocious exchange of fire, then a lull as the sky began to lighten. "With all the smoke in the air, everything looked very red," noted Kwiecien. The lull ended when an RPG suddenly whooshed in, and a trooper shrieked as he lay dying, "I'm hit, I'm hit—my God, they blew my legs off."

It was close, but the NVA were again pushed back, leaving seven bodies in exchange for the one friendly KIA and eleven WIA. Kwiecien had been told in training that there is a tendency to fire your weapon high at night. "Our people were good, though," he wrote. "They kept their fire low, and when it was over we found several dead dinks with their feet shot off at the ankles. Another very young enemy soldier had been hit by the blast from a claymore mine. It had blown his uniform off and he was hanging, dead and naked, with his arms outstretched, from a tree. He looked like Christ on the Cross."

Hard Luck Alpha finally humped off the hill after being relieved by Charlie Company. The embattled position became known as Re-Up Hill, after the numerous survivors who subsequently reenlisted to get out of the field. "Officers didn't have any choice, of course, but I don't think any of us who stayed were critical of those who decided to take that way out," wrote Kwiecien. "You just did what you felt you had to to survive, and if that meant re-upping, so be it."

There had been a similar wave of reenlistments, incidentally, in the 2-506th Infantry after the original battle to take FSB Ripcord.

Following a drunken respite at Eagle Beach, Captain Mitchell and A/2-501st took over the perimeter at FSB Granite. The firebase had been penetrated by sappers a month earlier. Intelligence presently predicted another attack, and Hard Luck Alpha waited for it in a state of benumbed calm. "We just accepted the fact that they were coming and there was nothing we could do about it until they got there," explained Kwiecien. "Looking back on it, our attitude seems strange since our company strength at that point was in the low thirties at most. There were so few of us that troops from the battalion mortar platoon were attached as reinforcements."

After four nights of waiting, the attack began two hours before midnight on April 29, 1970. "There was some confusion when the shooting started on the other side of the perimeter," wrote Kwiecien, "but the word spread quickly: 'Dinks in the wire.' "

The new battalion commander, Lt. Col. Otis W. "O. T." Livingston, a rawboned, old soldier from Columbia, South Carolina, who had fought as a platoon leader in Korea, jumped into a foxhole himself and opened fire with his M16. Most of the sappers leading the attack died in the wire as Alpha Company raked it with fire and detonated its claymores and phougas. According to a prisoner taken the next morning, the supporting U. S. artillery fire killed the enemy assault commander and broke up the two infantry battalions standing ready to follow the sappers in.

It was a long night, nonetheless; a handful of sappers, smeared with charcoal and naked except for loincloths, had managed to penetrate the perimeter. They intended to do as much damage as possible before being killed, and there were intense little melees as each sapper was eliminated with grenades and M16s. Eighteen enemy bodies were counted at dawn, but the defenders of Granite lost seven WIA and seven KIA, as well as an infantryman who was blown to bits and listed as MIA.

Livingston's exec and sergeant major, along with numerous others who were getting the perimeter reorganized, were wounded when the enemy mortared the log pad at the approach of a Huey. Kwiecien and his shake 'n bake platoon sergeant were among those hit. "A medevac came in and some of us got on," recalled Kwiecien, who had a piece of shrapnel in his back that would keep him in the rear for three weeks. "The chopper drew more mortar fire, so it went around, touched down again, immediately took off so the mortar rounds could land, then darted in and picked up the rest of the wounded before the enemy could put another salvo in the air. The pilot really did a nice job of faking the dinks out."

As reinforcements arrived, "the firebase was completely socked in," recalled 1st Lt. Blair Case, FO, A/1-506th, which walked onto Granite that morning. Chinooks with sling loads of ammunition followed the Rao Trang River to get in under the low clouds, then swung north toward Granite. "Once they reached the base of the mountain with Granite on top," Case wrote, painting a surrealistic scene, "a soldier with a radio stood on the edge of the firebase and 'talked' them up through the clouds. We could hear but not see them far below us, then, eventually, the rotor blades, engine housings, and fuselages would appear through the fog. The enemy dead were hooked under one of the Chinooks in a cargo net and dropped along the path of the retreating North Vietnamese."

The scene of battle abruptly shifted. Colonel Bradley had previously been tasked to support one of the joint operations periodically launched to disrupt enemy infiltration past Khe Sanh in northwestern Quang Tri Province. The ARVN were to provide the ground troops, and the Screaming Eagles were to secure a firebase to provide artillery support. Bradley used a company attached from another brigade to reopen a debris-strewn Marine base named Henderson. Behind the attached company came an ARVN 105 battery, the 155s of B/2-11th FA, and a regimental TOC from the 1st ARVN Infantry Division, which took control of the South Vietnamese units combat-assaulting into the hills west of Firebase Henderson.

The attached company spent five days patrolling the unfamiliar and unsecured area around Henderson and preparing as time permitted defensive positions on the firebase itself until relieved by Captain Mitchell and A/2-501st on the morning of May 5. The battalion recon platoon under 1st Lt. Richard A. Hawley, Jr., arrived late that afternoon. Company A had been brought back to strength with about sixty replacements, and the idea was to let Mitchell integrate them with the battered veterans of Re-Up Hill and Firebase Granite in what was considered a relatively quiet AO.

Hard Luck Alpha never got that chance. It took the company all day to establish its positions and set up its claymores. There was no time to make use of the concertina wire that had been flown in, or to clear fields of fire in the brush growing right up to the edge of the wire barriers begun by the attached company. No security patrols were run, no listening posts deployed. Taking advantage of the situation, sappers, concealed by the heavy ground fog that shrouded the base that night, cut two paths through the flimsy perimeter wire. Behind the sappers came NVA assault troops. With a crash of AK-47 and RPG fire that shocked everyone awake, they darted into Henderson an hour before dawn on May 6, 1970.

The enemy moved swiftly and ruthlessly, one prong of the attack homing in on the A/2-501st CP and the ARVN TOC, the other the 155 parapets and the ammo-fuel storage area directly behind Hawley's recon platoon. "Many of the big guns were destroyed by satchel charges, some with barrels peeled back like bananas," it was later reported. One of the attackers cut loose in the dark with a Soviet-made flamethrower, torching a hapless infantryman who "ran off the hill screaming. He was never seen again. . . ."

Either the flamethrower or a satchel charge ignited a fuel fire, which, in turn, detonated the ammunition in the storage area in a titanic blast. At the heart of the explosion were a thousand 155mm shells belonging to B/2-11th FA. The brigade after-action report implies that the ammo had not been properly entrenched with overhead cover, a not uncommon problem on new firebases as shells were delivered faster than revetments could be built. Turner recalls, however, that the U. S. ammo had been revetted; the inferno started because of exposed ARVN ammunition. Bradley would concur, writing: "Turner and I had observed ammo supply pallets sitting in the open adjacent to the ARVN 105 positions as we flew over the firebase two days prior to the sapper attack. All exhortations to the senior ARVN commander and his U. S. advisors to revet the ammo or 'shoot it up' fell on deaf ears as Mitchell's troops reported exposed ammo when they occupied their defensive positions." Turner added: "Colonel Bradley was just livid because if they had revetted the ammo as instructed, one satchel charge wouldn't have ended up destroying most of the firebase."

Most of the recon troops were killed in the ammo explosion, as was their platoon leader, Lieutenant Hawley, the "goat" of the USMA Class of '68. The devastation was so complete, the survivors were so shell-shocked, that when the enemy withdrew before first light, many ambled away at sling arms. Some of the overconfident NVA were picked off by infantrymen who were still functioning.

Livingston landed that morning with B/2-501st, even as ammo continued to cook off and the base was subjected to mortar and recoilless-rifle fire. There had been twenty-five U.S. and three ARVN KIAs and, between the two forces, fifty-five WIA. Given that the enemy had time to carry away their casualties, only twenty-nine NVA bodies were accounted for on and around FSB Henderson.

Colonel Bradley choppered in shortly after Livingston with Major Turner and Captain Hopkins, his fire-support coordinator, and Sgt. Maj. Raymond L. Long, the brigade sergeant major, only to have a mortar round explode behind his command group as it dashed from the LZ to the ARVN TOC. "As we got to the bunker, Sergeant Major Long stepped aside at the entrance to let me go in first," recounted Turner. "As I moved past Long, I grabbed his left arm to pull him into the bunker. Hopkins was close behind me. At that instant, the mortar round hit slightly to the rear. Long went down like a polled bull. Hopkins and I were blown into the bunker, Hopkins on top of me. He had been hit in the legs and buttocks while I got only a few slivers in the neck and face." Turner crawled back out of the bunker, pulled Long inside, "and tried to revive him without success. He had been hit in the base of the skull by a small sliver from that damn mortar round. He died in my arms. . . ."[1]

The enemy kept up the pressure. The next major action involved 1st Lt. Donald R. Workman's company, D/1-506th, after it combat-assaulted onto the site of an old firebase, Maureen, seven klicks south of Granite. The three platoons moved off the hill in three different directions, the 2d Platoon under 1st Lt. Lawrence E. Fletcher returning to Maureen to set up an NDP in the middle of the abandoned firebase after heavy contact with the NVA below the hilltop on May 5. Fletcher spent the next day, May 6, on patrol. Running out of daylight before a new night defensive position could be found, Fletcher opted to return to Maureen. The sappers who crept up the hill that night infiltrated the perimeter without detection, and when the satchel charges began exploding—the attack started shortly before dawn on May 7—Fletcher and his radioman were the first to be killed. The platoon sergeant was also killed. The platoon's brand-new medic, Pfc. Kenneth M. Kays, a reluctant soldier—denied conscientious-objector status, he'd fled to Canada when drafted, returning only when the army guaranteed him service as a medic—was running across the perimeter to reach the wounded men screaming for help when a satchel charge blew his left leg off below the knee. Not realizing what had happened to him, Kays jumped back up, only to fall head over heels when he tried to keep running and his left foot wasn't there to support him. He secured a tourniquet to the stump, then dragged himself from casualty to casualty, shielding these men he barely knew with his own body as he treated them. The platoon lost six dead and twelve wounded. The half-dozen able-bodied survivors frantically threw grenades at the enemy to their front and fired behind them at those inside the perimeter.

Leaving four bodies, the sappers pulled back at first light as Workman and the platoon that his command group was accompanying arrived, having been delayed by an ambush en route. Kays was found on the side of the hill, weak from loss of blood as he huddled beside the soldier he had left the perimeter to reach after the man had been blasted down the hill. For such dedication, Kays would be awarded the Medal of Honor.[2]

Next, during the night of May 28–29, the NVA tried to penetrate FSB O'Reilly but, caught in the wire after one of the approaching enemy triggered a trip flare, were chopped to pieces by the Cobras that methodically rolled in under the light of an orbiting flareship. Three ARVN were killed and fifteen wounded, light losses compared to the official body count of seventy-seven enemy—two NVA were also taken prisoner—and the capture of two Chinese radios, three Soviet flamethrowers, eight RPG launchers, and twenty-nine AK-47s.

The attack on Granite had been visible in the night sky to the troops on Ripcord, who expected to be hit themselves. It hadn't happened by the time Captain Williams and Company B relieved Company C on rainy, muddy, miserable Ripcord on May 14. Williams had no sooner gotten his company into position than Lieutenant Delgado reported that one of his men had been injured. The circumstances were a sign of the times. The problem was a trooper from Company C who had missed the combat assault back to the bush. "It was a black guy," said Williams. "He holed up in a fighting position with some of my black soldiers, got stoned, and decided to throw a grenade. He didn't throw it very far, and shrapnel hit one of my men, a very good man, in the leg."

After checking the injured soldier, Captain Williams stormed down to the position where the frag-happy malingerer was ensconced, and shouted, "Come out of there, boy." It was the wrong word to use in the time of Black Power. "He came out of there like a mad badger," recalled Williams, "and went into a furious tirade. Delgado reminded him that he was talking to a captain, and he said he didn't care who he was talking to, I was just a white honkey motherfucker." When the malingerer threatened Williams's life, the captain went to report the situation to Lucas and was instructed to use as much force as necessary to bring the out-of-control trooper to the TOC. Williams did, informing the malingerer that if he tried anything he would be shot dead on the spot by the sergeant whom Williams had picked to stand ready at his side with an M16. It was obvious that the sergeant would have relished shooting him. "With that, his whole attitude changed and he timidly marched up to the TOC," noted Williams. "I guess he got what he wanted because Lucas had him helicoptered to Camp Evans and thrown in the stockade. He got sent to the rear. He got out of there."

There soon followed another bizarre incident. Company B's fighting positions on the perimeter were shelled several evenings in a row, right at sundown, by someone firing a grenade launcher from inside Ripcord. The source could not be identified because the fire always stopped after two or three rounds. The grunts surmised that it was coming from a pot-smoking support trooper, and they called the phantom the Mad 79er. Finally, one of Company B's most popular soldiers, a little Italian guy who owned a barbershop back home—when he gave haircuts on an old ammo crate, taking the time to do it right, he made many guys feel as though they were human again for the first time since they'd been drafted—was wounded by the friendly fire. "I got a bunch of people together the next night," said Williams. "Everyone took their rank off, and we just had flak jackets, no shirts, plus our steel pots and weapons, and we sat outside and waited for the guy with the grenade launcher to start shooting. There was going to be no quarter. That sort of low-life bastard didn't deserve any. Evidently, the word got around because there was no M79 fire that night or any other night thereafter."

There were many nights when noises were heard in the wire or the ground radar detected movement. Company B would lob frags and M79 fire down the hill while the 81mm crews dropped in some HE. At odd times during the night, even when all was quiet, there would be so-called Mad Minutes in which every available rifleman, machine gunner, and grenadier would cut loose for sixty seconds to deter infiltrators. "[T]here are beaucoup gooks all around," Sergeant Tolson wrote home in a letter dated June 5. "Three days in a row now we found tracks just outside our wire . . . Last night the guy in the hole next to mine was looking through his starlight scope . . . and he saw a gook on his stomach right at the wire." The mortars coincidentally put up some illum at that time. The flares released by illumination rounds make a popping sound before igniting. "As soon as the round popped," Tolson continued, "the gook got up and ran behind a big rock. About the time he got up to run, the guy next to me opened up for all he was worth, guys were shooting and throwing hand grenades, but this morning when they went down and checked it out it was the same old story, just tracks. . . ."

Captured documents spoke of numerous sappers being killed while attempting to breach the wire at Ripcord. Sergeant Tolson's letter made reference to two NVA, captured after a firefight with another company, who "said that they have been sending people up to the wire to find an easy way to get in and so far they haven't found it. One of the prisoners said that they were at the bottom of the hill that the firebase is on and before they could do anything they had 20 dead out of his company due to close in mortar and artillery fire that is shot all night just to keep the gooks away."

The hard days of laying wire continued. With all the vegetation having been cut down, the firebase was blisteringly hot when the monsoon finally blew over. "The only bright spot was if we'd gotten mail on the resupply bird," noted Sergeant Rubsam of Bravo One. "We'd go inside our little bunkers at the end of the day, and burn the wax wrappings off mortar rounds to read them by at night. It really stank up the place, but it relaxed you to read about home."

Entertainment was provided on a nightly basis by U. S. Air Force C-47 Spooky gunships—also known as Puff the Magic Dragon—which could be seen circling to the south, pouring streams of red minigun fire into enemy truck convoys and anti-aircraft sites in the A Shau Valley. There was an air force directional beacon and a Marine tactical aircraft antenna on Ripcord, "and we ran both fighter-bombers and B-52s into the A Shau and the Warehouse Area," noted Koenigsbauer. "There was no question in our minds that between the air power we were bringing in and our own ground operations, which were uncovering the caves and bunkers the enemy used to shield themselves from artillery and air attacks, we were seriously disrupting the enemy's ability to resupply their units in the coastal plains. We were definitely an obstacle to their plans—a thorn, in hindsight, that they were going to remove at any cost."

CHAPTER 8

The Forever War

There exists no clear picture of Andre Lucas. Reserved by nature, he was different things to different people. "We had a good battalion and a good battalion commander," said veteran platoon leader Steve Wallace. First Lieutenant Fred H. Edwards, the battalion engineering officer, described Lucas, a tall, slender, dark-complected man with dark eyes and black hair, as having "an unmistakable air of poise and authority about him. He had a very professional, quiet demeanor. I don't think I ever heard him raise his voice. He was stern without being overbearing, and always seemed to be in total control. In short, a complete professional."

Others found Lucas's tactical judgment suspect and noted that he "led" his battalion from the uninspiring safety of his command ship. "We didn't know who the hell the guy was," said one grunt.

Andre Cavaro Lucas, son of a career officer, was born in Walter Reed Army Hospital in Washington, D. C., on October 2, 1930. He spent his early years on military bases before his father retired as a colonel in Santa Monica, California, at the beginning of World War II. An aircraft manufacturer during the war, the elder Lucas moved his family to Le Pouligen, France, in 1946 to stay with his wife's mother. The younger Lucas joined the army in 1948 and soon secured an appointment to West Point with the Class of '54.

Lieutenant Lucas married his fiancée, a no-nonsense, upper-middle-class woman from New York City, on graduation day. Having earned his jump wings and ranger tab, he served a 1955–58 tour in Germany, including a stint with the 10th Special Forces Group. Lucas was subsequently assigned as an instructor at the ranger school in the snake-infested swamps near Eglin Air Force Base, Florida, in 1958–59, then spent two years with the U. S. Army Infantry Training School at Fort Benning in 1959–61, and a year with the Tactics Department at the U. S. Military Academy in 1961–62.

Captain Lucas went to Vietnam from West Point, a plum assignment in 1962. Advisor to an ARVN ranger battalion, he didn't need an interpreter, able as he was to converse fluently with his counterparts in French. Lucas's combat tour netted him the Silver Star and Bronze Star Medal for Valor. He next served as a company commander and staff officer with the 82d Airborne Division at Fort Bragg, North Carolina, in 1963–64. On the fast track, Major Lucas attended Command & General Staff College at Fort Leavenworth, Kansas, in 1964–65 and the L'Ecole D'Etat Majeur in Paris in 1966. Duty with European Command Headquarters and promotion to light colonel were followed by service as a brigade executive officer, battalion commander, and division operations officer with the 24th Division in 1967–69, first in Germany, then at Fort Riley, Kansas, when the division relocated to the United States.

Bidding farewell to his wife and two boys, Lieutenant Colonel Lucas began his second combat tour in November 1969, cooling his heels initially as a brigade exec before getting the 2d Battalion, 506th Infantry, 101st Airborne Division on March 4, 1970. "Lucas, Koenigsbauer, and Davis were obviously in sync with each other, and were a great team to lead any battalion," wrote Chuck Hawkins, who thought Lucas brisk and to the point. "He wasn't into lengthy discussions. You said what you had to say, and then you went about your business. If you made a mistake, Lucas would chew you out and that would be that. He didn't hold anything against you afterward—but you'd better not make the same error again."

Lucas found it necessary to relieve a number of officers in the battalion of their duties. He believed that to make such cold-eyed decisions, a leader must remain aloof from his subordinates. It was a command philosophy that fit Lucas's personality, which his admirers describe as dignified and cheerful, though formal, his detractors as bland and uncharismatic. "Lucas was close with only two people—me and Sid Davis," noted Koenigsbauer. Lucas might share a beer with his XO and S3 when back at Camp Evans, but never with a captain or a lieutenant. He never asked his subordinates about their families, never discussed his own personal life. "Lucas was a little more detached than most battalion commanders," said Koenigsbauer. "He was nevertheless on excellent terms with his company commanders, clicking especially well with Williams, Rollison, Hawkins, and Vazquez. Lucas made a major effort to nurture those relationships. He would listen, and he never discouraged discussion during the planning of an operation, but once a decision was made he expected professional execution and loyalty. Much has been written about why units fight. It is my opinion that the company commanders in the 2d of the 506th fought hard for Lieutenant Colonel Lucas."

The ace of spades being the informal symbol of the battalion, Lucas drew one on the side of his helmet and went by the call sign Black Spade. "Lucas liked being in command. I think he enjoyed danger," observed Hawkins. Fond of quoting from his readings, the colonel once pronounced to his officers: "In our chosen profession, death is our handmaiden." For all that, Lucas's CAR15 submachine gun, the preferred weapon of battalion commanders, went unused and was actually rusty. "I wondered what sort of an example that was to set for soldiers," wrote Hawkins. "Lucas never humped the boonies with me or my men. There was no reason for him to do so, and I think he enjoyed the freedom of his command ship more—or being able to quickly go where he wanted to. He seemed to be on the go a lot, but when your battalion is as far flung as ours was, you have a lot of places to check."

Like the grunts who saw the battalion commander only in the rear or on the firebase, Capt. Jeffrey D. Wilcox was unimpressed with Lucas. Promoted to command of the battalion support company after duty as a rifle platoon leader, Wilcox, a West Pointer, took the opportunity to discuss tactics with

Lucas. Wilcox expressed his concern that it might be wiser, given the withdrawals, to rely almost exclusively on firepower to avoid casualties instead of finding, fixing, and fighting the NVA. With an air of bravado that Wilcox found disturbing, Lucas tried to reorient the captain's thinking by telling him that losing people was "all in the game."

Black Spade had a point. The discussion nevertheless left Wilcox with the impression that the superaggressive Lucas saw the war as some kind of live-fire exercise, his chance to look good and move up the ladder. There is a little of that in most career officers. The issue was complicated in Lucas's case, argued the colonel's detractors, because he did not always make good tactical decisions, such was the disconnect between the war as it was on the ground and the war as it appeared from Black Spade's C&C. The withdrawals also put a twist on the issue. While demonstrating their ability to destroy the enemy, unit leaders also had to avoid taking the kind of losses that would embarrass MACV. It was a real dilemma. There was, in fact, a desperate quality to the whole career game at that stage in the war. Whereas many so-called professionals who'd already gotten their tickets punched tried to avoid further combat duty lest something happen to wreck their careers, those such as Lucas who needed a combat command to survive professionally scrambled to impress their superiors and gather what laurels were still to be had before the war wound down completely.

The result was that Hawkins could write that "Lucas had courage, nerve, and was strong minded," while also being of the opinion that he was "a bit of a 'yes-man.' I think I used the word 'kowtow' in a letter home to describe his attitude towards 'senior brass.' "

"Lucas wanted to make general," said Capt. Fredrick L. Spaulding of the brigade staff, "and his attitude was always, 'Yes sir, yes sir, three bags full, sir.' It was kind of sickening sometimes."

Lucas was unique only in the transparency of his careerism. Spaulding, an up-from-the-ranks mustang on his third tour, saw few career officers stand up and be counted when they disagreed with the party line: "I thought, this must be the New

Army. It wasn't the way I was taught by the World War II and Korean vets who were my officers and NCOs when I first joined the Army. The attitude of the officer corps in Vietnam was, 'What's in it for me?'"

The competition was fierce. It wasn't enough for an ambitious officer to finish his six months with a good efficiency report. It had to be "immaculate," noted Turner, the brigade ops officer, "to get that next promotion and that next command." Lucas was considered one of the division's stars, but his need to rise even higher above the rest resulted in another incident in which he crossed swords with Wilcox. Division was concerned that the rear was soaking up too many people, "so at a particular time one night each week," recalled Wilcox, "every battalion had to send up a report declaring how many personnel it had on its firebase and out in the field." The report was called the Foxhole Count. According to Wilcox, "Lucas's policy was to load a Chinook on the reporting day with as many cooks, armorers, clerks, drivers, et cetera, as could be rounded up and fly them to Ripcord, where they would spend the night in a bunker before being returned to Camp Evans." Wilcox thought it a dangerous ploy, given the vulnerability of Chinooks to ground fire, and questioned Lucas "about why we simply didn't either tell the truth or give a false report without actually moving people around and putting them in jeopardy. Lucas brushed me off, saying that this was yet another dimension of 'playing the game.'"

Major Koenigsbauer saw nothing of the self-serving careerist in Lucas; he admired him unreservedly as an "intense, focused, businesslike officer—very decisive." Donning headsets, Lucas would ride on the right side of his command ship, with his S3 and artillery liaison officer (arty LNO) on the left, each of them wearing a flak jacket and sitting on another in case of ground fire. "Location was critical," noted Koenigsbauer; the command-ship pilots knew the terrain, "but it was not convenient to be on the intercom with them, and Colonel Lucas wasn't the type to constantly ask where he was, so he had a large plywood map-board made with a compass mounted to one side. That map always kept him oriented."

Captain Williams recalled that "when you were on a combat

assault, Major Koenigsbauer was there on the radio, talking you in. You trusted him, it was just there in his voice, and you knew if you ran into trouble, Lucas would back you up one hundred percent.

"Lucas was always correct in his manner," Williams continued, "but he never talked down to you. He had a good sense of humor and did not make things unnecessarily tense like I've seen some commanders do. We were all very close. There wasn't any animosity or intense competition between the company commanders. We weren't just a numbered battalion, we were a team, and I was always impressed by how everyone from the top down would work together to accomplish the mission."

Leadership throughout the division was superior. General Wright, survivor of three years in Japanese prison camps after the fall of the Philippines, and a veteran of the Korean War, was on his second Vietnam tour, as were most of his battalion commanders, brigade commanders, and key staff officers. Though the 101st was airborne in name only as of 1968, the army hierarchy was determined to keep it in top form. Colonel Hugh A. MacDonald, a veteran paratrooper, served as division chief of staff for an unprecedented three years, 1969–71, providing a strong sense of continuity. In addition, at the end of Wright's year in command, May 25, 1970, he passed the colors not to a newcomer but to Hennessey, a fellow West Pointer promoted in-country to major general. Virtually every officer from captain up, and many of the lieutenants, too, wore jump wings, as did the majority of the senior NCOs. One of the top sergeants in Koenigsbauer's operations shop had parachuted into Normandy with the 101st. Such men were members of a legendary airborne elite. Like the 1st Cav, the Screaming Eagles had a reputation such that hard-charging officers, be they new lieutenants or seasoned professionals coming back for more, fought to be assigned to it rather than end up in a half-steppin' outfit such as the 4th or 25th or, worse, the disaster-prone Americal Division.

The division was nevertheless not all it had once been. The war had gone on too long, and second-string players were arriving on the scene. Brigadier General Sidney B. Berry, USMA '48, a two-war, three-tour man who served as assistant division commander for operations (ADC-O), 101st Airborne Division, during the Ripcord siege, wrote a letter to his wife decrying "the surprisingly low quality of the colonels who write to seek brigade command." One such colonel was a West Pointer with "no CIB; no previous tour of duty in Vietnam; 25 years service and no combat. He must have worked hard to avoid combat. Now he wants to command a brigade of Screaming Eagle soldiers. Like hell he will."

The change in the division's character was most apparent at the platoon level, as described by Lieutenant Noll of A/2-506th:

> The senior leadership was definitely hardcore airborne, but 99 percent of the lieutenants and troops in the field were draftees, myself included. We weren't paratroopers. We weren't professional soldiers. The troops were no different than those assigned to any other unit. They had gone through Basic and AIT, then were shipped over to Vietnam. A lot of them had a ninth- or tenth-grade education at best, and their training, rudimentary as it was, didn't really sink in. Platoon leaders had the problem of trying to teach these kids in the middle of combat operations how to patrol, how to set up an ambush, hell, which way to point the goddamn claymore. . . .

The division's line units nevertheless displayed a level of competence not often seen in other draftee outfits of the era. There was more to it than good leadership. Given its institutional mind-set, the 101st Airborne was the only division still aggressively taking the fight to the enemy during the withdrawals. The war in the jungle-covered mountains west of Hue was a "pure one, as wars go," noted Chip Collins—no civilians, few booby traps, "just us, the elements, and the NVA"—and the troops had to be professional if they wanted to survive out there. "The mountains scared people," explained Lt. Stephen Wallace. "In the mountains, you stayed one step ahead of the enemy or they would clean your clock."

First Lieutenant John H. Smith, a gung-ho, career-minded

platoon leader in D/1-506th, found that his men had little enthusiasm for the war or the 101st. "They often referred to the unit patch as the Pukin' Buzzard," he wrote. "Nevertheless, when we assembled on the helipad at Camp Evans to be CA'd into the jungle for another operation, you could see a determined look in everyone's eyes—not because we were great, motivated soldiers, but because we knew it was us against them once we landed."

Lieutenant Kwiecien commented along the same lines:

> The people weren't the hoods from the movie *Platoon* or the psychos from *Full Metal Jacket.* They were just a bunch of very ordinary young men who realized that the best way to stay alive was by being good at your job. There were very few gung-ho types, just a general determination that if we had to be out in the woods we were going to be good at it.
>
> After being assigned to the rear, I had a chance to talk with the E6 who'd taken over my platoon. He was a shake 'n bake and had heard the horror stories about the troops in Nam not caring anymore, smoking dope, et cetera. He said that the level of professionalism in the platoon blew his mind; they had good noise and light discipline, knew how to cross an open area, knew how to set up at night, automatically assumed defensive positions during breaks, et cetera, et cetera. I was proud as punch.

The soldiers were so good that Kwiecien came to appreciate how young they were only when he encountered two E6 platoon sergeants he knew in the company orderly room after Ripcord. In the field, "these guys were all business, very tough, serious, and professional," but in the rear, "the pressure was off, and I was amazed to see that they were really just a couple of kids, kind of giggly and silly kids at that, like you might see at a college frat party."

Such youthful sergeants were not unique. Given that many regulars coming back for a second or third tour pulled strings to avoid further combat—"the rear areas were full of E7s and First Sergeants running PX S, supply rooms, etc.," wrote one disgusted lieutenant—most of the noncoms in the field were Noncommissioned Officer Candidate School grads out of Fort Benning. Despite their inexperience, "a remarkable number of these so-called shake 'n bakes performed quite effectively," wrote General Berry. "We would have been in terrible shape without them, and many were actually better than the Regular Army NCOs they replaced."

The shake 'n bakes did their best to fill the gap, though many felt that they were in over their heads. "I always thought that I would have been one hell of a fine squad leader," mused Sergeant Rubsam of B/2-506th, "but I never served in that position." Instead, Rubsam, a married man drafted out of college, ended up with a platoon. "I guess I was the platoon leader. Actually, it was more leadership by committee. There were three or four of us who talked everything over and planned things out. I remember staying up every night with my group, waiting our turn to call in defensive targets. It got everybody used to handling mortars and artillery. That kind of on-the-job training was a real boon for me. Luckily, too, we didn't see much action my first two months, which allowed me to get my feet on the ground and get to know my people before Ripcord broke."

Contact was infrequent for Lucas's entire battalion after Ripcord had been established, and there developed a scripted pattern to its operations. "The enemy could read us like a book," lamented Koenigsbauer. One company was always committed to firebase security. The rest would be out in the hills. Division had tasked the Currahees with constructing three landing zones per day, so while two platoons from each of the three companies in the bush ran RIFs, the third blew down enough trees to clear another one-ship LZ. "When the explosions went off, you'd hear monkeys whooping and hollering off in the distance," noted a platoon leader. Meanwhile, those platoons on patrol basically trekked along ridgelines from eight in the morning until four in the afternoon. At that point, each would grab a piece of high ground and begin digging in, hacking down fields of fire, and rigging claymores and trip flares. "It was a real project," recalled Sergeant Judd, a shake 'n bake squad leader in Company B. "That was half our day's work. Humping was one part, and setting up for the night was the other."

There were moments of great beauty in the mountains. First Lieutenant Lee E. Widjeskog of Company A recalled that when his platoon crossed the Rao Trang River, wading across with the assistance of a rope, "the water was fast flowing, with rapids, and looked [to] all the world like a trout stream in the Rocky Mountains." On another occasion, the platoon happened upon a fifteen-foot waterfall cascading into a clear pool of water. Unseen birds called to one another high in the enveloping canopy. "We used the area to clean up and eat lunch before continuing on," wrote Widjeskog. "It was a peaceful and lovely respite from the war."

Mostly, though, the mountains were a bitch. It was rough country, and the grunts, humping rucksacks that weighed up to a hundred pounds when full—units were resupplied every three days—were reduced to rubber-legged exhaustion as they chopped their way through vines and thorn bushes and dense thickets of bamboo. Hands were covered with cuts. Headaches buzzed under steel helmets. Shoulders and necks ached from the rucksack straps and ammo bandoliers cutting into them. Patrols were tormented by mosquitoes, plagued by leeches. "Whenever we stopped for breaks, guys would check all exposed skin to see if a leech had hooked on for a meal," noted Widjeskog. If a leech went unnoticed, it would drop off when it had its fill, leaving a bleeding sore, "and it was not unusual," Widjeskog added, "to wake up in the morning with dried blood on your face and hands where leeches had feasted during the night. Between the leeches and various scratches, it was no wonder guys caught bacterial infections like jungle rot and cellulitus."

It was a brutal existence, but the troops tended to make the best of it. There was much comradeship among the grunts, and always an undercurrent of humor. What the troops did not have was an aggressive fighting spirit. It was too late for that. "Grunt logic argues that since the U. S. has decided not to go out and win the war, there's no sense in being the last one to die," wrote John Saar of *Life*. The 1st Cav and Screaming Eagles might have been the two best outfits still in-country, but neither was what their flaky brethren had been before the withdrawals when the leadership slots had been filled with pros and the troops had thought they were fighting to win. Saar interviewed a tough young cav sergeant who'd seen heavy combat in 1967–68 before coming back for a second tour in 1970. "We make a lot less contact now, and guys are a lot more afraid," the sergeant said. No one wanted to die for nothing. Bunker complexes were found but not reported. Night ambushes were faked, sometimes with the collusion of sympathetic platoon leaders. There was also a lot of "reconning by fire"—shooting up suspicious areas with M60s, M79s, and 81s before moving in, the better to chase away the enemy without a fight. The mood of the troops was, fuck it, the war's been going on for twenty-five years. We ain't gonna win it today, so don't go lookin' for trouble.

It was a difficult time to be a commander. Consider the case of Lt. Col. Charles J. Shay, CO of the 2-502d Infantry (the O-Deuce) in the 1st Brigade, 101st Airborne Division. Shay was the model for the "ass-kicking" battalion commander in John Del Vecchio's *The 13th Valley,* and General Berry described Shay in a letter home as a "strong, direct, aggressive, sometimes blunt and untactful soldier" and "the best battalion commander in the division."

Chuck Shay was a New York Irishman. He was sixteen in 1945 when he lied about his age to join the Marines in an unsuccessful attempt to get into World War II. He joined the army the day after the Korean War began, and after OCS commanded a company in the 2d Division 1952–53. He was wounded by mortar shrapnel and finally evacuated with gunshot wounds to both legs. Shay was an ARVN advisor in 1960 and 1964–65, and after three months of staff duty with the 101st he commanded the O-Deuce from May to December 1970.

Shay was short, squat, and profane—"a fire-eater," noted Fred Spaulding, "who carried a damn shillelagh around with him, banging it on things." Correspondent Arthur Hadley found Shay—call sign Shamrock—a popular commander admired by officers and grunts. But for all that, taking care of problems that should have taken care of themselves, and trying to motivate troops who knew they were fighting to no useful end, had left the colonel "wasted, drained, almost somnambulant" by the end of his tour. "It's different now," Shay told Hadley one night on the battalion firebase. "When you praise a man for being a good soldier, he looks at the ground and shuffles his feet. It's not much fun anymore."

However low morale had slipped in the field, it was infinitely worse in the rear. "Camp Evans was sliding towards anarchy by the summer of 1970," noted Lt. Blair Case, an artillery forward observer with the 1-506th Infantry. "The mood was ominous, almost hostile, and the rear-echelon types seemed to go out of their way to demonstrate a lack of military courtesy. At night, marijuana smoke would drift through the hootch areas like a heavy fog. Racial tension was near flash point. There were a lot of Black Power salutes and all-black hootches where whites were not welcome. Other hootches displayed Confederate battle flags."

Discipline had been eroding ever since Tet, as the troops, increasingly draftees and part of a generation in revolt, brought to Vietnam as never before the very problems tearing the country apart. There was, for starters, the drug mess. Marijuana began to outclass alcohol as the drug of choice in 1968–69. Most platoon leaders, unwilling to ship half their guys to the LBJ Ranch, as the troops sardonically referred to Long Binh Jail, drew the line when it came to pot in the bush but turned a blind eye during stand-downs.

The grunts tended to police themselves in combat, though some refused to play by the rules. The problem became noticeable in Captain Hawkins's company, for example, during the 2-506th's deployment to the Firebase Rakkasan AO after Ripcord. There being a distinct lull in enemy activity as the rainy season began, some grunts saw no reason not to get smoked up in the bush; one GI from Company A was out on OP when he fired up a joint instead of staying alert, and for that he died, shot in the chest at point-blank range by the point man of a passing enemy patrol who swung up his AK-47 before the kid even thought to reach for his M16.

Such lapses were rare in the bush. It was usually on firebases that things got loose. One night on Rakkasan, Chip Collins of B/2-506th found "five consecutive bunkers with guards asleep or zonked out [on drugs]." First Lieutenant John R. Fox, a three-tour helicopter pilot with the 101st in 1970–71, reported that "when the sun began to set, the smell of marijuana would drift across the firebases." It was disquieting in the extreme "to wonder if the man watching the wire was as high as a kite." Unsure how much discipline they could enforce without starting a mutiny, most battery commanders just prayed that the sappers didn't attack during their six months in the field. "They were getting their tickets punched," said Fox. "They needed the command time for their careers, but they wanted to get it over with without making waves. There was no long-term accountability in Vietnam."

That was one perspective. Another could be found in the case of Capt. Charles R. Brooks, USMA '68, who commanded B/2-320th Field Artillery with the kind of informal, people-oriented approach that got results out of the new-style draftees. Brooks was aided immeasurably by First Sergeant O'Neill, who "looked like a Cro-Magnon man," noted Pfc. Frank J. Parko, but who "was actually a pretty cool dude. He was a lifer and a taskmaster, but he'd sit down and shoot the shit with you—and he'd walk through incoming mortar fire, yelling orders, keeping things organized." Brooks and O'Neill couldn't make the drugs disappear, but they did get across the message that "there was a time to do it and a time not to do it," as Parko put it. "Our battery was pretty tight. You had the rednecks who liked their beer, and the dopers who would quietly go off and do their thing, but nobody bothered anybody, and when the shit hit the fan, everybody was there. Everybody helped each other out."

Not so in the rear, as Parko discovered when wounded on FSB Kathryn in May 1970. There had been a brief mortar attack earlier that day during a football game on the log pad. The fire came from a nearby knoll. Later, at dusk, as Battery B was finishing a hot meal delivered in mermite cans, "that whole hill lit up with mortar flashes," recalled Parko. "The first attack had been a registration mission." Amid the counterbattery fire,

Parko, jumping into a perimeter foxhole, put up flares and popped away with his M16 until a near miss gave him a fierce concussion and peppered his arm with shrapnel. Parko was evacuated to Camp Eagle, where "everyone was uptight because of all the spit-and-polish lifer shit." Benumbed by the monotony of their duties, and wired on pot, speed, and way too much booze, the support troops—known to the line troops as REMFs, as in rear-echelon motherfuckers—were literally at war with one another, lifers against draftees, blacks against whites, drinkers against the dopers. "It was nuts," said Parko. "I mean, we were watching some Civil War movie, and a fight broke out between guys from the North and the guys from the South."

Some officers were real hawks when it came to busting people for drugs, especially, and most justifiably, when checking the bunker line at forward base camps such as Evans. Many, however, prudently ignored the groups that gathered at night to pass the weed. "The officers and NCOs didn't mess with the pot heads," said a squad leader in the 2-506th Infantry. "They wanted to go home alive."

The threat of fragging was always in the air, especially because the line companies dumped their duds and troublemakers in the rear. "Misfits were plentiful by 1970," wrote Lieutenant Smith of the 1-506th Infantry. Reassigned to Camp Evans after serving his time as a platoon leader, Smith eventually requested a job on the battalion firebase, because "I preferred to take my chances with the NVA."

There was another reason that the drug crackdown was not wholeheartedly enforced. The Regular Army runs on caffeine, nicotine, and alcohol, as the saying goes, and many junior officers weren't convinced that the marijuana preferred by the young draftees was such an unacceptable alternative. "It was hard to get too ugly about marijuana," mused one gunship pilot, a West Pointer, "while we were polishing off bottles of Jack Daniel's in the Officers Club."

Another West Pointer, a career officer who commanded a mechanized infantry company from the 9th Division during the 1970 Cambodian incursion, told the author off the record that "if the guys were going to do anything when we came in on standdown, marijuana was preferable to alcohol. Marijuana mellowed guys out, while drinking led to violent brawls. It was a real dilemma for the leadership that what was legal was worse than what was illegal."

Marijuana was one thing, but heroin, better known as smack, came on the scene big in Vietnam that summer, making it to Camp Evans around August or September 1970. "Guys were buying heroin right outside the front gate that was ninety-five percent pure," recalled Capt. James D. Harris, M. D., battalion surgeon for the 2-506th Infantry. Mainlining was not required with such high-grade heroin. It could be snorted or, more typically, smoked in a menthol cigarette. "They'd snort that stuff," Harris said, "and they wouldn't even be able to stand up. We had troops who were addicted, and we had some overdose deaths on base. It was a horrible situation."

Sergeant Lin L. Bashford, company clerk for D/2-506th:

> The dopers in the company rear knew I didn't tolerate drugs, so they hid it from me. Once, though, I walked into the barracks when I was putting together duty schedules, and I caught them snorting smack. I threatened to turn them in, and they got right in my face: "Go ahead and report us—you'll never make it back home if you do." It wasn't an idle threat, and I said, "Just get rid of the shit, I don't want it around."
>
> The worst encounter I had was with the company's Kit Carson Scout. He was well respected, but after Ripcord he was so scared you couldn't hardly trap him into getting on a helicopter—and then I caught him bringing heroin in to sell at Evans. He was on his little Vespa motor-scooter, and I don't remember if he was showing the package to somebody, or what the deal was, but he had a white brick of the stuff under the seat—it wasn't broken down yet—and I took him into the orderly room and called the MPs. They took the evidence and hauled his ass off. On his way out, in cuffs, he told me in that Vietnamese lingo, "I kill you, sonofabitch, I kill you." He was ousted from the Kit Carson program, but I didn't sleep very well for a long time because the Scout was an ex-sapper who could have gotten through the wire any time he wanted.

Drugs and live ammunition did not mix. Del Vecchio wrote in *The 13th Valley* of "Demented Fuckers" who settled scores by "plantin['] frags." Chip Collins bitterly noted that "you never knew when you were in the rear when some asshole was going to get drunk or drugged up and start rippin' off with his '16."

Collins saw his first dead American before he'd even cleared the replacement center at Cam Ranh Bay on his way to the 101st: "A guy was shot in the back of the head with a .45 while watching an outdoor movie. It had been dark, hot, and crowded. No immediate suspects. Drug deal gone bad? Race related? Jealousy? What?"

Like drugs, race relations were a problem that got worse the further removed a unit was from combat. "We never had racial problems in the field," wrote Lieutenant Case, FO of A/1-506th. "Once the helicopters landed, nothing mattered except survival and everyone eagerly did their part." As a sign of the times, one platoon did have an all-black squad. The company commander, Capt. Harold Echols, a black officer known as Spartan because he'd gone to Michigan State on a football scholarship, frowned on that kind of separatism. The white GIs, however, noted Case, "didn't take it as a sign of racial animosity. They thought the blacks wanted an all-black squad simply to demonstrate solidarity." Case continued:

> As soldiers got short, it was customary to find them a job in the rear. One night in the field, my radioman brought two black soldiers to me. They complained that the first sergeant, an Hispanic, would accept only white soldiers for jobs in the rear, and that black soldiers had to stay in the field right up to their DEROS [date eligible for return from overseas].
>
> The first sergeant, they said, claimed he picked soldiers who could best handle the clerical work back at base camp, and it was not his fault that the best-qualified usually turned out to be white. They felt anyone, no matter what their level of education, could handle most of the base camp jobs, and they wanted me to intercede with Spartan. It might seem strange that they would come to me since I'm white and Spartan was black, but infantrymen seem to treat FOs as

someone outside the chain of command who can act as an intermediary.

I talked to Spartan, and he called all the black soldiers in the platoon together. They sat talking in the dark for a long time. Spartan repeated the process each time the CP rotated to another platoon on resupply days when helicopters were available. I don't know what was said in the black caucuses, but I do know that afterward soldiers rotated to the rear based solely on the number of days they had left in-country.

A serious racial incident erupted when Company A returned to Camp Evans on June 4, 1970, prior to the 1-506th's deployment to the Ripcord AO. When six blacks took over an entire tent for themselves, a white GI shouted a racial insult at them from the company street. The tent's occupants promptly punched out the GI. As reported by David Warsh of *Newsweek:*

> [T]he next hour saw rumors fly and tension mount until a second scuffle sent at least two hotheads—one black, one white—rushing for their weapons. For a time, black and white troopers faced each other across rows of barracks in a confrontation that threatened to flare into a racial fire fight.
>
> In the end, no firing occurred, but before peace was restored, some whites told the blacks that the next day's training session in ambush techniques would turn into the real thing—with black troops as the sitting ducks. The next morning, as the company began its trek to the nearby gullies [outside Camp Evans] where the ambush practice was to take place, fifteen black enlisted men flatly refused to go. "We were threatened," [a black GI] told me. "We asked the officers to get the people who threatened us. They didn't."

Captain Echols convinced six of the GIs to rejoin the company; the other nine would not budge. By making their stand when they did, the nine were left safely behind when the 1-506th assaulted into the Ripcord AO. As Warsh wrote, the battalion commander, tempted to charge them with mutiny, instead filed charges for "simple failure to obey an order, a much milder rap." Then, to make a point, he had the "Evans Nine" shipped to the LBJ:

> After five days at Long Binh, the defendants were returned to their base for a court-martial. All of the men pleaded guilty, but only three—those with records of previous offenses—received jail terms . . . The other six defendants received suspended sentences and fines and were reduced in rank.
>
> Last week, as the Evans Nine waited for their sentences to be reviewed, tension ran high at Camp Evans. To the distress of whites from other units . . . their black comrades performed elaborate, black-power handshakes [the Dap] in the mess halls before sitting down to eat. "[Dappin'], that's just another way the brothers have of showing unity, of coming together," one black told me. Meanwhile, except for the Evans Nine, the troopers of Alfa Company, black and white, were back in the field, laying ambushes for the North Vietnamese in the tortured mountains near [the] A Shau [Valley].

There were troops "rumored to be Black Panthers," noted Case, "who acted as agents provocateurs, trying to persuade black GIs to refuse to return to the field." The Black Power movement had indeed come to Vietnam, and Chaplain Fox recalled that when the 2-506th received an influx of in-country transfers after Ripcord from units being pulled out of the country, they included "a group of black militants who immediately set about intimidating the black guys in our unit not to associate with the white guys. They really made it tough on the black guys who weren't with their program."

The results of such agitation were spectacular. Like many others, Sergeant Rubsam of B/2-506th was shocked by the number of black replacements who angled for medical profiles that would keep them in the rear, or simply refused to function and ended up being reassigned as cook's assistants in the battalion mess hall. "If nothing else," added Rubsam, "they would just buy some marijuana, turn themselves in to the first sergeant, and say they wanted a dishonorable discharge. They wanted out of the Army. As they told us, they had a war to fight when they got home."

The magnitude of the problem is revealed in a letter that Sergeant Bashford wrote home in September 1970 in which he bitterly noted that of the twenty black GIs assigned to D/2-506th, twelve were on profile or awaiting court-martial for refusing to go to the field. "In a situation where a lot of guys were looking for a way out of the bush," concluded Lieutenant Case, "it made you admire the black soldiers who resisted the temptation and went back to the fighting. They had an out but didn't take it."

If camaraderie still knew no color in combat, there was mostly fear and hatred between the races in the rear. "Most of the blacks hung together, and most of the whites felt intimidated to some degree," wrote Lieutenant Smith. They had reason to be. The Black Power movement was, at its core, thuggish, and gangs of black REMFs would "try to start fights with us whenever we came in on standdown," said Frank Marshall, a laid-back white M79 grenadier in A/2-506th. "I still don't understand it." The gangs would also jump the line at the mess hall; on one rare occasion, the Currahee recon platoon blocked the door en masse. Collins remarked that "that kind of everyday tension in the rear was nerve-wracking." He thought the command structure was intimidated by the militants: "The officers and NCOs had a see-no-evil-hear-no-evil attitude, and would only react to the most significant incidents for fear of stirring up more trouble."

As bad as things got sometimes, the 101st "shined in comparison to other units," said Capt. Michael S. Lancaster, USMA '67, a Cobra pilot with D/158th Aviation during Ripcord and Operation Lam Son 719, the push into Laos in early 1971. "We teamed up with the 5th Mech and the Americal Division during Lam Son 719, and they just didn't have the same set of rules we did. It was spooky how bad they were. It was like something out of *Apocalypse Now*."

Lieutenant Fox recalled that when the 101st displaced the 5th Mech at Quang Tri during Lam Son 719, "there were people who had not moved out with their units. They were still there, wandering around, doing drugs, just hanging out. No one was in charge of them, and nobody came to get them. They had total disrespect for anyone in authority." In fact, two majors from a 5th Mech armor battalion had recently been shot in the head, one fatally, by a pistol-toting REMF when they tried to shut down a disruptive all-night party in an all-black hootch. "Our sergeant major had to go into some of the hootches with a baseball bat to clear the stragglers out so we could move in and get set up for the operation," said Fox. "I was in a hootch by myself one evening, and this young black soldier walked in and wanted to know where 'Buddy' was. I told him that Buddy wasn't there. He got belligerent—he wanted to know where Buddy was. He had an M16 slung over his shoulder and a six pack of beer in one hand. He was obviously high, and I finally drew my .38 and advised this individual that he had better leave. I kept that pistol loaded and ready beside my cot at all times when we were at Quang Tri."

Thus did the American military straggle out of Vietnam. In distinct contrast, the North Vietnamese Army was a professional force from beginning to end. "I respect every man I killed over there," one Currahee platoon leader would reflect. Draftee grunts at that stage of the war tended to admire more than hate their foe. The NVA were in for the duration. They were seasoned soldiers, and they were willing to die for their cause. "I have nothing against that little man out there," a black trooper told John Saar. "They're fighting for what they believe in, and you can't knock that. I lie on my air mattress at night and I say, what am I doing here?"

Despite horrific losses, the enemy kept coming. "They fought hard and they won, that's all there is to it," said Captain Michaud of the 2-319th FA, who was particularly impressed with the sappers his cannoneers killed on Firebase Granite. "They penetrated the wire and came on in knowing there was no way back out. You've got to respect someone who has that kind of bravery and determination."

The communists were willing to live a primitive existence in the jungle. They made it their home. Second Lieutenant Sheldon C. "Barney" Wintermute, USMA '69, FO, D/1-506th, recalled "pushing through some incredibly thick triple-canopy, and thinking to myself, God, we must be the first human beings that have ever been here—and then all of a sudden there were these beautifully cut steps going up the side of the mountain."

The enemy had spent years preparing their positions, and some were truly impressive. "We found a large hospital complex built into a natural stone formation," said Sergeant Rubsam of B/2-506th. "It had running water piped through bamboo to the different rooms. It was solid rock, so we backed off as I recall and destroyed the place with long-range fire from a battleship or cruiser in the South China Sea."

The jungle hid the enemy, nullified the allies' firepower. No matter how many bombs were dropped, noted Chuck Hawkins, the jungle "just sucked them up like so few drops of water into a dry sponge. There was an eerie, mystical quality to those jungle-covered mountains. To watch the sun rise and begin burning off the fog, each mountain peak an island, is absolutely breathtaking . . . and frightening. I still get cold chills when I think about the terrain and what we and the enemy did there. . . ."

Captain Lancaster, the gunship pilot, recalled that "when you flew down those twisting, turning valleys leading to the A Shau, the air sort of turned green and you had this feeling that we don't belong here, this is not our turf." Lancaster was leading a two-ship recon down a river when "we flew over a bunch of people who were in the water swimming. They were not civilians. There were no civilians out there." There was, however, the occasional U. S. Special Forces team with Cambodian and Chinese Nung mercenaries, "so we swung around to see what the hell we had," Lancaster recounted. "Those guys were scrambling out of the water by then, and as we came back by, we saw little gardens and cornfields and marijuana patches. The NVA used to grow that shit. I said, 'Out, now.' We marked it on the map, reported it—and left."

Both sides were preparing for the battle to come. When Lucas and the division artillery (div arty) commander flew out to recon Firebase Bradley, a position at the north end of the A Shau Valley that was to be reopened to support Operation Chicago Peak, artillery rounds began hitting the mountaintop. The div arty colonel, concerned that the premature prep fires would tip off the NVA, ordered a cease-fire. It developed, however, that the fire was actually coming from camouflaged 152mm howitzer positions in nearby Laos. "The NVA knew we were coming," noted Hawkins, "and were pre-registering their heavy weapons." It was a chilling development.[1]

As Lucas established a foothold to the north, Lt. Col. Roy J. Young's 2-502d Infantry, from Col. John D. White's 1st Brigade, reopened FSB Veghel in the mountains east of the A Shau Valley. Young was soon engaged in a four-day battle to take Hill 714. The NVA had bunkers on top of the mountain and more on the three knolls leading to it. "Each time we forced them off one complex, they simply fell back to the next one, set up, and waited for us," said a frustrated company commander. In the end, for all the fire support called in, it came down to grenades. "[W]e were killing NVA still in their bunkers," a sergeant told a division combat correspondent. "They had everything their way and we beat 'em."

Next came a three-day battle to take nearby Hill 882. Chuck Shay assumed command two days later, on May 6, when Young replaced Dyke as G3. Defeated in open battle, the enemy stung the O-Deuce in ambushes and night attacks before the battalion was pulled out on May 24. By then, it had accounted for two hundred NVA but had itself lost approximately thirty KIA and two hundred WIA.

The O-Deuce was replaced by the 1-327th Infantry, which found itself shadowed by unseen enemies as it pushed on from Hill 882. A Huey pilot asked the element it was extracting after dark to mark its position with a strobe light. Four strobes went on at various points. The extraction was canceled. Another night, an English-speaking NVA got on a platoon's internal frequency and "asked who they were, where they were, what they were doing," noted the battalion journal. The platoon "answered all questions[,] giving false info."

A platoon from B/1-327th, in deep bush with no available landing zone, arranged to have a Huey kick out its resupply of water, rations, and ammo at treetop level. A smoke grenade was popped to mark the platoon. The slick never arrived. The platoon leader asked about the delay. "I requested green smoke," the pilot answered. "It was popped, and I delivered—

activity was observed on the ground." The resupply had, in fact, gone to NVA who had been monitoring the radio and popped a green smoke of their own.

Company B was ambushed the next day when it unknowingly approached another bunker complex on another hilltop. It took four days to take the position. The final act was a napalm drop, which hit both sides. "Moving forward after the napalm burned itself out, we were within the bunker complex before we knew it," wrote Pfc. Ted McCormick, a grunt in the lead platoon. "Two dead NVA lay half-buried in their exposed bunker, which had taken a direct hit from a 500-pound bomb. Burned fatigues and equipment lay everywhere." The complex was impressive, complete with ammunition caches, rows of concertina where sappers practiced their skills, and "a 'highway' as wide as a city street that cut through the triple-canopy jungle," noted McCormick, "the very top of the canopy left intact to conceal it from the air. After the battle, we moved off the hill and set up in the valley below. At night, we could plainly make out red flashlights as the NVA spotted a trail, moving into position we know now to attack Firebase Ripcord."

The war in the mountains did not breed atrocities. The enemy there was made up of regulars, not the despised guerrillas who sowed booby traps and hid behind villagers. If captured, a wounded NVA could expect to be treated by a Screaming Eagle medic with the care that a good infantryman deserved. Such attitudes could not diminish the raw brutality of the war. The claymore mine is inherently brutal. So are white phosphorus and napalm, which sucks air from the lungs and adheres to human flesh "like shit to a blanket." The M16 delivers rounds with such supersonic velocity that a dime-sized hole in an NVA's forehead meant the back of his head had disappeared in an explosion of gray matter. People hardened, became numb, found humor in the grotesque. During the rainy season after Ripcord, A/2-506th was holed up above the flooded O Lau when a dead North Vietnamese "from a shallow, up-river grave was washed loose and floated by our perimeter," wrote Hawkins. "Got hung up on a branch in the middle of the torrent, and swayed there like a drunk until a couple of [M79] thump gunners decided to use the corpse for target practice. Does that sound gross and despicable? Maybe it does. It certainly wasn't the niftiest thing the company ever did. But if the tables had been turned, I'm sure Mr. Charles would have done the same for us."

That the enemy could be ruthless was confirmed to the Currahees when one of their reconnaissance teams made contact on Triple Hill on the morning of May 28, 1970. Two recon men were wounded by rocket shrapnel from a supporting Cobra. In response, a medevac from the 326th Medical Battalion, 101st Airborne Division, came to a hover over the team and lowered a jungle penetrater through the canopy. The casualties were strapped onto the little seats attached to the jungle penetrater, but as they were being hoisted back up, the North Vietnamese fired an RPG at the medevac, ignoring the red cross on the door of the Huey.

The RPG scored a direct hit, igniting the helicopter's fuel cell. "My God, they've hit the medevac," the recon team leader called out on the radio. "It's on fire, out of control, and going down."

The crew chief operating the hoist had the presence of mind to fire the system's explosive cutter, which blew the cable and dropped the jungle penetrater back to the ground like an anchor. That saved the lives of the two men strapped to it, because a moment later the Huey crashed into the side of the hill and went up in a fireball.

The entire crew of four was killed. Two other recon teams had linked up and were presently rushing to the scene. "[W]e were all numbed by the reality of what had just happened," wrote Sp4 John Mihalko. They pushed on in a fury: "Saving [the other team] was of the utmost importance, but we also wanted to exact a measure of revenge. The loss of the Medevac set a lot of angry and determined Screaming Eagles in motion. Radio traffic was hot and heavy. A line unit was being prepared for insertion into the fray. . . ."

Recon got there first. Ralph Motta was on point and Mihalko was walking slack as they came up the hill on an enemy high-speed trail. "There was a huge boulder just off the side of the trail. Just as we reached it, we both saw the NVA gunner with an RPG pointed right at us," wrote Mihalko. They dived behind the boulder an instant before the RPG slammed into it. The RPG gunner fired again. Doc Speed rushed up—another rocket hit the boulder at that moment—peeked quickly around the boulder, then lobbed several frags up toward the rocks from which the gunner was firing his RPGs. No more rockets. Company D was clattering in at the base of the hill, meanwhile, and shortly assaulted past the recon element. Following the grunts up, Mihalko cautiously checked the RPG gunner's position. The gunner had been killed by the grenades. "I took a very long look at the face of the man who had calmly and deliberately destroyed an unarmed Medevac." There was another dead enemy soldier at the top of the hill, and "a very terrified NVA prisoner. He looked almost pitiful, standing there stripped down to his underwear, pondering his fate. There was talk of blowing him away for what had happened to the Medevac, but cooler heads prevailed. A bird flew in with an interpreter. He was questioned for a while and then whisked away, much to his relief."

Based on intelligence reports of an enemy buildup in the area, Lieutenant Colonel Lucas inserted Captain Williams and Company B onto Triple Hill at the end of the battalion stand-down at Camp Evans. The first six days of the mission were unproductive. Twenty bunkers were found on the seventh day. Lieutenant Delgado and Bravo One pushed north the next morning, June 22, to a hillock from which Sergeant Tolson's squad was dispatched to check a trail. While following it, "one of the guys noticed a trail marker cut into a tree," Tolson wrote home. It was identical to a marker found near the bunker complex, and further investigation revealed a small pile of mortar rounds tucked between the roots of a big tree "with a small thatched roof over the top of them to keep them dry. They were laying on a raised platform made out of twigs woven together[,] and [what] looked like a seat [was] on top of that where the gooks could leave a trail watcher to guard the stuff."

Leaving his squad at the cache site, Tolson was hiking up the hill to get Lieutenant Delgado when "the bushes started moving to my left rear," his letter continued. "I dropped down into the bushes and made it back to the squad as fast as I could. They had seen the same thing and were all hiding behind bushes and trees. . . ."

Even as Tolson braced for a firefight, Lieutenant Delgado, on his way down the hill to refill canteens from a nearby stream—he had not alerted Tolson, totally confusing the situation—spotted a line of figures moving briskly through the trees. Two Vietnamese with steel pots and M16s, apparently Kit Carson scouts, were in the lead, followed by a shirtless, blond-headed individual with an M60.

Someone in Tolson's squad let out a whistle. Delgado answered with a booming "Currahee," thinking that Tolson couldn't identify him in the heavy vegetation. Tolson thought the answering call had come from the element rustling the bushes—apparently another squad was coming down to join them—but was perplexed when the shout of "Currahee" was answered from the bushes with "Okay."

After a pause, Sergeant Tolson shouted, "Who are you?" There was no answer. Delgado, in fact, was no longer there; the lieutenant had assumed that the "Okay" was confirmation from Tolson that they had heard and identified him. Thinking that he had just missed being killed by his own guys, Delgado had hurried back up the hill.

"We whistled again," continued Tolson's letter, but "nothing happened except the bushes kept moving down one ridge and up and over the other one until they were out of sight. We figured there were six people in all but didn't know who they were."

The incident produced conflicting versions. Whereas Delgado reported that the white machine gunner was third in line behind two Vietnamese, a brigade-level report, echoing the lieutenant's account that the enemy had U. S. gear and U. S. weapons, placed the blond man himself on point, adding that the other five "were wearing helmets and their nationality could not be determined."

Sergeant Judd had his own perspective. "I could see pith helmets bobbing along in the brush," he recalled. "There were maybe five uniformed NVA soldiers—and behind them was a light-skinned blond with his shirt off, carrying an M60. He had it on his right shoulder with his right hand on the muzzle, the butt of the weapon up in the air. He was head and shoulders taller than the five little NVA in front of him. He wasn't tied up or anything. He was at the tail end of the group, trotting right along with them."

Judd would have opened fire but for the startling apparition. "It didn't compute," he said of the white NVA. "They were already moving at a good pace, but when Delgado yelled 'Currahee,' they instantly broke into a dead run and disappeared without even looking back." The Caucasian was apparently the one who yelled "Okay," hoping to give the GIs pause as the strange group made its getaway. Tolson's squad hustled up to Delgado—that's when the pieces of the puzzle were put together—then went back down "to look at the tracks those guys left and some were bare footed and the others were sandal prints," wrote Tolson. "We called the C. O. on the radio and he said there weren't any G. I.s out there except us."

Lieutenant Delgado and part of Tolson's squad took off in hot pursuit, splashing across a nearby creek. They found stumps where the enemy had cut down trees to build bunkers, then a trail with fresh tracks. "[T]hat was enough encouragement because we were off and running down the trail," wrote Tolson. Following the trail up a hill, "[w]e found a bunker but the tracks went past it." Delgado handed Tolson his flashlight to check the bunker, then continued the pursuit alone. Delgado came pounding back down the trail in short order and, jumping behind a tree, swung his weapon back the way he had come, shouting, "The gooks are coming back."

The patrol waited for five tense minutes as the enemy moved around them, heard but not seen. When it seemed safe, Delgado gave the word to pull back. Delgado returned as quickly as he could with the entire platoon, but the enemy had vanished. It will be forever unknown if Bravo One had spotted an American defector or an East Bloc advisor to the NVA. "We made a joke out of it with some of the black guys," recalled Lieutenant Wallace. "We joked about firing up the Honkey, or Getting Whitey."

Captain Williams brought the whole company together the next day, and they went in the following morning, June 24, with a very uptight Sergeant Judd on point. "I felt like I was leading a company of country peddlers for all the noise we were making," he recalled. Fanning out in the hushed cathedral gloom under the canopy, Company B found twenty-five bunkers. The company was also on the lookout for the blond individual with the NVA. Williams had passed the word to his troops that higher command wanted the man taken prisoner if possible, prompting Pfc. Donald E. Colbert of Bravo Three to write home: "Our Capt. said if we see him [the white NVA] not to shoot to kill[,] but I've got news for him. . . ."

Running out of daylight, Williams dug in on another hill, then resumed the sweep the next morning. Finding still more bunkers, the troops also "mistakenly checked bunkers that we'd already cleared the day before," said Judd. "The NVA used leafy branches for bedding, and we found fresh green leaf beds in the bunkers. They had blatantly come back and slept in the bunkers below our NDP." Sometime during the afternoon, the enemy stole into the vacated overnight position and, looking for discarded ammo and food, dug up the foxholes that the grunts had filled in before moving out. They didn't find anything; Williams was death on policing night positions, requiring his troops to cup up empty C-ration cans so the enemy couldn't use them in making booby traps. "We decided to leave a little present for them in case they came back," said Judd, who helped set up an elaborate mechanical ambush—six claymores daisy-chained together where two trails crossed at the top of the hill. "It was a masterpiece." The troops heard the claymores thunderclap in the dark from their new NDP. Williams called in artillery. "We went over there the next day," recounted Judd, "and found hamburger and shreds of clothing embedded in the trees—but not a single body or piece of equipment. They couldn't get all the spattering up, but they had cleaned up everything else."

Three days later, another NVA patrol in U. S. gear was spotted. It was, all in all, a decidedly spooky area. "[W]e have found a total of 75 bunkers," Tolson wrote home. The complex was "so big you can get lost in it, I know because I was lost for 3 hours yesterday. We have uncovered small quantities of rice and marijuana. We have seen gooks but can't get them because they keep a pretty good distance and when you raise your rifle they disappear in the bushes. They have been around our perimeters at night but we never find out until the next morning when we send people out looking for signs of gooks and they find footprints. The people in the know seem to think that there is a Bn. of gooks heading this way from the south and there is just a small party up here trying to fix things up before the Bn. arrives. If this is true I certainly don't want to be around when they get here. . . ."

PART THREE

An Escalating Situation

Ripcord was just another exercise for us. We were the swing battalion. We bounced from brigade to brigade, getting inserted into whatever area was hot at the moment.

—Lt. Col. Otis W. Livingston, Jr.
Commanding Officer
2d Battalion, 501st Infantry
101st Airborne Division

CHAPTER 9

Cat 'n Mouse

The exploration of the bunker complex ended when the enemy began mortaring Ripcord, and Lucas in response instructed Captain Williams to assault and seize Hill 805. Mission accomplished, the troops dug in and, as described, repelled a night attack of their own before watching in shock as the sappers overran Company C on Hill 902. The mountaintop literally glowed in the black void for all the illum popping overhead, and the satchel charges exploding all over it looked like an eruption of flashbulbs to Company B.

Even as the sapper attack fizzled, the enemy hit Company B again. The troops, having gone to 100 percent alert, were just starting to stir from their positions as the sky began to lighten and the NVA, unseen among the trees on the north slope of the hill, opened fire out of the twilight gloom with AKs and RPGs.

One startled grunt grabbed his helmet with one hand and his M16 with the other as rounds cracked past. He lunged for his foxhole, then disappeared headfirst into it with a furious, "Goddamniiiiiiit."

Williams brought in mortar and artillery fire amid the crackle of M16s and M60s and, finally, Cobras, which rolled in on the now-silent north slope only to take fire from the southeast side of the hill. One Cobra made repeated passes, expending its entire load in an unsuccessful attempt to silence the single NVA firing on it with an AK-47. While a patrol swept around the hill, finding several hastily vacated bunkers where the fire had come from, tac air went in on suspected enemy positions around Hills 805 and 902.

Meanwhile, a rigger team from the division support battalion prepared to extract the CH-47 shot down the day before, but when a Chinook from A/159th Aviation attempted the hookup that morning, it was hit by .51-caliber fire and crash-landed next to the aircraft it had come to recover. It would be able to depart that evening, however, repaired with parts from the disabled Chinook.

The jets also prepped landing zones for the 2d of the 501st out of Phu Bai. Attached to Colonel Harrison that morning, Livingston moved a small CP into Lucas's TOC—"Andre was a grand fellow to work with, very active, very aggressive," Livingston recalled—and began assaulting his companies along the ridge running southeast off Hill 902. During the insertion of Company C, a gunship making suppression runs accidentally wounded three men. Company A landed on Hill 902 after the remnants of C/2-506th were lifted off, coming in through 82mm mortar fire. Two men were slightly wounded, including Lieutenant Kwiecien—"a shell landed pretty close to me and I picked up a scratch on the arm and a face full of dirt." Because Kwiecien could hear the mortar tube from his position, the company commander turned their supporting ARA over to him. "The Cobras made a couple of runs and the mortar fire stopped," Kwiecien later wrote. "I don't know if we hit them, came close enough to scare them off, or if I was entirely off in my guesstimates and they had just had enough fun for a while."

As the company began moving off the mountaintop, Kwiecien noticed on the ground a damaged photograph of "an older couple with a rather attractive Italian-looking young lady. It really made me sad to see that, because for the photo to be torn and discarded meant that its owner had been killed or wounded when the company we relieved was hit. Here was this nice looking set of people and the guy they cared about was either badly hurt or dead and they didn't even know it yet. I regret not picking it up since I'm sure it ended up as a souvenir for some dink."

* * *

The enemy continued shelling the firebase on the second day of the battle. There were several wounded who required evacuation, and there was much counterbattery fire. There was also more antiaircraft fire on the resupply Chinooks. One gunner set up his .51 in a dugout in a little clearing only a hundred meters northeast off the top of Hill 805. "I don't know if he didn't realize we could see him through the trees or what his problem was, but he didn't pay any attention to us," said Sergeant Judd. "He was totally focused on Ripcord."

Private First Class Ramon Santiago quickly put the NVA in the sights of his M60. "He took off running, but I know he was hit at least three times," said Judd. "You could see his body take the hits."

Judd's squad found a blood trail but no body. It is likely that the gunner had help getting away; though only the one NVA had been seen, three rucksacks had been left behind. The tripod-mounted .51 was evacuated by helicopter and put on display at Camp Eagle.

Company B was mortared from the slope of its own hill at dusk. A patrol was dispatched, but the enemy vanished. Another patrol found more fresh bunkers on another part of the hill. "We were constantly in contact and on edge around 805," wrote Chip Collins. "Patrols moved very slowly, literally creeping along for safety's sake, and the people walking point were scared to death."

Company B had another tough night of mortar and RPG fire, then continued its patrols in the morning; they found an ammo cache. That same morning, gunships and smoke ships led an effort by C/159th Aviation to recover the disabled Chinook on Ripcord. While the Cobras suppressed the antiaircraft sites around the firebase, CH-47s flew off with each of the disabled aircraft's rotors, at which point a third Chinook lifted out the aircraft itself. Major Koenigsbauer watched astonished as "the blade suspended underneath one of the Chinooks started to fly by itself as it got away from the firebase—that is, it started to rotate, pick up momentum, and actually rise up towards the bird. The pilot punched the blade just in time." The CH-47 carrying its disabled sister set its load down at Camp

Evans, noted the 159th journal, then "ran out of fuel on short final to POL and crashed[,] so we recovered one and lost one. Both aircraft [were] returned to Phu Bai by CH54 [Sky Crane]."

The third day of the battle was the final day of patrol for a recon team that Lucas had previously dispatched in response to the enemy buildup north of Ripcord. Led by Sgt. Robert O. Granberry, Jr., the team had been inserted two klicks east of the bunker complex discovered by Company B; it had found on its second day out a black commo wire snaking down the draw through which the recon troops were moving. It was Hai, the team's Kit Carson scout, who actually spotted the wire in the thick underbrush. Holding it up with a look of sheer terror on his face, Hai moved his fingers like legs to indicate that the enemy would be patrolling the line. He sputtered that they should get out of there: "Beaucoup NVA. *Di di mau, di di mau.* Beaucoup NVA, beaucoup NVA."

Granberry reported the find, expecting to be replaced by a line company; he was instead informed that a slick was being dispatched with a tape recorder and alligator clips to tap into the line. The team backtracked to its insertion LZ, which was against all the rules. After the equipment was delivered, the recon troops—wondering if higher command was setting them up for annihilation but hoping that they had found something important—tapped the line and took turns listening in with headphones. There were no voices, just static, and the team finally moved off to find a position on a hillside above the draw from which it could observe the wire. Their presence having been compromised by the helicopter, Granberry recalled that "we were convinced we were all going to have our throats slit before morning. I really had to calm everybody down. We posted watch like we did on any other patrol, but a lot of guys took it on themselves to try to stay awake all night."

Another slick arrived in the morning to take out the first set of tapes and deliver more. All told, the recon troops maintained the wiretap for most of four days, from June 29 to July 2, waiting to be discovered and wiped out. They ventured from their cover only to change tapes. The mission was not the recon platoon's way of doing things. "Line companies were too big and loud, but our little recon teams could cruise and bruise right in the enemy's backyard," noted Mihalko. "We initiated most contacts because the NVA didn't even know we were there. We walked right into one of their little camps once and fired 'em up as they sat there cooking rice. They didn't have guards out because they felt safe." To men accustomed to operating with such stealth and cunning, "sitting in one place with helicopters coming and going was fuckin' nuts," concluded Mihalko. "That kind of stuff really gave us a case of the ass about Colonel Lucas."

Sergeant Granberry was finally given an extraction point to the north late on July 2, and his team moved to it along a steep and narrow ridge, passing an old, overgrown LZ. Granberry called battalion, suggesting his team leave from there, but battalion was adamant that he move to the designated LZ. The team pushed on, hitting a high-speed trail. "It had fresh footprints on it," noted John Schnarr. Following the trail downhill as dusk approached, Granberry stopped a hundred meters short of the designated LZ, then took Mihalko on a two-man recon. The LZ was on a small plateau at the foot of the ridge. "As we approached it, there was a bunker staring at us," wrote Mihalko. No one was home, but the position was so new that when Mihalko pulled some leafy camouflage off the roof "sap was still coming out of the stems. . . ."

Extraction was set for the next morning. Mihalko walked point after sunup on July 3 but, upon reaching the south side of the LZ and just starting past the bunker there, he saw a bareheaded NVA in green fatigues, an AK-47 slung over one shoulder, standing at the edge of the trees on the north side. The enemy soldier had his head cocked, listening to a passing Huey. When he began walking unawares across the clearing, Granberry signaled the team sniper to drop him with his scope-mounted M14.

Three quick shots and the NVA was down, falling out of sight. Unbelievably, he began shrieking in pain. "My God, he's not dead," someone blurted to the sniper. "Where'd you shoot him?"

"I shot him in the stomach."

"What? Why didn't you shoot him in the head?"

"I wasn't sure if my rifle was zeroed."

"Well, shit," came the disgusted reply.

With the gut-shot enemy soldier continuing to scream and moan—stomach wounds are agonizing—Granberry finally snapped at the sniper, "Hey, you shot him—you go finish him off."

The sniper darted into the clearing and silenced the man with a bullet through the brain. Not sure if they were dealing with a lone trail watcher or something bigger, Granberry requested permission to pull back to the overgrown LZ. The request was denied; the extraction ships were already en route to the team's present location. With no choice but to secure the clearing, Mihalko had his slack man, Doug Jacoway, do a little recon by fire with his M203—an M16 with a tubelike 40mm grenade launcher fitted under the barrel. Encouraged by the lack of response, the two started across the LZ.

Jacoway continued to fire grenades on the way across. Nothing moved. Mihalko felt himself relaxing, but as he neared the cover of the trees, an RPD machine gun opened fire from a hidden bunker. Dropping flat, Mihalko noticed that the center magazine in the ammo bandoliers crisscrossing his chest was blown open. He lifted the bandolier and saw to his mounting horror that there was a corresponding hole in the magazine underneath. He gingerly lifted the second bandolier, but there was no wound, no blood, only three bumps in the back of the second magazine where the three rounds that should have killed him had finally stopped.

The firefight turned into a stalemate. The machine gunner poured it on, as did several other enemy soldiers with AKs, but the clearing was slightly crowned; for all the vegetation being shredded right above Granberry's head, his group was actually safe from the RPD. The enemy, too, was unreachable. "I don't think we even fired back," recalled Schnarr. "I know I didn't because you couldn't see low enough on the other side of the clearing."

The enemy finally ceased firing. Granberry requested a Pink Team. Meanwhile, Jacoway and Mihalko, who amazed everyone when they called out that they were okay, hunkered down in a slight depression behind a felled tree, knowing that if they tried to run back they would be cut to ribbons. Mihalko heaved a couple of frags, cursed himself for letting the enemy know that he was still alive, then lay bathed in sweat under the noon-day sun, tormented by flies, for thirty to forty minutes before the arrival of the Pink Team.

Able to think of no other options, Sergeant Granberry, probably the best team leader in the recon platoon, proposed to the Cobra pilot that he fly straight at the RPD but not fire: "If you come in like you're making a gun run, that machine gunner will probably get his head down—and I can get my two guys off the LZ."

It sounded suicidal, but the pilot agreed. He made an orbit to get his bearings, climbed to three thousand feet, then turned the aircraft on its side and started his dive, screaming in at top speed, to frightening effect. Mihalko looked over his shoulder at the Cobra coming straight at him and bellowed at the top of his lungs to Granberry, "Junior, don't let him shoot—I'm alive."

Granberry shouted that the gunship was a decoy, and Mihalko and Jacoway low-crawled back like frantic lizards. It was time to make a gun run for real, and Granberry popped red smoke to mark his position. "I can't shoot," the pilot said. "You're too close to the target area. Can you move away from the LZ?"

"Negative, we're pinned down," Granberry explained. "We're dead meat one way or the other. Just go ahead and fire."

"Well, I need your initials," the pilot said.

"Romeo Oscar Golf," Granberry answered, thus officially relieving the pilot of responsibility in case of mishap.

The recon troops, at the prone, clasped their hands behind their heads to protect their skulls as the Cobra rolled in, unleashing rockets, then further chewing up the scenery with its minigun and automatic cannon. The racket was so fearsome that it was impossible to tell whether the enemy was returning fire. As the gunship pulled up, the lead extraction slick immediately started its approach into the smoky LZ. Everyone was uptight, having seen the NVA survive Cobra strikes before. Granberry asked, "Who wants to go first?"

Mihalko volunteered. He reached the Huey just as it settled into a five-foot hover. Mihalko grabbed a skid to pull himself aboard, but the door gunner suddenly waved him off. Mihalko couldn't hear anything over the roar of the blades and didn't know what was going on, but he let go, then stared for an instant in disbelief as the Huey climbed away before rushing off the open LZ.

"Junior, what the hell happened?" he shouted.

"The RPD shot the slick up," answered Granberry. "Both pilots got hit and they made a command decision to haul ass."

Granberry began getting desperate as he called in additional Cobra strikes, to no effect. When the Cobra finished a run, the LOH would buzz down to check the damage, only to draw more fire each time.

Battalion finally instructed Granberry to move back up the ridge to the overgrown LZ that he had wanted to use all along. The recon troops hit the high-speed trail at a trot and were soon climbing aboard the extraction slicks. The helipad at Camp Evans was crowded with people who had monitored the team's fight on the radio, and Mihalko held up the captured AK in a victory salute as he jumped off his Huey. He was mobbed by giggling Kit Carson scouts who stuck their fingers in the bullet holes in his ammo magazines as Hai excitedly recounted the events of the mission to his friends in Vietnamese. Finishing the story, Hai grabbed Mihalko's arm and, using the Vietnamese word for "kill," exclaimed, "John, you number one GI—NVA no can *cocadau* you."

Captain Wilcox, commander of the battalion support company, was hastily brought forward to replace Hewitt after Company C was hit by the sappers. Wilcox met the troops on the helipad at Ripcord as Lieb brought them in, then led his new command down the ridgeline pointing to Hill 805. After spending the night at the end of the ridge, Wilcox continued on to 805 with instructions to relieve Company B. Chip Collins was shocked at "how hollow the guys in Charlie Company looked when they came into our perimeter—like dead men walking. If any one thing ever showed me how hard combat was on people, it was seeing Charlie Company after they got overrun. They were just torn apart and it really showed."

It was a clear, blazing hot day, though a storm front could be seen advancing over the mountains to the west. With Wilcox in position, Captain Williams gave the word for Company B to start moving down the southwest slope of 805. The first platoon in the column, Bravo One, started out only after a troubling incident involving Bob Judd, whose squad was to lead the way, and a certain Sergeant Johnson, whose turn it was to walk point but who refused to do so. Phil Tolson, for one, wasn't surprised, remembering that Johnson, a cocky type, was generally regarded as a "lazy, worthless, do-nothing piece of shit. I don't know how he kept his rank."

Everyone was already uptight, and tempers flared as the platoon sergeant told Johnson to get his ass in gear. "I told ya I ain't walkin' fuckin' point," Johnson said hotly, not caring how loud he got.

It was a bad scene. Finally, Pfc. Robert S. Utecht, a normally mellow hippie type with beads and a peace sign around his neck and a headband under his helmet, snapped, "Fuck it, I'll walk point."

With that, Utecht stormed past Johnson. Judd fell in behind his friend in the slack position. Half a klick later, at which point Utecht was coming up out of a draw, Judd noticed a freshly sawed-off tree stump. He looked up to warn Utecht, and at that instant a muzzle flash blazed from a bunker at the top of the rise about fifty meters ahead. Utecht flew backward as if jerked off his feet by a cable. Judd emptied his M16 as he dove for a log. Changing magazines, he heard his grenadier fire two rounds almost simultaneously—*thoomp-thoomp*—an impossible feat with a single-shot grenade launcher. When one round exploded near the bunker and the other down in the draw, he realized that not only had the grenadier fired, so had a North Vietnamese soldier with a captured M79.

There was no more fire. Judd looked over at Bob Utecht. He was lying in a lifeless sprawl under his rucksack. "Bob didn't see that stump because he was stomping and going too fast," recalled a grief-stricken Judd. "He was still mad about

Johnson. That was the only time we ever really let our guard down—and they nailed us."

Captain Williams told his best platoon leader, Wallace, to take charge of the situation. Lieutenant Delgado wasn't up to it, and his platoon was apparently frozen. Tolson wrote home that although a "few of us did what had to be done," at least three GIs in his squad "hung back and they [will] get court-martialled for cowardice."

All was quiet as Wallace rushed down to the point of contact; he suspected that the enemy had again hit and run. Taking no chances, however, he had a trooper cover him as he advanced on the log bunker at the top of the rise. The frag that Wallace threw glanced off the firing port and came bouncing back, forcing him to dive for cover.

Williams and his forward observer, Lieutenant Andrasson, had run up their long antennas, meanwhile, and were calling for fire support when the storm front finally closed in. As it started to rain, a tree near Captain Wilcox suddenly exploded with a crashing flash that turned the whole hilltop orange. "I felt as though I had been punched in the gut, and was doubled over at the waist," recalled Wilcox. "Paul Burkey had been physically knocked down, and was sitting beside me with his legs sprawled out in a V." The explosion was so loud that Wilcox thought an RPG had hit the tree, but "we quickly realized it was lightning . . . from brilliant sunlight, we went into a black, monsoon-like downpour within seconds."

The long antennas attracted most of the charge of the lightning strike. The electricity that coursed down Williams's antenna and through the handset he had pressed to his left ear blew out his eardrum and knocked him unconscious. "The next thing I recall was coming to under a poncho in the rain, and the medic picking the poncho up and looking at me," said Williams, whose head was throbbing. Andrasson had also been knocked out. "They were really dazed," recalled Wilcox. "It was scary because there would have been no way to get a medevac in if their hearts had stopped."

As Wallace came back up the hill with Bravo One, he received some nonsensical radio messages along the way from Williams, who, unable to shake off the effects of the lightning, finally passed the word to Wallace that he had the company that night. "The captain was bald, and his head looked like a red lightbulb," noted Sergeant Judd. "The veins were standing out. He acted like he was drunk, but, luckily, he wasn't really hurt all that badly."

People crouched behind boulders or in waterlogged foxholes, expecting more trouble. "It was raining so hard nobody had dry cigarettes," recalled Wallace, who kept his in a waterproof plastic case. "I smoked Lucky Strikes and Camels, and a lot of people were so bad up—you get shaky, you want some nicotine—that they were bumming them off me even though they wouldn't ordinarily smoke nonfiltered cigarettes."

When the storm blew over at dusk, a medevac landed for a trooper who'd caught some M79 shrapnel. Sergeant Johnson also went out on the Huey. "Bob Utecht had been well liked, and everyone knew that what had happened was Johnson's fault," said Judd. Utecht was trussed up in a poncho to be evacuated on a resupply ship the next day, the evacuation of KIAs being a logistical—as opposed to a medical—responsibility. The times being what they were, an ugly mood was made absolutely incendiary by the fact that Utecht was white and Johnson black. Judd remembered that "no one said anything directly, but it was understood that Johnson wasn't going to survive the night, and someone had the smarts to send him to the rear."

Several stratagems, all relying on firepower, massively applied, were quickly developed to better defend Ripcord. One new procedure involved using the Quad-50 at the northeast end of the base for counterbattery fire, in addition to the 81s and 105s. "Many of the enemy mortar positions were 'reverse slope,' meaning that they were on the backside of the hills surrounding the firebase," said Koenigsbauer, "requiring the Quad-50 to fire almost straight up in an indirect mode." The torrents of fire arcing over the hills must have been effective as they rained through the canopy on the other side because the NVA made the Quad-50 a primary target. "You could watch mortar rounds being walked right up to the gun position," noted Koenigsbauer. "The weapon was repeatedly damaged, and there were some casualties among the crew."

Lucas was so impressed with the Quad-50 that he eventually requested a second one be flown out to Ripcord. To add additional bark to the perimeter positions in the interim, Koenigsbauer had the battalion transportation section send forward several .50-caliber machine guns from Camp Evans. The transportation section had them to spare; each of its two-and-a-half-ton trucks in the rear was authorized a ring-mounted .50, but they were rarely if ever installed, noted Koenigsbauer, "and usually lay rusting in the backs of the trucks."

Trained as an armor officer, Major Koenigsbauer was actually more familiar with the .50 than standard infantry weapons, and he personally set up the additional machine guns on tripods and test-fired them at various strategic points around Ripcord.

By coincidence, one distant spot of jungle that Koenigsbauer blasted was occupied by NVA, who returned fire with a .51-caliber machine gun. The operations officer saw dirt kick up as one round, spent of energy—the enemy was also firing from maximum range—thudded harmlessly into the ground in front of his position. He picked up the still-warm bullet and pocketed it for a souvenir.

The enemy seemed especially active at night, lights blinking in the hills around the firebase, things rustling in the perimeter wire. The result of such nocturnal activity was "a very, very aggressive defensive-fire plan that was executed on a nightly basis," said Koenigsbauer. Though the mortar platoon was split with three tubes on O'Reilly, the six crews on Ripcord managed to fire more than five hundred rounds a night. The mortar tubes never got cool during the battle.

Helicopters were a primary enemy target, and bringing in the daily resupply demanded close coordination between the 2-506th staff and the 159th Aviation Battalion. All of it was conducted on a secure net, given the likelihood that the NVA were monitoring the radios. When the CH-47s, sent in groups of two or three, were two minutes from the firebase, the ground-mounted .50-cals and the Quad-50s, plus the mortars, recoilless rifles, and 105s, would commence firing on the known or suspected mortar and antiaircraft positions around Ripcord. To ensure that there would be no interruption or gaps in the suppressive fires, which were continued until the aircraft had departed the area, the flight paths were carefully charted to avoid overflying if at all possible the friendly ground units in the hills.

Though casualties on the firebase were initially light, Lieutenant Colonel Lucas himself was wounded on the Fourth of July 1970. Lucas and Koenigsbauer were standing thigh deep in the stairway leading down into the TOC, scanning the hills for mortar positions—the shelling that day had included tear-gas rounds—and calling in fire with the PRC25 radio that the ops officer had placed at ground level in front of them. Unheard over the high winds and the general din of outgoing fire as it came in, the mortar shell that exploded on the helipad about twenty-five feet to the right front of Lucas and Koenigsbauer startled them and splattered them with dirt. Koenigsbauer's radio was destroyed, one piece of shrapnel smashing into the body of it, another clipping off the antenna a mere six inches above the major's head. In the excitement, Lucas, on Koenigsbauer's right and thus closer to the explosion, did not realize he had been grazed until Koenigsbauer noticed the blood running down his forearm. It was a superficial injury. After having it treated and bandaged by the battalion surgeon in the next conex over, Lucas, contrary to his image as a self-promoting careerist, made no attempt whatsoever to secure a Purple Heart.[1]

Captain Raymond A. Williams, the battalion's artillery liaison officer, was also wounded on day four while conducting a crater analysis in front of the TOC. Diving back inside when a round exploded in his face, Williams realized he was still alive and merely peppered with little pieces of the shell casing because it had been CS, tear gas, not HE. The troops had only lightweight M28 gas masks that provided limited protection and quickly fogged up. "The NVA, of course, did not know how effective their tear gas was," said Koenigsbauer, glad the enemy did not launch a ground attack behind the CS. Lucas had his exec, Major Davis, send forward on an emergency basis the bulky but reliable M17 gas masks kept in storage at Camp Evans. The masks arrived before the day was done. "We carried them from then on as the enemy began hitting us with CS on an almost regular basis," noted Koenigsbauer. In return, brigade authorized the use of CS artillery rounds in the defense of Ripcord.

Captain Rich of B/2-319th FA, shrugging off additional flesh wounds received while doing some crater analysis of his own on day four, put his 105s into action late that afternoon when three 82mm rounds came in from Coc A Bo Mountain, more than four kilometers southeast of Ripcord. Rich, an expert artilleryman, quickly delivered counterbattery fire that resulted in several satisfying secondary explosions, as observed through binoculars.

Shortly thereafter, Major Koenigsbauer, standing near the pathfinder bunker at the top of the base as he continued to watch for firing positions—he would be awarded the Bronze Star for exposing himself thusly—turned toward Hill 1000 at the same instant that a recoilless rifle punched off a round from high up the slope. Koenigsbauer saw the smoke and was able to follow the round in flight, losing it only just before it impacted in the base trash dump. Koenigsbauer rushed to Rich—there was a second puff of smoke then, which they both saw—and the battery commander had two tubes lowered to return fire. The enemy got off two more rounds, then went silent as the cannoneers slammed a half-dozen shells directly into their target, either destroying the recoilless rifle or driving its crew into one of the many bunkers dotting the hills.

The reserve battalion suffered a demoralizing blow on day four when a platoon from C/2-501st, following a trail at the far end of the ridge running southeast from Hill 902, walked into an enemy-style mechanical ambush. The NVA had daisy-chained five 82mm mortar rounds together, three on one side of the trail, two on the other, and the resulting explosion wounded five and killed five, including 1st Lt. William L. Sullivan, the platoon leader.

Captain Wilcox and C/2-506th combat-assaulted that day onto Triple Hill. Though they didn't find the recoilless rifle that had been firing on Ripcord from that location, they did come across several abandoned enemy positions near boulders that had been cracked by bombs or counterbattery fire. Fresh graves had been blown open, revealing two dismembered NVA.

Already shaken, C/2-501st came under attack during the night of July 4–5, taking satchel charges, plus AK and RPG fire, from all around its NDP. With a flareship lighting up the jungle and Cobras rolling in, the enemy was kept at bay, making a final abortive rush at dawn. Five NVA bodies were found, with weapons, but the company suffered one more KIA and twenty more WIA.

Following Wilcox's departure, Captain Williams and B/2-506th ran several patrols, then set up for another night on Hill 805. "Staying in the same place four days was unheard of," said Sergeant Judd. "We felt like we were a decoy for Ripcord." The uptight troops watched, unamused, as star-cluster flares began bursting in the night sky as the REMFs at Camp Evans celebrated the Fourth of July. Meanwhile, the enemy fired a single RPG at Bravo's NDP, which "hit the big boulder at the very top of 805," recalled Judd, "and spiraled straight up into the air, spewing sparks. After traveling a certain distance, it self-destructed with a loud boom—and we cheered. It was our own Fourth of July fireworks."

The reserve battalion ran into more trouble on the fifth day of the battle. Captain Donald R. Goates, the new commander of Alpha Company, moved out that morning with two platoons, leaving Kwiecien to secure a knoll five hundred meters southwest of the top of Hill 902, which was being used as the company patrol base. Cutting southeast from the patrol base, Goates's element had moved eight hundred meters and was in the saddle between Hill 902 and Hill 975, a large mountain that was the object of that day's patrol, when it came under machine-gun fire from a bunker not far up the opposing slope. Attempts to outflank the bunker resulted in more casualties, and Kwiecien, monitoring the radio, "could tell they were in trouble. Goates was bringing in Cobras, but they weren't having any effect, and after a couple hours of this, he told me to bring my platoon down and to try to get them out of this mess."

Lieutenant Kwiecien got word as the platoon began moving that a trooper in SSgt. Joe E. Ludwick's squad had seen something. Hoping that the enemy hadn't gotten between his people and the rest of the company, Kwiecien passed the word for everyone to sit tight and keep their eyes open. Sergeant Michael R. McCoy, another squad leader, shortly spotted a bareheaded figure moving through the brush outside the platoon circle and cut the man down with his M16.

The man turned out to be Joe Ludwick, the tough, cocky squad leader having plunged into the jungle in pursuit of whatever it was his trooper had seen. It had been a brave but foolish maneuver, and though an anguished McCoy blamed himself for the mishap, no one else did. Ludwick, moaning loudly, in terrible pain—he would lose his spleen—was lifted out in a basket lowered by a hovering Huey. There was no fire during the long medevac process, forcing Kwiecien to conclude that the original sighting of an enemy soldier had "just been a case of nerves. On the other hand, a couple of NVA may have seen us and left to report our presence, but if I had to choose between the two, I'd say they were never there."

Finally getting down the mountain, the platoon paused behind a rise while Kwiecien, concerned about running into enemy and friendly fire if they weren't careful, coordinated the next move with Goates. Kwiecien was sitting next to a machine gunner named Ramseur and an ammo bearer named Hernandez, who had their M60 pointed over the top of the rise. They suddenly turned to Kwiecien: "Sir, we got two NVA comin' this way."

"You sure they're not ours?"

"Yes, sir," answered Ramseur.

"Kill them," Kwiecien said, and returned to his radio. Ramseur and Hernandez looked at each other with smiles that really weren't smiles, then wasted the two unsuspecting North Vietnamese.

Goates continued to direct a steady stream of Cobras on the bunker that was firing on his two-platoon element. Goates had a dozen wounded. Several medevacs were driven off by heavy AK and .51 fire that seemed to come from every direction. "One pilot was hovering overhead," noted Kwiecien, "when he very calmly said that he had to break station because his peter pilot [copilot] had just taken a round through the chest and he wanted to get him to the hospital. We stopped trying to get medevacs in after that."

Goates presently instructed Kwiecien to bypass his pinned-down element and take out the enemy bunker from the flank with LAWs. "Stupidly, I had only one LAW in the platoon," Kwiecien wrote. "What it came down to was one shot, one chance, or else. . . ."

After crossing the saddle, Lieutenant Kwiecien told his best squad leader, Sergeant Bartlett, to push on up the slope with his men. If the way was clear, Kwiecien would bring up the rest of the platoon and the precious LAW. While moving uphill, Bartlett ran into NVA who were coming down the jungled hillside. "I don't know if this force knew we were there, or if they were trying to outflank the company and unintentionally hit Bartlett's squad along the way," explained Kwiecien. There was a brief firefight, punctuated by the explosions of numerous satchel charges. The squad pulled back after one of the satchel charges went off in Bartlett's face, damaging his eardrums and flash-blinding him. Kwiecien watched as "a very nervous-acting kid named Sims, whom I had been afraid would break when he experienced combat, hung back, exposing himself to both the enemy fire and our return fire to help his blinded squad leader back down the slope. You cannot tell ahead of time who will be brave and who will not. I put Sims in for a Silver Star."

Two of the gunships strafing the bunker in front of Goates swung over to assist Kwiecien. When Kwiecien told the pilots to put their ordnance into the slope just above where he had popped smoke, they asked Goates for his initials. "It was going to be very close," noted Kwiecien. Bartlett lay with his head almost in Kwiecien's lap, helping him coordinate the Cobra fire even as the platoon medic got a bandage around his eyes. "The gunships rolled in with both HE rockets and flechette rockets," recalled Kwiecien. "I later learned from some pilots how inaccurate flechettes were. The situation was even dicier than I had thought at the time."

Following the gun runs, Kwiecien started forward with two squads up and one back; he encountered only a single NVA, who drew the fire of almost every keyed-up grunt in the forward element when he peeked out from behind a tree. As Kwiecien passed the body, he remembered the time when he was a kid and his father, an infantry veteran of World War II, "got very drunk and talked about going into a town which had just been shelled. He said that German bodies were scattered all over. The concussion from the shells had popped their heads open and lying next to each exploded head was a brain." The dead North Vietnamese was in a similar condition: "It looked like someone had neatly removed the top of his head with a can opener and exposed his brain. The top of his head was lying next to him. The poor guy didn't even have a weapon."

Having moved far enough up the slope that Kwiecien thought a shot on the bunker possible, he formed the platoon into a hasty defensive perimeter and sent two men forward with the LAW. He followed. Keeping low, the two grunts peered over the crest of a small rise and whispered back that they thought they had the bunker in sight down below. Kwiecien asked if they were sure, concerned that if they wasted the LAW the platoon would have to attack down the slope to take the pressure off Goates. They said they were pretty sure. "Okay, go ahead and shoot, but make it count," Kwiecien replied. The two troopers must have scoped out the correct bunker, because after their LAW flashed down the hill, there was no more machine-gun fire from the bottom of the saddle.

Alpha Company pulled back up the side of Hill 902. It was dusk by then, too dark and too risky to attempt to medevac the numerous wounded. As the company got reorganized, Goates asked Kwiecien for his position. "Seventy-five meters to your November," he answered, but when he released the transmit bar on his handset, he could hear someone saying, "break, break, break."

Kwiecien repeated his message, but again the transmission was covered with the chant of "break, break, break."

It was Goates. "If you let 'em know where we are, they'll attack us again," he shouted. Kwiecien was dumbfounded. If you didn't want to know where the fuck I was, he thought, why'd you ask?

Goates was on his second tour. Beefy and bespectacled, with a crew cut, he didn't look like a model paratrooper, but he seemed to know his stuff. Kwiecien now wondered if Goates had been unnerved by what was the company's first big action since he had taken command a month earlier. Actually, Goates would explain, he had attempted to cover Kwiecien's transmission, "because I was taught that you gave a direction, never a distance, in the clear in an NDP situation, especially when you were pulling in after a firefight."

The previous company commander, steady, cool-headed Captain Mitchell, had been beloved by Alpha Company. Like many officers who replace a respected predecessor, Goates was being viewed with an especially critical eye by his command. Kwiecien never thought he measured up. One of the company radiomen also had his doubts about Goates. During a subsequent stand-down, the radioman and Kwiecien fell into a conversation about Goates with Captain Mitchell; according to Kwiecien, the radioman said that " 'Goates almost got us all killed out by Hill 902 [on July 5]. If it hadn't been for Lieutenant Kwiecien and his platoon, we all would have died out there.' Jim Mitchell just turned and looked at me. I think it was the proudest moment of my time in the Army."

Alpha Company pushed uphill to its patrol base in the morning and a medevac lowered a jungle penetrater through the canopy. Sergeant Bartlett was being placed aboard when the Huey suddenly took fire and banked away. There was no choice but to leave the blinded squad leader behind. After arty was called in, another medevac settled into a hover overhead. It too was driven away, as was a LOH that tried to dart in. All three helicopters took hits. "We could distinctly hear three AK-47s," wrote Goates, "and they seemed to be no more than two to three hundred meters away. I wondered if Charlie was moving parallel with us, and we could not see him or he us because of the density of the jungle. From the sounds of the gunfire[,] Charlie was on the same level as we were on the slope of Hill 902."

There was a small clearing below the patrol base. To give the medevacs a chance to avoid some of the fire by landing instead of hovering with a jungle penetrater, 1st Lt. Richard W. Driver secured the clearing with his platoon. Goates requested chain saws to remove a huge tree that would have blocked any attempted landing. Kicked out from a Huey, the saws did no good, the chains quickly clogging up with wood shavings. Goates placed charges around the tree—it was now late in the afternoon—but the enemy attacked before he could detonate them. Goates told Kwiecien to move down on the flank of Driver's platoon to cover the withdrawal to the patrol base. Goates recalled being concerned that enemy sappers might attack as night fell and shouting to his men to have grenades ready because it would be virtually impossible to see the enemy well enough in the dark to hit them with M16s.

According to Kwiecien, what Goates actually shouted as his platoon moved to support Driver's was, "These are sappers—M16s won't kill them—you have to use grenades to blow them apart."

It was a dubious call to battle. "Here's Goates telling his men that we're fighting Superman and our weapons are worthless," recalled Kwiecien. "I was kind of pissed, so I just stood up in full view of anyone who wanted to take a shot at me and started firing my supposedly worthless M16 to cover Driver's movement."

Alpha Company re-formed at the patrol base, and under sporadic fire from all sides from an unseen enemy who got close enough to lob satchel charges into the perimeter—fifteen men were hit—blasted back into the darkening jungle. It was Goates's impression that the NVA were "testing the perimeter in preparation for an attempt to overrun us during the night." Goates requested tac air. The Phantoms came in at dusk. "The enemy fire dropped off dramatically after the air strike," wrote Captain Goates. "I believe the air strike is what kept Charlie from coming in that night. . . ."

The action petered out completely two hours later, after dark. A flareship was overhead, and gunships were making rocket runs. The next morning, a lone enemy soldier was brought under fire within fifty meters of the perimeter. Goates appeared on the scene and shouted at the NVA, who was slumped behind a tree, to *"chieu hoi."* Getting no response, Goates, armed with a pistol, worked his way to a vantage point from which he could see that the man was not holding a weapon, whereupon he moved in on the NVA. It turned out that the enemy soldier, slung with satchel charges, his AK-47 dropped nearby, was dead. "Goates was as happy as a little kid," recalled Kwiecien, who thought it highly irresponsible that the company commander had personally gone after that NVA. "If there had been a sizable enemy force out there, instead of just one private, or whatever he was, the entire company CP could have been wiped out as they stood at the edge of the perimeter."

If Goates wasn't on the verge of coming unglued, thought Kwiecien, he was rushing into battle without thinking, so eager was he "to look good and get the decorations that would enhance his career. The men thought he was insane. I was running scared under Goates," Kwiecien admitted, "and I know it negatively affected my performance as a platoon leader. I couldn't see dying because the guy in charge didn't know what he was doing. . . ."

Recalling the incident with the enemy soldier, Goates offered a perspective that Kwiecien lacked when he noted that "the platoon CP on that side of the perimeter told me they thought they had an NVA who was wounded. I told them to make sure. No one was willing to check him out, so I did. If I wasn't willing to take that kind of risk, how could I expect the troops to? It might have been a stupid move all things considered, but the next time I said, 'Check it out,' somebody might think back to the time the Old Man checked out that NVA on Hill 902. . . ."

By early afternoon, Goates had blown down the tree that was blocking the clearing and was bringing in medevacs. Most of the wounded were finally lifted out, but eleven more men were hit in the process, Goates among them, as the NVA plastered the LZ with 82mm mortar fire at the approach of each Huey. The medevacs kept coming. Livingston ordered Goates aboard one so he could see the extent of his injuries—a single fragment buried in his shoulder muscle. After being treated on Ripcord, Goates went back out on a resupply slick. "I insisted on returning to my unit," he wrote. "I knew that if I could keep down any infection with penicillin tablets, I could stay with my company and get the command time I desperately wanted and felt I needed for my career."[2]

Livingston wanted to combat-assault another company in to

reinforce Goates, but brigade denied the request. Instead, and the word came straight from General Hennessey, Goates was to make a rapid march to the north the next morning to clear the area for an impending B-52 Arc Light. Goates tried to get out the last of his wounded at dawn on July 8, but the medevac took hits and pulled off. An attempt to back-haul the rucksacks and weapons piled up on the landing zone from those casualties that had already been evacuated, as well as a 90mm recoilless rifle previously brought out to the company by helicopter to help it defend its position, was also unsuccessful. Incoming mortars set fire to one of the packs, and as the flames spread to others, ammo and grenades began cooking off. Goates ordered several GIs to recover the weapons, but they balked in the face of the exploding ammunition. Goates tried to get the recoilless rifle himself, "but just as I reached around a tree for it, there was a major explosion and I quickly backtracked. I couldn't reach the recoilless rifle, and lacking an incendiary grenade, I couldn't destroy it. We were forced to abandon it intact."

Alpha Company moved the half klick to the top of Hill 902, then swung onto a high-speed trail that dipped into a saddle before it ascended the ridge knifing down from the top of Coc Muen Mountain. It is a two-kilometer trek as the crow flies between the two peaks. The route took the column—which included walking wounded, who had to keep up as best they could—past a bunker complex on the side of the ridge facing Ripcord. "The enemy had a beautiful shot of the base from that spot," wrote Kwiecien, "and the site was littered with spent casings from a Chicom recoilless rifle."

The column proceeded without flank security, risking ambush in order to move more quickly. The tension was terrific. At one point, the sergeant ahead of Kwiecien in the file turned to him and said plaintively, "We're not going to get out of this, are we, sir?"

Looking the sergeant in the eyes, Kwiecien, who was convinced they'd had it, lied: "Sure we will; don't worry about it."

The top of Coc Muen would have put Goates just at the edge of the safety zone required around B-52 strikes, but because the company was still pushing uphill as the appointed hour neared, the Arc Light had to be diverted to less lucrative targets farther south. Goates halted on a small rise as dusk fell and sent 1st Lt. Rex Gerlinger's platoon to the next rise up the ridge to secure it for an NDP. Before Goates could move up with Driver and Kwiecien, the NVA slipped between the main body and Gerlinger. Cut off from each other, each element set up where it was. Goates, informed by brigade to expect an attack, told his platoon leaders to keep their people on alert all night. "If we snooze, it will probably be our last snooze," he intoned. Lieutenant Kwiecien was angry and wrung out, unfairly blaming Goates for the decision to withdraw under fire from the patrol base below Hill 902. "We were out there to fight, not run," as Kwiecien would put it. "Running and hiding is not good for a unit[;] the men lose confidence in themselves and their ability to fight. A couple of people came to me and told me there were discussions going on among the men about refusing to go back out in the field if we ever got out of there."

Kwiecien was monitoring the radio around one that morning when he heard Gerlinger's platoon sergeant trying to raise the company CP. According to Kwiecien, no one at the command post answered the radio. Convinced that whoever was on radio watch had fallen asleep—Goates would deny this—he finally got on the horn himself with the platoon sergeant. Speaking in a whisper, the sergeant explained that there had been a possible penetration of his perimeter. He wanted some illum so he could sort out the situation. Kwiecien went looking for Goates with murder in his heart, but in the pitch-black night he stumbled not across the captain but the company FO. The artillery lieutenant, busy calling in artillery on the trail they had followed to their present position, brought in the requested illumination. It developed that there had been no penetration, only a GI having a nightmare inside the NDP.

The pressure eased the next day. Alpha Company cut a landing zone on the slope of Coc Muen, got all the wounded out at last, then continued its forced march, making it two klicks northeast to a bit of high ground adjacent to the knoll between Ripcord and Hill 1000. The B-52s came in behind them, dropping strings of five-hundred-pound bombs. "You could feel the ground shudder as those big babies slammed in," noted Goates. Meanwhile, tac air went in on the patrol base—one suspects that the enemy had already recovered the recoilless rifle abandoned there—and the bunker complex where the expended shell casings had been found. Alpha Company spent two nights in Ripcord's shadow, getting resupplied. "Morale went up, but was still on the low side," wrote Kwiecien, who was relieved when "someone came over to me and said that the men had dropped their plan to refuse to go back out in the field. They were concerned that if they followed through on it, their platoon leaders would get in trouble, and they didn't want that."

To clear the way for the Arc Light, Livingston pulled Companies B and C up to positions near Hill 805. When the bombs stopped falling, the battalion reconnaissance platoon, led by 1st Lt. Victor E. Arndt, combat-assaulted atop Coc Muen late on the afternoon of July 9 with a platoon from Bravo Company. The insertion, made amid high winds, came under fire from the surrounding high ground. As the two platoons moved down the ridgeline running northeast from the top of the mountain, an attached sniper team zapped a North Vietnamese spotted above them on the LZ.

Eager to verify the kill, the snipers got permission from a reluctant Lieutenant Arndt to run a patrol back up to the landing zone with some of his recon troopers. The rest of the two-platoon force continued downhill, stopping at dusk to set up a night defensive position. It was dark by the time the patrol returned; no enemy body had been found. Tragically, the patrol walked into one of the mechanical ambushes that had been rigged around the NDP. The point man, one of Arndt's people, was killed instantly, his legs blown off. Two other men were seriously wounded in a mishap that could have been avoided with better communication between the separated elements. The medevac that landed took aboard the wounded and flipped out a body bag for the KIA. When the patrol continued the next day, recon had to carry its dead comrade along the way, two men in front, two men in back, with the sticks that had been slipped through the loop handles of the body bag over their shoulders. The body was finally taken out on a resupply slick.

PART FOUR

Hill 1000

I have always felt that I came through my experience in Vietnam in good shape, but Hill 1000 did create years of intermittent nightmares for me.

—1st Lt. John A. Flaherty,
Company D, 2d Battalion, 506th Infantry
101st Airborne Division

CHAPTER 10

First Blood

The new mission was simple. As Lucas explained to Sergeant Granberry and acting assistant team leader John Schnarr, their recon element was to move off the firebase, past the next hill to the west—the battalion commander traced the route on the acetate-covered map in his operations center—then up onto enemy-occupied Hill 1000. Neither artillery nor air strikes had silenced the mortars dug in near the top. To employ the supporting arms to better effect, Lucas needed the recon team to pinpoint the exact location of the mortars.

Granberry and Schnarr exchanged dubious glances after being dismissed. What seemed logical to the colonel sounded reckless to the recon troops, and they basically decided among themselves that they weren't going to rush into anything. They were going to take it slow up that mountain, and if it proved impossible to reach the mortars without being detected, so be it.

Taking a patrol trail down through the wire, Granberry had progressed six hundred meters by the time dusk fell, and his team set up for the night in the saddle below Hill 1000. When the shelling began again in the morning at the approach of a CH-47 bringing in a sling load of artillery ammunition—it was now the sixth day of the battle—the recon troops could hear a mortar tube some four hundred meters above them on the easternmost of the two small knolls at the top of east-west Hill 1000. The troops on the firebase could not hear the shells over the high mountain winds, so at the thump of each outgoing round, Granberry would alert the TOC duty officer, "You're going to be taking incoming."

Granberry also provided an approximate distance and direction for counterbattery fire. As far as the recon troops were concerned, they had done what they'd been sent to do. The duty officer instructed Granberry, however, to move up the hill to pinpoint and, if possible, actually destroy the mortar position. "Tell the sonofabitch to kiss our ass," the usually levelheaded Schnarr said to Granberry. "We're not going up that hill. They're fuckin' nuts."

"We gotta go," said Granberry, "but we'll play it by ear."

Doug Jacoway took the lead, because perennial point man and assistant team leader Mihalko was attending a leadership course at Camp Evans in preparation for taking over a team of his own. Granberry's radioman and sniper also had business in the rear and had been replaced by men from other teams. Their Kit Carson was absent altogether, still shook from the wiretap mission.

The last seventy-five meters or so to the top of the hill had been blasted by arty and tac air, and the naked trees and churned-up earth offered little cover. The recon troops slipped into a large bomb crater at the forward edge of the remaining vegetation. As they were discussing their next move, the mortar crew atop the knoll dropped another round down the tube. Granberry was again on the radio to the operations center: "More incoming on the way."

The team watched the shell impact over on Ripcord. "They're right above us here. We can hear 'em talking," Granberry reported. "The grid coordinates are three-three-four-one-nine-four."

"Roger, understand," answered the duty officer.

"I can adjust artillery or a mortar fire mission."

"Negative on that. We want you to assault the position."

Granberry restated his call sign to remind the duty officer that he had only a small recon team, adding, "but I can adjust fire. Over."

"Negative. Take your element and assault the position."

"That's not a good idea," Granberry objected, thinking of the enemy infantrymen who would be securing the mortar position.

The duty officer, speaking bluntly himself, replied without equivocation: "Your mission is to assault that enemy position."

It was Schnarr's impression that the duty officer was relaying instructions from Lucas, who had flown over the recon team at one point in his C&C. After all the high-caliber munitions that had been expended without apparent effect on the hill, one can imagine Lucas's enthusiasm that a recon team had managed to maneuver within striking distance of an identified target. The team's attack would have the element of surprise on its side. In addition, the duty officer assured Granberry that he was not as alone as he imagined: "We're moving a platoon from Delta Company into position directly behind you to reinforce your attack if necessary."

Captain Rollison and Company D had begun moving off the firebase early that afternoon, replaced by Company B, which had marched to Ripcord from Hill 805. The assault order was given late in the day, at which time Rollison's grunts, coming over the little hill west of the firebase, were descending into the saddle leading up to Hill 1000. Sergeant Granberry nevertheless thought the attack order so unwise that he was willing to risk a court-martial over it. "The Army isn't a democracy, but this team is," he said after getting off the horn with the TOC. "If you guys want to turn around and walk off this mountain, then that's what we'll do, and we'll just take our lumps when we get back to Ripcord."

"Aw, fuck it," Jacoway, a real wild man, finally said as they crouched in the crater. "Let's give it a shot, let's see what happens."

That broke the spell. "We shouldn't risk the whole team," said John Schnarr. "I'll take somebody, and we'll try and get closer and see what the situation is, if it's something we can do or not."

Schnarr moved out with "Dixie" Gaskins, a quiet kid from the Deep South who had a rebel nickname despite the fact that he was black. There was no cover straight up from the crater, so with Schnarr in the lead, the pair worked their way into some vegetation on the right that arched to the left on its way to the top of that eastern knoll. Starting on his hands and knees, Schnarr ended up low-crawling as the brush gave way to burned, stubbly patches of undergrowth no more than two feet high. Gaskins prudently dropped back as Schnarr bellied through the stuff a few feet at a time, stopping to watch and listen before moving another few feet.

Schnarr followed the undergrowth to a point directly above the crater, then started straight up toward the top. He stopped again to see what he could see, thinking maybe we can pull this off, maybe the mortar wasn't protected by any infantry. Suddenly he heard people speaking in Vietnamese. Peering through the brush, he saw the face of an enemy soldier. The man was wearing a pith helmet. I can take him, Schnarr thought, shouldering his M16. Before squeezing the trigger, however, he followed the eyes of the man in his sights and saw that he was conversing with a second NVA. Another half-dozen enemy soldiers seemed to materialize as Schnarr focused on the scene; their pith helmets were visible as they moved about in some kind of entrenchments dug amid the deadfall just below the bald top of the knoll.

Schnarr had the impression that there were even more enemy soldiers that he could not see. He was hugging dirt, totally exposed amid the low brush; had one of the NVA glanced in his direction, it would have been all over. He motioned to Dixie to start moving back. Gaskins scooted backward through the brush, then stopped to wait for Schnarr, who, joining him shortly, whispered, "There's a bunch of 'em up there. We gotta get outta here right now."

Instead of retracing their route through the brush, Schnarr and Gaskins rushed straight across the open area in their haste to get back to the crater where the rest of the team was waiting. It wasn't a smart move. The top of Schnarr's and Gaskins's heads were exposed for only a moment before they dropped below the enemy's line of vision, but that was enough. Schnarr and Gaskins had no sooner reached the crater and were crouched at the edge of it, ready to continue downhill—Schnarr was hurriedly telling Granberry what he'd seen—when the enemy simultaneously fired three RPGs down at them. One landed just below the crater, the other two just above. All seven recon troopers were wounded in the fearsome blast. Schnarr and Gaskins were blown into the crater. Schnarr took a piece of shrapnel in his chest, more in his upper back. Feeling something burning as he came to his senses, he reached for it and pulled the severed end of his dog-tag chain out of the side of his neck. Gaskins had taken the brunt of the explosions and was in worse shape, with big chunks of muscle blown out of his back.

Private First Class James D. Neff, the team radioman, had been sitting in the crater with his back to the top of the hill. Shocked dumb by the explosions—unaware, in fact, that he'd been hit in the face and leg—he tore out of his rucksack and started running down the hill so fast that he forgot the handset was still hooked to the shoulder strap of his web gear. The cord stretched tight behind him before jerking itself loose from the handset. In a blind panic, Neff got hold of himself when he heard someone calling for help and saw the team medic, a cocky new man, stumbling after him, blood squirting from a shrapnel wound in his jugular vein.

Neff pulled the medic back in the crater even as Schnarr shouted at him, "Get on the radio and get Delta Company up here."

Neff rolled his rucksack over. The radio inside had a big shrapnel hole in it. At that, Granberry scrambled out of the crater and started down the hill. Schnarr shouted, "Junior, where the hell you goin'?"

"I'm gonna get Delta Company."

"They'll come up, they'll come up."

Granberry bolted down the hill anyway. Everyone just freaks out sometimes, thought Schnarr, who held nothing against Granberry.

"The idea that I might lose Dixie because I had obeyed an insane order was too much for me to handle," Granberry later wrote of the incident. "When I went for Delta Company, it was because I needed to do something, anything to keep Dixie alive. . . ."

The medic started out of the crater, too, and Schnarr screamed at him, "No, we need you here." The medic said he was hurt. "Put a compress on it," Schnarr snapped. "You need to work on Dixie."

To stop the bleeding, Neff had to secure a field dressing so tightly around the medic's neck as to almost choke him. The medic had already lost so much blood that he repeatedly passed out as he bandaged the gaping wounds on Gaskins's back and started an IV.

Granberry, meanwhile, reached Company D's lead platoon. The platoon medic rushed up to him and told him to sit down.

"What?" Granberry said, dazed and confused. "Why?"

"Take your shirt off and sit down," the medic repeated.

Granberry was shocked upon peeling off his shirt to see that it was soaked with blood across the shoulders and down both sleeves. Though he hadn't felt a thing, Granberry's back and the backs of his arms were thoroughly peppered with little fragments.

The grunts were organizing a patrol to pull the recon team back. Granberry wanted to lead it because he knew exactly where his guys were, but someone replied, "You ain't goin' nowhere but to the aid station. We've got a dust-off on the way."

Granberry was evacuated on the spot. Back up the hill, Schnarr and Jacoway, who had taken shrapnel in one hand, hunkered down at the forward edge of the crater, ready to pop anyone who started down toward them from the top of the knoll. Concerned that the enemy might be trying to outflank them, Schnarr had Neff use their thump gun to lob high-explosive shells not only along the crest of the hill but also into the brush off to the right. No enemy appeared, however. There was no additional enemy fire, so Jacoway and Neff argued with Schnarr, who wanted to stay put until the grunts got there, that they had to get back down the hill before the enemy thought to cut them off.

Schnarr asked the medic if Gaskins could be moved. "Yeah, we gotta get him out of here," the medic said. "I can't do anything else for him. But I'm not sure how we're going to move him."

"I'll carry him," said Schnarr. Hefting Gaskins on his back, he led the way down the hill, calling out, "Currahee, Currahee."

Moving toward the answering shouts from the grunts, Schnarr, walking slowly under his load, was almost at the bottom of the hill when he ran into the point man of the patrol starting up the hill.

Neff glanced back at Jacoway, who was bringing up the rear, as they were about to slip into the cover of the trees below the crater and saw that his buddy had stopped to fire his M203 thump gun back up the hill. "What the hell are you doing?" Neff exclaimed. Jacoway was furious. "They ain't gonna get away with this," he spat. Neff, not wanting to bring anything else down on their heads, pulled him along. "C'mon, let's just get the hell outta here."

After forming a hasty defensive position in the saddle, Captain Rollison instructed SSgt. Gary A. "Ranger" Radford, a highly respected platoon sergeant who was airborne and ranger qualified—rare for a young shake 'n bake—to run a patrol up the hill to retrieve the radio, rucksacks, and weapons left behind in the crater by the recon team. Of special concern was the team's scope-mounted sniper rifle. The scope was a classified item, and Radford was to make sure he either recovered or destroyed it.

It was almost dark. The last thing Rollison told Radford before he moved out was, "Don't get in any firefights. Just get the gear and get back. We'll deal with whatever's up there tomorrow."

Easier said than done. As soon as the patrol reached the crater, it became engaged, and Rollison barked to no one in particular, "That goddamn Ranger never listens to a fuckin' thing I tell him."

It wasn't much of a firefight actually. Accustomed to fighting an enemy that hit and ran, neither Radford nor another platoon sergeant who'd tagged along, SSgt. George K. Strasburg—he was the one who actually low-crawled out to the crater after the patrol got into position—expected trouble. Strasburg was utterly shocked when a rocket-propelled grenade exploded against a nearby tree as he reached for one of the rucksacks. Thinking himself seriously injured—the concussive force of the blast was that strong—he rushed back behind cover. The enemy atop the hill opened fire in the next instant with AK-47s. "Let's get the fuck outta here," Radford shouted when he heard a round hit the bottom of the mortar tube. Radford bolted downhill in a panic, followed by the rest of the patrol, only one or two members of which paused long enough to return fire. The enemy hurried them along with a second RPG. The mortar crew also put three quick rounds in the air, trying to catch the patrol as it rushed down the slope.

Rollison questioned Radford when he got back as to why he had made contact. "I didn't," Radford replied. "They hit us. The good thing was they didn't have time to set up a real ambush. I don't think they expected anyone to go back up there so quickly."

Rollison pulled his people back up onto the middle hill and coordinated some 81 and Quad-50 counterbattery fire from Ripcord. It was dark by the time he was ready to bring in another medevac. The pilot had to break away when the flare used to mark the landing zone blinded him, but he was able to land on his next attempt and take aboard the four most seriously wounded recon troopers, leaving Schnarr and Jacoway.

When Granberry's medevac landed, the team leader vented at the first sergeant who was anxiously waiting on the helipad at Evans. "There's an officer on Ripcord that's gonna die," Granberry raged, thinking not of the colonel but of the duty officer who'd actually given the assault order. "If I ever find out who he is, I'm blowin' his fucking brains out."

CHAPTER 11

Fighting the Good Fight

Per the colonel's instructions, Captain Rollison got organized during the night for an early-morning assault on the easternmost of the two knolls atop Hill 1000. Following extensive prep fires, Rollison's two full-strength platoons were to converge on the knoll, Delta Two from the southeast, Delta Three the northeast. The company command group would follow the assault platoons, trailed, in turn, by the reserve platoon—the understrength Delta One.

Before moving off the firebase, every man in the company had been resupplied with a full load of ammunition and at least eight fragmentation grenades. "We knew it was going to be tough," said 1st Lt. James R. McCall of Delta Two, "but they were going to give us as much artillery as we could handle. We were going to follow the arty up and shift it across the top of the hill as we neared the crest, and we were going to move in quickly while we had the enemy stunned and dazed, eliminate any resistance, and take the hill."

That the company prepared for the assault with confidence was due to Captain Rollison. "He knew his shit," as Radford put it. "I served under five COs during a year and a half with Delta Company, and you couldn't get any better than Captain Rollison."

Rollison was the most combat-savvy company commander

in the battalion during the battle for Ripcord. His lieutenants loved him. His grunts trusted him to get them home alive while kicking a little ass along the way. "Rollie talked the talk and walked the walk," as Chuck Hawkins put it. Rollison was tall and lean and spoke with a deep southern accent. He was forceful, almost intimidating, gregarious, too, and colorful in his use of language; the NVA were "little devils," and to call an air strike on them was to "bring some scunion on their ass." Rollison packed a shotgun and operated with an aggressive flair that was legendary among the Currahees. "Rollie once set a trap with himself as bait," recounted Hawkins. "He set out maybe a dozen small ambushes in a circular pattern around his position, then he and another guy plinked C-ration cans with a .22 target pistol he had. This went on for two or three days. The enemy never took the bait, but that's the kind of thing he'd do."

The son of a carpenter, Gabe Rollison had grown up poor on the outskirts of small-town Hinesville, Georgia. He enrolled in the ROTC program at North Georgia College and became a resident football star. He was commissioned in 1966, whereupon he married his sweetheart and volunteered for jump school, ranger school, and Vietnam.

Lieutenant Rollison pulled a 1966–67 tour as a platoon leader and company executive officer in a rifle battalion headquartered in the Michelin Rubber Plantation near Saigon as part of the 4th Division before being switched to the 25th Tropic Lightning Division.

Following his two years of service, Rollison got into the insurance business with his father-in-law. It wasn't for him. "One day," he told Hawkins, "I looked in the mirror when I was shaving and I saw a fat roly-poly insurance salesman staring back at me."

Rollison went back on active duty. Returning to the war a captain, he was determined to secure command of a rifle company after reaching the Screaming Eagles replacement center at Camp Evans. He began his politicking with Andre Lucas of the 2-506th Infantry. Lucas informed him of an opening on his staff. "Colonel, with all due respect, I can't use it," replied

Rollison. "I came back here to do what I do best, and that's leading men in combat. I want a company. If you don't have one for me, I'll find a battalion that does."

Lucas liked what he heard and told Rollison that he was going to send him out to Company D, then operating in the foothills from FSB Jack. "My guidance is very simple," said Lucas. "Take care of your people and kill North Vietnamese." Turning the tables a bit, Lucas then asked, "What do you expect of me, captain?"

"Sir, don't run my company—let me run it."

Lucas cracked a smile. "That's fair enough."

Captain Rollison took over Company D on March 6, 1970, his predecessor having been sent packing by Lucas. "I got off the helicopter and he got on it," recalled Rollison. "He hadn't taken care of his people. He hadn't cared enough to set the standards and make sure his people toed the mark." When Rollison walked around the muddy firebase, he found troops with "filthy weapons and machine guns that wouldn't fire; when I went down in the CP, the chief RTO's radio had C-ration cheese down the face of it and all over the knobs. It was obvious he hadn't cleaned it in some time. They looked raggedy. My impression was that I'd taken over a pretty ineffective, poorly disciplined, rag-bag outfit."

There tended to be more searching and avoiding during patrols than searching and destroying. Contact being rare in any event, the smell of marijuana drifted from many a position when the sun set on the platoon NDPs. Rollison set about rebuilding the company in his image. He had the help of a good first sergeant, plus two highly motivated lieutenants, Bud Romig in Delta One and brand-new Jack Flaherty in Delta Three. Jim McCall, another hard charger, got Delta Two after Rollison fired the previous platoon leader. "I gave the guy four hours to get ready for a daylight patrol, the simplest, most fundamental military mission, and he couldn't get it together," explained Rollison. Checking the patrol before it left the wire, Rollison was dismayed that the troops had dirty weapons and wore boonie hats instead of helmets, not to mention that "the radios weren't on the correct frequency. Half the radios didn't even work, which they tried to hide from me, and there was only one map and compass in the whole damn platoon."

When Rollison visited Romig's and Flaherty's platoons in the field for the first time, he gave each the same speech he'd given the platoon on Firebase Jack. "He let everyone know that things were going to be different from then on," recalled Flaherty. The rest of the battalion was committed at that time to the original assault on Ripcord. Rollison had three weeks before Company D went in. "That was our shakedown period," he noted. Weapons were zeroed, and basic patrol, ambush, and river-crossing techniques were rehearsed under combat conditions. "Basically, I got 'em out in the woods and just ran their asses off," said Rollison. "I told 'em, 'We're gonna winnow out the chaff here, and find out who can function and take care of his buddy, and who can't.'"

Rollison went by the book, requiring his men to shave every day, believing that troops who looked sharp were sharp. The fundamentals were stressed to include moving every day and digging in, deploying claymores, and registering artillery every night. "Rollison knew every one of his soldiers by name, and could tell a man a joke and then chew his butt if he needed it," recalled Lieutenant Flaherty. "Every man in the company knew exactly what was expected of him. Morale soared. I loved being a part of it." Flaherty, an OCS man, decided to go career because he was so impressed by Rollison. "Rollison taught me how to be a platoon leader, and he expected me to teach my men as he was teaching me. The offense was touted as the best defense, and the troops carried lots of ammunition and grenades. Water and food had second priority in our rucksacks. The men were proud of how tough their company commander was. He was seen as hard but fair."

However conventional his tactics, Rollison's methods were anything but. If, after digging in, someone got too loud, laughing or goofing around, the captain would stand up in the center of the perimeter, his voice booming furiously: "Okay, you just told 'em where we are, so, c'mon, come and get us, you sons of bitches."

Most of the guys quickly got the message. Rollison was checking the lines one night, however, when he saw a man sitting in full view at the edge of his foxhole, lighting what looked to be a joint. Slipping up behind the trooper, Rollison grabbed him by the hair on the back of his head, put his seven-inch Gerber fighting knife to his throat, and whispered some profound words in his ear about the importance of light discipline and staying alert on guard.

Rollison's reputation began to flourish when Delta Company CA'd into the Ripcord AO and began killing more than its share of NVA. One of the many successful contacts began when the point squad of Lieutenant McCall's platoon, which was leading a company move along a ridge, exchanged fire with a small group of North Vietnamese. "We were moving through the jungle just like Rollison had taught us, being very quiet, very cautious," said McCall. The result was that the enemy, thinking they were dealing with a small patrol, ran right into a larger element they didn't even know was there when they tried to maneuver behind the point squad. "I already had a bead on the lead NVA when he spotted one of my guys," recounted McCall, armed with an M16, "and when he started to bring his AK-47 up, I squeezed off three rounds and dropped him right there." That night, McCall was pondering the fact that he had killed a man "when I got word on the radio that the Red Cross had called to notify me that my wife had given birth to our second daughter, so it was sort of a double dose of emotions."

After more than two months of hard campaigning in the mountains, Company D, which had inflicted many casualties but suffered a few, too, was trucked to Eagle Beach for two days of beer and sand during the battalion stand-down in June. A disconcerting incident occurred then that was probably related to the trooper whom Rollison had tried to scare straight with his fighting knife. The trooper was black. "There were two classes of black guys," said Pfc. Bruce W. McCorkle. "There were the ones who were really good soldiers, and there were the street guys who hung together and were never really part of the unit." The trooper whom Rollison confronted belonged to the latter camp. Afterward, the company commander heard through the grapevine that they were talking about fragging him. There were no attempts, and the issue seemed to have died a natural death until Rollison, on the way back to his hootch after a night of drinking at Eagle Beach, turned the corner of a barracks and was clobbered squarely in the forehead with a two-by-four. An officer from another battalion who happened to meet Rollison at that time observed that "both of his eyes were black and blue and swollen almost shut. He was trying to find out which GI had wielded the two-by-four. Maybe some of his soldiers considered him a little too hard charging."

Rollison was not intimidated, as evidenced by his handling of a street guy who joined Delta One shortly after Ripcord. The trooper immediately began agitating about the white man's war. When his platoon leader, a new lieutenant named Andrews—one of the few black officers of the day—told him it was his turn for LP, the trooper told Andrews that he'd better watch his back the next time they made contact. Given that the trooper had boasted of having done time for manslaughter, Andrews was concerned, as was Rollison.

Chewing the man out had no visible effect, so after the trooper threatened Andrews a second time, a fed-up Rollison took him on a little two-man RIF. Alone in the jungle, Rollison suddenly spun around, shoved his shotgun into the trooper's gut, and, flipping the safety off, told him in no uncertain terms that if he didn't square away he was going to meet a hero's untimely death.

The recalcitrant trooper injured himself some days later with a white phosphorus grenade while setting up a mechanical ambush. Packed off to the rear with painfully blistered buttocks, he sought out the battalion chaplain to describe the mistreatment he had suffered. He furiously threatened everyone up the chain of command with physical harm, to include the chaplain, apparently because he did not appear sympathetic, and soon went from jabbing his finger in the chaplain's face to thumping him in the chest with it. The chaplain finally threw a right cross that laid the trooper out cold. The story spread like wildfire in the battalion and was great for morale, though there were repercussions in the form of a congressional complaint from the trooper's gullible congressman.

* * *

Following the battalion stand-down, Rollison's people took over the perimeter at Ripcord. On June 28, prop wash from a CH-47 blew sparks from the 105 area, where a fire mission was in progress, into the mortar section's ammo bunker, igniting several powder bags. Fearing a major explosion, Rollison ordered everyone out of the area, then jumped into the bunker and began shoveling dirt on the fire. He was soon joined by one of his men who had rushed down the hill with the aviation fire extinguisher from the VIP pad. Disaster thus averted, Rollison was awarded the Soldier's Medal.

When the battle began and Wilcox replaced Hewitt, Lucas asked Rollison for his best platoon leader to fill Wilcox's vacated slot as CO of Company E. "Well, McCall's the craziest, meanest one I got," said Rollison. "Flaherty's the smartest and most calculating, and Romig has the most experience and is the calmest under fire."

Lucas took Romig. Shortly thereafter, on July 6, Delta Company moved out to support the recon team on Hill 1000. "When we turned the security mission over to Bravo Company, I was very happy and relieved," recalled Flaherty. The jungle seemed preferable to "being stuck on the firebase with the work details and incoming mortar fire. We had no idea that we were going to run into a major enemy fortification within a kilometer of Ripcord."

The morning of the attack was hot and cloudless. Lieutenant McCall and Delta Two advanced in column on the left flank, Lieutenant Flaherty and Delta Three on the right, the troops—rucksacks left behind in the overnight position—well spaced as they threaded uphill through the jungle. The pace was slow and cautious. It was three hundred meters to the top of the eastern knoll that was the company's objective. The last seventy-five meters were the most vulnerable, the underbrush burned away by air strikes, the slope crowded with tree trunks broken off at various heights and littered with the tangled and splintered debris of the felled trees.

The prep fires were lifted as the assault platoons started across the deadfall. The lead troops were twenty-five meters from the top of the knoll when a single shot rang out and Pfc.

Michael J. Grimm of Delta Three dropped to his knees and pitched forward onto his face.

It was 9:40 A.M. on July 7, 1970. George Strasburg, the platoon sergeant, instantly sought cover amid the deadfall. Returning fire, he didn't notice for some moments that Grimm was lying beside him, unmoving, facedown. "All of a sudden, the medic was there, pulling Grimm's shirt open, and he had a bullet hole in his chest directly over his heart," recalled Strasburg. There was no blood, Grimm's heart having stopped pumping when he was shot. The medic tried to find a pulse but finally looked up despairingly and shook his head. Grimm, married, age twenty, from Carthage, North Carolina, was dead. "I couldn't believe it," said Strasburg. "Grimm was a good friend of mine. He was right beside me as we were going up. It was like, we're talking one minute, and the next he's just lying there, and I didn't even know what had happened to him."

Flaherty got an excited radio call from a trooper in the point squad who reported the KIA in the clear: "L. T., Grimm is dead."

"Okay," Flaherty answered matter-of-factly, shocked that in the heat of the moment he didn't feel anything, couldn't think of anything to say, about losing one of the best soldiers in Delta Three.

Moments later, as the fire grew heavy on Flaherty's platoon, the enemy also hit Lieutenant McCall's platoon on the left flank. "We all basically knew what we were getting into when we saddled up that morning. Nobody wanted to walk point," noted Gary Radford, the rangy, blond-headed platoon sergeant of Delta Two. Specialist Fourth Class Lewis Howard, Jr., ended up as the platoon point man through an unfair process of elimination. "We were going to draw straws," explained Radford, "and a couple guys threw 'em down. They said they weren't walking point, they just flat-out refused. I didn't argue with them. What it came down to was if nobody would go, I'd have to do it, but other guys were willing to draw straws. Howard came up with the short one. He didn't say a word. I knew what was going to happen. I knew he was going to get it."

Radford was a white guy from Pittsburgh. Howard, a big, strong, soft-spoken kid who never complained and always did his job, was a black draftee from Macon, Georgia. Recently reassigned to a rifle squad, Howard had carried Radford's radio the previous six months. They were close friends. "I'll come and get you if something happens," Radford said, trying to reassure Howard.

Lieutenant McCall, after passing the crater where the recon team had left its equipment the day before, equipment that had since vanished, halted his platoon at a rock formation before pushing on to the top of the knoll. Howard and his slack man, Sgt. George McIntosh, got behind a boulder until McCall passed the word to move out. The point team hadn't gone another fifty meters—firing broke out at that point on the other side of the knoll—when several RPGs came whooshing in, the first one hitting the tree that Howard was moving past. Taking the brunt of the explosion, he dropped on the spot. McIntosh was badly wounded in the hip. As he scrambled for cover, he heard Howard cry out for a medic, but that was it. Howard neither answered those who called to him nor tried to crawl back toward the platoon. He might have only been unconscious, but, given the massive injuries he must have suffered, the impression his buddies had was that probably he had died almost instantly.

As the lead troops returned fire, Sergeant Radford moved up to join them. Radford, wounded and decorated with a Silver Star during the big battles of the previous summer, had extended his tour an additional six months, such was his loyalty to the men in his platoon. Seventeen months in-country, he had only a few weeks to go, however, when they went up Hill 1000. "I had short-timer's fever," said Radford, who had drifted all the way back to the tail end of the column after Howard took the point. "Hell, I think I placed myself next to the last guy in the platoon. I don't know if I was losing it or what, but I wasn't the same NCO I had been in the past." Feeling guilty, Radford led a squad uphill to drag Howard back but had to withdraw when the enemy began "firing RPGs into the trees above us, trying to get the shrapnel to spray down on us." Radford and his squad next tried to outflank the entrenched enemy. "We were able to move fifty or sixty meters over to the left, but we weren't able to advance up at them at all. As soon as they saw movement, they would start lobbing satchel charges down at us."

The situation was the same on the right flank. "The enemy positions were well camouflaged to begin with, and the prep fires added to it," noted a frustrated Lieutenant Flaherty. "With all the deadfall you couldn't see anything at ground level. We were returning fire blindly, but they were aiming at specific people."

Shouting directions over the din, Flaherty had the platoon work its way to the left until they had a fifty-meter front coming down the hill at an angle from Strasburg, who was the farthest forward on the right. "At that point, we started to maneuver over and around the deadfall to see if we could get at the bunkers," recounted Flaherty, who, like the captain, carried a pump shotgun. "We were shooting, throwing hand grenades, just trying to get a fix on where they were, when we started taking fire from additional positions. It sounded like we had four or five bunkers directly in front of us."

It was impossible to crawl under the felled trees. The only way to advance was to lob a frag and, as soon as it exploded, scuttle over the next log in your path, hoping the enemy had ducked at the blast. It didn't always work. Flaherty's radioman, Sp4 Thomas E. Gaut, started over one log only to be shot and knocked backward into Flaherty, who pushed him back over the log and came crashing down on top of him. They landed in a crater, which saved their lives because the enemy soldier who shot Gaut—from a bunker only ten feet farther up the hill that no one knew was there because he had waited for the right moment to reveal his position—couldn't depress his weapon low enough to finish off the two as he furiously hosed down everything around and just behind the crater.

When the enemy soldier finally stopped firing, Gaut looked at his bullet-shattered arm. "Aw, shit," he said in a stunned whisper.

"Don't look at it," Flaherty exclaimed, afraid the man might go into shock. "Don't look at it, it's going to be okay."

It was a terrible wound. The round had smashed into Gaut's hand, destroying the radio handset he was holding, then tore down his arm. His forearm was hanging on by only a few strands of muscle.

"Gaut's hit," Flaherty shouted to some troops who had been moving up on the right. "I need a handset for the radio."

"Hold on, we'll get one off another radio."

Meanwhile, Flaherty got a bandage around Gaut's arm, then tied a tourniquet above the radioman's elbow to stop the bleeding.

Someone was heading up with a spare handset, but Flaherty shouted, "Don't come up here because you're gonna get hit."

The trooper instead crawled to within five to six feet of the crater and tossed the handset to Flaherty. "Give me the radio," Gaut said, in a lot of pain but hanging tough. "I'll use my other hand."

Lieutenant Flaherty began lobbing grenades at the enemy soldier who had him pinned down. "Every time my arm came up, he would fire, which actually gave me a better fix on where he was." Flaherty's first few frags seemed to have no effect, but as his aim got better there were long lulls in the enemy fire after each explosion. "Frankly, I think I killed five or six people. I think the enemy positions could be reinforced from the inside with tunnels, so no matter how many you killed, they just sent somebody else in to pull the body out of the way and keep up the fire. That's my impression. I don't know for sure. I never saw a single NVA."

Spotting a bunker, George Strasburg, a low-key, absolutely dependable shake 'n bake who had been drafted out of college, rose from the depression where he had found cover, squeezed off a burst, dropped down, came up to fire again, and was shot in the head from a bunker he had been unaware of. "My helmet flew up, landed on the ground, and was sitting there rocking with a hole in it," remembered Strasburg. "I thought this is it, this is that split second between life and death, the moment before you leave your body. I hoped I was going up. It was the strangest sensation."

Coming to his senses, Strasburg realized he was on his back, his rifle across his chest, his legs pointed downhill. Not sure how badly he might be hurt, given the little fragments that had peppered the side of his head, he moved his feet back and forth, making sure they still worked, then held up his hands and did the same. Everything seemed okay. Retrieving his helmet, he saw how lucky he had been. An inch or two lower and the bullet would have gone through his forehead instead of tearing open the top of his steel pot.

Strasburg was lobbing grenades, careful not to throw too hard lest the frags go over the top of the knoll—the fight was that nose to nose—when the enemy sent a satchel charge his way. "It landed about ten or fifteen feet away on my left," he recalled. The satchel charge, a yellowish orange block of dynamite, "just kind of laid there, smoking, and I thought, good, it's a dud. I wasn't paying much attention to it, and all of a sudden the thing went off, and my ears were ringing worse than when I caught the bullet in my helmet. I couldn't hear anything in my left ear at all, but the satchel charge was all blast effect, no shrapnel, and I was basically okay."

Lieutenant McCall was also convinced that the enemy positions were interconnected with tunnels. Having pinpointed one bunker, the platoon leader and several of his troops worked their way close enough to toss grenades through the firing aperture. "I know we eliminated that bunker," said McCall. "The explosions actually blasted a body out of it, and we fired down in there to make sure nothing was left alive, but when we pressed on towards the next position, we started receiving fire from that same bunker."

During an attempt to get around the enemy on the far left flank, McCall saw Sp4 Dwayne H. Pace's gun team start across an open space, only to run into point-blank frontal fire from an unseen bunker. Pace began returning fire from the prone position, but the assistant gunner, Pfc. Charles E. Beals, a new guy from French Lick, Indiana, took a burst in the chest as he lay there feeding the M60.

"The machine gunner was stuck out in the open," said McCall, "trying to take care of Beals, who was actually dead, and keep his weapon in action. He kept firing until he ran out of ammo. . . ."

To get the heat off the machine gunner, Lieutenant McCall,

who had the platoon radio on his back so his RTO could fight as an infantryman, worked his way to within fifteen meters of the bunker from the right and let fly a frag. The NVA inside responded in kind. "I wasn't behind much. In fact, my steel pot probably saved my life," said McCall. He could see the stick-handled Chicom grenades flipping toward him; all of them landed to his front. He would squeeze flat behind his helmet, tucking his arms under him, then heave a grenade of his own after each explosion. Losing his helmet as another Chicom grenade sailed in, McCall "reached out and grabbed my helmet and put it back on, and the grenade went off while my hand was still on top of the helmet. Shrapnel hit me between my trigger finger and thumb, a deep, jagged graze right in that fleshy part. It was painful, but it wasn't critical. I started shooting with my left hand, and I could still throw grenades."

To move was to draw fire, so in short order the assault had bogged down. The lead troops could do no more than lob grenades as they hunkered, heads down, amid the deadfall. Captain Rollison started forward himself with part of the reserve platoon. Along the way, the company commander and the single radioman he had taken along, Rick Rearick, stopped behind a tree that was lying at an angle, pointed downhill. When Rollison jumped over it, a machine gun suddenly opened up, stitching the trunk and narrowly missing Rearick. Rollison vaulted downhill to get away from the fire. He landed on his shoulder and rolled into a shallow depression, where he kept his head down as the machine gunner fired all around his hideaway, spraying him with dirt.

From behind the log, Rearick blasted away, to no effect, with his M16. "Get your head down," Rollison finally shouted to the radioman, " 'cause I'm going to cook off a couple frags for about two and a half seconds, then I'm coming out of this friggin' hole."

Rollison pulled the pins on two grenades, one in each hand, released the spoons, counted off, flipped them over his head, then sprang up the instant they exploded. Madly pumping shotgun shells at the machine-gun position, he dashed back up toward Rearick. In the blur of dirt and debris flying in the air, it looked as though he got an NVA who stuck his head up to return fire. Making it to cover, Rollison grabbed the radio and excitedly reported, "I got the sonofabitch with my shotgun. I got him with my shotgun."

Continuing up to the right, Rollison got on the horn with Flaherty, who, still pinned down by the enemy dug in above his crater, reported that he was out of grenades. Rollison, who had plenty, crawled to a log about ten feet to the left rear of the crater.

It was approximately 10:45 A.M. Lucas had arrived by then in a LOH, better known as a Loach, and directed Rollison by radio from his perch as the captain began to blindly lob grenades.

Boom!

"Three feet to the right."

Boom!

"Okay, two feet to the left."

Boom!

"Not so close next time," Lieutenant Flaherty chimed in on the radio, his voice calm but pained. "You got me with that last one."

"Bad?" Rollison shouted back.

"I don't think so," Flaherty answered, unaware that his entire back had been peppered. "I got it in the back, but I seem to be okay."

Rollison's next two grenades were on the money, and Flaherty scrambled from the crater as soon as the enemy stopped firing, to thoroughly blast the position with his twelve-gauge shotgun.

Before the enemy could regroup, Flaherty grabbed Gaut under his arms, pulled him up onto his hip, and, pushing with his other foot, crawled around the log behind the crater and started down the hill. "I dragged Gaut ten, fifteen meters, then turned him over to a couple guys," said Flaherty. "By that time the medics had established an area down the hill where they weren't taking any direct fire, and people were bringing the wounded to them there."

Flaherty grabbed the radio, hustled back up the hill, and jumped behind a log with Rollison, who instructed him to keep up the fire while he, the company commander, tried to outflank the enemy on the right with the men he had brought up from Delta One. As Rollison's group started through the deadfall, an RPD opened up from a low-profile bunker that would have been impossible to see except that the machine gun was at ground level and the muzzle blast spit up dirt whenever the gunner pulled the trigger. "I kept my eye on the spot and asked somebody to hand me a LAW," said Rollison. "I hit the son of a bitch dead center. I think the LAW actually went through the aperture, but they apparently replaced the gunner through those damn tunnels we think they had because not more than two or three minutes later they were firing again from that position. I knocked it out again with another LAW."

Rollison's maneuver was soon stopped by heavy fire. Lucas orbited the knoll at fifty feet, the little observation helicopter taking multiple hits as the colonel radioed corrections to Rollison and others who were lobbing grenades and firing M79s.

Two LOHs from a White Team came on station at 11:25 A.M. and, buzzing around like angry bumblebees, delivered minigun bursts whenever they identified a target amid the deadfall on top of the hill. The enemy returned fire with AK-47s and RPDs, and at one point an RPG went sailing past the battalion commander's Loach.

One of the scout ships, probably the colonel's, dropped a gas-mask pouch full of grenades to Lieutenant McCall, who was still pinned down but out of frags, after the platoon leader heaved a smoke grenade to mark the bunker that was firing on him and gave his location in relation to the smoke. McCall explained the difficulty he was having eliminating the NVA in the bunker. "We'll hover over the bunker," the LOH radioed back, "and when he comes out to take us out, you take him out." The enemy soldier, unable to fire at the hovering Loach from inside his bunker, stepped out into an adjoining trench, exposing himself to McCall from the chest up as he blasted away with his AK. "The Loach was taking some pretty good hits," said McCall, who frantically threw the grenade he had ready. "Before the grenade even went off, I was firing my M16 to make sure I took that guy out completely before he got me or actually shot the helicopter down. It was a crazy moment."

George Strasburg was ordered to try to close with the enemy, an order that made sense to him because none of the grenades he had thrown had done any apparent good. Telling the closest troops, two guys he did not know from the reserve platoon, to follow him, the platoon sergeant crawled to the top of the knoll. There was a trail there that would have to be crossed to outflank the bunkers. Strasburg went first, exposing himself for a split second as he rolled across. Having crested the knoll at that point, he slipped downhill into the tall elephant grass on the reverse slope, realizing with a start that the other two men had not followed him across the trail. Strasburg could hear the scout ships buzzing around, ripping off an occasional minigun burst. For cryin' out loud, he thought, if they think I'm a gook out here, I'm going to get blasted.

Pushing down the grass around him so the pilot could see clearly that he was on their side, Strasburg waved at one ship that whipped past, then continued working his way through the elephant grass, staying low in a ravine. Moving uphill from the enemy's rear, Strasburg broke out of the elephant grass on his hands and knees and spotted the bare earthen top of a bunker about thirty feet above him. He put down his M16 and reached into the cargo pocket on his left trouser leg where he kept his map and grenades. He came up empty. He had already thrown all his frags. Oh, shit.

At that moment, an enemy soldier wearing a pith helmet stuck his head up from the bunker and looked in the general direction of Strasburg. Thinking himself a dead man, Strasburg slowly reached down for his M16 and slowly, in time-expanded suspended animation, brought it to his shoulder and sighted in on the enemy soldier's head. He squeezed off a three-round burst. The man disappeared in a flash, apparently hit. Before the enemy could figure out where the fire had come from, Strasburg scooted away through the elephant grass. He thought he'd find the two reserve-platoon guys back at the trail and together they could take out the bunker with grenades. The two turned out to be nowhere in sight, so he continued back-tracking until he ended up in the same depression where he'd spent most of the battle.

CHAPTER 12

Hitting the Wall

Lieutenant Colonel Lucas broke station after forty-five minutes to refuel and take aboard a resupply of fragmentation and smoke grenades for Company D. When the Loach shut down on the POL pad at Ripcord, Lucas and Major Koenigsbauer quickly discussed the situation, the operations officer offering to relieve a very wrung-out-looking Black Spade. "Grab thirty minutes and relax, sir," said Koenigsbauer. "I'll take the bird back up and keep the attack going."

Lucas declined, insisting that it was his responsibility. With that the colonel flew back toward the hill. Though the range was too great to see any movement except the helicopters, the ongoing action was visible from Ripcord. "We could faintly hear the small-arms fire, and see smoke and occasional flashes on the hill," wrote Fred Edwards, the battalion engineering officer. "We sat on the side of the firebase, following the course of the battle on the radio. You could get some appreciation for the intensity of the fire from radio background. The voice of every officer was astonishingly cool and professional in the face of the fire. I have always had the utmost respect for infantrymen, and this event solidified that respect."

Lucas dropped several cases of smokes and frags to the troops from an altitude of about fifteen feet. The LOH accumulated several more bullet holes as it hung suspended between the trees. Losing oil pressure—something vital had finally been hit—it was forced to return to Ripcord.

The action continued. Running out of options, Rollison popped smoke on the right flank and had Flaherty do the same at his location fifteen feet to the left. "Can you make a gun run from one smoke to the other?" Rollison asked one of the LOH pilots.

"If you really want me to," the pilot said doubtfully. The forward edge of Company D, as marked by the smoke grenades, was only a few meters from the bunkers that Rollison wanted strafed.

"Affirmative," Rollison came back. "Keep your fire just as close to my side as you can, but see what you can hit in there."

The Loach zipped by right on the deck, minigun blazing. "A couple of those rounds ended up six or eight inches in front of my smoke, which was getting a little bit tight," recalled Rollison, "but the guy knew what he was doing and no one got hurt. I think he made two gun runs across our front, and did a lot of good for us."

Flaherty, meanwhile, was working from position to position with several of his men, distributing the grenades and trying to get a handle on the situation. Everyone told him the same story: "No matter how many grenades we throw at these bunkers, no matter what we do, every time we stick our heads up, they're firing at us."

Flaherty crawled over to Rollison. "We're up against it," Flaherty said. "We're not getting anywhere. We're just expending ammunition."

Rollison had a quick radio conversation with Lucas, then turned back to Flaherty. "Okay, that's it, we're going to pull back."

It was time to bring in more of the heavy stuff. To help Rollison break contact, Lucas—quietly turning aside Koenigsbauer's repeated suggestion that he, the S3, go aloft—climbed aboard a replacement aircraft that had arrived an hour after the first Loach had been forced down. Before departing, Lucas directed that a platoon from Company B move on foot from the firebase and secure for the medevacs the overnight position to which Delta Company would be returning on the bald hilltop between Ripcord and Hill 1000.

Strasburg had dragged Mike Grimm along as he withdrew to where everyone else was clustered, then lost track of the body as he helped Flaherty get the platoon back down the hill. Captain Rollison crawled up to get the dead man, but as he reached out to grab Grimm's boot, an enemy soldier suddenly stood up from a bunker ten feet above him. Rollison took the individual for a Chinese advisor. He was big and tall and was wearing, in addition to khaki web gear, a distinctive khaki bush hat to which was pinned a big red star. He was gripping a drum-fed RPD in his right hand. In his left was a satchel charge. "He just looked straight at me and tossed it. It came arcing through the air," recounted Rollison, "and before it landed, I shot him twice in the chest, and he dropped down to his knees, and I shot him in the face." The adrenaline was such that Rollison crushed the walnut slide of his shotgun as he pumped off the shots, then, his left hand stinging with splinters, he "dropped the shotgun and plugged both ears and opened my mouth, and the satchel charge went off in my face. I woke up about twenty feet away. I'd lost most of the hearing in my right ear from the explosion. I also lost my shotgun. I got distracted by something, got turned around and never got turned back around. I loved that shotgun. That ol' Winchester was a sweet-shootin' gun."

As Flaherty's people edged away from the bunkers, one of his machine gunners maintained a forward position, laying down suppressive fire. The gunner presently shouted that he needed more ammunition, but his ammo bearer, Pat Dooley—not his real name—remained glued behind his cover. That was not surprising. Dooley, a nice guy and certainly no pariah among his comrades, always froze under fire. Bruce McCorkle, a radioman from the company command group, finally grabbed a box of belted ammo from Dooley and crawled up with it to the machine gunner.

McCorkle was joined by Sgt. Stanley G. Diehl and, passing their M16s to some of the guys heading downhill, they went to get Mike Grimm. The machine gunner was pulling back himself by then. It seemed to McCorkle that he and Diehl were the last friendlies on that side of the hill. McCorkle grabbed Grimm's arms, and Diehl his legs, but when they lifted him up, a machine gun fired into them. The rounds passed so close, the sensation was like that of being electrocuted, and they went to the ground, expecting to be killed in the next instant by the enemy soldier who had them in his sights. There was no NVA, however. Rolling over, McCorkle saw a Loach flash past over their heads and realized that the little helicopter had apparently been caught in a downdraft as it fired, putting a burst right through them. Miraculously no one had been injured, though McCorkle noticed a hole in Grimm's wrist that he hadn't seen before as they continued downhill with the body.

On the other side of the hill, Lieutenant McCall, pinned down again after another aborted attempt to move forward, was throwing the grenades that had been dropped to him in the gas-mask pouch to cover the withdrawal of Delta Two. Ranger Radford, controlling the move, was grief stricken that they had been unable to recover Lewis Howard, the platoon having progressed too far to the left of the bouldered area where the body of his friend was sprawled. Getting reorganized back among the trees, he was horrified to realize that Beals, the new assistant machine gunner, wasn't there either. Someone said he'd been hit. It was unclear in the confusion whether he was alive or dead, and Radford headed back to get him.

Beals was lying facedown, unmoving, where he had been shot. The M60 that Beals's gunner had been manning lay nearby, damaged and useless. Radford grabbed Beals but was suddenly knocked unconscious, his eardrums ruptured by a satchel charge. Radford snapped back to reality as Sp4 Joseph Gibson, his radioman, dragged him back behind one of the knocked-down trees. "Had Joe Gibson not followed me to find Beals," Radford would later write, "I may have also been left behind on Hill 1000."[1]

Out of frags again, McCall reported that he needed help, and Rollison turned over to him the Cobras from the 4-77th ARA, which had replaced the White Team at 12:45 P.M., shortly after Lucas had gone airborne again over Hill 1000. McCall used one of his last two smokes to mark the nearest bunker.

The fire-team leader of the Cobras asked, "How far are you from the smoke?"

"Fifteen feet," McCall said.

"That's not far enough," the team leader answered. "We need more room than that to operate."

"Okay, wait one minute, and let me see if I can pull back."

McCall jumped over the log behind him. The enemy had been waiting for him to move, and AK-47 rounds cracked past all around him as soon as he exposed himself. "That's about as far as I can go," McCall informed the ARA. "Go ahead and roll in hot."

As soon as the first Cobra unleashed its rockets, McCall was up and running, hoping the enemy was too preoccupied with the helicopters to open fire on him as he headed downhill through the deadfall, taking it in leaps and bounds. Only when he reached the safety of the jungle did he slow down long enough to notice that he had taken some light shrapnel in his elbows from the ARA.

If McCall wasn't the last man off the embattled hill, then Sergeant Radford was, peppered along the way in the arm and leg by rocket fragments. The Cobras broke station at 1:15 P.M. to clear the way for a forward air controller and a flight of Phantoms. Rollison reported taking heavy AK-47 and RPG fire from boulders overlooking the saddle across which he was withdrawing, and Lucas spotted movement southwest of the LZ being secured by Bravo Three. To keep Rollison from getting cut off, Lucas, trusting that the jungle would absorb most of the blast, had the FAC put the air strikes within three hundred feet on either side of Delta Company.

The price of the battle had been heavy. Against nine enemy kills confirmed from the air, Rollison had one KIA, two MIAs, and, not counting all the lightly wounded, thirteen WIAs. There was little doubt that both missing men were dead when the company pulled back, but, as Sergeant Strasburg noted, "It really played on our minds that we hadn't been able to get to them to make sure."[2]

Company D linked up with Bravo Three about five hours after first making contact on Hill 1000. "When we got back and looked at our watches, I couldn't believe we'd been up there that long," said Flaherty. "It seemed like twenty minutes. Time is so compressed when you're under fire. You're not conscious of anything. You just do what you have to do. You don't even think about it."

For doing what they had to do, Rollison, Flaherty, and McCall would be awarded Silver Stars, as would George Strasburg. All had been wounded. Flaherty, in fact, had been hit twice. Forgetting about the splatter of shrapnel in his back, Flaherty, upon reaching the middle of the hill, suddenly became aware of a wasplike pain in his left leg. The trouser leg was dark with blood. "I pulled my pants up," he recounted, "and there was a piece of shrapnel sticking out of my leg right above the top of my boot. It had hit the bone, but I never felt a thing when I was up on the hill. I don't know whether it was a piece of a bullet that had ricocheted off a tree, or shrapnel from God knows what, but I pulled it, and it kind of popped out."

Five seriously wounded men were quickly medevacked. Flaherty and seven other walking wounded were lifted out later that day by the log birds bringing in water and ammunition. "You got to go back and have them take a look at your back," Rollison told Flaherty, who was busy getting his platoon positioned on the perimeter, Bravo Three having been ordered back to Ripcord.

"No, I'll stay, I'm all right," Flaherty said, not realizing how banged up he was. "I'll have the medic take a look at it."

The medic who was there checked Flaherty's back, then looked at Rollison and said firmly, "No, he's got to go back."

Flaherty and Radford flew out on the same resupply ship, along with the body of Mike Grimm, which was wrapped in a poncho on the floor of the Huey. "I remember staring at him and just crying and crying," Flaherty later wrote. "I tried to stop when we landed on the pad at Ripcord but couldn't. I'm sure I was quite a sight."

Treated by the battalion surgeon, hastily debriefed by Lucas and Koenigsbauer in the operations center, Flaherty, dazed and suddenly exhausted, was next led to a helicopter heading back to Camp Evans by a lieutenant in crisp fatigues and polished jungle boots. He was wearing a branch insignia that the platoon leader did not recognize. The cabin of the Huey into which

Flaherty climbed was loaded with communications equipment; he assumed that it was Lucas's command ship. Strapping himself in alongside the strange lieutenant, Flaherty found himself blanking out as they banked away from Ripcord.

The lieutenant suddenly nudged him and shouted over the noise of the helicopter, "Put the headphones on."

"What, what?" Flaherty shouted back, greatly irritated.

"Put the headphones on."

Donning the headset, Flaherty got on the helicopter's internal intercom, whereupon he was questioned in great detail about the fight on the hill. What the hell, Flaherty thought. Who is this goddamn pilot? My back hurts, my leg hurts, I just got one of my guys killed, we got a bunch of people wounded. Not a good day. All I want to do is get patched up and get back to my platoon, and this guy wants to dissect the battle like it was a field exercise.

The questions seemed endless, and Flaherty, providing only grudging, monosyllabic answers at first, was finally drawn into an extended description of the attack on the hill. The voice signed off then with, "Well, Lieutenant Flaherty, thank you very much."

"Hold it," Flaherty said. "Who are you?"

"This is General Berry."

Looking up with a start, Flaherty saw BG BERRY stenciled on the back of one of the pilot's helmets and realized that their new assistant division commander was flying the command ship. The lieutenant at Flaherty's side was the general's aide-de-camp.

Berry dropped off Flaherty at the medevac pad at Camp Evans. First Sergeant Thompson, the outstanding first sergeant of Company D, met Flaherty there and, meaning to encourage the disheveled lieutenant, gave him a big slap on the back, not realizing that's where he'd been hit. The pain drove Flaherty to his knees. Grimm's body, having already arrived on the log bird, was on a stretcher laid across the back of a jeep parked to one side of the pad. The man's shirt had been removed, and Flaherty could see the one neat, little hole over his heart that had killed him. "I said a prayer by the jeep because he was a great guy," recalled Flaherty.

He went into the aid station and lay on his stomach as a surgeon dug the fifteen biggest pieces of shrapnel from his back. A like number of medium-sized pieces still needed to come out, but the doctor told him he'd been through enough for one day and they'd finish in the morning. The doctor added that he saw no point in cutting out the constellation of little speck-sized fragments embedded throughout Flaherty's back: "You're going to go through the rest of your life with that stuff in your back, but it shouldn't be any problem. Most of it will work itself out over the years."

Lucas landed to talk with Rollison. "The colonel was very agitated that we hadn't taken the hill," said radioman Bruce McCorkle, who could empathize to a degree. "We were in a position to take the hill. It was like we were on third base, and when push came to shove the order was never given to assault the bunkers with the standard fire-team rushes we had been taught in Basic and AIT."

Though frontal assaults had gone out of style with the restrictions on casualties, there was more to it than that. With the war as good as lost, not even troops led by a dynamic officer such as Rollison were prone to take the risks necessary to seize an objective such as Hill 1000. "While there were numerous acts of individual bravery on the part of the American soldier," noted McCorkle, "by and large they were related to rescuing others or providing cover fire, not risking life and limb to successfully overwhelm the enemy."

There was probably only a platoon, at most a company, occupying the bunkers at the top of Hill 1000. "The reason we did not take the hill was very simple," concluded McCorkle. "The NVA were willing to die for what they were fighting for. We were not."

Lucas ordered Rollison to launch another attack as soon as possible. "Rollison said there was no way we could do it that late in the day," recalled McCorkle. "He wasn't disobeying a command, but he was arguing his case." Rollison said he understood that taking the hill was key to the security of the firebase, but his troops needed rest and it would be wise to continue the prep fires through the night, given the strength of the enemy bunkers. Lucas relented, indicating that he would bring in Company C the next morning to reinforce the second assault. "There was a sergeant sitting there, and I guess a satchel charge had gone off near him because he was temporarily deaf," noted McCorkle. Before Lucas departed in his Loach, "he kind of insinuated that the sergeant was faking it, then came up behind him and shouted or clapped or something to convince himself that the guy really couldn't hear."

CHAPTER 13

Sideshow

Captain Wilcox and Company C had also made heavy contact the day of the attack on Hill 1000. At that time, Wilcox had been in command only six days. "I was somewhat in awe of most officers," said Bob Smoker. "They had the responsibility, and the perception I had was that they were a cut above. They were the elite." Wilcox, bespectacled, possessed of a boyish grin, seemed "more low-key than the other officers, more friendly, somebody that you could talk to on your own level. He didn't seem like a West Pointer."

Smoker, temporarily assigned as one of Wilcox's radiomen the day the thunderstorm hit them on Hill 805, would recall "standing in a few inches of water in a foxhole with the captain, and him turning to me and joking, 'What a great day to be a soldier.' "

Jeff Wilcox had wanted to be a soldier, or, more precisely, to attend West Point, since his childhood in Gary, Indiana. It was a dream that meant a lot to a kid from a broken family who didn't want to end up in the steel mills, and he was ecstatic when accepted into the USMA Class of '68. The dream did not survive Vietnam. When the moment came to board the bus that would take Wilcox to the airport with his orders for Vietnam, his wife blurted that he didn't have to go, that they could go to Canada. "She thought it was a stupid war, and I wasn't so sure that she wasn't right," recalled Wilcox. Not going, however, was not an option: "I wasn't gung-ho, but I wanted to see how valid our involvement was, and there was a part of me that wanted to prove myself. I also had to keep my word. I believed completely in Duty, Honor, Country."

Arriving as a lieutenant, Wilcox replaced the platoon leader from Company A killed during the first assault on Ripcord. The unit was in a quiet state of crisis at the time. The company commander, having never recovered from the shock of the original Ripcord battle, had taken to hunkering down on hill-tops for days at a time in an apparent attempt to avoid contact. To sit still was actually to invite attack, as Lucas repeatedly warned the captain. On May 14, Wilcox's platoon was indeed ambushed and its point man killed as the men started down a ridge from the company position. Wilcox hit the deck, shrugged out of his rucksack, and was coming back up when he saw a grenade land in front of him. His glasses protected his eyes, but one fragment sliced the side of his head and another caught him in the forehead. First Lieutenant Jim Noll, the company's most experienced platoon leader, rushed forward with one of his squads and linked up with Wilcox, who was stunned and half blind because of the blood in his eyes but still able to direct the 81s firing from the NDP. Some troops were returning fire; many others had their heads down. Noll kicked some ass to get everyone firing, then covered the withdrawal with an M79 while Wilcox and his platoon sergeant carried the dead man back to the NDP. Noll's last shot was a smoke round to mark the enemy for the Cobras.

Wilcox hoped that when he was promoted—because of the war, lieutenants were putting up captain bars in only two years—he would get command of Company A. "I feel a tremendous devotion to these guys," he wrote in a letter to his wife, adding that "because I am not gung-ho, they are safer with me in charge. I will absolutely refuse to take them somewhere I deem too dangerous. . . ."

Lucas thought to breathe new life into Company A by replacing the rattled captain not with Wilcox but with hard-charging Chuck Hawkins. Promoted with his class on June 5, Wilcox ended up in command of the battalion support company at Camp Evans. "[Lucas] said something about never placing a man who has been a platoon ldr in a company as CO of the same company," a disappointed Wilcox wrote his wife. Jim Noll, who respected calm, methodical, levelheaded Wilcox, wondered whether the real reason Wilcox didn't get Alpha Company was because "he was too smart, too devoted to his men, too able to see through bullshit, to successfully command an infantry unit, especially in Vietnam."

Butting heads with Lucas over such issues as the Foxhole Count further disillusioned Wilcox. By the time the young captain took over Charlie Company after the sapper attack on Hill 902, he was thoroughly disgusted with the war and his superiors. "In the absence of any real purpose to the whole war," he later wrote, "our operations had devolved into senseless exercises that benefited no one except officers trying to get the right career tickets punched."

As such, Captain Wilcox was of the same mind as the grunts in his new company, to include Rodney Moore, who would remark, "The commanders wanted body count, but we really didn't care if we killed anybody or not. We didn't know what the hell we were doing there. We fought so we could get everybody home alive."

Wilcox was on the helipad when the remnants of Company C were ferried to Ripcord from 902. Seeing Sergeant Burkey, platoon leader of Charlie Three, disembark from a Huey with the captured RPG launcher—made of mahogany, it was a beauty—Wilcox noted: "There was just something about the way he carried himself that I knew he was the guy to go talk to, and I was right, he was the ranking man in the company. I was the only officer, and I relied on him a lot when we went to relieve Bravo Company on Hill 805."

With seven months in the field, Burkey was a good man for a new company commander to lean on. "Burkey was a balls-out motherfucker," declared platoon leader Campbell. "He's the bravest man I've ever known, and the best NCO I ever saw in Vietnam."

Though Burkey never went regular, as some expected he would, he was a natural soldier. "He was born for it," mused Campbell. "He loved it. He wanted to be there." Burkey was the product of blue-collar Lowellville, Ohio. Volunteering for the draft, he made E5 out of NCOCS and E6 after the Khe Me Mountain action of March 1970, for which he was also awarded a Bronze Star. Burkey, smart, hot-tempered, and hard-core when it came to the discipline problems of the era, was almost twenty-one years old, but blond and dimpled he looked all of fourteen and initially had some trouble exerting the authority of his stripes. "I had to lead by example and show my people that I had my shit together," he noted. Wilcox thought Burkey was "a little cocky, and it really worked for him."

Wilcox was joined by another officer, Lieutenant Campbell, late on July 6, at which time the company was on a ridge that ran north from Triple Hill. Returning from R&R that day, Campbell, who'd done his time in the bush plus an extra month, was supposed to have a job in the rear waiting for him. When he checked in at the main gate at Camp Evans after hitching a ride from the Phu Bai airfield, however, the MPs had his name on a clipboard and placed a call to the Currahee rear. A jeep soon arrived to take Campbell to the helipad, and the driver informed him along the way that his platoon had been wiped out. After finding his weapon, ammo, and rucksack waiting for him, he was whisked out to the company without even stopping at Ripcord. "I think that most people would have become a nervous wreck after surviving as long as Campbell did in the field," wrote Wilcox, "only to be returned like that to the line. He never missed a beat. It was clear to me that he was deeply devoted to the troops and that the feeling was mutual. I was really lucky to have Jim Campbell and Paul Burkey as my subordinate leaders. I was inspired and supported by both of them."

On the morning of July 7, a Huey dropped Sergeant Judd from Company B, along with two of his men, Ramon Santiago and Dennis Bloomingdale, in Company C's NDP. Judd's team, escorted by a squad from Charlie Three, was to move to the north end of the company's ridgeline, then disarm the mechanical ambush that Judd and Bloomingdale had set up on the next piece of high ground, Hill 707, when their outfit had been working the bunker complex in the area at the end of June. There had been no time to retrieve the claymores when Bravo

Company was lifted out on the first day of the battle and combat-assaulted onto Hill 805.

It was imperative that the hazard be removed. Following a narrow trail to the end of the ridge, a five-hundred-meter march from the overnight position, the patrol moved down into the draw between the two hills, then up Hill 707. There were two enemy soldiers squatting on the slope—cooking rice, as the story was later told—but the squad from Charlie Three was moving in a quiet, well-spaced column, and its alert point team opened fire on the NVA before they had a chance to open fire on the squad from Charlie Three.

The enemy scampered out of sight. The grunts, moving uphill in pursuit, suddenly came under fire from a little bunker dug in at the crest of the hill. Sergeant Judd, who was left-handed, went to the prone position with his right shoulder against a tree and began firing his M16. Bloomingdale opened up from some boulders to his left. Santiago was to his right. "There must have been a bunch of NVA behind the bunker we were firing at," said Judd, "because all of a sudden RPGs started raining in on us. We had these rockets tree-bursting above us, and we were getting shrapnel like crazy."

One piece hit the funny bone of Judd's left arm, straightening the arm right out—he felt as though it had been hit with a baseball bat—and sending his rifle flying out of his grip. In a flash, Judd dove onto his M16, then back behind his tree, realizing only after he resumed fire that there was a small hole in his elbow. "That was the first injury. I got thirteen different shrapnel wounds from different explosions," noted Judd. "I was lying on my right side, firing up the hill, and I got hit in my ass and my left leg, and in my back, although I didn't know it at the time. I got some shrapnel in my left foot, too. I think that was from a grenade. There were grenades rolling down at us."

The patrol pulled back under the onslaught. Bloomingdale, badly wounded in the leg, shouted to Judd that he couldn't move. Judd, unable to drag his buddy back but unwilling to leave him as the rest of the guys edged back, kept blasting away with his M16.

Sergeant Burkey was at that moment rushing down the trail from the overnight position with Rodney Moore's squad, also from Charlie Three. Burkey linked up with his ambushed squad at the base of Hill 707 and, trading his M16 for an M79, started uphill on the trail with his radioman. Ramon Santiago tagged along to show them where to find Judd and Bloomingdale.

Burkey could hear someone—it was Bloomingdale—yelling at the enemy in the bunker to surrender: *"Chieu hoi, chieu hoi."*

"Me no *chieu hoi,*" the answer came back.

"*Chieu hoi,* you motherfuckers."

"Fuck you, GI."

"Come and get me, motherfucker."

Burkey's group reached Judd, and the wounded sergeant pointed to where Bloomingdale was hidden among the boulders: "I'm not the one that's hurt the worst. It's Dennis over there."

Burkey scrambled over and bandaged Bloomingdale's bloody mess of a leg even as the wounded man, in terrible pain and going into shock, continued to scream at the NVA.

Burkey couldn't use his M79. The shells spin-arm only after traveling ten meters. The enemy bunker was too close.

The call went up for Moore, who had an over-and-under M203. Moore hustled up the path, then crouched next to some of his guys who were downhill to the right of Burkey's forward position and asked if they could see the bunker. One who could heaved a frag, but the grenade came bouncing back and rolled onto the trail about ten feet from Moore, who went flat just before it exploded and peppered the buttocks of the man next to him with fragments.

Moore could hear the enemy soldier firing from the bunker but couldn't see a thing for the trees. The man ahead of him said he had the bunker in sight. "Let me in there," Moore shouted, and as the man slid back, Moore crawled forward. He still couldn't see the bunker. He got up on one knee to fire anyway but had no sooner shouldered his weapon than "a damn RPG exploded right in front of me, blowing the thump gun out of my hands and throwing me like ten feet back down the hill. I got hit in my legs and my left foot, and there was a hole in my right forearm the size of a dime. It was black. It didn't really bleed because the shrapnel was so hot it kind of cauterized the wound. I caught the biggest chunk of shrapnel right on top of my steel pot. The helmet had a dent in it the size of your fist, like someone had hit it with a sledgehammer. I was stunned. I was also lucky to be alive."

There was a lull in the enemy fire. Sergeant Burkey passed the word to pull back, then started dragging Bloomingdale down the hill with the help of Santiago and his radioman, Bernie Brown. They had to take it slow so as not to injure Bloomingdale further. "The enemy threw a couple Chicoms at us along the way," recalled Burkey. "They rolled on down the hill. We didn't get a scratch."

Reaching the draw, Burkey, to be awarded his second Bronze Star for the rescue, turned Bloomingdale over to a medic, then got on the horn with the 81s on Ripcord. Burkey started the mortar fire behind the enemy, then walked the rounds up to the top of Hill 707. Sergeant Judd reached the draw shortly before the mortar rounds began dropping in. "When they teach you low-crawl in Basic, you think you're never going to use it, but I did the hundred-yard dash on my belly," Judd later joked. His main concern was not the enemy but getting wasted by a keyed-up, trigger-happy grunt. Accordingly, Judd bellowed, "Currahee, motherfucker, Currahee, motherfucker" the whole way down the hill, recalling later that "those guys from Charlie Company, their eyes were as big as cue balls when I came crawling into their little perimeter. They were looking at me over the tops of their M16s."

Hearing the fire in the distance, Lieutenant Campbell, who had moved down the side of the ridge from the overnight position with the five men left in his platoon, moved back up and rushed over to Captain Wilcox. The new company commander was getting ready to join the action with the last squad from full-strength Charlie Three. "Your place is here," Campbell objected. "Let me get a team together, and we'll go over there and see what we can do to get Sergeant Burkey's people back to the LZ. It's better that you stay here and get us some gunships and medevacs on call."

Wilcox reluctantly agreed. Leaving his five survivors behind, Campbell crossed the landing zone in the center of the NDP to the side where that last squad of Burkey's was dug in. "All right, I need some of you guys to saddle up and go with me down the ridge here," Campbell announced. "Sergeant Burkey's in trouble."

Jim Campbell had previously commanded Charlie Three. He knew most of the men there, and they him. "Yeah, fuck it, L. T., I'll go with ya," Sp4 Gerald L. Risinger, a bead-wearing, hippie-style country boy from Kentucky, said without hesitation, popping off the log where he'd been sitting. "It don't mean nothin'."

The amazing thing, and Campbell would not have let the man volunteer if he had known, was that Risinger, a veteran of almost ten months in-country and the best point man in Charlie Three, was supposed to go in on the next resupply helicopter, slated for R&R, after which he was to finish his tour at Camp Evans. As Campbell recounted, he took off with Risinger in the lead, "and several of his buddies followed us. I didn't order 'em, I didn't say you, you, and you. I didn't have to. That's just the kind of guys they were."

Moving quickly to the end of the ridge, Lieutenant Campbell placed his volunteers along the trail to secure it for the return trip. "Risinger, I want you right here," he said, indicating a spot forward of the others that overlooked the draw between the ridge and Hill 707. "Keep your eyes open," Campbell instructed. "If the gooks move up, they'll be comin' up from this direction. Whatever happens, whatever you gotta do, you can't let 'em get up here because if they do everybody in the draw is going to be cut off."

As Campbell proceeded alone into the draw, an RPG whooshed over his head and exploded above him on the ridge. Campbell turned and called to his security team, "Is everybody okay?"

"We're all right, L. T.," someone yelled back.

Campbell hurried on. Sergeant Burkey was still calling in mortar fire when Campbell hooked up with him in the draw. The walking wounded were directed to move back up the ridge. Rodney Moore, trudging up the ridge, was shocked to see Risinger at the top and blurted, "What the hell are you doin' here?"

"I heard you guys needed some help."

"Yeah, but you're supposed to be out of here," Moore exclaimed, concerned. "You're supposed to be on that bird out of here."

Risinger sat down ten feet to Moore's left, disappearing from view in the heavy vegetation. A moment later, another RPG flashed straight across the draw from the crest of Hill 707.

Moore was peppered in the face with little bits of shrapnel. Bob Judd, who'd also made it up the ridge, was sitting, drinking from his canteen, when he saw the heat trail of the rocket coming at them. The blast sent him sprawling. He already had so many flesh wounds that he didn't know if he'd picked up any more, but he was unnerved upon retrieving his canteen to see that a big hole had been punched through the canteen cup. He flung the canteen away.

Risinger had been killed. Moore heard him scream and found that his buddy had literally been blown in half at the waist. His head, torso, and one arm were still connected to one another but not to his legs, and his other arm had been sent flying. It looked as though the RPG had landed right in Risinger's lap. "I can still see his hip bones sticking out of him," said Moore. "I had written a letter and given it to Risinger that morning because he was going back to the rear. He was a good friend of mine. His nickname was Chicken Man because he had long, skinny legs and kept his trouser legs wrapped tight around them with boot laces to keep out the leeches. His wife used to send him care packages with white chocolate. He was a helluva nice guy, and a great point man. He always called me 'sergeant,' I don't know why. He treated the rank with respect. Some of those guys did and some of them didn't over there."

Two badly wounded men were still in the draw. Getting them up the ridge would have been extremely difficult, so because the enemy fire had ceased after that last rocket, Campbell and Burkey decided to risk bringing in a medevac. There were no landing zones in the area, however. The medevac pilot had to instead hover, at eye level with the high ground to either side, and lower a litter basket through a small hole in the canopy. Both casualties could have been lifted out together on a jungle penetrater, but they were in no shape to hang on. They needed to go out in the litter basket. The medevac thus had to remain in its vulnerable hover for fifteen agonizing minutes, slowly lowering the litter basket, slowly bringing it back up with the first casualty—at the rate the winch unwrapped and rewrapped the cable, it seemed to take forever—then repeating the process for the second man. Burkey kept the mortar fire going the whole time, and a pair of gunships maintained a protective orbit around the medevac Huey.

There was no enemy fire. "Let's go," Campbell shouted after the medevac banked away. "Everybody, let's go. We're out of here."

To make sure no one was left behind, Campbell and Burkey were the last ones up the ridge. As everyone regrouped, Campbell asked about Risinger, who had not popped up with the other troops he had deployed along the trail. "Chicken Man's still over there where you put him, L. T.," one of the security troops said, unaware in the confusion that Risinger had taken a direct hit from an RPG.

Campbell, horrified at what he found, had several men remove their shirts to wrap the mangled body parts. "I didn't want anybody to see that," said Campbell, who took some meager solace in the fact that "I think we got all the pieces of Risinger's body out of there."

As Campbell's group started back down the trail, the gunships began rolling in on Hill 707. Sergeant Judd limped painfully along, a piece of shrapnel in the bottom of his left foot, using an M16 as a crutch. "When we were almost to the LZ, a big redheaded guy met us," said Judd. "He handed me a five-quart collapsible canteen. That was the best-tasting water in the world. I was stone thirsty."

The action had cost one dead and fifteen wounded. They went out a few at a time on medevacs and resupply ships. One of the troopers who had been left at the overnight position during the firefight, a lackluster soldier in the best of times, disappeared amid the hustle and bustle. "That sorry bastard climbed on a fuckin' helicopter and went in with a bunch of wounded soldiers," recalled Campbell. "He claimed afterwards that he was a conscientious objector. What he was was a no good son of a bitch."

Sergeant Judd was loaded aboard one of the Hueys. "The door gunner had a peace sign around his neck, and so did I," he would remember. "He held his out to show it to me and gave me an encouraging pat on the back—and that's when I knew I'd been hit in the back. I reached back there, and it felt like half a hardball on my back where it was swelled up around a shrapnel wound."

The slick landed at Camp Evans. When Judd climbed out, his left foot crumpled under him without warning. Two of the medics rushing to meet the helicopter caught him before he went face first into the tarmac. Laid out on a gurney in the aid station, Judd was surprised to see a friend of his appear to check on how he was doing. The friend, formerly a medic in the company, had already said his good-byes—his tour was over—but he was still in the rear, awaiting transport, when he heard that his old outfit had taken casualties. "We'll have you fixed up and back to your unit in no time," an aid-station medic said as he cut away Judd's ragged fatigues, getting him ready for surgery. At that, the medic on his way home slapped his hands over Judd's ears and jokingly admonished his colleague: "What are you trying to do, put this boy in shock?"

CHAPTER 14

Another Try

The prep fires resumed at eight in the morning. Captain Wilcox and Company C had been lifted only twenty minutes earlier into the landing zone secured by Company D on the hill between Ripcord and Hill 1000. Lieutenant Colonel Lucas had disembarked from his command ship soon thereafter and when the artillery began firing was in a huddle with Wilcox, Rollison, Campbell, and McCall. The plan that the battalion commander outlined for the second attack on the key piece of high ground called for both companies to move off the LZ on a trail that ran through the jungle along the northern base of Hill 1000. Company C, in the lead, was to move into position below the westernmost of the two knolls atop the mountain and Company D below the easternmost knoll. From there they were to launch a coordinated assault to the summit of Hill 1000.

Campbell questioned why Company C, down to thirty men, was being tasked to hit the far knoll, whereas Company D, with about fifty men, was to hit the knoll closest to the LZ. Campbell didn't want Charlie Company to get cut off or bogged down with a lot of wounded that it wouldn't have the manpower to carry back up the trail.

"Lieutenant Campbell, there are two bodies on that closer knoll," Lucas said, "and Delta Company wants to get them back."

Campbell could appreciate that, although he doubted that the bodies had survived all the shot and shell pounding the objective. The arty prep, which continued over the heads of the grunts as Company C, dropping rucks, led the way down the trail, involved 105mm, 155mm, 175mm, and 8-inch fire from Ripcord, O'Reilly, Barbara, and Rakkasan. Major Koenigsbauer controlled the artillery from the upper tier of Ripcord as the howitzer crews there, tubes lowered for direct fire, slammed shell after shell into the bald top of Hill 1000. The cannoneers had dubbed their target Hot Dog Hill, an irreverent reference to Hamburger Hill, and "took bets," noted one trooper, "on who would knock the last tree down."

In coordination with an orbiting forward air controller, Captain Lieb—the S3 Air—had Koenigsbauer, with whom he was standing, shut off the arty whenever another flight of F-4s came on station. The fighter-bombers dropped 250- and 500-pound bombs, plus napalm canisters, which blossomed like fiery red flowers. "It was so intense, you could feel the heat on Ripcord," noted Koenigsbauer.

Rollison got into position first. When Wilcox reported that he too had reached his line of departure at the edge of the trees below the western knoll, Lucas gave the order to assault—the time was 10:30 A.M.—and Koenigsbauer lifted the prep fires after a final stinging salvo of CS shells was fired at the top of Hill 1000.

Brigadier General Berry presently joined the S3 on the windy crest of the firebase to observe the attack—battalion and brigade command, meanwhile, were airborne over the battlefield—and expressed concern that the artillery was not firing. To prevent the enemy from moving up additional troops, Berry wanted fire shifted to the reverse slope of Hill 1000. Koenigsbauer explained that the 105s and 155s were standing ready to provide observed fire as requested by the assault companies but that the prep barrage had diminished the ammunition levels on Ripcord to the point that he thought it unwise to continue any unobserved fire until resupplied.

"Okay, so you've reached a critical point with the ammunition on the firebase," Berry replied sharply, lecture style. "In that kind of situation, use the other firebases, use the corps artillery."

Koenigsbauer had, in fact, been doing that, but he had not thought to continue using the long-range 175s and 8-inchers with troops moving onto the objective. Berry assured Koenigsbauer of the accuracy of the big guns, and in short order more shells were rushing through the sky overhead to explode behind Hill 1000. "In any event, I didn't think anything could have survived all the fire we put on the objective," recalled Koenigsbauer. "The enemy bunker complex was so extensive that the preparatory fires actually did very little damage. When the two assault companies crossed their lines of departure and we shifted the fire to the backside of the hill, the enemy troops came out of their bunkers and put up the same stiff resistance we had encountered the day before."

While getting organized, Wilcox had looked up the steep slope with Lieutenant Campbell. There was about 150 meters of deadfall between their tree line and the top of the western knoll. "It's a long-ass way up there," Campbell muttered. The company didn't have any real platoons anymore, so Campbell suggested that they "divvy up into a maneuver element and a support element." Wilcox said he would lead the maneuver element. "You're the company commander," Campbell objected. "You need to stay with the support element and direct the fire support if we get hit. You can always maneuver if we get pinned down."

Wilcox agreed. He would follow with Charlie One, designated the support element, while Campbell led off with Burkey's platoon, the most intact of the three, and what was left of Charlie Two.

As the assault element started out of the trees and up the hill, one of Burkey's squad leaders, burly but gentle Frank Bort—a former divinity student with a degree in psychology who'd been drafted and sent to the NCO academy—began reciting the Lord's Prayer.

Oh, man, I'm fuckin' dead now, Burkey thought, the gravity of the moment sinking in as he listened to the prayer. This is it, this is the last thing we're ever going to do. Burkey was so unnerved that he tore the staff sergeant stripes from his sleeves. The bastards ain't gonna know who they got when they're looking for targets.

Burkey moved out in front after the point team reached the top of the knoll, then turned left and started toward the edge from which they could fire on the opposing knoll, a hundred meters away across an open saddle. Burkey was about to step around a tree that had survived the prep fire when he heard the thump of an M79 being fired. The round hit the tree and bounced off without exploding. Burkey dropped flat, saved by a fluke, as an RPD light machine gun and several AK-47s opened up from the eastern knoll.

It was 10:50 A.M. on July 8, 1970. Lieutenant Campbell's people, most of whom were still strung out along the side of the hill, hit the dirt as bullets impacted around them with ferocious spurts of dust. The assault element laid down cover fire as the support element leapfrogged past. Ascending the bombed-out hillside was like running up a sand dune; the pulverized earth was as loose as potting soil. Sinking and sliding with every step, the troops gained the crest only after much effort. Specialist Fourth Class Steven A. Riley of Charlie Two, a big, rawboned country boy from Alabama, took a round through his arm along the way, but because it missed the bone, he merely wrapped a rag around the wound upon reaching the top of the knoll and began returning fire with his M16.

Wilcox and Campbell ended up in the same crater at the very summit of the knoll. They placed one machine-gun team forward to their left and another to their right and along with the handful of others who had made it up front—Burkey, Bort, Riley, Bob Smoker, and Phil Lormand—popped up to heave frags and fire quick bursts at the opposing knoll, dropping back down as the RPD returned the favor with disconcerting accuracy. The two machine-gun teams kept up their fire through it all. "They were in an excellent position to bring direct fire on the enemy and were smokin' the other knoll," recalled Campbell. Layne Hammons and his assistant gunner, Chuck Damron, had the M60 to the left of the command group's crater. "Hammons and Damron were incredible soldiers," stated Campbell. "Before the fight was over, they had burned out their barrel and fired every belt of ammo they had with them."

It was unclear what damage was being inflicted. Bort had an impression of where the enemy machine gun was but was frustrated that he could not silence it no matter how many shells he sent slamming into the area with his M203. There was no muzzle flash to zero in on, no tracers, no smoke, no dust. "That gun emplacement was perfect," said an equally frustrated Paul Burkey. "I mean the fuckers were in the side of the hill. Their line of fire was straight across the saddle into the top of our hill, and we simply could not see the hole the fire was coming from. The man behind that RPD wasn't some guy that went to the Ho Chi Minh School of Machine Gunnery—it was the fuckin' guy that taught the class."

The enemy had a clear view of their foe. Specialist Fourth Class Charles Schlueter, the machine gunner to the right of the command group's crater, took one RPD round through his shoulder; another round hit the smoke grenade on his web belt, setting it off. "I don't think his bullet wound was as bad as the burns he got from the smoke grenade," noted Bob Smoker. "Either he or his ammo bearer managed to unhook the thing and get rid of it."

Hanging tough, Schlueter resumed fire with the M60. Meanwhile, amid the intermittent AK and RPD fire, the enemy soldier with the M79 continued to lob rounds across the saddle. Captain Wilcox, hearing the shells—duds all—as they clattered down through the branches of a big denuded tree near him, initially thought they were taking long rounds from Company D. After Wilcox confirmed on the radio that it was not friendly fire, there wasn't anything to do as the enemy rained dozens of shells on the western knoll except listen for the sound of the weapon and hope that the next round wasn't the one that was going to explode.

As the firefight dragged on, Lieutenant Campbell was shocked at how little seemed to be happening with Company D. He could see a half-dozen figures just past the trees on the slope of the eastern knoll. Though still far short of the top of the knoll, one figure was ahead of the rest, urgently pitching grenades. The remainder of the company, however, hadn't even left the cover of the tree line.

Lucas, orbiting the action in his command ship, thought to bring in gunships, but Wilcox alerted him to the fact that an east-west pass at the enemy-held knoll would put Company C on the gun target line, and a north-south pass would endanger Company D.

Instead, a White Team from the 2-17th Cav daringly buzzed the knoll, raising hell with their miniguns amid the enemy ground fire. One of the LOHs, hit in the engine, had to set down at Ripcord.

To break the stalemate, Lucas instructed Captain Wilcox to seize the eastern knoll once and for all with a bold frontal assault. Campbell came up on the net to try to explain that there was no cover, that they couldn't even use the craters in the saddle because the enemy could place plunging fire into them from above.

"Get Delta Company to move up the hill," Campbell suggested to Black Spade. "We can lay down a base of fire for them—"

Lucas cut Campbell off and, getting Wilcox back on the horn, confirmed the assault order. Campbell was aghast. "This is insane," he exclaimed to Wilcox. "You've got to call the son of a bitch back. He doesn't understand what he's asking us to do. Tell him that we've got two machine guns up here, we've got grenade launchers, we can lay down all the support in the world for Delta Company. We're in a great position to cover them if they'll just move up the fucking hill, but we're going to get our ass handed to us if we get up and try to go across that saddle. There's just no way—it's suicide."

Wilcox made the call, and earned a sharp rebuke from the colonel for resisting a dangerous order under fire. "Jim," Wilcox said, turning back to Campbell, "we've got to carry out the order."

Campbell said he understood, and he began to quickly outline his plan to get his maneuver element across the saddle. Wilcox cut him off: "No, Jimmy, I'm going to lead the assault."

Campbell argued that a company commander was supposed to coordinate fire support, not charge RPDs. Wilcox didn't budge this time. "If I'm going to command this company for the next six months," he replied, "I've got to show these men I can lead them."

Before going over the top, Wilcox wanted to try once more to silence the machine gun that had them cold. Wilcox had Bort put his helmet on a stick and move it along the edge of the depression in which he had taken cover. The old trick drew fire, but Wilcox, ready with a LAW, could not get a bead on the source. "We did fire some LAWs, but just aimlessly," he noted. Campbell, who was to keep the cover fire going during the assault, was moving from position to position, getting everyone ready. When he told Burkey what was going down, the best noncom in the company sputtered, "You gotta be out of your fuckin' mind. How can we go after that RPD when we don't even know where the fuck it is?"

Captain Wilcox, stripped to his sweat-soaked undershirt in the heat, was wearing a steel pot, a pistol belt with two canteens and a lot of frags and smoke grenades, plus a couple bandoliers of ammunition for his M16. He presently slung a few LAWs over his shoulder. "I had it in my head," Wilcox recalled, "that if I could get close enough, I could put those LAWs in the right spot. . . ."

It was about 11:40 A.M. At a signal from Wilcox, their M60 gunners began laying a continuous stream of three-round bursts into the objective as the captain started forward with a group from Charlie Two and Three. The assault lasted all of fifteen seconds, just long enough for one man to be shot dead and three to be wounded. "The fire on us was just withering," said Wilcox. "We got up, went down, then immediately came scrambling back."

Specialist Fourth Class James E. Hupp, the man who was killed, had made it about twenty feet out into the saddle and had taken cover when he was shot as he raised up too high to fire his M79. "Hupp was one of my best friends," said Frank Bort of the friendly, easygoing draftee from Darlington, Pennsylvania. "I was firing. Hupp was up ahead of me to my right, and he got up to his knees, which I couldn't believe, to position himself to take a shot, and as soon as he did that he got machine-gunned right in the head."

Bort shouted for a medic. Private First Class Rickey L. Scott, a conscientious objector from Indiana who refused to carry a weapon, immediately left his covered position with the support element to answer the call. Only a day or two with the company, Scott was too inexperienced, however, to go about it the right way. "It was like I was in a surrealistic movie, not believing what I was seeing," recounted Bort, "because this new medic just comes walking over, standing straight up when he should have been crawling, and I'm screaming at him to get down, but he doesn't understand what the hell's going on, and then he gets shot in the head just like Hupp."

Captain Wilcox was deeply disturbed by Scott's death. When the medic had climbed off a resupply ship less than forty-eight hours earlier, Wilcox had thought it ludicrous that a conscientious objector had been sent to an understrength rifle company engaged in heavy combat. Wilcox questioned Scott about his unarmed status. "He explained himself succinctly. He was the genuine article," Wilcox recalled. "He was a very bright, well-spoken kid with deep political convictions about not killing people. He was also eager to fit in and do a good job as a medic. I liked him immediately." Unfortunately, Scott seemed more disconnected from the ways of war than even the greenest replacement. "The guy was so completely out of his element," noted Wilcox, "that the only thing I could think to do with him was to tell him to stay right with me. He got killed because he walked directly into a hail of fire, that's how clueless he was. Why in the world did the army think it was a good idea to make Scott a combat medic? Couldn't he have served his purpose as a medic in a surgical hospital back at one of the base camps? He had no place in a line unit in Vietnam."

The fitful exchange of fire continued. The troops were almost out of ammo and water when one of the scout pilots brought the situation to a crisis point by warning Captain Wilcox that a large enemy force was threading quickly through the jungle in his direction from the west. Lucas, monitoring the net, immediately ordered Wilcox and Rollison to break contact and pull back. "If we move off this hill, the stupid bastards are going to make us do it all over again tomorrow," Campbell said to Wilcox. "We're in a good position up here. Goddamnit, if Delta Company would just move up and take the other knoll, we can all get resupplied, we can get the wounded out of here, and we can hold what we've got."

"No, Jim," Wilcox said calmly. "We gotta get off this hill. If those gooks get between us and the LZ, we're through."

It was now approximately 12:40 P.M. Lieutenant Campbell lobbed smoke grenades into the saddle to shield the recovery of the dead, dashing out himself to help a Mexican Indian trooper struggling to drag back the body of Rickey Scott. James Hupp's body was brought in by Sergeant Burkey. Back under cover, Campbell noticed with a start that Company D was gone. Rollison had already pulled back to the LZ as ordered, "but he had a hell of a lot more men and machine-gun teams than us," Campbell noted, "and we'd thought Company D was going to cover us as we worked our way back across the barren hillside to the tree line with our dead and wounded."

From beginning to end, Company D had barely been involved in the second assault on Hill 1000. Only a handful of troops under Lieutenant McCall—the man whom Campbell had seen ahead of everyone else, throwing frags—had come under direct fire. McCall had moved up front because he felt that the situation demanded some leadership by example, and he had not stopped until reaching an open area, across which was an RPD emplacement as implacable as the one raising hell with Charlie Company. "Captain Rollison told us to hold in place," recounted McCall. "He was discouraging any acts of glory that would get more people killed, so we ended up taking some defensive positions, and more or less getting pinned down. I think at that point Rollison felt that Charlie Company was making substantial progress and that they would shortly take some of the pressure off of us, which would allow us to continue to advance."

Rollison never resumed the attack, however. Bruce McCorkle would recall "a prolonged shoot-out between our machine gunners and theirs," but no maneuvering: "Most of us were back down the hill among the trees and boulders. We didn't move forward and weren't asked to. The second day was nothing like the first."

How much of an effort Captain Rollison should have made to push Company D up his side of Hill 1000 after Company C secured the western knoll remains an unanswerable question. "Rollison wasn't going to do anything stupid," said McCall. "If we'd had a reasonable chance of success, we'd have taken it, but Rollison wasn't about to send my guys across that open area where we were stalled. We weren't going to get people killed and left out in the open again. We had learned our lesson the day before. We knew we couldn't destroy those bunkers and tunnels with what we had."

It was Campbell's impression that Rollison had felt himself going up against impossible odds and had deliberately held back so as not to get his company chewed up again. Campbell could sympathize. "Hell, man, if Rollison had told Wilcox when we were starting out that, hey, we're gonna lay down on this one, we'd have had Charlie Company laid down in that tree line, too," Campbell said. "It didn't make a shit to me. I wasn't that gung-ho. All we'd have had to do was fire off some ammo, throw some grenades, and report that we were pinned down. The colonel wouldn't have known the difference. That's what Delta Company was doing."

The problem, according to Campbell, was not that Rollison held back to save his own men but that he let Company C proceed up the hill unaware that it could expect no support from a bloodied and discouraged Company D. "He didn't tell us because he would have had to get on the radio to do so, and then Lucas would have known he was being bullshitted," Campbell wrote. "The goddamn mission that morning was to attack the hill in a coordinated two-company assault," he continued, noting that a single company had no chance of securing the objective. "I didn't like the mission any more than the next guy, but Charlie Company made every effort to carry out its orders. Men died in vain because Charlie Company went forward while Delta Company remained for the most part in the tree line with no intent to maneuver and carry out its part of the attack. I'm not on a vendetta for Rollison," Campbell concluded.

"He was a great soldier and a great combat commander. He was everything people said he was, but he wasn't that day. . . ."

It is possible that Rollison, still suffering the effects of the satchel charge that had blown up in his face the day before, simply wasn't in shape for the second assault on Hill 1000. Rollison would deny such an explanation, writing that although "in considerable pain and bleeding periodically from the nose and ears, I do not think my judgment was impaired." In Rollison's version of events—refuted in every particular by Campbell—the inexperienced Wilcox failed to heed Rollison's warning about the location of the RPD and thus got Company C pinned down in an exposed position from which it could not adequately support Company D's attack with covering fire. Rollison would also speak about a loss of communication between him and Wilcox that contributed to his reluctance to press on, the concern being that without proper coordination Company C might accidentally inflict casualties on Company D. For his part, Wilcox did not at the time feel himself abandoned by Rollison. "I had great respect for Rollison's abilities and looked up to him," he would write. "I had always assumed that Company D was just stuck like we were in an untenable position. Jim Campbell contends that we would never have been given the order to cross the open saddle if Company D had maintained its assault. I'm not so sure Rollison would have actually accomplished anything by continuing forward. Charging up a hill into machine-gun fire would have been as costly for Company D as our assault across the saddle. Given what had happened the day before, it seems reasonable to me that, without anyone being explicit about it, everyone in Company D would be instinctively reluctant to get back into the same fix. In retrospect, I'm not surprised that things worked out the way they did. . . ."

Captain Wilcox, concerned that they would collide with the enemy force maneuvering toward them if the company went straight back down the hill, instead directed his men to traverse the slope at an oblique angle from west to east, making sure to stay below line of sight from the crest at all times to avoid the continuing fire from the eastern knoll. More smoke was popped to shield the move. It was as tough going down as it had been coming up because of the loose soil and suffocating heat. Wilcox was at one point standing above everyone else on the hillside, shouting directions, when he realized that his head was exposed. With the cold feeling that he was about to go lights-out—he could almost picture the RPD gunner lining up his skull in his sights—he immediately ducked down.

Lieutenant Campbell remained on the knoll, alone, to return fire and pitch smoke grenades, for which he was later awarded the Bronze Star. When the withdrawing troopers got beyond range of his throwing arm, he clambered to a new position between the enemy and the rest of the company to keep them covered with more smoke.

The enemy fire petered out when the company reached the trees, at which point Wilcox cranked up the artillery. As the company regrouped, Sergeant Burkey—to win his third Bronze Star—went back up to help Campbell get off the hill. They linked up in a bomb crater. "What the fuck are you doing here?" Campbell blurted.

"Hell, L. T., I wasn't going to leave you on the hill by yourself."

Campbell and Burkey crawled down the hill to rejoin the rest of the company in the tree line as U. S. shrapnel whizzed overhead from the artillery barrage impacting atop Hill 1000.

Plans were quickly made. Wilcox would take the trail back to the landing zone with the wounded and the main body of the company, with security deployed on the flanks, while Campbell and Burkey and a small detachment brought up the rear, carrying the KIAs. Campbell hefted Scott's body over his shoulder. Burkey was too worn out to do more than drag the stocky, heavyset Hupp along by his wrists. The rear detachment quickly lost sight of the others. "We couldn't keep up. We were really dragging ass," said Campbell. Rollison's people had been back at the landing zone for almost an hour by then. "I was pissed," noted Campbell, "that no one in the chain of command had thought to send an element from Delta Company to secure the trail and help us carry our dead back to the LZ."

Sergeant Burkey was in a state of temporary insanity by the

time they reached the overnight position. He was angry that they'd lost two men for nothing, angry at the sight of the Company D grunts sitting around looking rested, smoking cigarettes, and eating Cs. Burkey stormed up to one kid in a foxhole and, brandishing his M16, shrieked, "You motherfucker, get over there and carry that goddamn body. I need some fucking help." The kid scrambled to action, as did several other nearby grunts. "I probably would have blown the sonofabitch away if he hadn't gotten out of that hole," Burkey recounted. "I was so fucking exhausted, it didn't connect in my head that he was on security. He was doing what he was supposed to do. I was the one who was wrong. Good thing I didn't shoot the bastard because it turned out I had four inches of mud in my barrel from stumbling and falling on my way down the hill. If I'd have pulled the trigger, we both would have been in trouble."

On his last legs, Campbell went down hard upon reaching the overnight position below the landing zone; he dropped the body of Rickey Scott in a heap. Someone handed Campbell a collapsible two-quart canteen, from which he greedily drank before lying down and lighting a cigarette. His exhausted reverie was suddenly interrupted by a trooper who ran up to him to announce, "The colonel wants to see you up on the LZ right now."

Campbell could not have gotten to his feet if he wanted to. "Go fuck yourself," he mumbled. "I'm not going anywhere."

Lieutenant McCall knelt beside Campbell to check on his friend. "What the hell happened to you all?" Campbell asked.

"I did the best I could to get up that hill."

"Was that you out there in front of everybody?"

"Yeah," McCall said, getting up to rejoin his platoon.

Having been requested ahead of time, a medevac clattered in when Campbell and Burkey reached the perimeter (the time was 2:15 P.M.) and took aboard four WIAs—three from Company C and a lone wounded man from Company D who had been peppered in the face by U. S. shrapnel during the prep of Hill 1000.

There was a fifth casualty, Steve Riley, who walked over to where Campbell was lying after the medevac departed. "They done shot me in the arm," the slow-talking country boy drawled, holding up his arm to show Campbell the rag he'd wrapped around the wound. "The colonel told me to get on the medevac, but I told 'im I wasn't goin' nowhere till I talked to L. T. I think I can still fight, L. T."

"You're the dumbest fucker I know," Campbell barked. "Get the fuck out of here." Riley trudged back up to the landing zone like a whipped dog, not understanding the concern behind the harsh words. He went out aboard a resupply ship that landed a few minutes later. Riley was one of Campbell's best, a high-spirited soldier willing to do anything asked of him, and Campbell would regret for many years that he had spoken so harshly to the young man the last time he would ever see him in Vietnam.

Lieutenant Colonel Lucas had alighted from his command ship almost as soon as Wilcox reached the landing zone, some fifteen minutes ahead of Campbell. The colonel strode briskly over to Wilcox and Rollison and, without preamble, barked out in a voice of confident bravado, "Okay, men, when can you be ready to go back up?"

The question completely broadsided Wilcox. "Back up?" he blurted. "Sir, we'd be crazy to go back up in the condition we're in."

McCall joined the huddle at Rollison's side. It was Wilcox, however—still in a fever pitch from the battle and offended that Lucas had not even bothered to consult his company commanders before ordering another attack—who did most of the talking. Another assault, he said, would be futile and would result in needless casualties. He advised Lucas that he had only twenty-two men left in his company, not counting him and Campbell, and they were exhausted and dehydrated. He heatedly suggested that his troops be allowed to rest for the night and the hill be subjected to another round of prep fires, particularly tac air, before they went back up.

Lucas was having none of it. Frustrated that the colonel seemed unwilling to accept the realities of the situation, such was his desire, as Wilcox saw it, to look aggressive to his superiors, Wilcox angrily threw his helmet on the ground.

The colonel's order spread like wildfire. An acting squad leader in Charlie One, a spec four, ran over to Lieutenant Campbell. "That stupid goddamn colonel," he exclaimed. "They're talking about us reassaulting the hill right now."

"Aw, bullshit, you don't know what you're talking about."

"I'm not bullshittin'. The crazy bastards, we ain't gonna do it. You gotta get up there and take care of it, L. T."

Campbell could feel the tension in the air when he joined Wilcox, and was taken aback when Lucas informed him of his intention to mount another assault. "C'mon down here, colonel," Campbell said. "You want to see these men? They're dead on their feet. Give us a chance to rest, and we'll do it tomorrow."

Wilcox nodded. "We'll get these men rested, colonel," he said. "We'll have a better chance of taking the hill if we do it tomorrow."

Lucas said he understood that they'd had a rough time of it but they had to keep the pressure on, that it was essential to the security of Ripcord that the enemy be pushed off Hill 1000. Turning from Campbell and Wilcox, Lucas asked Rollison for his input. Rollison replied that he fully understood the importance of taking the hill and quietly affirmed that he was ready to make another assault whenever the colonel gave the word. "It was the only thing Rollison said while I was at the meeting," commented Campbell, "and I think I made some sarcastic remark about whether that next assault was going to be like the one they made that morning. Lucas directed the conversation back to reassaulting the hill." Campbell was appalled that Lucas did not press Rollison for an explanation of why most of Company D had failed to leave the tree line. "Lucas was totally fooled about what had occurred even though he had been overhead and could see who had attacked the hill and who hadn't," wrote Campbell. "I suspect the problem was that Rollison was his favorite company commander. Lucas seemed unable to even distinguish the difference between the physical condition of Charlie Company and the physical condition of Delta Company."

In his rush to resume the attack, Lucas said nothing about bringing up reinforcements or working out a scheme of maneuver in which one company could call in Cobras without the other being on the gun target line. The objective was going to be secured only if both companies moved forward aggressively with close-in gunship support.

"Goddamnit," Campbell snapped in a tone that a lieutenant did not use with a battalion commander, "we've only got a few hours till dusk. It's going to take an hour and a half just to get resupplied and get back into position to attack from the tree line, and then what, are we just going to make the same assault from the same direction? It didn't work the first time with a twelve-hour arty prep and all those air strikes. What if we're still trying to fight our way up the side of the hill when the sun goes down? We'll never be able to get into a strong defensive position for the night and get our dead and wounded out. It's not worth the risk. We can take that damn hill tomorrow morning."

"Lieutenant Campbell, you're getting out of line here," Black Spade snapped with restrained anger. "You go back with your men on the perimeter, you sit down—and you cool off."

Wilcox grabbed Campbell by the arm and walked him part of the way back down the hill from the landing zone. "Jim, don't worry about it," Wilcox reassured Campbell. "I'll take care of this."

Seeing Campbell, the squad leader from Charlie One who had first alerted him to the problem rushed over to ask if the assault order had been rescinded. Campbell said that it had not, and the kid exploded: "We ain't goin' up that goddamn hill again today."

Campbell wheeled on the man. "Let me tell you something, you motherfucker. If I tell you to go up that goddamn hill again, you're going up that goddamn hill, you understand? What are you gonna do, let me and the captain and Sergeant Burkey go by ourselves?"

"Hell, L. T., we wouldn't do that, we wouldn't let that happen," the squad leader said, abashed. "If you say to go, we'll go, but we ain't going just 'cause that stupid fuckin' colonel says to go."

While Campbell had been on the LZ arguing with Black Spade, the acting squad leader and several like-minded troops had been rushing from man to man, trying to organize a full-scale combat refusal in Charlie Company. They were mostly ignored by their buddies, and it is unlikely the dissidents themselves would have refused a direct order to attack. "They were talking hard, but it was all bullshit," said Campbell. Sergeant Burkey agreed. "Going back up was fuckin' crazy. It didn't make sense. We didn't have anything left in us, and the guys were grumbling, but there's no question that push come to shove every one of us would have gone back up there and done what we had to do."

Push did not come to shove. Wilcox did not let it. "I don't think that hill's worth another soldier dying," he finally said to Lucas. "In fact, I don't think this whole war is worth another soldier dying." After some further comments about the utter waste and futility of the war, Wilcox went on to state that he could not in good conscience launch the second assault the colonel wanted. Wilcox would not later be able to recall the wording of his refusal; nor would Rollison and McCall, who were stunned. Sergeant Bort had been called into the huddle at that time, Lucas wanting to question the squad leader about the RPD emplacement he had seen. According to Bort, what Wilcox said was, "Sir, if you want to send me back up there, fine, I'll go alone, but I will not ask my men to go back up there. They are simply in no shape for another assault."

Bort was impressed. "The captain stood up for us," as he would later say. "He saved our lives. I thought he was one hell of a guy."

Black Spade was disappointed. "Captain," he said, dismissing Wilcox, "why don't you go over there and wait by my helicopter."

The meeting continued. Lucas again sought Rollison's counsel, and Rollison again emphasized that he was ready to launch another attack up Hill 1000 if the colonel so desired. Rollison added, however, that like Wilcox he thought it unwise to proceed that afternoon. "Sir, let's keep the artillery going all night long and just hammer the hell out of that damn place," he said. "We'll move up under the artillery as far as we can at first light and go from there."

McCall was surprised when Lucas next turned to him, a young lieutenant not normally consulted by colonels, and said, "What do you think?"

"I'm Captain Rollison's platoon leader," replied McCall, "and if you want us to go back up there, we will—but I'm not sure we can take that hill, to tell you the truth, sir. They're dug in deep. Instead of taking more casualties, I think we ought to neutralize the hill with arty and tac air. We should turn it over to the Air Force, and just bomb the shit out of it every day. If we can get the fire support we need to reduce Hill One Thousand down to Hill Nine-ninety-seven, that should take care of it."

It seemed to McCall that Captain Rollison, with a reputation that did not allow him to offer such advice, was visibly relieved that his platoon leader had, in fact, suggested they back off and call in the F-4s. "We didn't want to go back up any more than Wilcox," said McCall. "I think if we'd made a third attack, we probably would have shook hands good-bye. It was that bleak up there."

Lucas said he would think the situation over and get back to them momentarily. The meeting broke up. Wilcox had felt himself backed into his dramatic outburst. Rollison and McCall basically agreed with the points Wilcox had been making but were taken aback by the manner in which he had addressed Black Spade, a commander for whom they both had enormous respect. They also found Wilcox's veering into politics disconcerting. "The fact that Wilcox denounced the whole war indicated that he was suffering from fatigue and was distraught over his losses," stated McCall. "Any company commander watching his dead and wounded being loaded onto helicopters is going to get emotional, but it wasn't the time to philosophize about the war and debate whether or not we should be there. We had to neutralize that position, and we had to accept that like it or not we were going to lose some people. If Wilcox had confined his remarks to the tactical situation, he would have had much better results with Lucas."

Lucas had walked off from everyone else and sat down on a log. Rollison noticed that something was wrong with the colonel and, thinking he might have been injured somehow, walked over to him. "I felt a little uncomfortable, like I wasn't supposed to be there, and I looked at him, and I finally sat down next to him, and he was crying," remembered Rollison. "He had tears coming down his face. He was hurtin'." Rollison told Lucas that if he decided on another attack, the colonel could count on him. Lucas looked up at him and said, no, they weren't going to lose any more people but were going to instead attempt to reduce the enemy positions with firepower. "Lucas hadn't asked for that sonofabitch of an objective," said Rollison, "and that's why I didn't fight him. I knew that what he had to do as a battalion commander was unpopular. He was my boss and there was a job that had to be done, but he was incredibly compassionate. He had a tough veneer, and he had to have it, but he cared about every single man there. There was never any doubt in my mind about that."

CHAPTER 15

Guillotine

Captain Wilcox reckoned that he had gotten through to Lucas when informed that there was to be no second assault that afternoon. The colonel departed then, leaving Rollison to direct the air strikes while the two companies established a joint overnight position.

Three or four grunts approached Campbell. "L. T., we ain't gonna NDP with these chickenshit bastards," they grumbled. "They laid down on us up there. We'd be better off by ourselves."

"Nah, we need numbers here, fellas," Campbell replied.

As the air strikes continued, Wilcox sat against his rucksack, which was pushed up against a tree, boiling water for coffee in a pear can balanced atop another can in which he had lit a heat tab. The pear can shifted. Wilcox lunged forward to keep it from spilling—and when he did, a three-inch-wide, six-inch-long piece of made-in-the-USA bomb shrapnel slammed into his rucksack where his chest had been. Wilcox picked up the hot, jaggedy chunk of metal, wondering about the randomness of modern war.

Wilcox knew that Lucas considered him insubordinate, but he hoped the colonel did not equate his willingness to speak his mind with disloyalty. According to Colonel Harrison, Lucas had come to a much harsher conclusion about Wilcox. Harrison had landed to speak with Lucas shortly before the battalion commander flew back to Ripcord. "Lucas told me that

Wilcox had refused to move back into the attack up the hill," Harrison later wrote. "Lucas also told me that he had talked with Wilcox in private, and that Wilcox said he wanted to do the right thing, but he just couldn't make himself go back up that hill. There didn't seem to be any doubt in Lucas's mind that Wilcox was just plain scared shitless. It happens."

Lucas remarked in frustration that Wilcox was an academy grad. "He told me that he was really upset that a fellow West Pointer was a coward," Harrison's account continued. The brigade commander wanted to court-martial Wilcox. Lucas suggested instead that Wilcox be quietly moved to the brigade staff. "I don't want to make a big deal out of this with a court-martial. The quieter we can keep this the better," Harrison quoted Lucas as saying.

"Lucas wanted the situation handled carefully," Harrison wrote. "He did not want to relieve Wilcox right there where it would be obvious to everyone present that he was being fired because he would not lead his company back into the attack. Lucas thought it would be very bad for morale in the battalion if word got out that a company commander had caved in and had to be replaced under such circumstances. I agreed. Lucas said that he would make sure that Wilcox's career was over in his efficiency report. I left how and when Wilcox was to be moved to brigade rear as something to be worked out by Lucas, a seasoned leader with good sense."

Lieutenant Flaherty hitched a ride from Camp Evans to Ripcord aboard a log bird late that afternoon, but he missed the last slick taking ammo and water out to Company D. Lucas offered him a spare cot in his conex. When the colonel came in late that night to grab some sack time, Flaherty started to engage him in small talk. "Lieutenant Flaherty, please don't, please don't," Lucas snapped with an intensity that startled Flaherty. "I really don't want to know you any better than I do right now because I don't want to feel any worse than I already will if your name turns up on the casualty list."

It came as a shock to Wilcox and Campbell, who had spent the night turning over in their minds how to best proceed with the next day's assault, to be instructed in the morning to march back to Ripcord. At the firebase, Lucas informed them that fifteen replacements had been brought forward for their company. Each cherry—they stood out in their clean fatigues and bright, new web gear—was paired off with a veteran as the company humped down the firebase ridgeline in the direction of Hill 805. "Battalion called that evening to confirm that we had thirty-seven troops," recalled Wilcox. "We said, no, thirty-six, and they eventually figured out that the missing man was a new guy who got off the helicopter at the firebase, took one look around, and just got right back on the Chinook."

Company C dug in at the end of the ridge, opposite Hill 805. It was a long night, the mountain wind conjuring up visions of approaching sappers as it whipped noisily through the trees. If the veterans were uptight, the cherries were completely freaked out, and the grenades they began lobbing into the darkness served only to heighten the hysteria. Wilcox requested illum from Ripcord. "It was like keeping a night light on," he said. When a frag exploded inside the lines, Wilcox, concerned that maybe something really was out there, had the 81s start firing HE. It was finally determined that the explosion had been a grenade that hit a tree and bounced back at the cherry who'd thrown it. Wilcox wasn't about to get up and start walking the lines in such a trigger-happy situation. Instead, he called out to the troops from his CP in the center of the perimeter and "told the company to just settle the fuck down," he remembered. "I said we were going to continue firing illumination, and promised that if the enemy was moving towards us, we'd know. The guys started to get ahold of themselves at that point."

Lucas had Company C helicoptered to Firebase O'Reilly the next day to replace Company A. Lucas and the battalion executive officer flew out eight days later and spent the night with Wilcox in his CP. Lucas said nothing about their previous confrontation, and Wilcox thought it likely that the colonel grudgingly respected him for the stand he had made at Hill 1000. Lucas did bring up the subject of politics, and Wilcox, taking the dialogue to be a good-natured exchange between colleagues, expounded on his disgust with the war. The whole thing was pointless, he opined. If democracy, the thing they were supposedly fighting for, were to suddenly descend upon Vietnam, the other side would win the election.

At one point during the conversation, the exec informed Lucas that he had recommended him for a Silver Star. Lucas was puzzled and questioned the exec, who reminded the colonel about his having flown through heavy fire to spot targets and deliver a resupply of grenades to Delta Company during the first attack up Hill 1000. Wilcox was impressed that Lucas, whom he had pegged as the ultimate careerist, seemed to shrug the whole thing off as nothing more than what was expected of a professional soldier.

Wilcox was not especially impressed with the exec. "Nobody liked the major," he recalled. "He was an embittered fellow. Here was this guy with a lot of years in who wasn't going anywhere, surrounded by other officers who were on the fast track." The exec apparently hoped to salvage something for his troubles. After mentioning that he had started the paperwork to get Lucas a valor award, recalled Wilcox, "the major more or less suggested that since he had been so alert to making sure the colonel got the badges he needed for his career, some reciprocity might be in order."

Wilcox, struck by the unseemliness of the major's grasping, blurted, "I don't believe you're saying this in front of me."

When Wilcox saw Lucas off the next morning, he thought the colonel had decided to let bygones be bygones and move on anew. He was mistaken. Lucas flew back in the next day with Capt. Kenneth R. Lamb, the battalion personnel officer. Wilcox, greeting them on the helipad, was summarily informed by Lucas that he was relieved and that Lamb was, as of that moment, the new commander of Company C. Wilcox felt as though he had been slapped. He asked why he was being relieved. Expecting to be blasted for insubordination, he was surprised when Lucas instead said, "I feel that the men have lost confidence in you."

"Bullshit," Wilcox said. "I think you should ask the men." Lucas did not respond. "Do you mean I'm being relieved right now?" Wilcox asked.

"Right now, captain. Get on the helicopter."

Wilcox, throwing his rucksack aboard, was the lone passenger on the command ship, Lucas having stayed on O'Reilly with Lamb.

Emotion washed over Wilcox during the flight. He was angry at the colonel and oddly embarrassed, but mostly he felt disloyal for disappearing on Jim Campbell and Paul Burkey. He had not been able to thank them for what they had done. He had not been able to explain the situation with Lucas. He had not even been able to say good-bye. Quit fighting it, Wilcox finally thought as the helicopter neared Camp Evans. You're powerless here. It's done. Let it go. What the hell, at least I know I'm not going to die in Vietnam.

Wilcox sent an audiotape to his wife, noting that although he thought Lucas had made a wrongheaded decision, he harbored no animosity about being relieved of duty. He followed the tape with a letter after ending up in the brigade TOC: "Inside I guess I feel really shitty about being taken away from my company. Life is so much more worthwhile when you are helping a bunch of innocent kids live—instead of pushing pencils and playing with big wall-sized maps."

The animosity would come years later when Wilcox learned that Lucas had in his conversation with the brigade commander charged him not only with refusing an order but with confessing to being frozen with fear. Wilcox vehemently denies that he told Lucas any such thing and tends to view the accusation of cowardice as an attempt to scapegoat him for the failure of the attack. "Lucas had a right to relieve me," Wilcox would write. "He had no right to defame me to justify to his superiors why his battalion had not taken Hill 1000."

The incident defies resolution. It is difficult to imagine that Lucas would concoct so vicious a lie about one of his officers. It is equally difficult to imagine that Wilcox, who had led his company with great personal courage during the attack, had broken at the thought of facing those bunkers again. Neither possibility is inconceivable, however. Nor is it inconceivable that Lucas had decided to give Wilcox another look after tempers had cooled—whether Wilcox had suffered a momentary lapse of courage or had merely been insubordinate, his behavior was not unforgivable given the stress of combat—and for that reason visited him on Firebase O'Reilly. Perhaps their conversation that night tipped the scales against Wilcox. There is a theory, to which Lucas probably subscribed, that an officer who doesn't believe in the cause won't take risks, and an officer who won't take risks can't beat a determined enemy.

"Lucas agonized over whether or not to relieve Wilcox," according to Chaplain Fox. "That was a very difficult decision for him. He talked to me a great deal about it." Rollison thought the relief entirely justified, suggesting that "it was a self-fulfilling prophecy. Wilcox was in the wrong place, physically and philosophically."

Campbell thinks that Lucas did, in fact, misrepresent to Harrison what Wilcox said to him on the LZ. "To suggest that Wilcox was a coward is an act of greater injustice than the act of his relief from command," Campbell wrote. "I do not believe that Lucas actually believed Wilcox to be a coward. I do not believe that Lucas would have left Wilcox in command of a combat line company in that environment for one minute, much less eleven more days, if he truly believed him to be a coward. I have no problem with Lucas relieving Wilcox for insubordination," Campbell continued. "That is a commander's prerogative. I have a big problem, however, with branding a man a coward because he is insubordinate, you don't like him, or you think his views on the war are soft, especially when he had been fighting his ass off all day for you."

When Campbell attempted to engage the colonel in a discussion about Wilcox's relief, Lucas curtly dismissed him. Campbell thought it was Lucas and himself, not a new company commander such as Wilcox, who had something to answer for. "I hated Lucas for years for what he ordered us to do that day on Hill 1000," he said. "I also spent years trying to blame Lucas for what happened, but, really, I was accountable, too. His order to assault across an open saddle in the face of direct fire without close-in gunship support was absolutely stupid—and I was stupid enough to order it carried out. I knew better. I knew that Lucas didn't know what was happening on the ground because he had never spent a single day in the field with his troops. I didn't have the moral courage to refuse the order, though. The result was that Hupp and Scott went to their deaths trying to carry out an attack that I knew didn't have a chance in hell of succeeding. It was a needless sacrifice of brave men."

Campbell thought Lucas the most able of the three battalion commanders he served under in Vietnam. "Lucas and Koenigsbauer ran superb combat assaults," he stated, "but their refusal to get on the ground with the troops at crunch time was a real problem." It made no sense to Campbell that Lucas, with the entire maneuver force of his battalion going up Hill 1000, did not direct the attack from the ground, leaving his S3 people and arty LNO to organize the fire support from the command ship. "Hell, Major Koenigsbauer and Charlie Lieb, the S3 Air, had their shit together and could have easily handled the fire support." Campbell was convinced that Lucas, had he been on the ground, would not have ordered the disastrous assault across the saddle. "Lucas might also have been able to spur Delta Company into action," Campbell said, "in which case we might have taken the hill." Campbell did not doubt Lucas's courage, "but he never understood that you can't lead men from a helicopter. None of my battalion commanders did.

"The helicopter was the worst thing that ever happened to leadership," Campbell added. "The troops didn't hate the gooks. They hated the commanders flying around in their charlie-charlie birds giving orders without a clue as to what it was like on the ground. You need to be on the ground. You can't lead men in combat and expect them to have loyalty towards you if they never see you. That's why there was so much bitterness about Lucas among the troops. He was never there with a word of encouragement or a pat on the back, and he definitely wasn't where he needed to be when we went up Hill 1000."

Campbell's own bitterness boiling over, he wrote a letter in longhand at O'Reilly and gave it to someone flying to Ripcord to deliver to Lucas. The letter set forth Campbell's frustration with what had occurred at Hill 1000 and requested that Lucas either deliver as promised on a rear job or, alternatively, have him reassigned to another battalion. "I honestly don't know whether I was fit to command troops at that time, even under another commander," Campbell would reflect. "I wasn't the same person after Hill 1000. I had lost confidence in myself and I think I had lost the confidence of my platoon because of that insane order to assault across the saddle. I knew that I did not want to die or order my men to die for Lucas, who at that point I had absolutely no respect for, and who I did not then, and do not now, believe gave the slightest shit about me or my men. I told Lucas that I didn't want to serve under him anymore, that I couldn't carry out his orders anymore. I'd had it. Relieve me, reassign me, do whatever. I wasn't going to do it another minute for Andre Lucas."

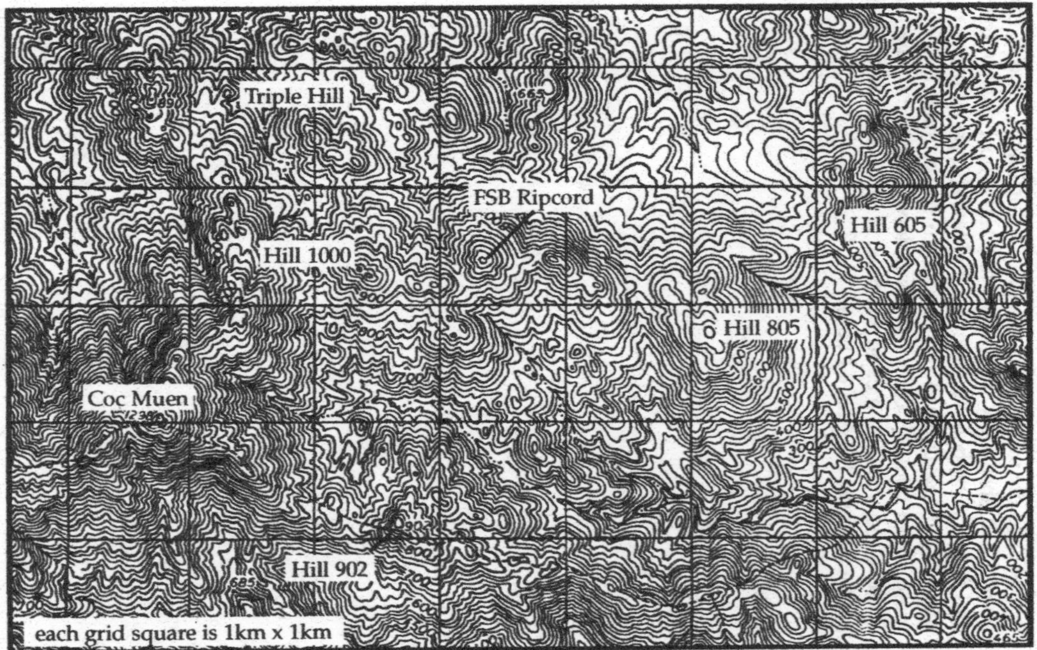
Triple Hill
FSB Ripcord
Hill 605
Hill 1000
Hill 805
Coc Muen
Hill 902
each grid square is 1km x 1km

PART FIVE

Maximum Pressure

Often times a special degree of valor is required to get yourself out of a situation that you wouldn't have been in in the first place if not for command stupidity.

—Capt. Christopher C. Straub
Company D, 2d Battalion, 501st Infantry
101st Airborne Division

CHAPTER 16

Into the Fray

Chuck Hawkins was a true believer—in his country, the war, and, especially, the U. S. Army. He also believed in himself. His self-assurance was honestly earned. Hawkins had grown up on a homestead in Alaska, ten miles by way of a dirt highway from the nearest town, Ninilchik, a little hamlet by Cook Inlet. His parents, both college graduates, were schoolteachers in town, but they liked the adventure of life in the wilderness and had themselves built the log cabin that was the family home. Hawkins and his brother learned at an early age how to fish, hunt, track game, and navigate the woods at night by the stars. After high school, Hawkins, wanting to do his duty and go to college for free—money became particularly scarce after his parents divorced when he was eleven—applied for and was accepted into West Point Class of '68.

Hawkins found his calling as an infantry officer and was fervent in his desire to go to Vietnam. Like many of his generation, he wanted to be the man his father had been in the big war, and his father had been a lot, a highly decorated platoon leader and a company commander with the elite 10th Mountain Division.

Lieutenant Hawkins took over the 2d Platoon, C/2-506th, in early March 1970. "I want to fight," he wrote home. "God help me but I want it so bad I would sell my birthright." Rugged in appearance, Hawkins was cocksure in attitude—"he was a strong-willed guy, very independent," said a fellow platoon leader—and he came on too strong for most of his draftee grunts. "My God, was that man gung-ho," said one. "He didn't fit in. He wanted to make a name for himself and we figured it was going to be at our expense."

Paul Burkey served as Hawkins's platoon sergeant. "West Pointers scared guys, and Hawkins had a definite gleam in his eye," said Burkey. "He wasn't just aggressive, though, he was smart, too. He had his shit together. I would have followed him anywhere."

Equally impressed, Lucas pinned captain's bars on Hawkins a week before his actual promotion date and placed him in command of A/2-506th as of May 30, 1970. Hawkins's predecessor had become gun-shy, and the company, though full of good people, lacked esprit. Lucas expected Hawkins to turn them around. This he did. Major Davis would write in Hawkins's efficiency report that "Hawkins was given command of the weakest company in the battalion and in two weeks time it was equal to the best."

It was a matter of leading from the front. Four days after taking command, Hawkins was accompanying a two-platoon move up the hill between Ripcord and Hill 1000. The point man spotted NVA on the trail he was following, got off a shot, then fell back when he realized his slack man had deserted him. The lead platoon leader, Lieutenant Widjeskog of Alpha Two, called in arty, then instructed the point and slack man to head back down the trail. They refused. Private First Class Wieland C. Norris volunteered to take point instead, and someone else stepped forward to walk his slack.

Widjeskog would always regret letting Norris take point. "Norris was new and could not be expected to react properly," the platoon leader later wrote. When Norris heard something, he did not instantly open fire like a veteran but glanced to the slack man for guidance. The enemy had set up an ambush, and Norris was shot through the heart as he turned; the slack man was shot through the shoulder. The platoon pulled back. "We again called in artillery, followed by gunships," Widjeskog wrote. "Things were happening fast and there was much confusion. The gunships managed to fire rockets close enough to hit one of my men with shrapnel. . . ."

Captain Hawkins had instructed Widjeskog to assault the hill but upon rushing forward found the grunts hunkered behind logs and trees. There was no firing from either side. "No one wanted to go up the hill for the third time," Hawkins wrote home, "so I grabbed one young fellow, put a grenade in his hand, and told him we were going to start crawling up the hill. I moved people to one flank and had them open fire, then I moved up to the kid with the grenade. The next man to join us was a wounded machine gunner, and I guess he made the others feel ashamed, because pretty soon I had two squads firing and maneuvering toward the enemy. By this time the NVA figured out that there were a few more of us than they could handle and were long gone. We secured the hill . . ."

Lieutenant Noll, the most experienced platoon leader in the company, had monitored the action over the company frequency and was impressed with Hawkins. Noll thought it important to let everyone know that. The new CO's reputation had preceded him, and the troops were apprehensive about serving under The Hawk. With that in mind, Noll got Hawkins on the horn and, using the phonetics for CO, said, "Good job today, Charlie Oscar."

"That was all he said, but it was enough," noted Hawkins. "Every RTO in the company heard the transmission and the word would spread. Before that moment I had been the company commander in name only, but now I was the company commander in fact."

Hawkins spent the night "giving a wounded man cigarettes and water and listening to him moan," his letter continued. "Five feet in the other direction our KIA 'slept' without a stir. . . . Norris had a wife and kid. A wife and kid. And he died doing a dirty, stinking job because no one had sense enough to do it right . . ."[1]

The situation remained grim. On Hawkins's eighth day in command, the enemy hit his NDP at dusk with AK-47s and RPGs. The platoon on that side of the perimeter, Alpha One, "reacted well," Hawkins wrote, "and using . . . fire and maneuver . . . drove the enemy off. Another man wounded, another man killed. . . ."

Following the big battalion stand-down, Lucas, wanting to give Hawkins some space to put his stamp on the outfit, sent Company A to Firebase O'Reilly. "I love every one of [my soldiers] and I don't want them to die any more," wrote Hawkins, who was twenty-three years old and suffering from migraine headaches. "So I push and I drive them . . . I will not lose more men. And when I leave this fire base I will have a company of killers who know how to survive."

Hawkins, meanwhile, chafed at sitting on a mountaintop in what seemed like the backwaters of the war as other units slashed into Cambodia. "This daring operation," he wrote, energized, ". . . has the flavor of victory. And a victory will bring us home. We will not win this war, the free peoples of Southeast Asia will win it[,] but we shall have laid the ground work for success. The Vietnamization concept will now have a chance to move ahead at a faster and more efficient rate. The South Vietnamese are capable soldiers. I am quite pleased with Cambodia and quite upset with student unrest at home. None of us here can understand it."

To Hawkins the anguish over Kent State seemed an insult to forgotten soldiers facing unheralded deaths in Vietnam. "[B]y not supporting us," he wrote in one angry letter from O'Reilly, the protesters were "aiding the enemy. I'm sick all right but let me tell you how I feel. There aren't enough grenades and bullets in my rucksack to kill the Gooks I'd like to see dead in a day. Nixon is OK. I've got men in my company who would extend to stay in the Army and in V. Nam if we were to make a thrust into Laos, Cambodia or North Vietnam. Can you imagine a beach landing in the Haiphong harbor or an airborne assault into the farm fields near Hanoi[?] I'd extend to take a company on something like that. As much as I love my wife and all you folks at home, I'd still extend . . ."

When Hawkins's old outfit, Charlie Company, was overrun the first night of the battle, the new commander of Alpha Company wrote his wife that it made him ill as he helplessly listened to the action over the radio. "I wish the NVA would hit O'Reilly," he continued, furious. "It would give me a great deal of animal pleasure to watch them die; tangled ribbons of flesh in the wire."

Hawkins was not displeased when Lucas instructed him to prepare for a combat assault onto the rocky hill immediately east of Ripcord. The LZ was to be secured by Company C, which would then depart on the lift ships to assume control of Firebase O'Reilly.

After Hawkins and Company A had progressed to the end of the ridgeline, Lucas explained, the battalion's extra rifle company, D/2-501st, under Captain Straub, a highly regarded infantry officer on his second combat tour, would be CA'd into the area, and together the two companies were to assault and seize Hill 805.

Hawkins's objective was the LZ on the western slope where Company B had landed on the first day of the battle; Straub's objective was the crown of Hill 805. Though the strategic hill mass had been hit with tear gas and subjected to numerous air strikes since Company B had marched off, it could be assumed that the enemy had reoccupied it. "We're as ready as we'll ever be," Hawkins wrote home.

Hawkins got a new artillery forward observer before the assault, 2d Lt. Steven A. Olson, to replace 1st Lt. Thomas J. Brennan, USMA '69, who had been reassigned to the 105 battery on Ripcord.

In the line platoons, Hawkins placed most of his confidence in Lieutenant Noll of Alpha Three. Jim Noll, age twenty-four, from Wabasha, Minnesota, drafted after his first year as a high-school teacher and sent to OCS, was calm, steady, "extremely savvy," noted Hawkins, "and not shy about sticking his face in a firefight."

Lee Widjeskog of Alpha Two, though green—he had joined the company after the first battle for Ripcord, commissioned by way of ROTC—was a smart, low-key individual with a lot of potential.

The situation was the same in Alpha One. The platoon leader, 1st Lt. William A. Pahissa, USMA '69, and the platoon sergeant, SSgt. Gerald B. Singleton, had just joined the company on O'Reilly, but both were sharp and highly motivated.

"Bill Pahissa impressed me immediately," recalled Hawkins of the tall, athletic Mexican American from Tucson, Arizona. One of Pahissa's best friends at the academy, Tom Brennan, had sent Pahissa a number of exciting letters about life in the Currahees. When Brennan informed him that Jeff Wilcox was to be promoted out of Alpha One, "Pahissa pulled whatever strings necessary to get to Vietnam ASAP," noted Hawkins. "On his assignment preference sheet he was very specific—he wanted to be assigned to 1st Platoon, Company A, 2-506th Infantry, 101st Airborne Division. He got his wish."

The assault was scheduled for July 10. "I am looking forward to it in a way," Hawkins wrote his wife. "It's funny, but I still find myself proving me to myself. Major Davis says to be careful and the Bn. CO talks to me like a son. You know they are worried too. . . . There are four officers and 70 enlisted men trusting in me and looking to me for guidance. They must have confidence in me, they must do as I say if they expect to survive and I can't show any signs of weakness. None. That's the hard part . . ."

Hawkins wrote in a last letter home of "look[ing] away from my map and grease pens. The sky is clear. Clean fresh air ripples my hair and my mind is lost in days gone by. Lonely country music wafts up on the breeze from a nearby bunker . . . Right now is the slack period before the birds come. Preparation is complete and the nervous talk and fiddling with weapons begins. Cigarette smoke rises heaven ward along with our prayers. This operation more than any other has me worried. I am carrying additional hand grenades, a claymore and a few other devices CO's usually don't carry. There is some big stuff out there. . . ."

Major Koenigsbauer had helped plan the assualt, but was no longer part of the battalion when it was launched, having been reassigned to division staff the day before, his six months with a line unit complete. Bill Williams took over as S3. In preparation for the switch, Koenigsbauer went over the firebase security and defensive-fire plans in great detail with Williams. It nevertheless struck Koenigsbauer as ludicrous that an experienced operations officer who enjoyed an excellent working relationship with his battalion commander was to be abruptly replaced in the midst of a major battle. "It didn't make any sense, but those were the rules of the game," noted Koenigsbauer. "I volunteered to see the battle through, but Lucas insisted I report to division as ordered. When the Loach picked me up, we shook hands, and I wished him luck. I said something to the effect that I wished I were staying, but Lucas made a major effort to keep my morale up, telling me that I was not abandoning ship, that I had put my time in, and that he had a good replacement as operations officer. He was adamant that I leave, and, of course, I did, however reluctantly."

The lift ships bearing Captain Hawkins and Company A set down in their turn on the rocky hill east of Ripcord. Red smoke marked the landing zone as there were enemy soldiers on the south slope of the ridge firing on the Hueys as they departed with Charlie Company. Hawkins brought arty in on the snipers as his lead platoon slipped down the spine of the ridge to secure a good NDP. Captain Straub, meanwhile, was planning that same day for D/2-501st's CA into the area from its present position near FSB O'Reilly. Straub was joined by 1st Lt. James M. Potter, his forward observer, who had been absent the previous week due to a badly infected cut on his leg that would not heal in the jungle. The resupply ship that brought Potter in took aboard a rifleman whose tour was over. "Straub and I conducted an aerial reconnaissance of our objective and the selected landing zone," wrote Potter. The LZ was on a knoll a kilometer northwest of the objective, at the base of a ridge knifing up to the top of 805. "As we flew over the area we received ground fire," added Potter. "I still remember the unmistakable sound of bullets 'cracking' as they passed between the rotor blades of the helicopter."

Upon returning to the company position, Straub and Potter were informed that the log bird "had made a supply stop at Ripcord on the way to Camp Evans, taking .51-cal fire as it landed," noted Potter. "The soldier on board from our company was hit in the shoulder and lost his arm. He had made it through his entire tour only to be shot during the last hour of his last day in the field."

By noon of the next day, Company A, having continued down the ridge, reached the hillock at the end and, after Noll disarmed a booby trap on the landing zone, set up another NDP. While more tac air went in on the objective, D/2-501st humped to an LZ of its own to take a resupply of extra ammunition. "We were told at that time that we were going to the Ripcord AO," noted Sgt. Raymond H. "Blackie" Blackman of Delta Three. In addition to the ammo, the slicks brought out soda, watermelons, and a hot meal in mermite cans. "I remember thinking that it was a kind of last meal for us," wrote Blackman. "After eating, we split up into platoons and NDP'd in separate locations down different trails from the LZ. At first light, we met at the LZ and waited for the birds. We didn't talk much. We knew this wasn't going to be a typical mission."

Captain Straub and D/2-501st began lifting out as of 7:55 A.M. on July 12, 1970. Three firebases were shelling the objective at that time, and a barrage of smoke was delivered immediately before the first slick landed to screen the LZ. In short order, Company D was moving in column up the ridge pointing to the top of Hill 805. The pace was brisk despite the sweltering heat, the tension palpable. There was no noise except the rattle of equipment. "You could feel the gooks," wrote Blackman. "I walked rear security and never felt so alone in my life. We could hear them prepping 805 in the distance and the explosions were getting louder as we got closer."

Company A started into the saddle between its NDP and Hill 805. Hawkins led with Alpha Three. "We are going to get hit," Lieutenant Noll told his men before they moved out. "You've got to have your finger on the trigger and be ready to respond immediately," he intoned, concerned about the large number of replacements in the platoon, "because as soon as we take fire we're going to get on line and assault into the enemy. If we don't, they'll trap us in that little draw and we'll be sitting ducks."

Noll was so convinced they were going to run into trouble that as the column started down the trail, he fell in line directly behind the point team. At 10:15 A.M., the point man, upon cresting a small knoll in the saddle below 805, encountered an enemy trail watcher.

There was a quick AK burst, then silence. Christ, he's dead, Noll thought as he scrambled up to the point man. Finding him in one piece, Noll urgently asked, "What the hell's goin' on?"

"Some little gook up there shot at me."

"Why the hell didn't you shoot him?" Noll snapped, upset because the point man was one of his veterans.

"I didn't think. I was so scared, I just ducked."

Noll rushed back to his platoon, angry that the guys had taken cover instead of deploying for an assault as instructed, especially because a gun team was keeping the enemy engaged from the flank. "Get up," Noll barked. "Get up, and get the fuck up that hill."

Enemy fire began zipping past as Lieutenant Noll charged forward, radioman in tow. Identifying where the fire was coming from, Noll opened up with his M16. His magazine was loaded with nothing but tracers. The troops were supposed to fire en masse wherever the platoon leader put the tracers, but none did because none had followed Noll in the face of the AKs and RPGs.

Noll was on top of the hill before he realized that the only man with him was his radioman. An enemy soldier popped up from behind a log at that moment, a startled look on his face, and Noll spun, raised his M16, and squeezed the trigger before the man could bring up his AK-47. The NVA flinched, evidently thinking he was hit, but Noll had already emptied the magazine in his weapon. As quickly as he ripped a fresh one from his bandolier and reloaded, the lucky North Vietnamese had already disappeared among the trees.

Lieutenant Noll went back down the trail, then, crazed with adrenaline, grabbed his new guys by their web gear, hauled them to their feet, and forced them up the hill. Noll was turning to say something to his radioman when a single shot rang out and he was knocked backward into a bomb crater. Unable to feel his left leg below the knee, Noll reached for his calf, which was throbbing, and accidentally slipped a finger into a small hole. He jerked his hand away; there was blood and a gob of meat on his finger. Thinking his lower leg had been blown off, he screamed for a medic.

The platoon medic, Sp4 Mark G. Draper, crawled up and,

concealed behind some brush, called to Noll, asking him what was wrong. "I'm hit," Noll yelled. "Get your ass out here and get me."

"You're okay," Draper shouted, knowing that wounds usually seemed worse than they were. "You crawl your ass over here."

Noll realized as he did so that he had landed with his left leg folded under him; it was just numb, not missing. After the medic bandaged his gunshot wound, he hopped into an old foxhole with his radioman and got Hawkins on the horn to request ARA.

The three or four enemy soldiers atop the knoll began lobbing grenades, and Noll's radioman was painfully wounded in the hand. When two Cobras arrived, Noll pitched a smoke grenade, then hunkered down as the gunships came in at his direction, pumping rockets. The North Vietnamese slipped away under the onslaught.

While the casualties were escorted back to the overnight position for medevac, Hawkins—who hated to be losing Noll—had Lieutenant Olson, the new FO, hit the enemy's likely escape routes with the 81s on Ripcord. Lucas, overhead in his command ship, was on the radio, urging Hawkins to keep the assault going without further delay. "Straub and I had been in communication and our move to the hill was well coordinated," Hawkins would write. "Straub reported that his movement was being shadowed by one or more enemy and we suspected [more] contact at any time."

It didn't happen. There was no fire as Company A secured the hillside landing zone or as D/2-501st, simultaneously emerging from the jungle, scrambled up the steep upper slope of Hill 805. There were merely some smashed timber bunkers to show that the enemy had been there, plus two dead North Vietnamese, nailed the day before in their spiderholes by a scout ship. "We were told to get rid of them so they wouldn't start stinking," recalled Blackman.

Captain Straub, senior to Hawkins by date of rank and experience, was nominally in charge of the dusty, windswept hill and responsible for coordinating all supporting arms except the 81s on Ripcord—Hawkins would use those—in case of the ground attack that Lucas told them both to expect that night. Straub established his command post among the big boulders at the peak so that it was protected on three sides. "Shortly after," noted Lieutenant Potter, the FO, "we were supplied with additional ammunition and grenades, plus shovels, axes, picks, and sandbags from a helicopter hovering at about fifteen feet, there being no place to land on the hilltop. Each soldier was supplied with about sixty magazines of ammunition, and each two- and three-man foxhole with a case of grenades."

There was barely enough room for the company on the crown of the hill. It was less than forty meters across from one platoon to another. "We were almost elbow to elbow in there," noted Straub. Digging was difficult in the rocky soil, and the troops, thoroughly winded from the uphill assault with full packs, settled for scooping shallow depressions from the old backfilled foxholes to be found among the stumps and scraggly trees. "My biggest mistake of the battle was that I didn't require more digging in that first night," wrote Straub. The men had been primed for a tough fight. The ease with which the objective had been secured had taken the edge off. No one believed that an attack was really coming, and no more than the normal number of claymores and trip flares were deployed. Still, the company had never before set up on a prominent terrain feature wiped clean of all natural cover, and there was a vague sense of uneasiness in the air as the sun set. "Blown up trees and branches covered the sides of the hill," wrote Blackman, "providing a million places for the gooks to hide. At the bottom of the hill there was a wall of green jungle. We were, to say the least, extremely vulnerable."

Captain Hawkins was approached two hours before midnight by Lieutenant Pahissa and Sergeant Singleton, whose platoon, Alpha One, was on that part of the perimeter facing Ripcord. Earlier, as the company had been digging in, Singleton had suggested implanting sensors back along the trail they had followed that afternoon to the hillside LZ. The plastic sensors, a new item of issue, resembled railroad spikes and came four to a camouflaged kit the size of a claymore bag, which also contained a receiving station with a headset. The spikes had transmitters in them and gave off a series of beeps when activated by the ground vibration caused by footsteps.

Pahissa and Singleton, along with a couple of troops, had placed the spikes at twenty- to thirty-meter intervals along the trail, starting two hundred meters down from the LZ. "I was sorta skeptical," recalled Hawkins, "but Singleton loved the things and just knew he was going to catch somebody that night by using them. . . ."

The new platoon sergeant was listening on the headsets when the sensors did indeed begin chirping like crickets. Accompanied by Pahissa, he presently rushed to Hawkins. "Sir, we've got beaucoup movement comin' up the trail," Singleton whispered.

Singleton excitedly offered the headset to Hawkins. "I believe you," Hawkins said. "Let's get the FO on it." Hawkins had Lieutenant Olson contact the 81s on Ripcord. To catch the enemy in the open, Hawkins told Olson to fire for effect without the usual adjusting rounds. "I let Straub know that we'd detected something," Hawkins later wrote, "and he told me that they'd just had a mechanical go off. The tension was building. About the time the mortar rounds began bursting to Pahissa's front, and we threw a bunch of rounds into the target area, maybe twenty or thirty, the enemy hit Straub from three sides with RPGs. The enemy column coming up the trail to attack the backside of our perimeter was busted up by the mortar barrage and never got into the fight. . . ."

When the attack began, Lieutenant Potter was standing on the north side of Company D's perimeter with map and radio, preparing to make some adjustments in the artillery defensive targets he had already registered around the hill. Potter was calling in the first of his new targets when a green star-cluster flare burst overhead without warning, the signal from the enemy commander to begin the assault. Within seconds, Potter had rocket-propelled grenades hitting the boulders and tree stumps all around him. He dropped flat and crawled some twenty meters back uphill amid the continuing explosions to Captain Straub's CP. Straub had given the command to return fire and was calling for a flareship and an ARA. "Four RPGs had hit the large boulder next to our foxhole," recounted Potter, "and fragments had peppered the back of Straub's radio operator. My air mattress, which I had been sitting on just twenty minutes earlier, was filled with holes."

Everyone was awake when the shooting started at 10:22 P.M. "We were on a self-imposed full alert," noted Sergeant Blackman of Delta Three, on the northern side of 805. Blackman was sitting, talking with a buddy at the base of one of the big boulders. "After such a long day and not much sleep the night before it was nice to kick back a little," he wrote. "It was real quiet and peaceful. When the RPGs started pouring in, we were taken completely by surprise."

First Lieutenant John D. Shipley of Delta Two, which was on the southeastern side of the perimeter, was slightly wounded in the sudden barrage of RPGs. "We were sitting around, drinking hot chocolate, when they hit. I gotta admit they kind of caught us off guard," recalled Shipley, in his first sustained action after almost two months with Company D. Unbeknownst to Shipley, a few of his guys had been quietly smoking pot at their positions. "We thought we were in for a gravy train on that hill, a rest," noted the platoon leader. "Sure, we got word to expect an attack, but we'd gotten those before and they often didn't develop."

The ferocity of the enemy attack was shocking. "There was a lot of confusion and not enough holes dug," according to Blackman, who rushed back down toward his foxhole with his buddy. "The battle was in full force before we ever reached our position, with loud explosions and small-arms fire hitting all over the hill."

Blackman's buddy took shrapnel in the back as they ran down the hill side by side. But he, along with Blackman, who tripped in the dark and ended up crawling into the foxhole, was soon returning fire. Everyone was, and the red tracers of a hundred M16s and M60s fanned out from the hilltop like the spokes of a wheel. "It was an impressive display of the firepower that a line company is capable of producing," wrote Blackman. "The noise was deafening."

It got louder as Lieutenant Potter requested mortar concentrations close around the perimeter from Ripcord. The 81mm crews also fired illumination rounds, one after the other as the parachute-born flares were quickly carried off by the high winds, "causing eerie shadows to dance around the tree stubble," noted Blackman. Captain Hawkins, in position two hundred meters west and ten meters below D/2-501st, could see enemy soldiers scurrying up the northern and southern slopes of Hill 805 in the flare light. It was an organized assault, with some of the NVA firing into Straub's position, green AK-47 tracers ricocheting off the boulders, while others made short dashes forward through the deadfall. Hawkins was surprised that the North Vietnamese would leave their flanks open to fire from his element on the LZ. "It was one of the few times I'd ever seen them attack without conducting adequate reconnaissance," he wrote. "We were in a position to devastate them. We had, in fact, prearranged sectors of fire with Straub to interlock with his defensive position. My machine gunners and grenadiers knew where to fire and where not to fire if we had to provide support."

The problem was that no one was firing. The troops seemed stunned, never having seen so many enemy at one time, and Hawkins rushed to an M60 gunner in Alpha Three, which faced the southern slope of Hill 805. "See them?" Hawkins barked. "That's the enemy attacking your buddies up there. You've got targets. You know where the friendlies are. Shoot to the right of the hill."

Hawkins dashed to a man with an M79. "Can you put a grenade up there every fifteen seconds?" he asked. The soldier said that he most definitely could, and Hawkins ordered, "Then do it now."

Alpha Two had a good view of the northern slope, and Hawkins scrambled over to Lieutenant Widjeskog. "Keep your fire on the slope to the left of the hill," Hawkins said. "Don't let up. We've got to provide some support. Get a thump gunner working, too."

As the troops began pouring fire into the enemy, Captain Hawkins, venturing onto the open landing zone for a better look, saw that RPGs trailing rooster tails of sparks were being lobbed into Straub's perimeter from a forested depression about two hundred meters north of Hill 805. Hawkins grabbed a LAW from a nearby position, then "went back to the top of the LZ," he wrote, "leaned back, took aim, and pressed the firing mechanism. Nothing. The LAW was a dud. I put the safety back in, put the LAW on the ground, then went back for another one and repeated the process. This one worked. I fired into the sky, waited, and a moment later the LAW round blew up in the depression with a satisfying crummmmp. There was an eerie silence, and I remember thinking to myself, well, that'll show 'em they can't fire with impunity."

Feeling rather pleased with himself, Hawkins was ambling over to check on Alpha One's situation when there came from the depression the sound of many, many rockets being fired all at once—*pop-pop-poppity-pop-pop-pop.* He began sprinting for the nearest foxhole, no doubt in his mind that those RPGs were headed directly for whoever had scored the direct hit with the LAW.

The nearest hole was occupied by Lieutenant Pahissa and Sergeant Singleton, who were still directing 81 fire along the trail leading up to the LZ. "I'm comin' in," Hawkins roared.

Hawkins tumbled into the hole as fifteen RPGs—Singleton had the presence of mind to count them—exploded in a great, rumbling mass twenty meters to the front of Alpha One, producing a chorus of startled exclamations: "Goddamn." "What the fuck? . . ."

Sergeant Singleton looked evenly at Hawkins. "I wouldn't do that anymore if I were you, sir," he said.

"And I didn't," noted Hawkins. "But those fifteen RPGs that missed us were fifteen RPGs that did not explode against the exposed positions of Company D."

The enemy, sheltered by boulders about fifty meters downhill on the southeastern slope, pressed the attack on Lieutenant Shipley's side of the hill with a barrage of RPGs. To keep the enemy from creeping forward under cover of the rockets, Delta Two swept the deadfall with a sheet of fire. Shipley's machine gunners, firing without pause, burned out their barrels and blistered their hands replacing them. The platoon radioman had "his arm torn up pretty badly by shrapnel," noted Shipley, but "the doc patched him up, shot him full of morphine, and five minutes later he was back in action, screaming, cussing, and lobbing grenades down the slope."

Captain Straub got his gunships fifteen minutes into the attack. The enemy began backing off. The troops continued to pour on the fire for another hour as three artillery batteries put up a wall of steel around the hilltop. "When the shooting finally stopped, there was a moment of complete silence," wrote Blackman. "My ears swelled up, trying to hear something. Someone called for a medic, not too loud, almost a whisper-yell, then there was another call, and another, and we realized that we had casualties." The wounded, a dozen of whom would be evacuated in the morning as an equal number with superficial injuries stayed on the hill, were mostly from Delta Two. "A few guys began moving around the hill to help," continued Blackman. "The sergeant who was our acting platoon leader ran up to check if we were all right. We stayed awake and down in our crowded foxhole the rest of the night."

Security patrols moved out at first light. There were bloody bandages to be found, plus a few rocket-propelled grenades and ammo magazines missed by the enemy as they had policed up their casualties and equipment in the dark. Lucas landed to speak with Hawkins and Straub. Company A, Lucas said, was to begin backtracking that afternoon into the draw between 805 and the firebase in preparation for reconnoitering the low area south of Ripcord. "We were rucked up and ready to leave when Lucas, who was back in the air by that time, called me directly and said I had a set of Phantoms to use any way I wanted," recalled Hawkins. "I told him I didn't have a target. He told me to pick a target and use them."

Hawkins, consulting his map, chose a spot six hundred meters to the west on a nondescript finger ridge branching to the south from the main ridge leading southeast of Ripcord. "It was on my planned route into the valley," noted Hawkins, "and because the spot was not in line of sight with Ripcord, but was down low on the finger, I figured it was as good a place as any for the enemy to have a cache." The FAC fired marking rockets, then "the first F4 went in," wrote Hawkins, "and KA-BOOM, we had smoke and flame and debris shooting into the air two to three hundred feet above the treetops. The FAC told us it wasn't the bombs doing that, but secondary explosions. We'd lucked out and hit an enemy ammo bunker. The Phantoms hit the target area for fifteen minutes before breaking station, and the FAC went nuts watching all the secondaries. He said that you could tell what you'd hit by the color of the explosion. Reddish yellow meant munitions. My troops and I enjoyed a ringside seat, looking right down on the area from the LZ. Guys were cheering. It was a pretty awesome sight."

CHAPTER 17

Holding the High Ground

Numerous air strikes were conducted throughout the morning and afternoon as Captain Straub's troops busily prepared for another night on Hill 805. Fields of fire were cleared. Bunkers big enough for five or six men were dug chest deep and covered with tree limbs and sandbags. As resupply ships came in, crates of ammunition and grenades were hauled up from the hillside LZ. Claymores and trip flares, also delivered in abundance, were set up in the deadfall on the slopes; sensors and mechanical ambushes were positioned astride likely avenues of approach. Concertina wire was staked all the way around the hilltop in a single belt about thirty feet below the perimeter.

First Lieutenant Joseph L. Guerra, recently recovered from wounds received with another company, was flown out to take over Delta Three. Guerra's platoon was positioned from ten to two, Shipley's from two to six, and Palm's from six to ten facing the saddle between 805 and the subhill atop which sat the resupply LZ.

As the troops dug in, a .51 below the hill fired on the CH-47s that approached Ripcord. Lieutenant Potter called in 8-inch fire, "but I could never get the gun crew to stop firing altogether. They would just move a little and fire again at the next Chinook."

Potter had plotted a routine number of defensive targets around the hill the first day, "adjusting selected targets with live fire," he wrote. "This allowed the batteries supporting us to record firing data—deflection, elevation, powder charge, and fuse setting—and assign target numbers for quick reaction if we had contact." Given priority for supporting fires that second day, Potter "spent four hours adjusting 81mm rounds over the surface of the hill in twenty-five-meter increments. Each time we adjusted on a piece of terrain from which we had received fire during the night, I recorded a target number on my map[,] and the mortar section on Ripcord recorded the firing data. I also refined my artillery adjustments, calling for close-in fire from Ripcord, O'Reilly, and Rakkasan."

Lieutenant Palm opted for foxholes and prone fighting positions instead of the bunkers with overhead cover favored by Delta Two and Three. It is unknown whether Palm thought it unwise to advertise his positions with moundlike bunkers or simply discounted the possibility of an attack across the open LZ. "Aside from laying wire, there was very little done to shore up our positions," noted Sp4 Richard R. "Rod" Soubers, who'd rejoined Delta One that morning after a week in the rear with a swollen knee. "My squad had dug sleeping positions that sloped back into the hill, but few foxholes. I didn't detect any sense of urgency or expectation, despite the fact that the other platoons had been hit the previous night. No one seemed to know how long we were going to be on the hill, nor for that matter why we were on the hill."

The mission, as it had been explained to Captain Straub, was to deny the enemy a dominant terrain feature from which they could observe and adjust mortar fire onto Ripcord. The unstated implication was that because the enemy would fight to regain the hill, holding it would provide an opportunity to fix the NVA and subject them to massed firepower. "I was basically told to go sit on a bald hilltop and wait to be attacked," said Straub. "I didn't accept that order with good cheer. It wasn't the way we operated. We weren't a company that did obvious things and set up in obvious places. The enemy didn't hunt us. We hunted them. I was very concerned then when we dug in atop 805 because we were giving up the initiative right at the start to the North Vietnamese."

The result would be the worst action of Straub's two and a half years in the war zone. A native of New York City, Straub was highly articulate, youthful and clean-cut in appearance, and had once considered entering the priesthood. He held a B.A. in English from Columbia University but, bored with graduate school and curious about the war, enlisted for OCS in late 1965. He arrived in Vietnam in February 1967 and led a rifle platoon and a recon platoon in the crack 2d of the 27th Wolfhounds. Extending his tour, he served as aide-de-camp to the commanding general of the 25th Infantry Division until September 1968.

Assigned next as a speechwriter for the commandant and assistant commandant of the Infantry School at Fort Benning, Straub instead volunteered for jump school, ranger school, and another combat tour, making it back to Vietnam in August 1969. After six months of staff duty, he assumed command of Company D, 2-501st Infantry, in February 1970. "Every captain in the battalion who wanted a company got a company," noted Straub. The fierce competition among junior officers for combat commands had evaporated. "Enthusiasm for winning the war was pretty much out of the officer corps by '69–'70," reflected Straub. For those few who asked to return to combat, "it was a question of doing your duty, and seeing the Army through, seeing the troops through."

There developed a special bond between Captain Straub and the grunts of Delta Company. "We all idolized him," said one. Straub was at once personable with his men, obviously committed to getting them home in one piece, yet serious about taking the war to the enemy and experienced enough to do it with skill. The troops responded. "In the context of 1970, Delta Company was an excellent unit," wrote Straub. It lacked that leavening of Regular Army NCOs that made for the kind of units Straub had seen in 1967. The company did, however, have an exec, 1st Lt. Ralph L. Selvaggi, and a top sergeant, 1st Sgt. John T. Schuelke, who provided excellent support from the rear, and in the field highly motivated platoon leaders and shake 'n bake sergeants. Straub also had Lieutenant Potter, USMA '69, son of a retired lieutenant colonel who had been a platoon leader with the same 501st Infantry at Bastogne.

"Potter had been to jump school and ranger school and was not only an exceptionally skilled forward observer, but also my assistant in running the company," wrote Straub. "We didn't look like a recruiting poster, but the troops were serious and professional, and because of that we had very low casualties."

As a platoon leader, Straub had not lost a single man killed. He did not intend to lose any as a company commander. "We prided ourselves in being unpredictable and surprising the enemy," Straub wrote. "Our point man always had the upper hand. We were never ambushed." During Company D's deployment to the Ripcord AO in April 1970, its point teams, moving with stealth and staying off trails, had killed many startled NVA during numerous meeting engagements in the jungle. Delta Company even captured a number of North Vietnamese; as a result, Palm wrote home, the troops "no longer have an unwarranted fear of them. Respect, yes; but not fear. Know your enemy . . ."

Captain Straub was emphatic about noise and light discipline. "We were not your normal, noisy, squeak-all-night-on-your-air-mattress company," he said. One night, Delta Company, hunkered in tall grass, was targeted for attack. "We were probed throughout the night," recounted Straub, but the attack never really got started because "as they probed, we'd kill one with a little burst of fire, and then another enemy soldier would appear and we'd kill him." Frustrated, the enemy finally faded away. "They never knew exactly where we were," wrote a gratified Straub. "When over a hundred heavily laden infantrymen can move into a position so quietly that the enemy can't locate their NDP, you know they're good."

Straub's original concerns about setting up in plain sight on Hill 805 had been largely academic. Enemy attacks, often predicted, rarely occurred. The night assault, however, confirmed the intelligence that Straub had been provided. "I became very angry at that point that this great company was being used in such a way," Straub wrote, meaning being used as bait to bring the enemy into a prepared kill zone. "I also became very determined that we would hold the hill."

By dusk, solid holes had been dug, and the troops sat waiting for the next attack, their weapons freshly cleaned and oiled and wrapped in towels to protect them from the eye-stinging dust on the windy hilltop. Straub pulled in his observation posts, passed the word for everyone to get under cover, then had the FO walk mortar and artillery fire to within fifty meters. "Straub wanted to show the NVA that we were ready," noted Blackman. "He also wanted us to know what we had available for support, assuring us that we weren't on our own out there. The shrapnel whizzed right over our heads. It made me feel better. . . ."

The night was cold and tense. It was hard to hear over the endless winds, and the flares that periodically popped overhead revealed nothing to the waiting grunts, for the sappers coming up the hill made expert use of the boulders and deadfall on the hillside. Most were within twenty meters, some even closer, when either a sapper or more probably one of the enemy infantrymen following them in triggered a trip flare. "By the time we were attacked, we were pretty tired," wrote Sergeant Blackman. "We'd been digging all day, then standing in our bunkers for a long time, trying to stay awake and alert. When the attack came, it seemed to happen all at once around the hill. The hill just exploded with incoming fire. . . ."

It started on the west side when Sp4 Dennis W. Belt, whose squad was on the right flank of Delta One's line, realized that there was a sapper at the wire thirty feet below his foxhole. "They're movin' down there," Belt hollered, squeezing off a burst from his M16.

It was 2:03 A.M. on July 14, 1970. The sapper rolled behind a log and cut loose in return with his AK-50. Sergeant William E. Jones, squad leader on the right flank, was sitting cross-legged near Belt's position. Only a few days with the platoon, Jones—a young regular, black, proud of his German wife, back for a second tour—had ignored Palm's orders to dig in that afternoon. "I don't know if he was lazy or if he thought he knew the ropes," recalled Belt, unimpressed. Jones presently commenced firing, then, leaning over the edge of the hill to get a better bead on the sapper behind the log, abruptly slumped forward, killed instantly by a shot that left one hole in the front of his helmet, a corresponding exit hole in the back. Unable to see what had happened to Jones in the dark, a grunt jumped beside him. "Sarge, are you all right?" No answer. The grunt shook Jones, pleading with him: "C'mon, Sarge, you're okay, aren't ya?"

Lieutenant Palm and his shake 'n bake platoon sergeant, rugged, stolid SSgt. Michael L. Cooksley, scrambled along the line, shouting directions as the platoon blew its claymores and opened fire on the sappers hidden in the deadfall. "The wind was howling so much and there was so much fire from our side," wrote Rod Soubers of the right-flank squad, "that a person couldn't be sure exactly where the incoming fire was coming from. All we could do was look for flashes or simply put a blanket of fire out all along our front."

Captain Straub and Lieutenant Potter began calling for fire support, the frightful whoosh, flash, and crash of mortar and artillery shells adding thunder to the ceaseless roar of small-arms fire. Straub himself was stunned by the "large amount of fire by both sides in [such] a small space . . . It was the most intense combat experience of my Vietnam service . . ."

Potter would later write:

> I adjusted 105mm artillery close-in to the south and west, and 81mm mortars even closer on the west side, where the main attack was taking place. Both of these came from Ripcord. On the north side I adjusted 155mm support from the ARVN battery on O'Reilly to about two hundred and fifty meters. Being on the gun-target-line, I was hesitant to adjust the fire much closer. Down in the valley on the south side, I used 8-inch artillery from Rakkasan. I had kept the 8-inch at a thousand meters the first night, but brought it in closer during the second attack.

Straub called for Quad-50 fire from Ripcord, and the red tracers formed a spectacular arc from one hill to the other as they rained into the deadfall in front of Delta One. Delta Company's grenadiers, meanwhile, fired flares, and the 81s on the firebase pumped out illum. Given the steady winds, however, the parachute-born flares and illumination rounds were quickly swept away from Hill 805.

To add to the sound and fury, gunships arrived at the thirty-minute mark from Camp Evans. Wrote Potter:

> Captain Straub had one of his RTOs mark the center of our position with a small strobe light, a reference point from which we gave the pilots instructions. The troops also marked some targets with tracers from an M60. The Cobras positioned their ordnance—miniguns, rockets, and 40mm grenades—with surprising accuracy, and having worked them in very close, fifty to a hundred meters, the first night, we brought them in even closer during the second attack.
>
> The effort required Captain Straub and I to work as a team, communicating with the platoon leaders on his radio net and the sources of all the fire support on my artillery net. The process worked well. We had as many as eight fire missions going at once. I had never been under such stress, but this allowed us to engage eight different targets simultaneously, and everyone involved—mortars, gunships, 105s, 155s, 8-inch artillery—were usually able to respond to our adjustments in less than a minute, sometimes as quickly as fifteen seconds. The gunships exposed themselves to great risk coming in as low as they did. We owe our lives to the pilots in the back seats of those Cobras and the gunners in the front seats.

Straub and Potter were in position among the boulders five to ten meters up from Delta One. The enemy was so close on that side—too close to be affected by the protective ring of mortar and artillery fire—that satchel charges flew over the heads of the troops on the perimeter and landed right in the CP. "At one point, four satchel charges exploded against the inside edge of the boulder about six feet to my left," wrote Potter, who, like Straub, won the Silver Star for coordinating the defense of Hill 805. "I didn't expect to see the sun rise in the morning. We were that close to being overrun. . . ."

Many battles were going on at the same time. Specialist Fourth Class Jack L. Godwin, with the center squad of Delta One, was firing away—this was probably before the gunships arrived, but the order of events could not be recalled precisely even the next day—when a satchel charge landed in his foxhole, blowing off his foot and lower leg. The two GIs in the hole to the left, eardrums ruptured by the blast, fled up the hill to take shelter among the boulders at the top.

The squad leader on the left flank of the platoon sent two of his men to fill the gap. One of them, Sp4 John L. "Red" Keister, ran to Pfc. Martin Cirrincione—the platoon sergeant's radioman had grabbed a position near Godwin—and asked where he should go, where he was needed most. "Right here with me," Cirrincione exclaimed. Almost as soon as the two began firing down the hill, Keister was shot just below the brim of his helmet and slumped dead against Cirrincione, who was splattered when the hole was blown in his buddy's head. The shot had apparently come from the sapper ensconced behind the log in front of Denny Belt. "He had me cold," recounted Belt, who, unable to raise his head, frantically lobbed frags at the sapper. Belt had a case of grenades, two-thirds full, and he "threw almost all of them that were in there. . . ."

Cirrincione screamed that he was out of ammo, and Sergeant Cooksley, appearing above him on the hillside, threw down a bandolier for his M16. Everyone was eating up ammo. "The machine gunner in the bunker to our left was sending out a steady stream of fire. The barrel was bright red and I could see the piston pumping," noted Sergeant Blackman of Delta Three. Blackman, his own weapon jammed, was alternately rolling grenades down the slope and loading magazines for the others in his bunker. The night was like a Bosch painting. "The sound of the incoming artillery rounds was absolutely unbelievable," wrote Blackman. "They sounded like train wrecks. The whole thing was unreal . . . the tracers from the Quad-50 on Ripcord and our small-arms fire, the Cobras circling like vultures, miniguns belching, explosions from grenades and satchel charges and RPGs, smoke, flares, dancing shadows. . . . This couldn't be happening. Such firepower, yet they kept coming. What drives these men we call gooks?"

Blackman's account continued:

> I remember glancing at the men in our bunker as I loaded magazines, taking note of how hard they were working at

trying to kill people and stay alive. It was only a quick glance, but the memory has stayed with me always. These were the men I ate with, slept with, and shared future plans with on a daily basis. To make those plans come true we had to survive the night. To do that we had to fight like hell. These guys, my friends, were shooting, throwing grenades, yelling for ammo, operating automatically, out of instinct. It was like living in a war movie except you could smell the smoke and feel the concussions from the satchel charges and RPGs. I remember their helmets rocking back and forth with each round they fired, and their concentration, their determination—there was no time for fear, though it was certainly there. The flashes from exploding satchel charges and RPGs, and our own grenades, caused no flinching or ducking down. There was a job to do and we couldn't hide. . . .

Lieutenant Guerra, only one day with the platoon but a seasoned veteran of Hard Luck Alpha, jumped into Blackman's bunker "and asked if we could tell where any of the NVA were. We pointed out a couple spots, and he got on top of the overhead cover and began shooting LAWs down at the suspected enemy positions. I remember looking up through the overhead cover from inside the bunker, and seeing him on one knee, a LAW on his shoulder, totally exposed amid the incoming fire. I thought that was a little crazy, but it was a crazy night. . . ."

Lieutenant Palm also exposed himself freely as he moved from position to position in his sector; he was finally hit while attempting to rescue Jack Godwin. Huddled at the bottom of his foxhole, the badly wounded Godwin had heard Palm calling as he approached, but Palm no sooner reached the position than he was shot in the chest at close range and fell in a heap on top of Godwin.

Straub got Lieutenant Shipley on the horn, telling him, because his platoon was not under direct attack, to dispatch four men to hard-pressed Delta One. Staff Sergeant James T. Hembree, the platoon sergeant, picked the four, including a machine gunner. Hembree immediately reconsidered, perhaps

Lt. Col. Andre C. Lucas, commander of the 2-506th Infantry (left), and his operations officer, Maj. Herbert E. Koenigsbauer, at Firebase Ripcord shortly before the siege of July 1970. (Courtesy H. E. Koenigsbauer)

Lt. Col. Lucas with a map that describes the attack launched on Hill 1000 by the 2-506th Infantry on July 8, 1970. (Courtesy C. W. Jensen)

Col. Benjamin L. Harrison on June 23, 1970, the day he took command of the 3d Brigade, 101st Airborne Division. (Courtesy B. L. Harrison)

Brig. Gen. Sidney B. Berry, assistant commander of the 101st Airborne Division (center), poses with new aide, 1st Lt. Victor E. Arndt (far left, wearing glasses), and his command-ship crew, including his pilot, 1st Lt. John R. Fox (second from right, wearing pocket patch). Late summer 1970. (Courtesy S. B. Berry)

Brig. Gen. Berry talking with troops at Khe Sanh during Operation Lam Son 719. March 1971. (Courtesy S. B. Berry)

Brig. Gen. Berry with Maj. Gen. John J. Hennessey, commanding general of the 101st Airborne Division. January 1971. (Courtesy S. B. Berry)

Sp4 John Mihalko and Sp4 John A. Schnarr (right, holding M16) of the reconnaissance platoon, E/2-506th Infantry. August 1970. (Courtesy J. Mihalko)

Sgt. Paul E. Burkey, Sgt. Frank Bort, and 1st Lt. James H. Campbell (left to right) of C/2-506th Infantry at Camp Evans. February 1970. (Courtesy P. E. Burkey)

Sgt. Robert O. Granberry, a team leader with the reconnaissance platoon of E/2-506th Infantry, poses with a captured AK-50. February 1970. (Courtesy J. Mihalko)

Sp4 Schnarr says good-bye to his platoon leader at the end of his tour. December 1970. (Courtesy J. A. Schnarr)

1st Lt. John A. Flaherty (left, with shotgun) and Capt. Rembert G. Rollison of D/2-506th Infantry. (Courtesy J. A. Flaherty)

Pfc. Bruce W. McCorkle of D/2-506th Infantry (right) cooking C rations at a fighting position at Firebase Ripcord. (Courtesy B. W. McCorkle)

SSgt. Gary A. Radford (left) and Sp4 Lewis Howard, Jr., of D/2-506th Infantry. (Courtesy G. A. Radford)

1st Lt. Flaherty (sitting fourth from left without a shirt) at Firebase Ripcord on June 28, 1970, with members of his platoon, to include SSgt. George K. Strasburg (sitting third from left), Pfc. Michael J. Grimm (sitting behind Flaherty with bandages on his fingers), and Pfc. Thomas E. Gaut (second from right, looking at Grimm). (Courtesy P. E. McCloskey)

Capt. David F. Rich (left, wearing 1st Cav patch from a previous tour) was wounded seven times while commanding B/2-319th Field Artillery on Firebase Ripcord. (Courtesy C. W. Jensen)

A 105mm howitzer from B/2-319th Field Artillery returns fire on the enemy during the siege of Firebase Ripcord. (Courtesy C. W. Jensen)

Howitzers standing ready on Firebase Ripcord. (Courtesy C. W. Jensen)

Capt. Rich (right) getting one of his 105 crews into position at Firebase Ripcord. (Courtesy C. W. Jensen)

1st Lt. Fred H. Edwards (second from left, lying on sandbags) commanded the combat engineers from the 326th Engineer Battalion on Firebase Ripcord. (Courtesy F. H. Edwards)

Maj. Gen. Hennessey pins a Silver Star on Capt. Philip L. Michaud of the 2-319th Field Artillery for his valor during the siege of Firebase Ripcord. (Courtesy P. L. Michaud)

Black smoke rises from burning ammunition or fuel after an enemy mortar attack on Firebase Ripcord. (Photo by J. R. Fox/Courtesy S. B. Berry)

CH-47 Chinook delivering a sling load of supplies to Firebase Ripcord. (Courtesy C. W. Jensen)

A bulldozer tows away a 105mm howitzer destroyed in the Chinook crash of July 18, 1970, on Firebase Ripcord. (Courtesy D. Cox)

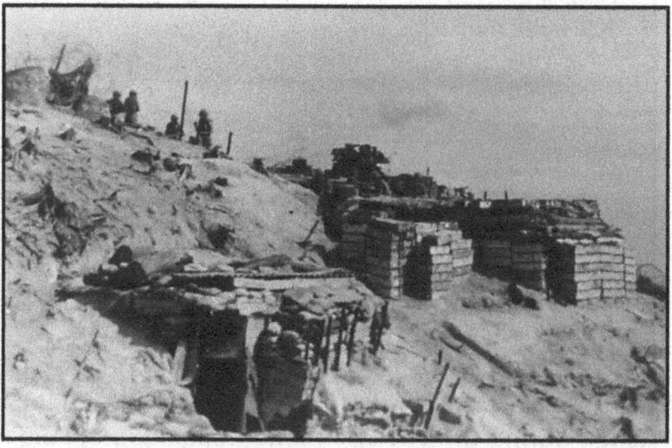

The Quad-50 (silhouetted in center of photo) at the northwest end of Firebase Ripcord. (Courtesy D. Cox)

Sgt. Raymond H. Blackman shortly before his unit, D/2-501st Infantry, was committed to the defense of Firebase Ripcord. (Courtesy R. H. Blackman)

Lt. Col. Charles J. Shay (left), commander of the 2-502d Infantry, during the Firebase Barnett operation of August 1970. (Courtesy C. J. Shay)

Capt. Charles F. Hawkins, commander of A/2-506th Infantry, shortly after the battle for Firebase Ripcord. (Courtesy C. F. Hawkins)

1st Lt. Lee E. Widjeskog of A/2-506th Infantry. August 1970. (Courtesy L. E. Widjeskog)

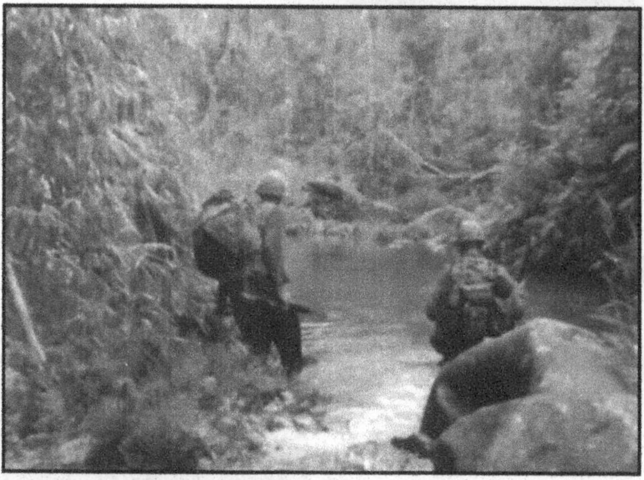

Troops from D/1-506th Infantry cross a jungle stream. Summer 1970. (Courtesy K. C. James)

Sp4 K. C. James of D/1-506th Infantry (right) at Firebase Kathryn. June 1970. (Courtesy K. C. James)

1st Lt. John H. Smith of D/1-506th Infantry at Firebase Kathryn. June 1970. (Courtesy J. H. Smith)

Capt. Donald R. Workman, commander of D/1-506th Infantry. (Courtesy K. J. Loke)

Sgt. Gilbert C. Rossetter of D/1-506th Infantry at Camp Evans before the insertion into the Ripcord area. July 1970. (Courtesy G. C. Rossetter)

1st Lt. Randall Thompson and Sgt. Robert J. Wise (right, wearing glasses) of D/1-506th Infantry sometime after the Ripcord operation. (Courtesy R. J. Wise)

A medical evacuation Huey comes in to land during the siege of Firebase Ripcord. (Courtesy C. W. Jensen)

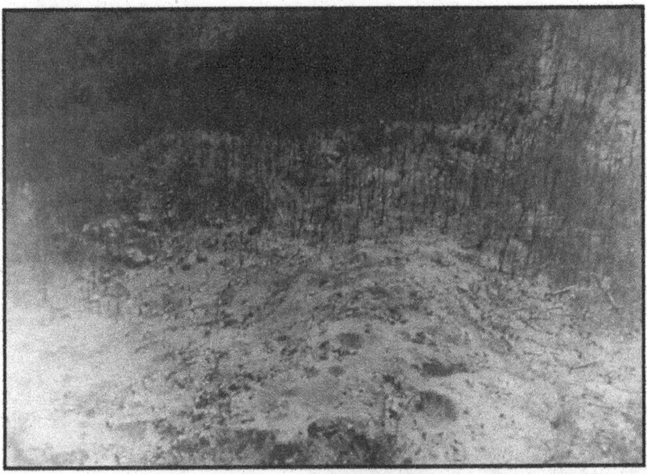

Firebase Ripcord after being evacuated and then bombed out of existence by the U.S. Air Force. (Courtesy S. B. Berry)

seeing the flash of fear in the kid's eyes. "Never mind," he said, taking the M60. "I'll go myself."

Sergeant Hembree, slung with extra ammo for Palm's platoon, led his three reinforcements to the west side of the hill and was maneuvering into a position to clean out several NVA from behind a boulder with his M60 when he was killed by a shot through the neck. Hembree, a twenty-six-year-old Regular Army NCO from Georgia with a Korean wife, had been with Delta Two for eight months and was the backbone of the platoon, the pro whom lieutenants and troops alike leaned on and learned from.

Private First Class Keith E. Utter, also of Delta Two, caught a bullet in the head and, like Hembree, was posthumously awarded the Silver Star for rushing to the aid of Delta One. As it could best be pieced together after the fact, Hembree and Utter, like Jones, Keister, and probably Palm, too, had been shot by the sapper behind the log. The sapper, lying still, holding his fire until he had clear targets, picked off his victims with single shots or quick bursts, leaving most of the defenders unaware in the confusion that one of their attackers had gotten in so close to the perimeter.

Sergeant Warren R. Hanrahan, another of Hembree's reinforcements, jumped into a foxhole upon cresting the hill. Just below, Sp4 Ronald W. Grubidt, Delta One's medic, was in another foxhole with a wounded man, "calling for some covering fire to get his man out," recalled Hanrahan. "I started down toward his hole when I got hit in the right side of my neck." Hanrahan survived by a fraction of an inch, the bullet passing between his jugular vein and spinal cord, which was nonetheless bruised, temporarily paralyzing his right arm. "It's kind of fuzzy in my memory," continued Hanrahan, who was losing blood and unable to speak, "but the [wounded] man and I crawled back up the hill, helping each other. We stopped in a hole awhile. My [M16] had gotten smashed when I got hit, but the other man gave me [his M16]. I had to shoot with my left hand, [and] I remember he told me I might as well go [back] across to the other side with that kind of shooting."

The center of Palm's line was basically being held by Sp4

Roger Myles, machine gunner, and Pfc. Angel Arimont, assistant gunner, who, feeling all alone, such were the casualties, laid down a continuous sheet of M60 fire from the foxhole immediately to the right of Godwin's. Their fire abruptly stopped. Myles shouted that he had a jam. "Roger always took good care of his weapon, so the jamming could not be attributed to carelessness on his part," noted Rod Soubers. "He had complained, in fact, about having a bad barrel weeks before 805, but was never issued another one. . . ."

Hoping to help, the machine gunner on the right flank, Sp4 Paul G. "Rat" Guimond, a tough, sarcastic kid from Chicago who had recently married a Thai girl on R&R, left the foxhole from which he had been blazing away with his own M60 and raced down the line toward Myles. Sergeant Drew Gaster reached out to trip Guimond as he went past; failing that, he began "yellin' for him to stay down," Gaster recalled, "because he was runnin' standin' up. . . ."

It was probably the sapper behind the log who nailed Guimond as he passed behind Belt's foxhole, and he tumbled twenty feet down the slope, ending up in a sprawl between friend and foe. Denny Belt and Rod Soubers waited until the latest flare blew out of range, then, hoping the darkness would cover them, rushed down to get Guimond. They were almost there when Belt suddenly froze and yelled that he was hit and couldn't move. One round had taken him in the stomach, nicking his spine on its way out his back; another round had shattered his left hip. Soubers hefted Belt over his shoulder, barely noticing the bullet that creased the side of his steel pot, and hustled back up the steep slope, legs pumping in the loose earth. Soubers later wrote that Belt was "cussing a blue streak as I carried him up the hill, since the pain of his stomach wound was so intense. After I got him up to a level spot above our position, I wrapped a poncho liner around him while at the same time yelling for a medic. I then went back to our position on the line, hesitant to go back after Rat given the intense fire we were getting . . ."

The platoon medic, Doc Grubidt, scrambled from one casualty to the next with his aid bag. At some point, he and several grunts carried Jack Godwin from his foxhole to the collecting point that the other medics had established among the boulders at the top of the hill. Grubidt pulled Palm out of the same foxhole as Godwin, but it was too late to do anything for the platoon leader, and Grubidt cried out in anguish, "Oh, my God, the lieutenant's just died in my arms."

Lieutenant Palm won a posthumous Silver Star. Despite the heavy casualties, Delta One was still holding. Myles had gotten his machine gun back into action, and Drew Gaster, assisted by Pfc. Rodney B. "Nose" Collins, had taken over Guimond's M60.

Rod Soubers took up a position with his best friend, Sp4 David R. Beyl, who methodically lobbed M79 shells into the deadfall when not answering the muzzle flashes winking from the trees on the far side of the LZ. Sergeant Cooksley—wounded when a bullet smashed through the magazine in his M16, spraying bits of metal—moved along the perimeter, noted Soubers, "giving help when he could and giving orders, and in general taking charge of the platoon. . . ."

Denny Belt was holding his gut, writhing in agony as he waited for Grubidt to get to him, when he saw in the light of a flare that the man who'd been in his foxhole when the attack started was crouched behind a boulder a few feet farther up the hill. "Come down here and put my rifle in my hands," Belt implored, terrified that the enemy was going to dart through the decimated line and kill him as he lay there, helpless, paralyzed from the waist down. The man behind the boulder said that he had something in his eye and couldn't see, then disappeared. "The son of a bitch split on me," Belt would recall bitterly. "He never took any part in the action at all, and wouldn't even move a few feet to help me. What makes me madder, he was always the gung-ho type until then."

At some point in the action, Captain Straub received support from six Marine A-6 Intruders, a jet fighter-bomber specifically designed to hit targets obscured by darkness or bad weather, guided in this instance by the navigational beacon on Ripcord. "I just had to give range and direction from 805 to have the bombs placed with accuracy, even in total darkness," noted Straub. Each Intruder released twenty-eight 500-pound bombs at a time. "It was a spectacular sight," said Straub, "and it broke up the attack on us."

At the forty-five-minute mark, a CH-47 flareship out of Camp Evans arrived. "Captain Straub gave instructions to the pilot in order to adjust each flare drop so the wind would carry the flares to where they would silhouette the enemy," wrote Potter. "Constant adjustments were needed because of the winds. . . ."

The enemy fire slowed, then dried up completely at 3:20 A.M. Staff Sergeant Raymond T. Dotson, platoon sergeant for Delta Three, appeared at the entrance of Blackman's bunker. "First Platoon's been hit hard," he said. "There are men laying all over the side of the hill. I need one man to come with me. We have to reinforce that side." The grunts in the bunker looked at one another, too stunned to answer. "C'mon," Dotson barked. "I don't care who goes, but we gotta go now. They need help over there."

Blackman was closest to the entrance, so, having just cleared his jammed M16, he climbed out to follow Dotson. They went first to the top of the hill, then started down toward Delta One. Blackman, stumbling against something, realized that "there were three men lying in a row at my feet, covered with poncho liners. You could see their boots. I knew they were dead but didn't want to believe it, and my first thought was, how can they sleep through all this?"

Dotson shouted at Blackman to come on, then pointed to a prone fighting position: "You stay here and keep your eyes open."

Blackman saw that there was only one man in the hole to his left and the foxhole to his right was empty. I hope my damn M16 doesn't jam again, he thought. I should have brought more frags.

Taking advantage of the lull in the enemy fire, Sergeant Cooksley and Rod Soubers hastily put together a plan to get Rat Guimond. "Mike [Cooksley] said that he would have the whole [platoon] put out covering fire if I and another guy would go after Rat," Soubers would later write. Cooksley cautioned Soubers to make his move when the area was fully illuminated "since the gooks would be laying low in order to avoid detection. . . . During the course of the battle it [had] bec[o]me evident [to Cooksley] that the NVA were using the cover of darkness for movement. Whenever the flares were up[,] the NVA were apparently crouched low and motionless."

Cooksley and Soubers moved along the line, getting everyone organized to lay down the cover fire. Blackman saw someone he didn't know stop and talk to the guy to his left, then the man—it was Soubers—came over to his position. "Rat's down there and he's still alive," he said. "I want you to help me carry him up."

Blackman went cold. "Where?" he mumbled.

"He's right down there," Soubers snapped, pointing to an inert shape lying just on their side of the concertina wire. "Can't you see him? He's still alive, damn it, and when I come back, we're gonna bring him up."

The man disappeared, then more illum popped overhead and Blackman saw him to his left, rushing downhill at an angle toward Guimond. Blackman hesitated, terrified. Soubers turned, screaming at him, "Get some balls about you, man, and help me."

Blackman slid down the hill after Soubers. Grabbing an arm each, they dragged Guimond back up the steep slope and laid him on his back near Denny Belt. Guimond had been shot in the temple and had blood all over the side of his face. Doc Grubidt placed a bandage against the wound and told Blackman, lying next to the unconscious Guimond, to hold it in place until the medevac arrived. "Damnit, Rat," Blackman pleaded, "don't die, man."

The medevac that arrived at 3:40 A.M. was unable to land because of the boulders. The pilot instead lowered a basket while holding his aircraft steady in the buffeting winds over a strobe light that marked the perimeter. "There is a strange silence when a helicopter is hovering overhead—all you hear is the rotors," wrote Sp4 Gary L. Fowler, senior company medic. Once the basket touched down, it was carried to the casualties—Fowler loaded Guimond first, Denny Belt on top—then carried back so that Fowler could reattach it to the cable dangling beneath the Huey. Fowler worked fast as the grunts on the perimeter laid down suppressive fire and gunships streaked in, miniguns blazing, rocket pods flashing, expecting the NVA to slam an RPG into the medevac at any moment and send it crashing down atop the company.

To save time, Fowler loaded only Jack Godwin into the basket lowered by a second hovering medevac. As the first medevac neared Camp Evans, meanwhile, Belt "could feel Guimond breathing hard under me—and just as the hospital hut came into sight, I felt him gasp his last breath, and he died. . . ."

Captain Straub spent what was left of the night controlling an air force C-130 that had come on station during the second medevac and flew lazy eights over the area for the hour and a half till dawn, discharging a succession of large flares to discourage another attack. No one slept. When the sun finally came up, all the claymores that hadn't been used during the attack were detonated on Straub's command so that new ones could be emplaced in safety, the thunderclap a finale of sorts to the battle. "The hill now had an eerie stillness to it," wrote Rod Soubers. "We walked around almost in a daze as smoke from the many small fires that had been ignited by the firefight was whipped around by the wind."

Soubers's friend Dave Beyl walked down the line to see how the rest of the platoon had fared. Learning only then about Lieutenant Palm, Beyl returned with tears in his eyes to tell Soubers. Physically spent, emotionally overwrought, Beyl and Soubers sat on the side of the hill, heads down, crying. They fell silent after a time and looked out over the dense vegetation between the hill and Ripcord. "Well, Rod," Beyl finally said, "at least we made it through."

Many of the grenades thrown down the hill during the attack had failed to explode. Some of the duds now began to cook off in the smoldering deadfall. Nose Collins was injured by one of the unexpected explosions and was evacuated in a medevac basket.

Security patrols found a bag of satchel charges that had been lost in the dark, along with an RPG. Five shot-up bodies had also been left behind, a sure sign that the enemy had been badly hurt, for they always made every effort to recover their fallen comrades. One of the dead men was the sapper behind the log, his right hand blown off, apparently from a grenade he had tried to throw back.

With a squad securing the landing zone so that a chopper could touch down, Straub had Doc Fowler determine which of the remaining wounded required evacuation. Fowler sent six men out, to include troops with blown-out eardrums and Warren Hanrahan, a bandage wrapped around his throat. Those suffering from what were in comparison superficial fragment wounds, and there were many, stayed on the hill. "I wouldn't let anyone be medevacked unless he had a really serious wound," said Straub. "Anybody who could pull a trigger and throw frags was going to be of immense value when the next attack came. I didn't get any resistance on this. Nobody complained, nobody pleaded to be sent out. They were willing to stay with the unit until this mess was over."

Observation posts were reestablished. Log birds shuttled in with ammo and claymores and wire, plus twenty hapless replacements. The log birds left with the dead, who had been carried in body bags down to the LZ. Lucas and his artillery liaison officer also landed, bringing mail, medical supplies, and two starlight scopes for Straub. Lucas, apparently having detected the depression in Straub's voice when he reported his casualties, made a point to reemphasize to the company commander the importance of holding the hill. "Lucas talked to me and bucked me up," recalled Straub. "He gave me a good little pep talk, which I needed. He got me thinking positively and made me stop feeling sorry for Delta Company. And then he went around to every position and talked to everybody, sat in foxholes and talked with the troops. That was super."

CHAPTER 18

Piling On

The strength of the enemy positions on Hill 1000 and the ferocity of the attacks on Hill 805 came as a revelation to Colonel Harrison. Contact had previously been too sporadic, the shelling of the firebase too intermittent, to suggest to the brigade commander that a major engagement was in the making. The actions at Hills 805 and 1000 began to bring the situation into better focus. "However, we still did not have a good fix on the size of the force opposing us or a clear picture of the enemy's intentions," wrote Harrison. Was the action around the firebase mere harassment, a diversion to draw attention away from something big about to happen somewhere else, or were the NVA, in fact, preparing a set-piece battle to destroy Ripcord?

"It's easy now to reconstruct the enemy plan, but it was a most frustrating mystery then," admitted Harrison, who was new to the area, having only replaced Bill Bradley on June 23. "As intense as the attacks on Hill 805 were, there was no evidence of mass numbers of enemy troops being involved. There were, in fact, no sightings of large enemy troop movements anywhere in the area. Not even a company-sized unit had been spotted at that stage. We were still desperately looking for targets. Clearly, we had a paucity of good intelligence."

The terrain allowed the enemy to mass without notice and inflict heavy casualties without warning on isolated units.

"You need troops on the ground to see what's going on in the jungle," wrote Harrison. "On the other hand, you simply cannot spread troops out too far in that kind of environment in an effort to locate the enemy." When Harrison assumed command of the brigade, he found that the line battalions sowed the jungle with platoon patrols. "There was no way in hell that those understrength and widely separated platoons could have supported one another if hit by a large enemy force," Harrison contended. "I ordered that until further notice units were to operate in company-size elements. One might argue that had I allowed the platoon patrols to continue we may have gained more intelligence more quickly about what was happening in the hills around Ripcord. I considered that and rejected it as too high a risk. Others may have different views.

"What could have been done?" Harrison wrote, dissecting the battle. "Perhaps the best chance of improving our intelligence in that situation would have been more intense reconnaissance by air cavalry of the many routes into and out of the A Shau. I said then, and I'll say now, I would gladly trade two battalions of infantry for one squadron of air cavalry. As it was, our one squadron of air cavalry was stretched very thin in a large division AO."

Lieutenant Colonel Robert F. Molinelli's 2-17th Cavalry had deployed to Quang Tri City, in fact, during the first week of Ripcord in response to intelligence indicating that the replacement-filled 9th Regiment, 304th NVA Division, was going to cross the Laotian border into South Vietnam near Khe Sanh. On July 8, one of several Pink Teams braving a heavy overcast that the enemy had hoped would ground its foe's helicopters caught a two-hundred-man NVA column as it marched down a thin trail in tall, concealing elephant grass. The result was a turkey shoot as swarms of scouts and gunships converged on the scene, hosing down the fleeing enemy with rockets and miniguns. Three shaken prisoners were scooped up by the squadron's ground troop. The body count was 139. The area was subjected the next day to B-52 Arc Lights.

To further exploit the situation, Colonel Harrison was given operational control of Chuck Shay's 2-502d Infantry, which reopened FSB Shepherd for a battery of ARVN 105s. Harrison himself moved a jump CP to Camp Carroll, another of the old U. S. Marine bases facing the DMZ. Molinelli's pilots continued to rack up numerous kills. Two battalions from the 1st ARVN Infantry Division inserted into the area captured piles of abandoned enemy weapons and rucksacks and counted a hundred more NVA bodies strewn amid the cratered rubble left by the B-52s. The enemy regiment having been destroyed before it even had a chance to fight, the ARVN and Screaming Eagles returned to Thua Thien Province on July 15.

Harrison wanted to wreak the same type of havoc on the enemy in the Ripcord AO. As Harrison's awareness of NVA strength around the firebase grew, so too did his determination to defeat the foe where they stood. It was a battle that made sense to the new brigade commander. "My understanding of the division mission," he later wrote, "was that we were to deny the enemy a chance to prepare an area from which they could launch another Tet-type offensive on the populated coastal area. It was also desired that we inflict as much hurt on the enemy as we could before we withdrew from Vietnam entirely and left the ARVN holding the bag."

Lieutenant Case, the brigade commander's acting artillery liaison officer, witnessed a vivid demonstration of Harrison's commitment to hold Ripcord. It came during a meeting with General Berry during one of Harrison's daily trips to Ripcord. "There was an upper and a lower landing pad at Ripcord," wrote Case, setting the scene. "The lower pad wasn't as zeroed in as the upper pad, but landing at the lower pad meant you had a longer walk to the safety of the battalion TOC." The brigade command ship "always landed at the lower pad," noted Case, and those on board would "stride single file to the TOC amid the incoming that usually began when a helicopter arrived. Colonel Harrison set a leisurely pace. Whatever staff officers made the trip that day walked behind Harrison, with me, the junior officer, last in line. Helicopters, incidentally, didn't wait on the pad at Ripcord, as they would at most firebases, but lifted off and circled the firebase to escape the incoming."

Harrison was already headed for the operations center on the day in question when Berry's command ship followed the brigade commander's onto the lower landing pad. Harrison and

Case met Berry as he came uphill, and the three proceeded toward the TOC. "As I followed Berry and Harrison, mortar rounds started coming in as usual," recounted Case, "but they mostly impacted in the wire on the slopes of the firebase. Berry and Harrison obviously wanted to discuss the situation in private, rather than in the presence of Lucas," Case continued. "About halfway to the TOC, they saw a soldier emerge from a sandbagged conex. Harrison and Berry stepped inside the conex and shut the door behind them. For a moment, I felt as though I'd been left out in the rain, only it was raining mortar rounds instead of raindrops. Realizing what they had done, Harrison opened the door and motioned me inside. There was barely room for the three of us in the conex and we had to scrunch up against the metal walls. Pressed up against a brigadier general and a full colonel, I felt very rank conscious." As Case listened, Berry informed Harrison that he had spoken to higher headquarters—none of the three can now remember whether Berry was referring to XXIV Corps, USARV, or MACV—and the upper echelons were determined to hold Ripcord. "Yes," Harrison exclaimed, slamming his fist into his palm.

"It was the only time I saw the colonel really animated," noted Case. "My impression was that Harrison had expected a decision to abandon the firebase. These quotes are far from exact, but Harrison then said something to the effect that, We've got to hold the firebase. We can hold. We can't let them win here." Harrison further maintained, recalled Case, "that if the NVA knocked us off Ripcord, they would start picking off our forward firebases one by one. I silently agreed. At any rate, I came away with the impression that Berry and Harrison felt Ripcord had as much symbolic as strategic significance. I think they viewed the battle as a test of wills with the North Vietnamese."

Case's narrative presents Colonel Harrison as a stolid and courageous officer. The image is accurate. Harrison's battalion commanders found him a "calm, levelheaded, and highly competent brigade commander," to quote one. The brigade staff loved him. "Colonel Harrison was an old-fashioned soldier's soldier," stated Fred Spaulding, the air operations officer. "He was firm and demanding and completely in charge, but also low-key, the kind of commander who worked with his people as a team. He never drew attention to himself or sought accolades from above like so many of the ticket-punchers." One junior officer found the colonel "gruff but compassionate." Spaulding was particularly impressed that Harrison "still believed that a leader was supposed to pick up a rucksack and rifle and get out with the troops. He spent a lot of time out on the firebases, and even a few nights out in the boonies with the line companies. Harrison cared a hell of a lot about his troops, but he also knew that his job was to find the enemy and go after them, and that's exactly what he did at Ripcord."

Ben Harrison was the son of an elderly country doctor in Truman, Arkansas, who died when the boy was ten. Ben entered college at sixteen but ran out of money and left after two semesters "to join the Army and see the world," he recalled, "but primarily to get the GI Bill so I could come back and finish school."

An instructor at the adjutant general's school, Harrison made sergeant first class during his 1946–49 enlistment, whereupon he returned to the University of Mississippi to major in psychology. He served as an infantry platoon sergeant in the reserves while a student, attended jump school, and, as a member of Ole Miss's ROTC program, was commissioned upon graduation in 1951.

Harrison served six years in infantry units before going to flight school in 1958. As a lieutenant colonel, he commanded the 10th Aviation Battalion, 1st Aviation Brigade, for a full year, 1966–67, during his first tour in Vietnam. The battalion supported the then-separate 1st Brigade, 101st Airborne Division, which had preceded the rest of the division to the war zone, in the rugged mountains of II Corps. It was a year of intense combat, during which Harrison earned numerous awards, including the Silver Star and two Distinguished Flying Crosses. Because the aviators not only flew for the infantry but shared their remote and often-mortared forward base camps, Harrison was pinned with a CIB by the Screaming Eagles.

As a brigade commander, Harrison flew his own C&C

Huey. He did so with casual expertise. Lieutenant Colonel Bobby B. Porter, who assumed command of the 1-506th Infantry during the Ripcord battle, recalled an incident involving Harrison's flying skills from the monsoon season of late 1970. One of Porter's platoons had discovered a weapons cache while operating off FSB Rakkasan. The platoon was instructed to remain with the cache until helicopters could evacuate it. Low clouds socked the platoon in for two days, however, preventing the numerous pilots who tried from reaching the position. By the third day, the platoon was in serious need of resupply, and Porter went to the brigade TOC to discuss the matter with Harrison. "Let's give it another shot," Harrison said.

"This time, Colonel Harrison flew the mission himself," noted Porter, who went along and "observed Harrison literally 'walk' his helicopter across the tops of the jungle trees until he was over the platoon. We roped water, rations, and radio batteries into them, plus enough TNT to clear an LZ. Harrison spoke to the platoon leader by radio, instructing him to blow and clear a one-ship LZ, and that we would be back to pick up the platoon and their weapons cache. We then 'walked' the helicopter back to Camp Evans." By the time the platoon had cleared a landing zone, "the ceiling had lifted just a bit," wrote Porter. "Harrison was able to guide several helicopters to the platoon's location, and after a few round trips in and out of the location, he had recovered the platoon and a sizable weapons cache. This is just one minor example of the type of combat commander and helicopter pilot we had in Ben Harrison."

Though General Berry was, like Harrison, new to the division, his reputation was well known. "Sid Berry was outstanding his entire career," wrote Harrison. Berry had been well rewarded for his excellence. "Fairly early in one's career, usually by the rank of captain, the cream rises to the top and the fast-burners are recognized by the hierarchy," noted Harrison. Those so recognized, and Berry was one of them, "get the early, below-the-zone promotions. They also get special attention from the assignment personnel in the Pentagon, who try to provide them the right professional development opportunities—in other words, that combination of staff, school, and command assignments required to enter the upper echelons of the United States Army."

Berry's renown was such that he was profiled by Lewis H. Lapham in *Life* magazine. Lapham described Berry as "a lean and athletic man, not particularly tall and with graying hair cut severely short. His strong face has the impassive cast of a man accustomed to command, an impression enhanced by the thin line of the mouth and the aggressive forward slant of the jaw. It is a face that would lend itself to [being carved] in stone or mint[ed] on coins. . . . I was struck not only by his military bearing but also by an air of exuberant self-confidence that I found inexplicably disturbing and only later came to recognize as a necessary characteristic of the warrior hero. I use the word without irony. Having read the full record of the general's life, I can image him at Thermopylae. . . ."

Raised by his stern, widowed father—a country lawyer and judge who expected great things of his only son—Sid Berry of Hattiesburg, Mississippi, had originally been commissioned with the West Point Class of '48. He was posted to occupation duty in Japan in 1949 and commanded a rifle company in the 25th Infantry Division during the first terrible year of the Korean War, winning two battlefield promotions and coming home in 1951 a twenty-five-year-old major with a Purple Heart, a Bronze Star, and two Silver Stars.

Berry's performance under fire opened doors for him. He was sent to graduate school at Columbia University, taught history at West Point, and, still a major, commanded a mechanized infantry battalion in Germany that had been rated subpar before he turned it around. He attended jump school, ranger school, and Command & General Staff College on his way to making lieutenant colonel. He was selected by Robert S. McNamara to serve as a military assistant in the office of the secretary of defense, one of those prestige positions that mark a rising star, and accompanied McNamara during four trips to Vietnam between 1961 and 1964.

Promoted to colonel after graduating from the Army War College, Berry was assigned in July 1965 as senior advisor to the 7th ARVN Division in the Mekong Delta. He was wounded by a loose grenade while inspecting two captured sampans filled with ammo meant for the VC. As his tour wound down, Berry resisted reassignment to the United States, arranging instead, through his acquaintance with Maj. Gen. William E. DePuy, commanding general (CG), 1st Infantry Division, to take command of a brigade in the Big Red One. DePuy was a hard man to work for. He was, in fact, infamous for his ruthless elimination of subordinates who did not meet his exacting standards. "DePuy was a brilliant, demanding division commander with a solid combat record from WWII," wrote Harrison. "He stated that he would not allow officers to learn how to fight at the expense of his soldiers. They had to be professionally competent when they joined his division. The record reflects that he relieved thirty-nine lieutenant colonels during his one year in command of the Big Red One."

Berry commanded a brigade under DePuy from June 1966 until completing his extended tour in January 1967. The young colonel habitually joined his troops on the ground when they made contact, and earned two more Silver Stars during heavy action in the tropical rain forests of War Zone C northwest of Saigon. Berry exposed himself to enemy fire so routinely and fearlessly that DePuy would tell Lapham that he'd had "no right to survive."

Berry's more than successful command of a brigade in combat won him an early promotion to brigadier general and assignment as assistant commandant of the Infantry School at Fort Benning from 1968 to 1970. "This is a highly sought after position and is considered a great honor by all infantry officers," noted Harrison. Berry was, in fact, being groomed as a future Army Chief of Staff. Senior officers at the Pentagon said as much to Lapham as the writer from *Life* did background research for an article about the process by which a man becomes a general. At the suggestion of those senior officers, Lapham used Berry as his case study, quoting DePuy to the effect that "Sid Berry expresses the ideal of the American soldier. He is what the profession would like to believe itself to be."

Lapham's article, based on conversations with Berry at Fort Benning in the spring of 1970, was a bittersweet portrait of the general as ascetic, ramrod straight in bearing and manner, a reserved, deeply patriotic, and religious man somewhat aloof from his contemporaries, though not lacking in humor and a streak of soldierly sentimentality, who had given himself totally to his profession and his own ambitions. "I know I short the family, but they get conditioned," Berry said coolly. His wife was a devout Quaker. Their home struck Lapham as "unusually silent. The general's two young daughters remained obediently out of sight; his 17-year-old son, who wears his hair long and subscribes to peace movements, played the guitar very softly in an upstairs room. . . ."

Brigadier General Berry returned to Vietnam on July 2, 1970, as assistant division commander for operations, 101st Airborne Division. "Berry visited me and my brigade every day and was frequently critical, but that was no surprise," noted Harrison. "There was no doubt in anyone's mind that General Berry was going to be a very tough taskmaster." That was the role of a division commander's right-hand man. Whereas Berry struck some subordinates as overzealous in his fault-finding, Harrison tended to ascribe such harshness to the lessons he had absorbed with the Big Red One: "It is not unreasonable to assume that Berry thought that DePuy had it right; no one deserves a second chance, fire the SOB, and get some competent professional to replace him."

Harrison further noted that the imminent publication of the Lapham article, which appeared in the September 25, 1970, issue of *Life,* put "considerable pressure on Berry to perform in an exceptionally professional manner and succeed, as portrayed, as the brilliant star of a new generation of Army generals."

The heat was on from the moment Berry reached Camp Eagle. "I liked Sid Berry," said Col. David E. Grange, CO, Division Support Command (DISCOM), 101st, during Ripcord. "We got along well and he took good care of me professionally—but he was a tough guy to work for. He was very professional, very demanding. I mean there were no gray areas with him. It was black and white."

Lieutenant Fox, who came to admire Berry greatly while serving as his command-ship pilot, offered this portrait of the general:

General Berry loved the soldier. He had great compassion for the soldier. When we landed at a firebase, usually unannounced, he would ignore the battalion commander when he came running up to greet him because he didn't want to talk to him at that time. General Berry wanted to get down to the bunker line and talk to the soldiers. He put them first. He wanted to see what they saw, understand what they understood, know what they knew. If it was near lunch time, he wanted to know what was for chow, and whatever that young man in the foxhole was eating, that's what he would eat. If it was C-rations, the general's favorite was beans and franks. The rest of us stayed away until General Berry had finished touring the base and talking to the soldiers, then he would rejoin us at the battalion TOC and receive a briefing. The briefing meant more than it would have otherwise because by talking with the troops, General Berry understood the morale of the unit and what the soldiers were expecting in terms of enemy activity. His conversations told him just how well a battalion was communicating intelligence about the enemy down to the privates.

Berry was a fanatic for details. He had a bulldog temper, noted Fox, when he discovered laxness in a unit:

As the old saying goes, the troops only do best what the boss checks most, but believe me, General Berry checked everything most. He was tireless. When he wasn't out on one firebase, he was monitoring the battalion nets in the command ship on our way to the next firebase. Whenever contact was made anywhere in the division area, he would go there as fast as possible to see what was going on and provide whatever support was needed. General Berry made a lot of people mad. They felt they were being watched over their shoulders, but it kept them on their toes. General Berry told his officers that this is the standard and you will adhere to this standard and I will hold you to this standard.

I remember one incident in which we landed on a hilltop the same afternoon that a company had combat-assaulted onto the site to open a new firebase. We came back three days later and General Berry was shocked to see soldiers sitting around on the perimeter, smoking and really not doing anything in particular. General Berry went down to one of the soldiers and asked him where his fighting position was. The soldier pointed to a shallow foxhole. There were no sandbags, there were no cleared fields of fire, there was no concertina wire, there were no claymores. This was three days after the company had opened the firebase, and it should have been done in three hours. General Berry hauled the company commander down into the TOC and ran everybody else out. I thought I was going to see that young captain come flying out of the bunker in pieces and parts because General Berry was just furious that he had exhibited such poor leadership and such lack of concern for his soldiers to not even have them prepare adequate defensive positions for their own safety. General Berry had the battalion commander bring out a new company commander and escort the other officer off the firebase, and he stayed there until that new captain actively had people digging foxholes and setting up concertina wire.

Berry enjoyed being photographed—the function, as his detractors saw it, of an overblown ego. Captain Michaud, battery commander with the 2-319th FA, was left a little cold when the cameras began clicking during one of Berry's visits to FSB Rakkasan. "It was during the monsoon, and we'd been living in the rain and mud for weeks on end," recalled Michaud. "Berry got off his helicopter all spit and polish, and jumped into a fighting position knee-deep in mud while his aide stood at the edge of the position taking pictures of him. That wasn't the kind of thing your typical general did."

Berry assumed an aggressive stance when conferring with subordinates, feet well apart, arms crossed over his chest, head tilted back to one side, eyes narrowed to skeptical slits. "Berry was not one for small talk or chitchat," noted Colonel Harrison. "He did not talk with anyone so much as question them, and his style was to be on the offensive, to take the initiative and set the terms."

Lieutenant Colonel Porter of the 1-506th, a future general

officer himself, recalled that "one got the feeling of being in a 'gotcha' situation when conversing with General Berry. I'm sure he didn't intend to, but he projected somewhat of a pompous attitude. I had no reservations, however, about his tactical competence."

Captain Hawkins of A/2-506th saw only strength in Berry's persona and considered the assistant division commander "one of the few generals with any real guts." Hawkins elaborated:

> Once, after Ripcord, when we were working the FSB Kathryn AO, General Berry landed his C&C ship in the midst of a CA I was conducting. His aide kicked out a ruck and an M16 and took off with the ship. Berry told me he would be spending the night and not to worry about him, he would join my CP after the dust had settled. He spent the next four hours talking to and working with the troops. He helped them assign sectors of fire, construct foxholes, fire in defensive targets, debrief recon patrols, you name it. Then he and my RTO dug his foxhole at my CP and we settled in for an evening of discussion. Our big bitch was radio call signs for artillery forward observers, which remained the same and allowed the NVA to identify the units after listening to the FO for a few minutes. Three days later Berry had the Signal Security Instructions/Signal Operating Instructions (SSI/SOI) completely revamped.

Colonel Walter H. Root's memories of Berry are instructive. The commander of the 2d Brigade of the 101st Airborne Division wrote: "Sid Berry had well developed notions of what a combat commander should be—what he should look like, act like, talk like, think like. Sid lived up to those standards in every way himself, and had some trouble concealing his disdain for those who didn't."

Root thought Berry's disdain sometimes misplaced. On the occasion of Berry's first visit to Root's brigade, he met Root out on one of the firebases in the 2d Brigade AO. Root, in turn, introduced the general to the battalion commander on the base. The battalion commander saluted smartly, and Berry asked, "How are things going?" The battalion commander replied,

"About as well as could be expected, sir." On the way back to his helicopter, Berry said to Root, "That officer should be relieved of his command. Anyone satisfied with the status quo has no business commanding troops in this division." Root was taken aback, though he did not think Berry entirely serious. "Berry's comment was intended, I guess, to impress me," recalled Root. "It didn't. I thought it a very extreme response to someone who was just trying to be modest. Not all of us are showmen. The battalion commander concerned was actually a favorite of mine and the division commander. Berry mellowed a lot in the ensuing months, and better than any other commander I have known, he could get in front of a group of men and make them feel that there wasn't anything they couldn't accomplish."

General Hennessey, the division commander, had been forced to postpone Operation Chicago Peak, the offensive into the Co Pung Mountain area that Ripcord existed to support, because of the air cavalry squadron's discovery of the enemy regiment near Khe Sanh. Chicago Peak, already postponed several times by corps, had finally been scheduled to begin on July 10. The pressure was considerable to get the operation rolling so that as much damage could be done to the enemy as possible before the seasonal approach of the monsoon once again forced the division out of the mountains.

"I spent the morning flying in the nose of a Cobra gunship out over the Ashau Valley[,] reconnoitering the area of operations in which we'll launch our next major operation," Berry wrote home in reference to Chicago Peak. "Got a good look at the excellent, well-traveled roads the NVA use to haul their men and equipment through Laos and the Ashau Valley right into the area where we are now fighting them [that is, the Ripcord AO]. . . . This is going to be a difficult operation. The enemy seems to be there in real strength and with many antiaircraft weapons. We are going into his vitals, his supply bases that he has established via Laos."

The operation could not begin until the Ripcord fight had been finished. To accomplish that, Hennessey and Berry planned to maximize the pressure on the enemy around

Ripcord. The taking of Hill 805 by A/2-506th and D/2-501st had been part of that plan, as had the increased use of supporting arms around Ripcord.

The plan next called for Lieutenant Colonel Livingston's 2-501st Infantry, the division swing battalion, to assault and seize Hill 1000. The key terrain feature had been hit with numerous air strikes since Lucas's two aborted assaults had revealed the depth of the NVA defenses, but "you cannot suppress a determined enemy indefinitely with firepower alone," noted Harrison. "At some point the only real solution would be U. S. infantry on the high ground."

The swing battalion was lifted out of the field on July 11 to get resupplied and reorganized at Camp Evans. Livingston flew in from the TOC he shared with Lucas on Ripcord to brief his company commanders. The attack that Livingston outlined called for a rolling artillery barrage, behind which Companies A, B, and C, and the battalion reconnaissance platoon, converging on the objective from different angles, were to push the NVA off Hill 1000. It was the only time in memory that the battalion was actually being called upon to operate as a battalion. "Captain Goates was ecstatic," said Jim Kwiecien of A/2-501st, who would recall with distaste someone making the excited suggestion that "we round up some pins so we could stick 101st patches to the eyes of dead dinks."

Lieutenant Arndt's recon platoon combat-assaulted into a hot LZ atop Coc Muen Mountain during the afternoon of July 12, followed by Companies B and C. Several men refused to board the slicks when it was Company A's turn to lift off the pad at Camp Evans. Two were from Lieutenant Kwiecien's platoon, new men badly shaken by their baptism by fire the previous week on Hill 902. "They sheepishly admitted that they were afraid to go back out," wrote Kwiecien, who, busy getting the rest of his platoon saddled up, only vaguely noticed the two being "walked off with someone escorting them. I was later informed that one of them, a sergeant who gave the appearance of being really sharp, but who was in reality a heavy-duty doper, was court-martialled and spent some time in LBJ. I would assume the same thing happened to the second man, which is too bad because I think he would have turned out differently if he'd had a less brutal introduction to the war."

A third man in the platoon had also considered opting for Long Binh Jail over Hill 1000. "Hoffman was kind of a gentle guy with a Master's in history," recalled Kwiecien. Though Hoffman was certainly frightened, "his problem was more intellectual. He told me the day before the assault that he didn't like the person he was becoming as a grunt. I asked the battalion surgeon to talk to him, and he came around." Kwiecien and Hoffman ended up in the same unit in the States after their tours in Vietnam. "I was very happy he made it out alive," noted Kwiecien, "because if I had to pick who wouldn't have made it, it would have been him. He's probably a professor somewhere now."

Captain Goates and Company A combat-assaulted onto Triple Hill. The LZ was being secured for them by Captain Rollison and D/2-506th. Delta Company had humped to Ripcord two days earlier. By the time the troops had been resupplied, several men had been seriously wounded by incoming recoilless-rifle fire. What was left of the company moved off the base with mortar shells exploding in the perimeter wire to either side of the column.

Delta Company fought its way to the top of Triple Hill the following evening, pushing off a squad of NVA. There had been a Caucasian with the enemy, presumably the same one spotted in the area three weeks earlier by B/2-506th. "I personally saw him at the top of the hill while we were still at the bottom," stated Rollison. "He was wearing a bush hat and aviator shades. I assumed he was a Russian advisor. Without taking my eyes off him for fear I would lose sight of him in the vegetation, I borrowed an M16 from one of my RTOs, sighted in, aiming uphill, and squeezed off a single shot. When we took the hill, we found a large blood stain where he had been."

Lieutenant Colonel Livingston and a small field command group accompanied Alpha Company as it moved off the LZ and set up an NDP on another of the knolls composing Triple Hill. "A battalion commander had actually donned a rucksack and gotten on the ground with his troops," wrote Kwiecien. "The men positively loved him for this. It just impressed the hell out of them. I mean, here's this old guy, he had to be about forty, struggling with a ruck just like the grunts."

After digging in at dusk, Livingston, a former tac officer at the ranger school, discussed with Goates the possibility of conducting a night recon of the objective. "Livingston wanted to make such a recon, but only with volunteers," noted Goates. "I tried to put together a group of men who were willing to tackle such an assignment, but was only able to come up with about ten men, myself included. Livingston thought it unwise to go with so small a group. Livingston, incidentally, had planned to accompany us had we gone. He had a set of . . ."

The next day was spent prepping the objective. Lieutenant Arndt's recon platoon began the cautious advance on Hill 1000 early the following morning, July 14, approaching from the southwest while Captain Goates and Alpha Company edged in from the north. The recon platoon, moving down the ridge that knifed off Coc Muen in the direction of Hill 1000, was still a full kilometer from the objective when its point man turned to Arndt and whispered that they had NVA to their right front. Quickly looking where the point man indicated, Arndt too saw an enemy soldier. The man was only forty meters away, casually walking from one position to another within what appeared to be a bunker complex.

"What do you want me to do?" the point man asked.

"Shoot the bastard," Arndt answered, moving to bring the rest of the platoon up even before the point man cut loose with his M16.

The enemy immediately returned fire. Arndt was rushing back up to the front when rocket-propelled grenades began exploding in the treetops, and he was suddenly blown backward over a log with a little bit of shrapnel in his right shoulder and a lot in his left leg. The recon platoon had nine men wounded in total by the RPGs.

The worst casualty was lifted out by jungle penetrater. Lieutenant Arndt brought in the Cobras soon thereafter, but all attempts to maneuver were met with more enemy fire, as was a medevac that hovered over a clearing a hundred meters back from the bunker complex to which some of the wounded had been moved. The Huey, stitched across its fuel cell and tail boom by a burst of AK-47 fire, managed to make an emergency landing on Ripcord.

Four hours after contact had first been made, two medevacs landed in the insertion LZ atop Coc Muen. "Those of us who were wounded had to crawl away from the bunker complex," Arndt wrote. "You couldn't stand up and expect not to get shot." The enemy took the mountaintop landing zone under fire at the approach of the medevacs, which "stopped just long enough for us to jump in, then took off again as fast as those Hueys could go."

Livingston had previously instructed Capt. Robert G. Stanton, commander of B/2-501st, to bypass the recon platoon and hit the enemy from the flank. Six and a half hours into the action, at which time Stanton was three hundred meters north of the recon's position, the lead platoon of Bravo Company encountered still more enemy bunkers on the northeastern slope of Coc Muen, down near the draw separating the mountain from Hill 1000. The point man was within fifty meters of the camouflaged bunkers when the shooting started. The platoon leader, 1st Lt. Robert L. Worrall, was hit several times. The platoon medic was also hit; a radioman pulled him to cover and, unshouldering his shot-up radio, grabbed the medic's aid bag and took over treatment of the wounded until he too was hit. The medic from the next platoon in the column rushed forward to help and became a casualty himself. In a few chaotic moments, Bravo Company had one KIA and eleven WIA.

In coordination with his wounded lieutenant, Stanton had a pair of Cobras from C/4-77th ARA rocket the bunker complex so the lead platoon could break contact. Three NVA were reported killed in the action. The first set of Cobras was replaced by a second set when it broke station to refuel and rearm. After the ground elements again popped smoke to mark their positions, the rocket runs continued. The Cobras, diving from north to south through the draw between Coc Muen and Hill 1000, began taking fire from a .51-caliber machine gun positioned at the southwestern base of Hill 1000.

Captain Goates, standing by in reserve on the western side of the hill and overlooking Stanton's action in the bunker complex, instructed Lieutenant Driver's platoon, Alpha One, to destroy the .51 while Kwiecien and Alpha Two advanced on a mortar firing from somewhere near the gun position. Goates, still energized about meeting the enemy in conventional battle, "was up front," recalled a chagrined Kwiecien, "telling the squads where to go and what to do himself, totally ignoring his platoon leaders."

Alpha One, in the lead, engaged a pair of enemy soldiers in spiderholes upon cresting a small ridge and, moving forward, eliminated them with grenades. Next, and the action was then at the eight-hour mark, one of the Cobras took more fire from the .51 while making its break to the left as it came out of a rocket run. It responded with four quick 40mm rounds from its chin-mounted grenade launcher. The rounds missed their target, exploding instead between Alpha One and Alpha Two, which had advanced to within two hundred meters of the enemy machine gun. Five men were wounded in the mishap, including Driver and Kwiecien. It is unclear whether Goates had failed to inform Stanton, who was controlling the rocket runs, that he had an element advancing past the smoke grenades previously used to mark his position or, if so informed, Stanton had neglected to explain the maneuver to the section leader of the Cobras. In any event, the aircrews continued making their runs for B/2-501st, unaware until a subsequent investigation of the incident that they had fired up A/2-501st.

Lieutenant Kwiecien, paying no attention to the gunships as his platoon advanced on the enemy, did not himself realize they were taking friendly fire when the grenades suddenly exploded in front of him. Something hit his shoulder like a rock from a slingshot, and he assumed that it was, in fact, a rock sent flying by the explosions. Everyone crouched where they were to see what was happening. Kwiecien reached into his left breast pocket, flipped open his plastic cigarette case, and pulled out a cigarette. It was cut in half. He pulled out another cigarette. It too was cut in half. Alarmed, Kwiecien pulled out the case itself and saw that a piece of shrapnel had gone through it. "I looked at the spot on my shoulder where I had felt the impact," he later wrote. "Nothing. I next looked inside my shirt.

There was a black and blue mark about the size of a silver dollar where I had been hit by a single piece of shrapnel. There was very little blood, though."

Kwiecien realized then that Chau Ngoc Tu, the platoon's Kit Carson scout, was lying in the open, moaning in pain. Thinking they had taken enemy fire, Kwiecien scrambled forward to pull Tu to cover, but when he tried to pick up the scout—with one arm behind his back, the other under his legs—the injured man let out a shriek, and screaming in Vietnamese let it be known that he hurt too badly to be moved. Tu's left leg had been chewed up by shrapnel, and a broken bone had split through the skin from a compound fracture.

Sergeant McCoy and the platoon's other scout, Kai, moved up to help Kwiecien. Kai gave Tu holy hell in Vietnamese, and McCoy, who had picked up the language without benefit of formal training, told Kwiecien that Kai was scolding his fellow scout for acting like a baby. McCoy picked up Tu and carried him out of harm's way as both platoons began pulling back on order. "The big attack," noted Kwiecien, "had been called off."

CHAPTER 19

Regrouping

Captain Goates was provided a flight of Skyraiders from the Vietnamese Air Force. The stubby, prop-driven aircraft, ideal for close air support, dropped cluster bombs to cover Alpha Company's withdrawal to Triple Hill. "It was the only time I saw cluster bombs used," wrote Kwiecien, who had been informed by Goates that an enemy force had been spotted moving in pursuit of Alpha Company. "I remember thinking that the cluster bombs were sure taking care of anything behind us. Despite being wounded in the shoulder, I was still humping my ruck, and it hurt like hell. . . ."

Lieutenant Colonel Livingston choppered over with his field CP to spend the night in the NDP which was being established by Bravo and Charlie Companies and the recon platoon several hundred meters back up the ridge from the bunker complex at the base of Coc Muen.

The enemy mortared the overnight position near dusk from the top of Coc Muen, and a medevac took automatic fire, one round hitting a rotor, as it lifted out with Bravo Company's WIAs. Alpha Company's casualties, meanwhile, were medevacked from Triple Hill. Kwiecien recalled that when the Huey landed at the 85th Evac, "some earnest young medic came running up to me to help. He stopped dead in his tracks about three feet away and asked if I wanted to take a shower first—that's how bad I smelled."

Lieutenant Kwiecien had been wounded three times during his three months in the field. The third wound was far more serious than it looked or felt. "Apparently, the shrapnel had barely missed an artery and some nerves," noted Kwiecien, who ended up with a medical profile and reassignment to brigade staff. Kwiecien was still being treated at the evac hospital when a Vietnamese baby was rushed in, having been medevacked from one of the lowland villages after crawling into a mechanical ambush. "Half his face was gone," wrote Kwiecien. "I could see the baby's X-rays from my gurney, and the paths the claymore pellets had taken through his body looked like a street map. I decided at that point that there couldn't be a God. It would have been okay for something like that to happen to me, after all, I was trying to kill people, but not to a kid like that. I stuck with my atheism for a number of years, but God finally reached out and brought me home."

Lieutenant Colonel Lucas received an alert from division G2 at 6:20 P.M. on July 14. As recorded in the battalion log, it read: "Recent intelligence [presumably, intercepted enemy radio transmissions] and very recent agent reports indicate strong possibility of sapper attack on FB Ripcord tonight. Highly reliable agent [presumably, a team from the division LRRPs] reported obs'[erv]ing en[emy] sapper force vic[inity] Ripcord and making final attack preparations."

The alert was received shortly before the evening briefing, in which Lucas spoke from a small podium in his TOC. "The briefings were very organized and surprisingly formal, given our situation," noted Fred Edwards, the battalion engineering officer. "We were always kept well informed." Speaking to the predicted attack, Lucas said that he welcomed it. "I want the bastards to come up this hill because if they do we're going to kick their ass," declared Black Spade. Edwards would later muse that "if anyone else had said such a thing, I would have thought the bastard was crazy. Lucas, however, instilled a lot of confidence just by his bearing, and he made it sound completely logical that we were going to clean their clocks if they attacked.

"We felt helpless amid the incoming," Edwards continued.

"The only way we could strike back at the enemy was if they actually tried to get through the wire, and as gut wrenching a prospect as that was, it had to be better than facing the random hell that rained down on us every day. There was no fear in anyone's eyes, just grim determination. Everybody had complete confidence that we would destroy the enemy in their tracks."

General Berry typed a letter to his wife that night:

> 2230 Tuesday, 14 July 1970 [Camp Eagle]
>
> Why am I writing at this hour? Because I'm so angry with two commanders—actually three—that I can't sleep. And because I expect an attack on Firebase Ripcord tonight or in the early morning and have been planning the defensive and offensive fires that will catch the enemy in their preparation and advance to attack.
>
> I may relieve a battalion commander [Livingston], perhaps another [Lucas], and possibly a brigade commander [Harrison]. Or to be precise, I may recommend their relief to General Hennessey. The brigade commander and his two battalion commanders have neglected to use sufficient supporting fires—air and artillery—in support of their soldiers on the ground. . . . This is particularly unacceptable when I personally have been instructing them each day to use heavier amounts of fire and telling them how to do it. . . .

Berry was the author of a widely distributed pamphlet, *Observations of a Brigade Commander,* which enjoined commanders to "expend ammunition like a millionaire and lives like a miser."

Putting words into action, the new assistant division commander had, among other things, ordered enough 81mm ammunition be shipped to Ripcord as of July 13 to increase the number of mortar rounds being fired around the base each night from five hundred to a thousand.

To return to Berry's terse letter:

> . . . believing that the two battalion commanders inadequately plan and use supporting fires . . . [and] further

> believing that the brigade commander should take personal control of the situation, I sent him to spend the night on Firebase Ripcord . . . I told him that I'll check every two hours to see that he has employed a heavier volume of fire around his troops each subsequent two-hour period.
>
> Forgive this "I" business, but that's the way it is. General Hennessey expects his ADC, Operations, to run the division's operations; and that's what I'm doing. With a vengeance. By Big Red One standards, the 101st Airborne Division has a long way to go. By Bill DePuy's standards, half the battalion commanders and two of three brigade commanders would have been relieved during the 12 days I've been here. . . . It's criminal to tolerate a weak commander. Soldiers deserve the best leadership, and they can't influence the quality of the leadership assigned to them. But I can, and I will. . . .

Harrison recalls that he had already planned to spend the night on Ripcord when instructed to do so by Berry. In any event, Harrison flew to Ripcord with Maj. James E. King, the new brigade operations officer, plus the air force major who served as the brigade's air liaison officer and Lieutenant Case, the acting arty LNO. "I spent most of that night drinking coffee in the crowded battalion TOC," noted Case. "I didn't think the NVA would launch a ground attack against a fully alerted firebase."

To make sure they did not, Harrison assured Berry, as indicated in the brigade log, that "[we] are employing 360° arty fire & 81mm around Ripcord & fri[endly] positions; are also having basketball [USAF flareship] on sta[tion] & 3 CH-47 [flareships] in reserve [at Camp Evans]. We will have FAC's ready to bring in air [in the event of attack] . . ."

The enemy attack, when it came, was launched not against the firebase but Captain Straub's embattled position on Hill 805. When hit, Straub immediately fired a red star-cluster flare to signal Capt. Ray Williams, Lucas's arty LNO on Ripcord, "and within 2 or 3 minutes they were receiving [preplotted] defensive fires from 105's, 155's, 81mm's, and quad 50's," read an after-action report prepared by Williams. "Due to the highly accurate and heavy concentration of defensive fires, D/2-501st sustained only [two casualties] . . ."

Berry commented on the battle in a subsequent letter home:

> No attack on Ripcord last night. But we put out sufficient artillery, mortar, and grenade fire[,] plus air strikes[,] to discourage any planned attack. Also, some commanders learned something about planning and using supporting arms. . . . Thank God for my training in the Big Red One under Bill DePuy. More than ever now I realize what a superb outfit we were. And I realize how much I learned from DePuy and the BRO. My aim is to transfer those lessons, practices, and standards into the Screaming Eagles. . . .

Considerable friction developed between Berry and Harrison. Berry was dubious that Harrison's command of an aviation battalion had adequately prepared him to lead an infantry brigade in combat. (Harrison would have argued that his combined infantry-aviation background well qualified him for command in an airmobile division.) Berry's displeasure extended to Harrison's staff, which he found extremely weak in terms of experience and military schooling. As the stalemate at Ripcord continued, he became increasingly impatient and short tempered during meetings in the TOC at Camp Evans. During one meeting, Major King began to make a tactical suggestion, only to be cut off by Berry, who, already knowing the answer, archly asked the operations officer, "And when did you graduate from Command and General Staff College?"

"I haven't been there yet, sir," King replied, his anger barely concealed. Berry moved on with a dismissive, "Uh-huh."

Fred Spaulding was flabbergasted by the exchange, considering that King had served as S3 of a line battalion for six months before moving up to brigade, a qualification more important, he thought, than Command & General Staff College. "They didn't even teach Vietnam there," Spaulding noted, "and I remember thinking, well, what the hell, just because some of us don't have CGSC diplomas, all of a sudden we're not worthy enough to speak our minds?"

Berry recommended to Harrison that King be relieved. Harrison demurred, thinking King a solid combat officer. But whatever protection Harrison tried to offer his staff, Berry's continuous ripostes nevertheless had a demoralizing effect. "General Berry was a martinet, the kind of arrogant ass who would relieve you for not kissing his ring," said Spaulding. "It was also my impression that he was prejudiced against officers who weren't West Pointers."

Captain Echols, recently assigned to brigade, dejectedly told Lieutenant Case, his former FO, "We're all going to be fired."

"Ripcord was pretty much shaping up as a debacle," Case wrote, "and my impression was that everyone's head, except mine, was on the chopping block. The captains and majors had careers to worry about. I did not. In sum, there were a lot of officers working in the 3d Brigade TOC who were very concerned not only about Ripcord itself but also about how the battle was going to affect their careers."

The wisest analysis of the situation was probably offered by Chuck Shay, whom Berry considered the best battalion commander in the division. "Sid Berry and Ben Harrison were both first-class guys," said Shay. "Berry was an up-front guy. He told people exactly what he thought, and, of course, he was confronted by people who told him back what they thought. So until everybody got to know everybody better, there was probably a little intolerance on both sides. The best of intentions have to be worked out man to man."

Captain Straub, like his men, was haggard and hollow-eyed by the time of the third attack on Hill 805. "I basically stopped eating and sleeping after the first night," said Straub. "I couldn't stop checking on things and thinking about what else we could do to prepare for the next attack. I forced myself to eat. There was zero hunger. I was just going on water and cigarettes and a very intense desire to get the company through this." Straub was consoled only by "the very good fire support we were getting, and the guts of the troops. They fought like tigers and showed how much they cared for each other."

According to Lieutenant Shipley, Straub had tried, during Lucas's visit on the morning of July 14, to secure permission to move D/2-501st off the bald hilltop. He was unsuccessful. "There wasn't any hope," stated Shipley. "The NVA were watching and could see our casualties being medevacked out each day. They knew and we knew that it was only a matter of time before we were overrun."

The observation posts were pulled in at dusk. The waiting began, the company at 50 percent alert. As noted by Captain Williams, Straub fired a red star-cluster flare when the RPGs started shrieking in—the third attack began at 10:53 P.M. on July 14—bringing down a wall of mortar and artillery fire while the troops, many already injured in the previous attacks, heaved grenades and laid down a sheet of M16 and M60 fire from their foxholes and makeshift bunkers. The third attack came mainly from the south and southeast, where Shipley's platoon, Delta Two, was positioned. Straub had been provided during the day with two 90mm recoilless rifles. One faced the LZ across which the previous attack had come, and one was set up near Shipley's CP. Shipley presently warned his men away from the rear of the weapon, given its ferocious backblast. While the platoon leader loaded, the trooper assigned as gunner began punching off flechette rounds known as Beehives. "Each Beehive shell sends out thousands of tiny steel darts in an expanding cone of fire," noted Shipley, "ripping through anything and anybody in their path. They'll go right through a small tree."

The effect on the enemy was devastating. Straub and his forward observer, Lieutenant Potter, were also in for a shock as close as they were in the crowded perimeter to the recoilless rifle. "The backblast of each round would blow my chin-strapped helmet to the side of my head," noted Potter, who was crouched beside a boulder, radio pressed to one ear, hand to the other, as he helped coordinate the supporting arms. "Rocks and dirt were blown all over our command post. It was sort of like sticking your head in the back end of a jet engine after feeding the front end with gravel."

The sappers continued to work their way forward in the face

of all the fire being thrown at them, covering one another with AK-47 fire as they darted from boulder to boulder until they were within throwing range of Delta Two. Satchel charges began exploding inside the lines with head-ringing blasts. Shipley's medic, in position just below the platoon leader, told him the next morning about a satchel charge that had almost landed in the platoon CP. "He just happened to raise his arm one moment," recounted Shipley, "and an incoming plastic explosive hit his arm and fell back outside and blew up. Except for his raised arm, the explosive would have landed in my position and blown us all up."

Specialist Fourth Class Gary L. Schneider of Delta Two was firing an M60, which was a key target for enemy fire, when his bunker took a direct hit from an RPG. There were four men in the bunker. The blast blew them all out of the position. Two were injured, Schneider seriously. The others were unscathed, thanks to their helmets and flak jackets, but one of them—terrified, and strung out from lack of sleep—went temporarily insane at the sight of his wounded buddies. "He clutched my leg, screaming hysterically," recalled Shipley, who could barely control his platoon's fire and keep the recoilless rifle loaded with the trooper hanging on him. "I thought he was going crazy. It took about half an hour before we got him quieted down."

The enemy hit the perimeter with tear gas. The troops didn't know where it came from—some of the satchel charges were probably embedded with crystallized CS—but suddenly people were choking, crying, unable to breathe, and able to resume firing only after donning gas masks. The air soon cleared on the windy hilltop, and the claustrophobia-inducing gas masks were ripped away.

Everything happened fast, without thought. When an explosion started a fire in the deadfall, which was as dry as kindling, and lit up the positions on that side of the hill, "we ran down with a couple canisters of water and put it out, right in the middle of the firefight," recounted Shipley. "The whole night was crazy like that. I probably should have been dead a hundred times."

At Captain Straub's direction, the two Cobras that had been

scrambled began making minigun and rocket runs at 11:14 P.M. The troops kept up their fire, cursing the NVA. "We were screamin' and cussin' and throwin' grenades," said Shipley. "The enemy must have thought we were a bunch of idiots, screaming down the hill at them like that, but it worked on them psychologically. They were so close, we thought we were going to have hand-to-hand combat. We'd already made up our minds that we'd fight to the last man. We weren't going to be captured. In the midst of the firefight, fear was not a problem. We had complete control, most of us. It was before, and after, that we were scared."

The attack subsided as flareships lit up the area. Straub requested a night medevac for Schneider, who was unconscious and going into shock, his breathing weak, his pulse fading. Shipley's platoon medic methodically pumped Schneider's heart while Doc Fowler, the senior company medic, performed mouth-to-mouth, keeping him alive, if barely, until the medevac arrived at 1:12 A.M. The pilot spent forty minutes trying to maintain a hover long enough to lower a basket. The howling winds made it impossible. Low on fuel, the pilot finally had to break station, reporting to Straub before departing that there was only one pilot in his company capable of holding an aircraft steady under such conditions. "Hang in there. We're gonna call for him."

While waiting for the second medevac, Delta Company began taking 75mm recoilless-rifle fire, plus some 82mm mortar fire, thirty-six rounds in all. Most of the recoilless-rifle shells hissed past the little bouldered hilltop to explode harmlessly on the lower slopes. The mortar fire was more accurate. "The enemy would bracket our position," noted Lieutenant Potter, "one short, one long, then one in the middle. It was nerve-wracking because our overhead cover could not stop the direct hit of a mortar shell. . . ."

Gunships swooped in on the firing positions. The fire stopped. The two medics had continued their lifesaving work on Schneider the whole time, oblivious of the bombardment. "He was bleeding internally," Fowler later wrote, "and each time I breathed into him, I got a mouthful of blood. I cannot describe in words what that was like. I spit the blood out and continued the artificial resuscitation. When the second medevac arrived, we still had a pulse."

That second medevac came on station at 2:41 A.M. The enemy greeted it with automatic-weapons fire despite the flares and the suppressive fire being laid down by mortars and gunships and, most furiously, the grunts of Delta Company. "The pilot reported to me that the winds were up to sixty knots," recounted Captain Straub. "He nevertheless held his aircraft as steady as a rock over the blinking strobe that marked our position, taking enemy fire all the while as we strapped our wounded man into the basket that had been lowered. I never saw anything braver in the whole war."

The enemy's fire on an unarmed medevac killed Gary Schneider. "The medics had kept him alive for hours," said Shipley, "but he was killed while being hoisted up in the basket. They found several bullet holes in him when the medevac landed at Camp Evans."

The area fell silent. Straub scanned the night with a starlight scope as flares continued to pop overhead. The troops waited in their positions, exhausted, unable to sleep, chewing Tootsie Rolls. It was still two hours before dawn when several trip flares went off only fifty meters in front of Delta One. Everything cranked up again—M16s, M60s, M79s, and the recoilless rifles, plus more arty, more ARA. The enemy backed off without returning fire. "We were nearly out of ammo by then," noted Potter. "If the NVA had pressed the attack, they would have had us. . . ."

Security patrols moved out in the morning, finding blood trails and chewed-up equipment among logs and trees that were saturated with flechettes. Hueys touched down on the landing zone below the top of the hill with everything needed for another day in position—ammo, frags, claymores, flares, rations, radio batteries, medical supplies, canisters of water foul with purification tablets. As the company got reorganized, "the captain called me to one side and asked me to wash my face," recalled Fowler, who produced a small mirror from his personal gear and saw that "the horror of war was all over me. I had dried blood all around my lips and nose, my teeth were red, my hands were stained, my uniform had blood all over it. I washed myself, got some other clothes, and tried to put it behind me. We were staying on the hill, and we knew we were going to get attacked again when the sun went down. . . ."

Berry tried late that morning to join Lieutenant Colonel Livingston at his command post on the narrow ridge knifing down from Coc Muen Mountain. The landing zone inside Livingston's perimeter was too cluttered to allow a helicopter to land on terra firma, but Lieutenant Fox, the command-ship pilot, thought he could hover low enough over the deadfall and between the tree stumps so that Berry could safely disembark. Fox, careful not to let the wind push him into any trees on the way in, was about twenty meters from touchdown when he realized that there was a black soldier lying on his back at the edge of the landing zone. He was the only man Fox could see, the rest being concealed in the thick brush. The man was firing a CAR15 with one hand and frantically waving the helicopter off with the other. Fox could neither hear nor see what was happening on the ground, but the door gunner on the opposite side of the aircraft, Sp4 Thomas J. Chase, saw muzzle flashes winking at him from the underbrush and he shouted a warning over the intercom. "Lieutenant Fox was one hell of a pilot," recalled Chase, noting how Fox banked to their right and dropped down into the valley below the ridge so quickly and so sharply to avoid the fire that "one of the general's aides, who didn't have his seat belt on, almost flew out of the aircraft."

Berry instructed Fox to make another attempt to land, but Fox again had to break away in the face of heavy fire. Fox thought the incident an inspiring example of the risks Berry was willing to take to get on the ground with his soldiers. "When we flew back to refuel, I noticed that I had taken a round right in my ammo box," said Chase, who had quite another take on the incident. "It was foolish. It was an unnecessary risk for a general. There had been something like four or five generals killed in Nam already at that time. We didn't need a sixth. Berry scared me. He thought he was John Wayne."

In a letter home, Berry noted that as his helicopter departed the area, "I jestingly accused Livingston by radio of giving me an unfriendly reception just so I couldn't land and harass him."

Berry had, in fact, wanted to get on the ground to take Livingston aside and tell him in private that old ties notwithstanding—the two had been on good terms since Lieutenant Livingston had been a tac officer for Major Berry's class at the ranger school—he was prepared to relieve him of command should he not use the firepower available to him to better effect on Hill 1000. Chase described Berry as having been "incensed" as he monitored the previous day's failed attack over the radios in the C&C Huey. Livingston's own officers thought the problem was not the improper use of supporting arms but the tenacity of the enemy and the restrictions on taking anything but light U. S. casualties. "If Livingston had been relieved, it would have been a massive injustice," said Jim Kwiecien. "The guy was a fantastic battalion commander."

Livingston called in artillery, then the resupply ships bearing the ammunition needed before the 2-501st Infantry again maneuvered toward Hill 1000. One of the first slicks to attempt to land had its tail shot off by a .51 and crashed down the ridge from the LZ. The pilot lost his leg in the crash. The resupply effort was disrupted not only by enemy fire but also by the high winds. Captain Goates watched from atop Triple Hill as one resupply ship started toward his position from Ripcord. "Halfway there, the wind blew the Huey in a 360-degree circle," Goates wrote, "shaking it like a dog with a toy, and forcing the pilot to return to the firebase. I don't think I have ever seen wind move an aircraft like that before or since."

The attack was held up as more arty, as well as ARA and tac air, was directed against various confirmed and suspected enemy positions. It was not until approximately 2 P.M. that Livingston's recon platoon began moving toward the bunker complex between Coc Muen and Hill 1000. Meanwhile, the site of the shot-down resupply ship had been secured by a line platoon, and a CH-47 arrived to extract the disabled Huey. The mission was aborted under heavy fire, the pilot of the Chinook banking away with six bullet holes in his aircraft as the two escorting Cobras rolled in on the NVA.[1]

The recon platoon made contact in the bunker complex, still occupied despite the pounding it had taken, at 4 P.M. Instead of reinforcing the action, Livingston pulled his people back and resumed firing artillery on the area. Loath to spend a second night in the same location, Livingston then moved his field CP, the recon platoon, and Companies B and C four hundred meters up the ridge toward the top of Coc Muen Mountain. Similarly, Company A, which had tentatively advanced toward Hill 1000 during the day, humped a klick west of Triple Hill to set up a new NDP.

Livingston's cautious approach was in keeping with the guidance he was getting from Harrison, who was, in turn, responding to Berry and Hennessey. "We had identified Hill 1000 as being very strongly defended, but we were not directed at that time to make another assault," recalled Livingston. "I think the enemy force on and around the hill was a lot larger than brigade and division had expected. We were up against a formidable, dug-in enemy, and the concern was that Hill 1000 could become another Hamburger Hill. Nobody wanted to be responsible for that. The division was still in a state of shock over Hamburger Hill, so there was some indecision in the operation at that point, a lull of sorts as the upper echelons sorted the problem out and decided how best to proceed." Livingston's impression was that division hoped firepower alone would drive the enemy off the hill, but, given the position's tactical importance, "it was not inconceivable that the word would come down to go take that hill. I was ready to go, and so were the troops."

Harrison, apparently disappointed that Livingston had not taken the objective on the first try and thus resolved the dilemma, informed Livingston after the battle that, like Berry, he had contemplated relieving him of command. "I was completely floored," recalled Livingston, unsure what he could have done differently and unimpressed with Harrison's contention that by taking his CP to the field he had disrupted the brigade commander's ability to confer with him face-to-face and better coordinate the action. Harrison's ire made more sense to Livingston when he learned of Harrison's concern that he might himself be relieved by Berry. "Everybody tends to relieve everybody when things go bad," Livingston noted philosophically.

Harrison's rebuke nevertheless left a bad taste in Livingston's mouth and confirmed the negative impression he had formed of Harrison when he first met the latest brigade commander to which his swing battalion had been attached. The meeting took place in the TOC on Ripcord. "Harrison's major concern at that moment in life was to prepare Andre Lucas and me for an imminent visit from General Berry," recalled Livingston. "He was quite agitated as he laid out how we should react when Berry arrived. Harrison wanted to butter up General Berry. I could understand that, but he was going so overboard that I came away thinking that the only concern this latest colonel I was working for had was how he looked to his superiors. I didn't like Harrison from that first meeting, and I think he sensed it. Harrison and I did not have a particularly good relationship during Ripcord."

The decision on whether or not to continue the attacks would have to be made without General Hennessey. The division commander departed Camp Eagle at 6:30 P.M. on July 15 for a twenty-day leave that had been scheduled well in advance of the action at Ripcord. Berry had been informed upon joining the division that he would shortly be its acting commander, and he had spent much time when not out with the line units bringing himself up to speed on Operation Chicago Peak. The ambitious summer offensive, drawn up by Wright and Hennessey, was to be launched by Berry. "So now I'm in command of a division," Berry wrote home. "Another man's division . . . Which has some built-in inhibitions. . . ."

Berry went on to note that two marriages had been planned around Hennessey's leave: that of his son, 2d Lt. John Jr., Infantry, USMA '70, to the daughter of Maj. Gen. George S. Blanchard, CG, 82d Airborne Division, and that of his daughter to his son's former roommate at West Point. After marrying off his oldest children, Hennessey would "help pack out . . . his wife and two [younger] children to Clark AFB in the Philippines," wrote Berry. "Wow! General Hennessey will have to return to the combat zone to rest."

Unremarked upon in Berry's letter was the disaffection felt by many in the division that Hennessey had not canceled his leave, given the increasingly volatile situation at Ripcord and the potential for heavy casualties at the start of Chicago Peak. It cast a certain shadow across a bright career. Hennessey, an academy man, USMA '44, had served in the European theater of operations in 1944–45. He became a master parachutist and aviator after the war and, a recognized fast burner, was picked in 1963 to command the first battalion activated in the 11th Air Assault Division. Trained as the army's first airmobile division, the 11th was redesignated the 1st Cavalry Division before deploying to Vietnam in 1965. Hennessey commanded a brigade in the division, as well as the division support command, before returning to the United States in 1966.

During General Hennessey's eighteen months as ADC-O and CG, 101st Airborne Division, 1969–71, he was regarded as a calm, composed, methodical professional of superior tactical acumen. "He was the epitome of the quiet man who just 'woke up every morning and went to work,'" noted Colonel Root. Bobby Porter of the 1-506th concurred: "I had nothing but the highest order of respect for and confidence in General Hennessey. He was a great role model as well as a great combat division commander."

Given Hennessey's sterling reputation, it is puzzling that he would turn over the single biggest battle of his command tenure to a brigade commander and an assistant division commander who had between them only five weeks of experience in the Screaming Eagles' AO. "I'll tell you, it was the weirdest thing, Hennessey going on leave like that," recalled Colonel Grange, an infantry veteran of World War II, Korea, and three tours in Vietnam. "General Hennessey was a good division commander," continued Grange, groping for an explanation, "but I don't think he was as troop-oriented as some generals are. It seemed to me that he didn't feel comfortable around troops and for that reason tended to stay in his headquarters. He nevertheless made good tactical decisions, and I've always been indebted to him personally for giving me a brigade after I commanded DISCOM. Those were two great jobs."

Others were less muted in their criticism. One officer would state off the record: "It was obvious that Hennessey was protecting himself. Should the situation at Ripcord completely deteriorate, he would be able to say, well, you can't blame me, I wasn't even there."

Captain Hawkins of A/2-506th was also bitter: "For a long time I thought it was outrageous that General Hennessey had gone home for his daughter's wedding during Ripcord. In retrospect, I think we were far better off having a man of General Berry's caliber step in in the place of a man who obviously didn't care that much about us."

Colonel Harrison thought such criticism completely unjustified, noting that Hennessey had not taken the leave due him during his first tour and arguing—the point would strike some as fantastic—that "there was no compelling reason for him not to take a normal leave during his second tour; the gravity of the situation at Ripcord was not at all clear by the time Hennessey left on July 15. . . ."

Harrison felt that Hennessey supported him completely, on the battlefield and in his skirmishes with Berry. "Jack Hennessey was a model airborne officer, tall, erect, and except for his prize-fighter nose, handsome," Harrison later wrote. "Where he did not fit the airborne persona was that he was quiet and reserved. He demanded calm order and discipline. The general officer's mess at Camp Eagle was as stiff as a gentleman's club in London." Hennessey was the only commander Harrison ever knew or heard of who enforced a closed-door policy with his subordinate commanders. Hennessey called them on the radio; they did not call him. Nor did they see him in his office at division headquarters without first making an appointment with the division chief of staff. Small matter, thought Harrison, given that "Hennessey's leadership was flawless. He visited all parts of the division area routinely and frequently, skillfully flying his own helicopter. Although private and reserved by nature, he exhibited warmth in conversations with the troops, always with a ready smile. He had splendid relationships with the ARVN and the Vietnamese officials in Thua Thien Province. All said, he inspired confidence and was everything one would wish [for] in a division commander." The army agreed. Hennessey would go on to retire with four stars.

* * *

Captain Straub's company had spent July 15 laying wire, rigging claymores, and otherwise preparing for the next attack on Hill 805. Lieutenant Potter arranged with Captain Rich, the 105 battery commander on Ripcord, to have one of his howitzers dedicated exclusively to neutralizing an outcropping of boulders about fifty meters from Company D's perimeter on the south slope of 805, from which numerous RPGs had been received during the first three night attacks. "Rich took a radio to the howitzer position and talked directly to me," recalled Potter. "For safety's sake, as we would be just fifty meters east of the final gun-target line, we got everyone under cover, then Rich and I walked shells up the hill until the howitzer was sighted in exactly on the spot that had been giving us trouble. Rich then directed that ammunition be prepared and the sighting not be touched in anticipation of that night's attack."

One of the company's resupply ships took fire as it came in to land that afternoon. The engine failed as the pilot attempted to pull away, and the Huey made a hard landing on the side of the subhill LZ on the west slope of 805. Delta One secured the crash site, and a CH-47 escorted by Cobras attempted to extract the Huey. The Chinook was forced away by heavy fire from a .51-caliber machine gun.

The pilot and copilot of the Huey were evacuated, but two very scared and very pissed-off door gunners were left behind for the night; they, their immaculately cleaned M60s, and all the ammunition that had also been recovered from the slick were put in position with Delta One to cover the trail leading up from the LZ.

Lieutenant Selvaggi, the company exec, arrived shortly after the resupply ship went down, having been called forward by Straub to take command of Delta One. Straub had instructed Selvaggi, a former platoon leader in the company, to bring with him every able-bodied man he could find in the company rear. "I went in with five or six men, a couple of whom were cherries," recalled Selvaggi. "I was scared. They were petrified. No one spoke during the flight."

Selvaggi got a good look at Delta Company's positions as the Huey approached the LZ. After disembarking, Selvaggi's group hiked quickly to the top of 805, passing along the way the sapper who had inflicted so many casualties during the big attack and who lay where he had been killed, bloated and rotting. A severed arm lay on the ground nearby. The smell of decomposing flesh and expended ammunition and burned, smoldering trees was overwhelming.

"Once inside the perimeter, I had to sit down for a couple of minutes before I could talk," noted Selvaggi, winded by the climb, shocked by the scene. Straub briefed Selvaggi on the situation, but the company commander's eyes told the story. Everyone on the hill actually had red eyes from the wind and dust and lack of sleep. There was trash and debris everywhere. Selvaggi noticed one "thin, red-haired soldier who seemed to be in a trance. His eyes were red-rimmed and bulging, and his face was covered with soot and dirt. He was walking about aimlessly, staring blankly, and mumbling incoherently. I thought he must have been the soldier who went into shock during the previous night's attack on Delta Two."

The fourth attack on Hill 805 began at 2:46 A.M. on July 16, when the approaching sappers tripped a mechanical ambush in front of Delta One. The enemy was only fifty meters from the perimeter, and a ferocious exchange of fire quickly built up on the west side of the hill and the southeast side where a trip flare exposed the approaching enemy to Delta Two. As if by rote, Straub and Potter began coordinating close-in fire support all around the hill—mortars and artillery and dazzling streams of Quad-50 fire from Ripcord. In response to the RPGs flashing in from the rocky outcropping, "Straub ordered all the troops to get their heads down," recounted Potter, "and I called Captain Rich to fire the howitzer we had previously sighted in. We got the first shell within a few seconds, and after a few more, we never took another RPG from that spot."

The attack was over in twenty minutes. There had been no friendly casualties. The first flareship that had been requested came on station at 3:15 A.M., revealing almost immediately a fresh group of NVA moving up the north slope of Hill 805. The Cobras that had also just arrived rolled in hot on the reinforcements, breaking them up 250 meters from Delta Company.

There was another lull, then, at 4:13 A.M., the blast of another mechanical ambush, this time to the north. The enemy reinforcements were apparently still trying to work their way up the hill. The perimeter again exploded with M16 and M60 fire, and the 90mm recoilless rifles boomed out more flechette rounds. Moments later, the night flashed as Marine Intruders began dropping loads of 500-pound bombs south and southeast of Hill 805. "After the fireworks ended," noted Selvaggi, "we continued lobbing grenades down the slope in front of us, every so often, just in case."

Nothing further developed as gunships and flareships orbited the hilltop, keeping the enemy at bay until morning, when more resupply ships arrived with more ammunition and more jets flashed past, dropping more bombs. As most of the troops wearily began putting out more claymores, more wire, and more trip flares, a security patrol found two dead enemy soldiers on the south slope of the hill and recovered some weapons and satchel charges and grenades. Soubers recalled that another patrol that had been dispatched to check the downed slick on the landing zone discovered that "a plate containing the chopper's logo was missing. The NVA had apparently managed to take it during the night for a souvenir."

CHAPTER 20

To What End

There was a terrible accident at dawn in Captain Goates's overnight position west of Triple Hill. Goates was awakened moments before it happened by the sound of a tree, badly damaged by aerial rocket artillery, squeaking in the strong winds that had blown all night. Suddenly, there was an especially strong gust of wind. "This time the tree cracked," wrote Goates. "I was wide awake now, but the tree was already falling as I dove out of the way." The tree came crashing down atop Pfc. Richard R. Timmons, who was sacked out about ten feet from Goates. "Timmons never knew what hit him," noted Goates. "The tree cut diagonally across his body. His head, face, and one hand, which were above the tree, were a deep purple color, while the hand below the tree was as white as a sheet. It took four or five of us to lift the tree and pull him out, but as quick as the medic got there, it was too late to attempt to revive him. Timmons was the only man I lost while I was a company commander."

Livingston's battalion spent July 16 working its way around the enemy bunker complex between Coc Muen and Hill 1000. The battalion CP and Company C were digging in north of the complex at dusk, and Company B to the south, when Livingston was informed by brigade that there would be no more assaults on Hill 1000. The entire 2-501st Infantry, in fact, including its detached Company D on Hill 805, was to be extracted from the Ripcord AO.

"I was very surprised when we were directed to withdraw," said Lieutenant Colonel Livingston. "I was ready to keep on going, man—there was still a fight out there—but somebody up above had made the decision to not launch any more assaults up Hill 1000."

The decision had been made by Berry after he and Lieutenant Colonel Young, the division G3, flew to Camp Evans late that afternoon to discuss the situation with Colonel Harrison in the 3d Brigade TOC. Fred Spaulding recalled that it was a particularly contentious meeting, with Harrison arguing forcefully that control of Hills 805 and 1000 was key to the security of Ripcord. If the enemy held the high ground, their mortar and antiaircraft fire would eventually make prohibitive the cost of even resupplying the firebase. It was time, said Harrison, not to withdraw the reserve battalion but to commit additional forces to the Ripcord AO.

In response, according to Spaulding, Berry did not so much address Harrison's tactical concerns as speak to the displeasure that higher command had begun to express about the resources being consumed to maintain Ripcord. There had already been more casualties than the political situation could bear, said Berry, more helicopters shot down and more mortar and artillery ammunition expended than could be justified, given the fiscal crunch under which the army was forced to operate as it withdrew from Vietnam.

The idea of increasing the number of ground sensors in the area so that supporting arms could be used more selectively and to better effect was discussed, as was seeding the high ground with persistent CS. "We don't need to have people fighting and dying on those hills," said Berry, ending the debate with Harrison. "We can, and we will, decide the issue with the firepower available to us."

During a subsequent meeting, Spaulding recalled that an officer from div arty made a comment—seconded by Berry—to the effect that they had to be careful how many 105 shells were fired during a maneuver related to Ripcord, given a cap on ammunition expenditure recently imposed by USARV. "I thought

Harrison was going to come unglued," said Spaulding. "I knew right then and there that it was all over. The writing was on the wall—you're not going to win a battle when higher command is more concerned with the price of artillery ammunition than destroying the enemy."

Berry would vigorously deny that any restrictions had been imposed. Lieutenant Colonel William A. Walker, commander of the 2-319th FA, the artillery battalion supporting Harrison's brigade, would nevertheless recall "being rather surprised by the questions I began getting from my superiors during the battle about why we were shooting as much ammunition as we were, and was it really effective, and could we not conserve? Evidently, a decision had been made somewhere up the chain to reduce the amount of artillery ammunition being fired," noted Walker, "and we were eventually restricted as to the amount of ammunition we could draw on a daily or weekly basis from the supply depot. The amount was substantially less than what we had been firing, and I remember being disturbed and arguing about the cutback. I also vaguely remember getting my hand slapped because my battalion managed to take more ammunition than we had been allocated so we could meet the requests of the infantry units fighting at Ripcord."[1]

Berry had returned to a very different war than the one he had fought as a brigade commander. Berry's plan, for example, to fire a thousand mortar shells per night around Ripcord had lasted only three nights, as recorded in Harrison's brigade log. Major Koenigsbauer could speak to the problem; his first task upon being reassigned to the division operations shop had been to recalculate the ammunition supply rate, given a cutback in the amount of 81mm ammo being provided the 101st by USARV. Koenigsbauer gave priority to Lucas and Livingston, the only battalion commanders then in heavy combat, but no matter how he did the math he ended up cutting by half the amount of 81mm ammo going to Ripcord as compared to what had been delivered during May, June, and the first half of July. "It was a travesty," he would bitterly recall. Koenigsbauer went to his boss, Lieutenant Colonel Young, who "empathized with me, but said that he had no choice, that higher command had decided that we had been firing too much 81mm ammunition. He had no flexibility in the matter, except not to provide ammunition to anyone else, which would have been a dereliction of duty since any firebase was subject to attack at any time.

"The cutback made it clear to me," Koenigsbauer continued, "that while the NVA were committed to taking Ripcord, we were not committed to defending it. Brigade was being held back by division, which was being held back by the next higher level of command, and so on. If higher command was not prepared to make available the ammunition necessary for the indirect-fire battle, they were certainly not prepared to commit additional ground units to fight the enemy around Ripcord. No one above brigade was prepared to take the enemy on in a major battle." It seemed to Koenigsbauer that higher command was prepared to "allow the status quo at Ripcord to continue until either the enemy pulled out or the effort became too expensive for us, at which point we would pull out."

The enemy began moving into attack positions around Captain Straub's perimeter soon after sundown. As Straub and Potter called in the fire support and coordinated the releasing of flares from a series of orbiting flareships, the troops responded with hand grenades and M79s to the movement and voices that could be heard below them on the slopes of 805. There was a sensor activation to the north of the perimeter and the detonation of a mechanical ambush to the west. The pilot of a LOH spotted flashlights on the east and northeast sides of the hill, within three hundred meters of the top, and called in arty and 81s. Secondary explosions flashed in the wake of a rocket run by one of two Cobras kept on station all night over 805. Straub was contacted by Lucas's operation center and warned that the enemy was massing for a major attack. The information came from the NVA themselves. "It just so happened that one of the radios in the TOC was set to the same frequency the gooks were using that night," noted Captain Williams, the S3 on Ripcord; when a transmission in Vietnamese was monitored, "a Kit Carson Scout was called over, and he listened to it. These guys were talking in the clear, no radio security at all, and the Scout said they were coordinating for a big attack later on that night against Hill 805."

The attack did not begin until 2:30 A.M. on July 17, six hours after the first movement around the hill had been detected, when a mechanical ambush and several trip flares went off in front of Delta One. The company, opening fire, immediately began taking AK fire and satchel charges in Delta One's sector and Delta Two's.

The fight had apparently been battered out of the enemy just getting into position, for their attack soon fizzled in the face of the overwhelming and unceasing fire of M16s, M60s, M79s, 90mms, 81s, 105s, 155s, ARA, and Quad-50s. It was just as well; at the end of the fifth attack in five nights, "you was totally burned out," recalled Sergeant Gaster of Delta One. "There was nothin' left in you. . . ."

Straub was resupplied during the morning and early afternoon, then directed to move to a landing zone on a knoll at the narrow northwestern base of Hill 805. Depending on how long it took to reach the landing zone, seven hundred meters away as the crow flies—a lot longer by way of the trail running down 805 and up to the top of the knoll—Company D would be extracted late on the seventeenth or early on the eighteenth. "We busted our asses filling in our bunkers," wrote Sergeant Blackman of Delta Three. "We wanted to get off the hill before they changed their minds and made us stay another night."

After the recoilless rifles were back-hauled aboard a slick, Delta One moved out, followed by Delta Three. Shipley's platoon remained to rig with demo charges the ammo and equipment that could not be carried. "It made a tremendous boom," noted Lieutenant Shipley. Delta Two rejoined the rest of the company where it was waiting in the jungle below the resupply LZ, having deployed in a small defensive circle bisected by the trail. What happened next "scared us and made us mad, too," recalled Shipley. "We were trying to sneak away with the woods full of NVA. Along came a helicopter [the time was 4:45 P.M.], no warning, no radio message to us. It tried first to land on the LZ with the downed chopper, took [AK-47] fire, then came over to where we were trying not to be seen and lowered a ladder to us." The first man to try to descend the flexible metal ladder, a lieutenant, fell to the ground from the helicopter's fifty-foot hover, amazed everyone by standing up, then collapsed, his foot broken. Several more equipment-laden figures scrambled down the ladder. "It turned out they were a communications team that had been dispatched [by brigade] to set up sensors around the hill," explained Shipley. "We told them they were crazy, to go ahead if they wanted to, but without us. They decided to stay with us."

The company maintained its position as Captain Straub brought in a medevac, which lowered a basket through the canopy for the injured lieutenant. One of the Cobras making suppression runs took AK fire as it circled past the southern slope of Hill 805. Straub called his platoon leaders together to map out their next move after the medevac; it was now almost 6 P.M. Delta Three had only just begun to move through Delta One to take the point down the trail when there was a big explosion back at the company CP. Everyone hit the ground and began returning fire as Straub, a piece of shrapnel in his left elbow—Potter, at his side, had taken shrapnel in his leg—grabbed the radio and reported to Lucas that he was under attack. It sounded as though they had been hit by an RPG.

There were multiple casualties. "The concussion effect of the explosion knocked me off my feet," Rod Soubers of Delta One later wrote, unaware at that time of the sliver of shrapnel stuck in the front of his helmet. It was the second time his steel pot had saved him during the battle. "Within seconds, I was out of my ruck, back on my feet, and instinctively firing into the bush on automatic while yelling at the stunned [and wounded] new guy on my left to do likewise."

Soubers glanced to his right where his best friend, Dave Beyl, was positioned and saw that he was sitting down against his ruck. "Rod, I'm hit," Beyl said calmly. "Get a medic." Soubers, rushing over, saw that Beyl had a hole where his upper chest was exposed because he had not zipped his flak jacket all the way in the terrible heat. "When I got to him, he was just staring straight ahead with a blank expression, apparently in shock and slipping into unconsciousness." Soubers was so upset that he was literally shaking as he pulled off Beyl's ruck and flak jacket, tore open his shirt, and ripped a section from his own shirt to cover the wound, "all the while screaming for a medic. Bubbly blood was coming out of his mouth and the hole in his chest. I got the hole in his chest covered and tilted his head back, continuing to yell for a medic." Soubers didn't know that their platoon medic, Doc Grubidt, had been severely wounded in both legs and the other medics were busy with the casualties around the CP. "As I looked up the trail," Soubers continued, "wondering where the hell the medics were, I saw two or three different colored smoke grenades filling the air with smoke. I continued to hold my torn shirt over Dave's wound and continued to yell for a medic until I was nearly hoarse. . . ."

Lieutenant Selvaggi ran back down the trail to the CP. Straub screamed at him to find out what was going on. The situation was wildly confusing; except for the first explosion, there didn't seem to be any more enemy fire. Selvaggi darted from person to person, asking what each had seen or heard, finally shouting for everyone to cease firing when he realized that they were not actually under attack. Instead, it turned out that Kim, the Kit Carson scout attached to Delta Three, had dropped a grenade at his feet and it had spontaneously detonated the three other grenades hanging from his web gear. Kim had been killed instantly, and his assigned buddy, Sp4 Wilfred W. Warner—the two had been flown out to reinforce the company during the third or fourth day on the hill—was grievously wounded in the chest.

Why the scout did what he did will never be known. There were those who thought that Kim, sick with guilt after so many of his former comrades had been killed during the night attacks, had meant to take Straub out when he blew himself up, an act of atonement and retribution. Most of the grunts were of the opinion, however, that Kim had meant to kill only himself, apparently convinced that the company was going to be overrun on its way to the extraction point, and was so deranged with fear at what would happen to a defector such as himself should he be captured that he pulled the pin on the grenade without even thinking of those around him. Kim, in fact, had tried to get medevacked before the company left the hill, complaining of sore feet. Soubers recalled the scout walking with "a noticeable limp" and later heard from others on the scene that "Warner had warned [Kim] that if he couldn't keep up with everyone else, he was going to leave him behind for the NVA. Whether this scared the scout into a state of suicide is difficult for anyone to say, but it does provide a motive."

Word of the self-inflicted disaster passed among the men in shocked whispers. Several troops from Delta Three were sent back up the trail to secure a small clearing for the medevac. "We walked past what was left of the scout," recalled Blackman. "People were cussing, and I saw Straub talking on the radio while a medic worked on him. It scared me to see Straub hurt. We needed him. . . ."

Doc Fowler had dashed down to where Soubers was shouting by then, and after getting Beyl bandaged up moved on quickly to the next casualty while Soubers and several others carried Beyl to the LZ. The clearing was too small for the medevac to land, and the pilot was hesitant to lower a basket, not wanting to hover in enemy territory. "Straub had to beg him to stay, assuring him that we were not under attack," recalled Selvaggi. Beyl, unconscious, his breathing labored, was loaded into the basket with a black GI who had "visible wounds on his head and much of his body," noted Soubers. "As the basket was going up . . . I said a silent prayer, pleading with God to help Dave pull through. . . ."

A second medevac arrived, as did a LOH, which was able to slip between the trees to land in the clearing. Between them they took out seven of the nine men who had been wounded, leaving Straub and Potter, who intended to stay with the company until the end. Dave Beyl and Wilfred Warner died from their injuries in the evac hospital, boosting D/2-501st's losses on Hill 805 to nine KIA.

After the wounded had been lifted out, Straub told Selvaggi to get the body of the scout evacuated. The scout was a mess, one arm blown off, his guts blown out. "Someone showed up with a poncho and helped me put the body and body parts in it," recounted Selvaggi. "We carried this sloshing poncho to the clearing." Another LOH came in but was still three feet off the deck when the pilot, unwilling to power down all the way to land in case he took fire, gestured to the grunts to throw the body aboard. "We tried to tell him the body wasn't all in one piece," wrote Selvaggi, "but he couldn't understand us and angrily gestured to throw it in. As we swung the load up into the chopper, the pilot started to move forward. He wasn't hanging around. The poncho started to unravel as we let go and was fully opened as it landed on the floor of the chopper. Body parts flopped all over the place. I think some of them slid right out the other side. The pilot never looked back."

It was too late by then to reach the extraction point, so Straub moved Company D several hundred meters down the trail. Hoping the darkness would conceal them, just as night fell they established an NDP around a small knoll on the side of Hill 805. Straub set up in the last place he thought the enemy would look for them, right in the middle of an old NVA bunker complex seeded during a previous operation with persistent CS. The tear-gas crystals, no longer overpowering, still made the area uncomfortable. "We couldn't dig in for the noise," said Lieutenant Shipley of Delta Two. "We had to keep quiet. We put out a few claymores. We were scared to death. We felt awfully alone in that jungle."

Sergeant Blackman described the company position as being "smaller than a normal platoon-sized NDP. I think that's when it hit me just how many men we'd lost over the past few days. We just kind of laid on the ground, no real positions or anything." Everyone was expecting to be hit during the night. "[O]ur morale was so low," wrote Rod Soubers, "I'm not sure we would have been able to adequately defend ourselves. . . . [T]he NVA missed a golden opportunity, but they may have been satisfied enough just to get Hill 805 back. . . ."

Moving out at first light, Company D continued down the trail and reached the extraction LZ by late morning. "We didn't have long to wait before the line of choppers arrived to take us back to Camp Evans," the account by Soubers continued. "We were never so happy to see a Huey as we were that morning. . . ."

Delta One went out first, one chopper load at a time, followed by Delta Two, by which time enemy soldiers could be seen moving downhill from the top of Hill 805, apparently in an attempt to find positions from which to fire on the extraction LZ. The NVA had gotten within range by the time the last elements of Delta Three were being lifted out. "I think the group I was with went out on the second or third to last chopper," recounted Sergeant Blackman. "When it came in, we started running toward it from behind. As I passed the door gunner, the bird took three rounds, maybe more, in its tail, very close to where I was. The pilot started to take off as I was climbing in the chopper. Jerry Bull and another guy pulled me in. Just as I turned to sit down, the bird, having reached treetop level, banked and dove to pick up speed. I started to slide out the door. I remember trying to grab ahold of something—anything. What a helpless feeling. As I slid out, Bull grabbed my rucksack frame and pulled me back in. He saved my life."

Shortly after the chopper carrying Blackman reached Camp Evans, the last one or two slicks arrived with the rest of the platoon. "The pilots and crews got out and started counting bullet holes in their birds," noted Blackman. "We heard that the last bird had to circle several times before it could get in to land because of the heavy volume of enemy fire. The last guys out said they could see NVA running up the side of the hill towards them when that last pilot came in through the fire to pick them up."

The entire Geronimo Battalion was lifted out that day, July 18: the headquarters elements from Ripcord and Companies A, B, and C from LZs on and around Triple Hill. Alpha Company discovered along the way a cluster of hillside caves strewn with blood-encrusted bandages from enemy casualties who had been treated there. It was a chilling sight to grunts whose nerves were drawn tight from fatigue and heavy combat, and Captain Goates thought it best to take point himself as they continued. "There was a stillness so profound you could cut it with a knife when I stumbled on a downed Huey further along in the jungle," wrote Goates. "It had been there for a long time, but as the remainder of the company passed by, the silence grew eerie. I was glad when we got past that point and were finally able to reach the extraction LZ."

The battalion was trucked to Phu Bai late that afternoon, at which point Captain Straub checked into the 85th Evac to have the shrapnel dug out of his elbow. Straub ended up naked on a gurney next to one of his M60 gunners, also naked, who had taken little shrapnel wounds all over his hands several days earlier. Because of Straub's policy of evacuating only the worst of the wounded, the gunner had stayed with the company until the end of the fight for Hill 805.

The man's hands were now badly swollen. "This is terrible," the attending doctor exclaimed. "Who left him in the field this long?"

"It was me, doc," Straub barked from his gurney, too tired to explain what they had gone through out there. "Send me the bill."

Straub was visiting his wounded in the enlisted ward at the 85th when General Berry arrived to present Purple Hearts. Straub had served as Berry's speechwriter at Fort Benning, and Berry, impressed with Straub's handling of his company on Hill 805, presently sought to engage him in a congratulatory conversation. "I really have nothing to say to you, sir," Straub snapped, suddenly seething. Straub would have preferred to present his grievances to Hennessey, whose leave-taking he thought appalling, but Berry, whom he had always respected, was there in the flesh, so Berry would do. Straub had thought the concept of using a rifle company to draw the enemy into a prepared killing ground around Hill 805 unwise from the outset. Having held onto the hill for most of six days, however, he couldn't fathom why they had suddenly given it back to the North Vietnamese. It made no sense to him that they had not been replaced on the high ground by a fresh company. It made no sense to him, in fact, that division had not massively reinforced the two battalions fighting in the Ripcord AO.

"You people forsake me and my soldiers," Straub said to Berry, his voice low and furious, his emotions at the breaking point. "You put us out there and just left us. We were statistics to you people, nothing but numbers, but I lost a lot of good men on that hill."

Straub said something about quitting an army as screwed up and poorly led as the one they had in Vietnam. "Now, Chris, I know you've been through hell out there," Berry interjected calmly, "but before you do anything irrational, just think about it. Don't make any rash decisions. You've got a good career ahead of you."

"I don't give a shit," Straub spat, but Berry, who understood what combat did to people and had absorbed Straub's venting without becoming angry himself, pressed on, reminding him that the army had already lost too many of its finest professionals because of the war. It needed people such as Straub to get back on its feet. "I know it hurts too badly now," Berry said, "but think carefully about whether you really want to get out when you're stationed back in the States."

Berry made a point of visiting Straub again before he was medevacked on to Japan. "I was cooler then," Straub wrote, "and we had a good discussion about NVA tactics and U. S. options in the Ripcord AO. I realized that he had done his absolute best in the Ripcord campaign to get the 2-501st and 2-506th all the support possible. Given the constraints from Saigon, no general in the 101st could have done better. It is an honor to have served under him."

The grunts of Delta Company, at least those who did not immediately reenlist to get out of the field, began at Eagle Beach to recuperate from their ordeal. There was splashing and laughter in the surf, a litter of empty beer cans in some of the hootches, the passing of the pipe in others. "Most of the guys had a good time, apparently trying to put the past week out of their minds," wrote Rod Soubers, who was in too much of a funk about Dave Beyl's death to join in. "I had lost the best friend I ever had. I suddenly felt all alone. . . . Instead of joining the rest of the guys, I would spend much of my time sitting on the beach, just staring out at the South China Sea. I kept asking myself why, why did Dave have to die? Dave had so much to live for, if anyone deserved to live it was Dave. Why couldn't I have been the one to take that piece of shrapnel? I felt there must have been something I could have done after he was hit to help him survive. We had depended on each other to get through the year, so for the longest time I felt that I had somehow let him down. It would take years before I would be able to put this feeling of guilt behind me, but the pain of his death will stay with me the rest of my life. . . ."

PART SIX

Siege

I was returning to Ripcord when I realized that the firebase was no longer an earthy brown, but almost black. Mortar rounds had exploded on virtually every square foot of the hill, charring it into a gray-black heap. It looked evil, malevolent. When the helicopter landed, it was like being dropped into an absolute hellhole.

—1st Lt. Fred H. Edwards
Company B, 326th Engineer Battalion
101st Airborne Division

CHAPTER 21

One Long, Mad Minute

Lieutenant Edwards, who commanded the combat engineer platoon attached to Lucas's battalion, kept a journal on Ripcord. Entries from the beginning of the battle reflected the general feeling that the situation was serious but not critical and sure to end soon. The mood began to change as the shelling continued unabated. Edwards was writing in his journal late on July 8 when the base went on alert, flares popping, 81s thumping, the Quad-50s pouring out streams of red tracers. Resuming the entry, he noted that "one of the sectors on the other side of the hill had some Dinks in the wire—had to put out the candle + go play army for a while. The Dinks got away, but worse, it appears that they were making a probe in preparation for a ground attack. . . . We'll get hit soon, I'm sure . . ."

Edwards, a bright, eager, young West Pointer, was surprised that the NVA were able to maintain their harassing fire for all the firepower being employed around Ripcord. "They've been averaging about 20–30 rounds a day in 5 or 6 volleys," Edwards wrote on July 9, adding that he "talked to some NBC correspondents out here (they didn't take any shots of me) and they said Ripcord was being played up pretty big back home + even called it a 'siege'—it's not that, but it is very unpleasant (+ unhealthy)."

There had been numerous injuries, but no one had been killed. Edwards wrote on the morning of July 10 that "I've had the dozer cutting helipads + POL slots for the past few days + it's coming along pretty well." Lucas had congratulated him, in fact, during the evening briefing. "[T]he Col said the Engrs were doing outstanding work under combat [conditions]—an exaggeration, but helped the ego considerably. Can't get any birds in for the 2nd day now," he continued, "because of high winds. . . . It'll almost knock you down if you aren't careful. Hope it lets up soon, because it's really going to put us in a bind w/o resupply of food and ammo . . ."

The winds were so bad on day ten that the scout ship in which Captain Williams and Tom Rubsam were riding was repeatedly spun around on its way to Ripcord from Camp Evans. Williams had made an administrative run to the rear, collecting Rubsam, his arm wound nearly healed, on the way back. Rubsam was glad to get back to the company but disappointed when informed that he was being reassigned to Bravo One, a new lieutenant having joined Bravo Two. Actually, Rubsam, whom Williams considered the epitome of the citizen-soldier—smart, calm under fire, and possessed of a real sense of responsibility—would soon be taking over Bravo One from Lieutenant Delgado. "Delgado wasn't a bad person, but he just couldn't make it as an infantry officer," according to Williams. "I always put some of my best NCOs in Delgado's platoon just to make sure he didn't get somebody killed, and finally ended up replacing him on the firebase with Sergeant Rubsam."

Upon reporting to the platoon, Rubsam climbed on top of the base's mess bunker to familiarize himself with the layout of Bravo One's positions on the eastern side of Ripcord. Rubsam, crouched down so as not to present too obvious a target, was about to climb off the roof when a 75mm recoilless-rifle round suddenly sailed right through the door of the mess bunker. "That was an accident," Rubsam said. "I'm quite sure they were aiming at me."

The enemy's imperfect aim might have spared Rubsam, but it killed Pfc. Victor L. De Foor of Bravo Three, who had just ducked into the mess bunker. "That haunted me for a while," said Rubsam, "but it was just something that happens in war, I guess. . . ."

Rubsam rushed into the smoke-filled bunker. De Foor was

unrecognizable, decapitated by a direct hit. The skin had been burned off his shoulders and chest. There were also several wounded men in the bunker whom Rubsam did not know. He raced to the company CP for help, and a number of grunts from De Foor's squad went to police up the body. "When the guys came back with tears in their eyes, telling how they had tried to pick Vic's scalp up," wrote Chip Collins, "we got with other units and agreed to take care of their bad KIAs if they would take care of ours."

The other men in the bunker were from Company D, this being the day that Rollison's battered command had humped to the firebase from Hill 1000 to get resupplied on its way to Triple Hill. The shelling had begun as Company D filed through the perimeter wire. "Four of us sought refuge in the mess bunker," wrote Sp4 Patrick E. McCloskey. "We were standing near the door, waiting out the incoming, when a guy came in to get coffee." It was De Foor, who got two cups, excused himself to get back by, "and was bending down slightly to get through the door," noted McCloskey, "when an explosion rocked the bunker. The four of us flew across the bunker and landed on top of one another at the back wall. The guy with the coffee landed on the countertop [where hot chow was served when flown out in mermite cans]. He absorbed most of the blast because he was filling the doorway when the round hit. He certainly saved my life because I was closest to the door. We all ran like idiots out the back door and up to the aid station where the medics looked us over. The war was over for me. I had taken a hit in the right lung."

Day ten was the first in which men were killed by the incoming fire. The shelling that had greeted Company D lasted from 9:45 to 10:15 A.M, during which time several enemy mortar crews around Hill 902, firing a few rounds at a time at odd intervals, placed twenty-five 82mm shells on Ripcord. Fourteen GIs were wounded badly enough to be medevacked. One of them, Pfc. Larry J. Plett of B/2-319th FA, hit while manning his howitzer, later died of his injuries in the 85th Evacuation Hospital in Phu Bai.

Two men were killed outright in addition to Vic De Foor. Private First Class Patrick J. Bohan, a pathfinder responsible for bringing in the medevacs that had been requested, lost his life when his radio malfunctioned and he left his covered position to secure another. Specialist Fourth Class Fredrick C. Raymond of A/2-11th FA was killed when it appeared that the shelling had finally petered out. "The battery commander called the hootch we were in, and asked for Raymond to bring a box of C-rations to the FDC [fire direction center]," recalled one GI. "Raymond didn't have his flak jacket or steel pot on. He was just going to run over there with the chow, but he got caught in the open between bunkers by a mortar round."

Lieutenant Colonel Walker, commander of the 2-319th Field Artillery, helicoptered in with his sergeant major during the shelling to check, as they often did, on Battery B. Walker was greatly impressed as Captain Rich, wounded yet again—his fifth injury since the battle had begun—kept his six howitzers in action amid the incoming, then leveled one tube for direct fire on a recoilless rifle that had begun firing on the medevacs from atop Hill 805. "Rich was a tough little knocker," said Walker. Rich was, in fact, something of a legend, a former E6 who had won a direct commission during his second tour and, at the time of Ripcord, was a veteran of four years in Vietnam. Rich, short in stature, thin of frame, was a cocky, abrasive bantam rooster—"Don Knotts with attitude," joked a contemporary—who referred to himself as the best artilleryman in the army and who intended, he often said, to stay in Vietnam until the war was over. Rich wasn't the type to prosper in the peacetime military. "He wasn't a paperwork guy," noted Walker, "but he was the perfect kind of high-energy combat officer to have out in a situation like Ripcord. He set the example not only for his own people, but for everybody on the base."

In a document to support a valor award, Lieutenant Colonel Walker described how Rich ran to the craters of each new salvo to determine back-azimuths, which, carrying a radio with him, he quickly called in to his FDC. "There the azimuths were used in selecting likely enemy mortar positions from locations obtained through previous visual reconnaissance and radar sightings," wrote Walker. "Precomputed firing data for the selected positions was sent immediately to the howitzers."

By then, Rich, having rushed back to his little forty-five-man battery, would be shouting at his guys to get out of the bunkers, made of ammo crates and sandbag-covered culvert halves, to which they sensibly retreated between fire missions. "Responding to his example," Walker continued, the "howitzer crews fell to their pieces and began delivering heavy counter-mortar fires within scant minutes of each mortar attack."

The cannoneers, wearing helmets and flak jackets but otherwise completely exposed within the sandbagged parapets around their crowded battery area—about the size of a basketball court—manned their howitzers in a state of nervous anticipation. They could hear little of incoming mortar rounds over the fierce winds, not to mention their radios and shouted fire commands and the sharp cracks of their own howitzers, which were cranked nearly straight up, given the close proximity of the North Vietnamese. Walker described how Rich moved from gun crew to gun crew "with encouragement, advice, and instructions. His courageous actions, totally disregarding the hazard of subsequent mortar attacks, inspired the men of his battery to suppress their fears." Because the howitzers were able to return fire so quickly and so accurately, "the mortar attacks were brief; in the majority of cases all rounds impacted within the span of a minute. By his gallant action Captain Rich was directly responsible for saving lives which would have been lost had the enemy felt secure in firing their mortars at will."

Most of the bunkers on Ripcord were solid enough to protect those inside from even direct hits. People usually went outside only when required, whether on working parties or when checking the wire for signs of enemy infiltration, as the infantrymen on the perimeter did each morning, sometimes drawing sniper fire from the lower slopes of Ripcord. At the first indication of enemy fire, everyone headed for the nearest shelter. Ripcord when being shelled resembled a ghost town. There were numerous close calls, however, given the unpredictability of the incoming fire. Captain Williams, the S3, was coming up the stairs leading out of the TOC, for example, when a shell exploded just on the other side of the blast wall at the top. "The concussion hurled me back down the steps and through the open conex door into the TOC," said Williams. "I slid across the floor and landed right at Colonel Lucas's feet, and I remember him looking down at me and making some sort of smart-ass comment about my having made quite a dramatic entrance. I didn't think it was real funny at the time."

In another incident, Captain Rich was directing the fire of one of his howitzers on an enemy position east of the firebase when a .51-caliber machine gun opened fire on the 105; a slug passed directly between Rich and Lucas, who was standing beside him observing the mission, embedding itself in the bunker behind them.

Lieutenant Colonel Lucas put his life on the line every day during the battle for Ripcord. In distinct contrast to his helicopter-seat style of command during operations, Lucas was in his role as base commander—King of the Hill, in the argot of the division—highly visible to the troops, recognizing perhaps that men being pounded day after day by an unseen enemy needed an extra boost. "When the shells were falling, you'd see Lucas out checking positions, basically letting the troops know he was around," said Lieutenant Wallace, acting commander of Company B. "It made you feel good that the battalion commander was willing to take the same risks as the troops. He was the type of officer who wouldn't ask his men to do anything that he wouldn't do himself."

One of the more vivid examples of the lengths to which the battalion commander went to make his presence known involved Sgt. Christopher Hinman of Company B. Hinman, a tough and reckless squad leader on his second tour, had been tasked to set up two M60s to help cover several resupply Hueys. The enemy began mortaring the base when the helicopters came into view. Hinman started blasting away, as did Sp4 Thomas E. Searson on the other M60, drawing in return heavy fire from a .51 caliber. Hinman took a ricochet in his helmet and was knocked aside, dazed. Lucas appeared from nowhere at that moment and, taking over Hinman's M60, joined Searson in laying down suppressive fire for the five full minutes it took the slicks to touch down in their turn, unload their supplies, and bank away at top speed from Firebase Ripcord.

The firebase medics also risked their lives freely and often. "They were just phenomenal," said Lieutenant Edwards. "Everyone on the whole damn hill would be hunkered down under the incoming, but if somebody hollered 'medic,' they were right there."

"I was really proud of my medics," said Captain Harris, the battalion surgeon on Ripcord. "A lot of them hated that war, but they all did their job. They weren't going to let their buddies down."

Captain Harris was something of a hawk himself, such was the impression made on him from treating numerous civilian victims of communist terrorism when he was assigned to a MASH unit in the Saigon area before being transferred up north to the Screaming Eagles. "That was a real eye opener," noted Harris, who, taking his job more seriously than the average draftee doctor, became a genuine hero to the men on Ripcord. To begin with, Harris was the only doctor any had seen on a forward firebase such as Ripcord. In addition, the short, stocky surgeon habitually joined his medics when they left the safety of the aid station to treat casualties; and when a medevac landed on the helipad in front of the aid station, he was usually at one end of one of the stretchers being hastily loaded onto the Huey. "I just didn't think it was fair to use my position as an officer and a doctor to send my medics out there if I wasn't willing to do it myself," said Harris, subsequently awarded the Silver Star.

Harris tended to downplay his own bravery, explaining that because the enemy didn't know which helipad to hit until an approaching chopper actually landed, and because it took twenty to thirty seconds for a shell to arc down for impact after leaving its tube, "you had a window of opportunity there to get your wounded safely loaded aboard. If everyone had their shit together, the medevac would be airborne again and we would all be back inside the aid station before the first shell hit the LZ."

The process was not always so smooth. Specialist Fourth Class Daniel C. Thompson, a wireman with the battalion communications section in the conex beside the aid station, often lent a hand during medevacs. In one instance, Thompson helped hump a stretcher out to a chopper, only to have mortar shells begin landing just as the group was making its dash off the helipad. "I was running like a football player trying to make a touchdown," said Thompson, "but I got nailed just before I reached the door of the aid station." Someone reached out, grabbed Thompson by his shirt, and jerked him inside the conex, where he made a crash landing on the floor. "I thought I was hit real bad, and the guys thought I was blind because I had instinctively brought my hands up to my face, but it turned out it was just little cuts on my face and forehead, that's all. The medic who checked me out asked if I wanted a Purple Heart. I said no. It wasn't the first time I'd picked up little dings from all the shit we were taking. I didn't give a damn about medals. I just wanted to do my time and go home."

It was on day nine that Sp5 Chris W. Jensen, in charge of a three-man team of combat photographers, arrived on Ripcord. "We had just come back from Cambodia," recalled Jensen, a photojournalism major who had dropped out of college to enlist, "when the word somehow got to our unit in Long Binh that there was bad stuff going on up in the 101st at a firebase called Ripcord. One of our officers must have heard something at the evening press briefing, so we decided to head up there and see what was going on."

After flying to Camp Eagle, Jensen and his team reported to the 101st's public information office (PIO). "They told us in no uncertain terms that they would not permit us to go out to Ripcord," said Jensen. "There was to be no media, military or civilian, out there."

As described in Fred Edwards's journal, a few media types had visited Ripcord early in the battle. As the situation worsened, however, a news blackout had been imposed by the PIO officers, apparently on order from a division headquarters concerned that Ripcord might turn into a public-relations disaster like Hamburger Hill. The blackout served only to further intrigue Jensen's people about what was going on out in those mountains, and they hitched a ride to Ripcord on a medevac. Lucas was clearly surprised by the appearance of three enlisted men wearing bush hats and loaded down with cameras. Jensen said he wanted to get out with one of the line companies.

"Lucas's response was absolutely not, things are really bad out there," recalled Jensen. "He offered to let us stay on the firebase, however. He was very gracious. He said they'd find us a bunker to stay in, and get us some steel pots and flak jackets."

Jensen and crew had several close calls of their own as they went about the next several days filming and photographing the 105s in action on top of Ripcord. There was the time a mortar round suddenly exploded where Jensen had just noticed one of his guys, Sp4 James Saller, standing to line up a shot. "The blast sprayed all this hot, wet stuff on my shoulders and the back of my neck," said Jensen. "I thought, oh shit, that's Saller, and I reached back to wipe the crap off my neck—and it was Spanish rice. The round had hit a mermite can full of hot food. Saller had moved from the area right before the explosion, and was perfectly okay, but lunch was ruined."

Saller's luck ran out a day or two later when he was splattered in the side with recoilless-rifle shrapnel. The third member of the team went out on the medevac with Saller. Jensen decided to stay on a few more days. "There was no feeling of impending doom on Ripcord," he explained. "There was a reasonable amount of incoming, and nobody was happy about that, but everyone was well dug in. People were in good spirits. Morale was solid."

Jensen's impressions were correct. There were a few men who either freaked out or decided to cut and run, including Sergeant Johnson, who, having been switched from Bravo One to Bravo Three after getting Bob Utecht killed on Hill 805, "simply skyed out on a resupply chopper shortly after joining us on Ripcord," noted Chip Collins, "never to return."

Most, however, were hacking it. "It was hairy, but we were young," said Danny Thompson, the wireman. "We had a little black dog called Rip. He was our mascot, and we went out during a mortar attack and ran around chasing him so we could put him on a helicopter and get him back to Evans. That just goes to show you some of the crazy stuff we did as kids."

Sergeant Rubsam recalled one of his squad leaders, Tolson, not only as a great soldier but as a great morale builder. "It was hard to get people out of their holes once they'd taken cover," said Rubsam. "Everybody would be hunkered down, but then all of a sudden you'd see skinny, pimple-faced Phil Tolson prancing back and forth, wielding an old trash-can lid like it was Captain America's shield, cursing and taunting the NVA. It was hilarious, especially to guys who were scared shitless, and it was a great motivator. It let people know that the shellings weren't the end of the world."

The only thing better than cursing the enemy was hitting them back. The opportunity presented itself to Sergeant Rubsam when a Huey landed on the refueling pad in his platoon sector and came under AK-47 fire from a bunker dug beneath a gigantic boulder on the rocky hill immediately east of Ripcord. A man sitting at the open cabin door was wounded before the helicopter could make its hasty departure. Using binoculars, Rubsam could see the silhouette of the sniper when he moved past the narrow firing aperture of the bunker, but the return fire being directed at the position seemed to have no effect, sheltered as it was by the overhanging rock.

Rubsam contacted Lieutenant Wallace, the acting company commander, and after much delay the artillery ceased firing so a Cobra could overfly the base to rocket the bunker. The gunship made numerous passes. None were on target. "I just could not get through to the pilot about where the bunker was," recalled Rubsam. When the pilot reported that he was going to have to break station to refuel and rearm, Rubsam desperately collected several LAWs, hoping to drop one close enough to the bunker to draw the pilot to the target. "I knelt on the hill and used this big old dead tree above the bunker as an aiming stake," noted Rubsam. Surprised by the accuracy of the first two LAWs he fired, he readied the third "with the idea that, hell, forget the gunship, I might actually be able to knock out the bunker myself—and that third LAW did indeed go right through the aperture. It tickled everybody in the platoon. The guys were just bored, watching the show, and when the rocket exploded inside the bunker it was standing-ovation time. I don't know if the enemy soldier was still in there, or if he had an escape tunnel, but we never took fire from that position again."

* * *

Because the enemy was so close, Captain Rich's battery fired numerous Charge One missions, meaning that the howitzer crews used only one of the seven powder bags, or charges, that came packed in a canister with each shell. The excess charges were an accident waiting to happen, and a working party began destroying them in a burn pit on July 16. It didn't take long for the high winds to whip sparks from the fire into the gun parapets and onto a big pile of charges. The resulting explosion blew Rich's exec, Lieutenant Brennan, across the battery area, badly burned, and he ended up in a heap against the tire of a 105. One of Brennan's academy classmates, Lieutenant Wintermute, USMA '69 and formerly of the 1-506th Infantry, was tapped to replace him and was flown out to Ripcord that night on a resupply Huey. Night flights to the firebase, infrequent because of the inherent risks, were almost always unopposed, the enemy only rarely exposing its mortar positions by continuing to shell Ripcord after the sun went down.

Lieutenant Wintermute was only nominally fit for duty, having been wounded, along with every other member of the platoon to which he was attached as FO, ten days earlier in the Rakkasan AO. Though it did not prevent Wintermute from calling in arty until the enemy broke contact, a big piece of grenade shrapnel had sliced open the head of his penis before burying itself in his thigh.

Wintermute was evacuated by jungle penetrater and treated at Camp Evans. Climbing in and out of helicopters since his release from the aid station had torn open the stitches in his thigh, however; the wound was packed with gauze before he was sent to Ripcord.

Lieutenant Wintermute's first morning on the base included the usual early-morning barrage, in this case a dozen 82mm shells, which fell short in the perimeter wire. Shortly thereafter, at 7:37 A.M. on July 17, there were two extralarge explosions, one inside the wire, one outside; the subsequent discovery of a mangled, extralarge mortar tail fin confirmed that the shells were from a 120mm mortar. "That got everybody's attention big time," recalled Chris Jensen. "That ratcheted everything up a little."

Manufactured in China and Russia, the 120mm was the largest mortar in Hanoi's inventory—"a pee-ringin' weapon," in the words of one officer. It was a heavy weapon with heavy ammunition, not easy to transport, not easy to replace if lost, and as such rarely employed by the enemy far south of the DMZ. Its sudden appearance on the battlefield—the first time that one had been employed in the division area in a year and a half—indicated that the NVA intended to destroy Firebase Ripcord.

Amid air strikes and counterbattery fire, the enemy dropped in two more 120mm rounds, then two more again. After an hour's lull, there were another two, wounding several men, including Captain Rich, who suffered powder burns in addition to catching a little piece of shrapnel in the corner of his right eye. Chris Jensen decided to pack up his cameras and get out while the getting was good. Before he hopped aboard a departing slick, he was given a large chunk of 120mm mortar shrapnel, which Lucas wanted him to hand-deliver to an officer from division intelligence who would be waiting for him on the pad at Camp Eagle. Jensen, incidentally, was summoned to the PIO office upon returning to the rear and reprimanded for having defied orders by taking his team to Ripcord.

Captain Rich was supervising another fire mission when, at 12:34 P.M., sixteen 60mm rounds were launched in rapid succession from one direction, twelve 120mm rounds from another, all of them impacting directly on top of Ripcord. Some of the 120s actually exploded inside Battery B's parapets, wounding eight cannoneers and putting Rich out of action with multiple shrapnel wounds to his legs, one of which was slightly fractured. The fire mission continued amid the incoming. "The men never left their guns," noted Lieutenant Wintermute. "I saw one round impact very close to one of the howitzers, literally blowing a crewman out of the position. He did a backflip—you would have thought it was a circus act—but immediately popped right back into the position, loaded the howitzer, and continued firing. They were all like that. They did an absolutely fantastic job. For all the stuff you read about bad morale in Vietnam, quite frankly, I never saw it."[1]

In addition to the counterbattery fire, gunships and tac air were scrambled to hit the suspected 120mm firing position almost four kilometers from the firebase on the reverse slope of Coc Muen Mountain. Captain Harris, meanwhile, recommended that Rich, wounded seven separate times, finally be evacuated, not only because of his fractured leg but, more importantly, so he could have exploratory surgery to ensure that no arteries had been damaged by a bad fragment wound in his groin area.

Lieutenant Colonel Walker selected Phil Michaud, CO, A/2-319th FA, on Rakkasan, to replace Rich for the duration of the battle and flew out in a LOH to pick him up and take him to Ripcord. "Whereas Rich was somewhat flamboyant, Michaud was very steady, very calm and cool under pressure," noted Wintermute. Michaud held the Silver Star from the first sapper attack on Granite. Another officer described him, admiringly, as "short and stocky, built like a damn rain barrel. He was forceful and outspoken, a football-player type."

Rich provided Michaud a hasty briefing in his culvert–half bunker about the enemy situation, the procedures that had been worked out for delivering ammunition and evacuating casualties under fire, and the status of the personnel in Battery B. "In the middle of the briefing, we got mortared," recalled Michaud. Rich and Michaud had no sooner exited the bunker to conduct crater analysis and get the 105s firing back than "that little hootch took a direct hit," noted Michaud. "It was completely demolished."

Having survived his last close call, Rich climbed aboard the colonel's LOH after the shelling and departed Ripcord. He was subsequently decorated with the Silver Star and Distinguished Service Cross. Rich's valor had taken such an emotional and physical toll, however, that Walker disapproved his request to extend once again and had him reassigned to battalion headquarters for the five months left on his tour. "Rich was one step away from being a basket case by the time I took over," said Michaud. "I don't know how long it had been since he'd had any sleep, but he was completely spent. He was just running on adrenaline. He was basically shell-shocked, and from what I saw, he stayed that way until he rotated out of Vietnam."

The other battery commander on the hill, Captain Baxendale

of A/2-11th Field Artillery, was also evacuated on July 17 so that a piece of shrapnel lodged in a bone in his neck could be surgically removed. Baxendale turned over the 155 battery to his exec, 1st Lt. J. Robert Kalsu of Oklahoma City, Oklahoma. "Kalsu was just a great guy," recalled Michaud. "He feared absolutely nothing. . . ."

Bob Kalsu, a tall, beefy hulk of a man who had gone to college on a football scholarship and played a season with the Buffalo Bills—he was their Rookie of the Year in 1969—was, thanks to his ROTC commission, one of only a half-dozen athletes who had to interrupt their pro careers to serve in Vietnam. Married to his college sweetheart, the father of a baby girl, everything going his way, Kalsu had wept the day he received his orders to Vietnam. He made the best of it, however, believing as a patriot and devout Catholic that one had to take the bad with the good. Extremely popular, Kalsu was a fine artilleryman and a gentle giant who rarely used profanity—"highly unusual considering the crowd," noted a fellow lieutenant—and enjoyed a remarkable rapport with his troops. "He was one of the very few officers completely at ease with the enlisted men, and they with him," wrote one GI, adding that Kalsu was "cheerful, fair, strong, seemingly indestructible, and one of the nicest people I have ever met." Another recalled that "Kalsu used to help us haul ammunition. For an officer, that was unheard of. A lot of the section chiefs didn't even hump ammo."

Captain Michaud was wounded only a few hours after relieving Rich by a ricocheting sniper round that took him in the back of the thigh. The bullet went in sideways, plowing all the way to the bone. "It felt like a red-hot poker had been jammed into my leg," said Michaud, who, informed by the medics in the aid station that the bullet would have to be removed in a surgical hospital, opted against being medevacked. "The walking wounded like myself," he noted, "got patched up and continued to drive. It didn't take long before the wound got infected and my leg turned black."

Toward dusk that same day, Michaud won a second Silver Star when he spotted smoke from a mortar tube that had begun shelling Ripcord. The firing position was on the crown of a little rocky knoll in the low ground southwest of the firebase, so close that the thump of each round could be heard as it left the tube. Michaud even caught a quick glimpse of one of the bare-headed NVA manning the mortar as he sighted the howitzer that was facing the knoll; Michaud was peering down the bore itself because the direct-fire sight had previously been damaged by shrapnel. "It was a major attack," recalled Michaud. "They were popping rounds on us like there was no tomorrow, but after three or four rounds of our own we were right on 'em, and then we pounded the position with another fifteen, twenty rounds. We got a direct hit. We could see pieces of metal go flying from the destroyed tube. It was no big deal. We immediately started firing other missions because it was coming in all the time and they just started peppering us from some other direction."

There had been relatively few fatalities on the firebase, none at all, as noted, until the tenth consecutive day of shelling, none again for the next seven days. "One life is too many," said Lieutenant Wintermute, "but for the amount of mortar fire we were taking, the casualties were unbelievably low. It was amazing."

The law of averages caught up with the defenders of Ripcord on July 18, the day that the battle, already something of a siege in spirit, became one in fact. Colonel Harrison flew in during a lull in the shelling late that morning and was standing at a bunker opening near the TOC, "talking with a sergeant as we both leaned on the stack of sand-filled ammo crates shielding the bunker entrance," he later wrote, when a "120mm round landed at the front base of the stacked crates. It blew both of us back about eight feet into the bunker. The sergeant was evacuated with blood coming out of both ears. A soldier leaning on crates in the same fashion at the next opening to my right [Sp4 William D. Rollason, a sniper attached to the 2-501st TOC] was killed instantly. My S-3 was approaching from the helipad to our left, and was wounded in the right leg." Like Major King, Harrison was also superficially wounded, though he did not report it: "I was bruised and had a terrible ringing and pain in my ears, and later discovered a nick in my leg. . . ."

Following the departure of the brigade commander, several CH-47s deposited supplies on the log pad on the southeast side of the firebase where the crown of the hill protected them from a .51 caliber that had begun firing on aircraft in the area from below the southwest side of Ripcord. The fourth or fifth Chinook to arrive, at 1:30 P.M., was piloted by WO1 Robert A. Barrowcliff of A/159th Aviation out of Phu Bai. Barrowcliff had already flown several missions to other firebases that morning when, upon refueling, he was dispatched to Ripcord with a sling load of 105 ammo he picked up at Evans. Barrowcliff was not in radio contact with Ripcord and, as such, was unaware of the threat posed by the machine gun. It would not have mattered—the pathfinders on the log pad had safely brought in the other resupply ships with hand signals—had Lucas not ordered the Chinook diverted with a smoke grenade to the 105 battery's ammunition supply point, about fifty feet from the log pad at the southeastern end of the base. The pathfinders had emphatically opposed the diversion, because an aircraft hovering over the ASP would be exposed to the machine gun below, but Lucas had overruled them, his prerogative as King of the Hill. By doing so, Lucas meant to protect the troops who would have to hump the ammo up to the battery area from the log pad, an extremely hazardous task, given the incoming mortar fire. Because the pilots could quickly position and unhook their loads, Lucas gambled that the enemy, at the receiving end of much suppressive fire, would be unable to hit the Chinook as it placed the howitzer shells directly in the wide trench in front of the main bunker in the ASP.

Lieutenant Colonel Lucas took a calculated risk, and he lost. He lost big time. Barrowcliff was settling into a thirty-foot hover when his door gunner, Sp4 Terry A. Stanger, behind the pilot on the left side of the aircraft, spotted three figures—in strange uniforms and wearing odd helmets—down in the vegetation at the base of the hill, directing, it appeared, some type of weapon toward the Chinook. Stanger immediately swung his M60 in the group's direction, flipped off the safety, and, as required, keyed his mike to ask Barrowcliff for permission to open fire. "We had been informed that there were friendlies outside the wire," noted Stanger, only two weeks in-country at that time. "I could tell those three weren't Americans, but I thought they might be ARVN."

The enemy gun crew opened fire at that instant. Lieutenant Edwards, the engineer platoon leader, was underneath the hovering CH-47, one of several men who, reaching up to grab the cargo net in which the artillery ammunition was secured, were physically guiding the sling load into the trench in front of the ammo bunker.

Edwards saw the .51 stitch the Chinook:

> If you have ever been near a hovering helicopter, you know that the noise is deafening. It's so deafening, in fact, that there was absolutely no sound as several bullet holes spontaneously appeared in the side of the Chinook. It was almost surreal—one second, it was a perfectly routine resupply mission, the next, there were these big bullet holes two to three inches wide. I was dumbfounded for a second before it registered that the Chinook had taken direct hits from a .51-cal. . . .

When the machine gun opened fire, the flight engineer, Sp4 Michael A. Walker, was lying on his stomach, peering through the hook hole in the center of the helicopter's floorboard, ready to press the button that would release the sling load once it was in position on the ground. Private First Class Charles L. Holmen, the crew chief, was manning an M60 at the right door, which was opened from the waist up, directly across the aisle from Stanger.

The burst of fire from Stanger's side passed through the aircraft and sparked a fire in the rear engine on Holmen's side; as Holmen noted, the crew was initially unaware that they were in trouble:

> The helicopter was about level with the top of the firebase on my side. I was watching to make sure we didn't clip any antennas with the rotors when I saw a pathfinder running towards us, frantically waving his arms. Something was

obviously wrong, and I leaned forward to look down the side of the helicopter—your peripheral vision is limited when you've got a flight helmet on with the visor down—and saw that the engine was on fire. Looking back inside, I realized that the cabin was full of smoke. It was so thick I could barely see the light coming in through the hook-hole where Walker was positioned. I hollered to the pilots that we were on fire. Of course, everybody was hollering on the radio by then. . . .

There was an intense flash of heat in the cabin as the entire aft section of the helicopter burst into flames, an auxiliary fuel tank having been ignited by the engine fire. Walker immediately released the sling load, as trained, so that the pilot could pull away from the ammo they were carrying before he crash-landed the burning helicopter. Singed by the flames, Walker frantically pushed past Holmen to climb through the crew chief's half-open door and jump to the ground from the still-hovering Chinook.

The enveloping wave of heat melted the outside of Stanger's visor. Barely able to see through the blurry plastic, the door gunner rushed into the cockpit, screaming that the helicopter was on fire. Barrowcliff and his copilot, Capt. Edwin W. Grove, had only just realized that something was amiss when Stanger burst in; at that same moment, the cockpit filled with smoke and the aircraft lurched forward, knocking Stanger headfirst into the center windshield. Stanger's arms got wrapped up in the controls, and Barrowcliff, unable to push the cyclic forward, decided that he had no choice but to set down where they were and hope they could get away from the burning aircraft before the main fuel tanks exploded. Stanger fell onto Grove as the helicopter tilted to the right. The copilot pulled the emergency release on his door, which jettisoned the entire door, along with Stanger, who'd been pushing off the door with his hand, desperately trying to get off Grove. Stanger described his sudden free fall:

It was just, boom, out goes the door with me in tow. I fell about fifty to a hundred feet down the mountain and landed on some empty ammo crates that had been thrown down the side of the mountain as trash. I hit pretty hard. The visor on my helmet slammed into the bridge of my nose, and I was half-blind for all the blood in my eyes. I was actually lucky, though, because if not for the visor I would have gotten a face full of nails from the ammo crates. As it was, when I stood up, my flak vest had ammo-crate lids hanging all over it. The nails had embedded themselves in the metal plate in the vest. I didn't realize it at the time—I didn't feel a thing—but the fingers on my right hand were all wrenched out of their sockets and bent in different directions from the fall.

All I could think of was my instructors at helicopter school who told us to get the hell away from a chopper's blades when you crashed. I took off downhill, the ammo-crate lids bouncing on my chest, until I thought I was clear of the blades. When I looked back up, I saw that the aircraft had come to rest on its side. The rotors had flayed themselves off against the ground. I tore my helmet off, unfastened the flak vest, and started climbing back up the mountain as fast as I could. . . .

The cannoneers from the 105 battery had barely survived the thrashing rotor blades. Captain Michaud described the scene:

We were in the rotor wash of that big bird. We saw the back end of it catch on fire, and watched the helicopter drop straight down on top of the ammo bunker it had been hovering over. The rear wheels landed on top of the bunker, but the front end nosed down into the trench in front of the bunker, and then the bird rolled to its right, and, of course, the rotor blades hit the ground and just tore themselves to pieces. The Chinook came down so fast that all we could do was jump for cover. I tried to squeeze into one of the little powder pits where we threw excess charges—they were about two feet by two feet by two feet—as the blades hit the ground, kicking dirt in our faces, slinging equipment and trash through the air. Pieces from the disintegrating rotors sliced right overhead, plowing into the howitzers, crashing down all around us. . . .

Barrowcliff and Grove exited the aircraft through the copilot's empty door frame after the blades finished destroying themselves; Holmen went up through the door gunner's window. Stanger rejoined them as they rushed to Walker, who had been knocked down by the helicopter when it rolled. Walker was flat on his stomach at the edge of the trench, right below the crew chief's half-open door, pinned down from the back of his thighs by the pontoonlike main fuel tank running along that side of the Chinook. The situation was desperate. The aft section of the helicopter, propped up on the ammo bunker, was burning out of control. "The fire was spreading rapidly along the fuselage towards that trapped crewman," recalled Michaud, who had dashed to the scene. "Because of the magnesium mixed in the aluminum, the skin of the helicopter was burning so hot the flames were almost white." Magnesium, noted Stanger, "burns like the sun. There's nothing that can put it out."

Lieutenant Colonel Lucas and Captain Williams raced over from the TOC; after ordering many of the troops converging on the crash back to cover so as to hold down casualties when the main fuel tanks exploded, they began building a sandbag wall between Walker and the oncoming fire. Barrowcliff removed Walker's flight helmet as soldiers pulled at his arms and chipped away at the rocky soil around him with shovels. "Walker was begging us to help him," recalled Stanger. "We were beside ourselves."

Holmen climbed back into the burning helicopter to secure the escape ax, then, back outside, swung it into the skin of the chopper, splitting it, but the ax bounced off the door frame above Walker. The enemy, meanwhile, began dropping mortar rounds around the stricken Chinook.

Michaud was one of those doing what he could:

> I remember jumping into the trench and crawling under the helicopter—there was just enough clearance under the nose—to see if there was any way I could get that crewman's

legs loose from underneath. I thought if I clawed enough dirt away, he could pull himself free, but I got soaked with boiling hydraulic fluid that was pouring out of the helicopter, and quickly gave up that attempt. . . .

Staff Sergeant Van F. Rosenkilde, a pathfinder, ran up with two fire extinguishers and handed one to Sergeant Hinman of Company B. Hinman sprayed the flames licking along the fuselage while Rosenkilde sprayed another pathfinder, Pfc. Nicholas A. Fotias, who was frantically trying to pull Walker out. "As long as he held the fire extinguisher directly on us," said Fotias, "it would keep the flames back, but as soon as he'd take it away, the flames would spring back to life."

Within perhaps five minutes of the crash, the main fuel tanks, which, topped off before the mission, held seven thousand pounds of JP4 jet fuel, exploded, engulfing the entire helicopter in flames. The machine-gun ammunition on board cooked off like strings of firecrackers. The wall of fire sent everybody running for their lives. Walker was left behind, still pinned under the Chinook. "I remember that kid's eyes, man, when the flames finally forced us back," said Fotias, still haunted. "They drug me away from him, and I was just looking at him, our eyes met, and he was just screaming. . . ."

Reaching cover, Michaud looked back at Walker. "All we could do was watch as he cooked inside his flame-retardant nomex flight suit," said Michaud. "You could see the steam coming out of his flight suit. It was the most terrible thing I've ever witnessed in my life. I even considered pulling my .45 and just ending it for him, but I couldn't do it. He was finally consumed by the flames. . . ."

Stanger scrambled into a bunker already occupied by three GIs, but it offered no refuge. Chunks of burning metal flew past the door as 105 rounds in the sling load began exploding and a stream of burning jet fuel ran toward the bunker from the blazing Chinook. Stanger asked one of the GIs where they should go, but the man was so terrified that, seeing Stanger's spec four insignia, he blurted that he was only a private and Stanger should tell them what to do and where to go. "Okay, where is the main bunker and who knows how to get there?" Stanger asked. One of the other men said he would lead the way to the TOC, the safest position on Ripcord.

The four of them dashed out of the bunker. Stanger immediately hit a concertina-wire barrier, which, as he tried to bull his way through it, tore off his gloves and snared his shirt and trousers. The other three men, not noticing, kept going. There was a tremendous explosion as the fire spread to the ammo bunker atop which the helicopter had crashed, and Stanger tore through the wire, shredding his legs, feeling nothing, fire and smoke all around, the concussion of an exploding shell knocking him down just as he reached the TOC. He blacked out for a second, then, looking up, saw a man with a cross on his helmet. It was Chaplain Fox, standing at the entrance, shouting at him to get inside, which he did, crawling in on his belly amid the continuing explosions. Holmen became separated from his fellow crewmen in the chaos, but Barrowcliff and Grove also made it to the TOC. There they weathered out the storm. "We had at least two direct hits from artillery shells that were blasted out of the ammo dump and exploded after hitting the roof," recalled Stanger. "They really shook the world. The concussion from one picked up one of the pilots as he stood there in the main hallway of the bunker and just laid him flat on his back."

Captain Harris described the destruction of his aid station:

> The artillery shells were blowing up one by one, and group by group. There were tons of explosions. They kept getting bigger and bigger, louder and louder, and, meanwhile, burning jet fuel had run down into the communications center and caught it on fire. The conex containers we were set up in were essentially fireproof, but we'd used dirt-filled ammo crates to build additional compartments around the conexes. We also used the crates for walls and desks and chairs. It was all that wooden stuff that was on fire.
>
> The aid station was right next to the communications center, and it began to fill with smoke as the fire worked its way down towards us. There was an ammo-crate wall between the aid station and the 2-501st TOC, and one of the guys—I

think it was Danny Thompson—chopped through it with an ax so we could get down the hall to the main TOC without stepping outside. Nobody was going to go outside. That would have been like jumping out of the frying pan and into the fire. The fire finally stopped at the main TOC. If the fire hadn't driven us out of the aid station, my medics and I would have all been killed. We didn't know it at the time, but the artillery guys had dug ammunition revetments at the top of the hill directly above and behind the aid station. When the shells in there detonated, the explosion just replaced the aid station with a big hole in the ground. . . .

The exploding artillery ammo included WP shells, which sent burning chunks of white phosphorus splattering down here, there, and everywhere, starting more fires. Tear gas from exploding CS shells permeated the southeast end of the base, and some of it drifted down into the TOC. "It was pretty bad," said Stanger, who, like most of those who'd sought shelter in the ops center, was without a gas mask. "The medics soaked four-by-four cotton pads in water and passed them out to hold over our mouths so we could breathe."

Holmen had already taken cover inside a bunker when "the tear gas came rolling in like fog, and I darted over to one of two conexes outfitted with communications equipment that were sitting back to back. The gas came in there, too, and I ended up going over the top of the radios and through this little opening into the next conex. Somebody in there gave me a gas mask, and that's where I stayed until everything settled down."

It took three hours for the ordnance in the ammunition supply point to expend its fury, with the more than two thousand 105mm rounds and accompanying powder charges stockpiled there. "Being in the middle of such carnage is almost beyond description," wrote Lieutenant Edwards, who was hunkered inside an underground bunker with several GIs. "The explosions were of such magnitude that you could literally see the bunker rise off the ground with each blast. I truly don't want to think about it. . . ."

Sergeant Rubsam was initially pinned down in a small bunker with his platoon sergeant and radioman as Beehive rounds cooked off outside, weakly but with enough power to pepper the sandbags with scores of darts. The tear gas that began wafting in convinced them that they had to get as far from the area as possible. Waiting for a lull, then hoping for the best, they made a mad dash for Impact Rock. Taking cover against the giant boulder, Rubsam's group was joined by several more grunts. Everyone was uptight, expecting the NVA to take advantage of the situation by slipping sappers through the wire. With adrenaline pumping as they waited for the ground attack, the grunts felt a ferocious need for sugar. "Somebody recovered a case of C-rations," said Rubsam, "and we dug through it, looking for peaches and fruit cocktail, anything with a high sugar content."

There appeared then a naked figure moving rapidly uphill in their direction, shielded by the boulders between which he was passing. It was impossible to get a clear shot at the man, so Rubsam, thinking that this was it, that the ground attack was starting, gave the okay to one of his grunts to pitch grenades down among the boulders. Undeterred, the figure continued forward. "He scared the hell out of us," recalled Rubsam, "but as he got closer, we realized he was an American. I couldn't believe it. I also couldn't believe we hadn't succeeded in killing him before we saw who he was."

The naked, barefoot GI high-stepped his way through the wire and, reaching safety, sat down. Medics rushed over as Rubsam questioned him and relayed his name and unit to the TOC. The GI, it turned out, had been asleep in his hootch when the top of the base began exploding; he had dashed down the southeast end to escape the inferno, tearing through the concertina, hurtling the hog-wire fence, and otherwise not slowing down until he reached the jungle below the cleared upper slopes of Ripcord. Moving in defilade, the man had made his way all the way around to the northwest end of the hill, which was not exploding, then started back uphill toward the perimeter. "If I recall correctly, he was an artilleryman," said Rubsam. "He was sort of in shock and had a bunch of cuts and scrapes, some of which were probably from our grenades, but he was in remarkable shape for what he'd been through and was obviously relieved to be back inside the wire."

* * *

Colonel Harrison, airborne over the firebase, which was hazy with smoke and tear gas and from which a column of thick black smoke rose high into the sky, was in radio contact with Lucas as they coordinated protective artillery barrages from Barbara, Rakkasan, and O'Reilly. When the tear gas dissipated enough to allow helicopters to approach the base, Harrison sent in slicks to deliver fire-fighting equipment and take out the wounded while gunships rolled in around Ripcord.

Amazingly, no one had been killed or even seriously injured by all the exploding ordnance, not even the trooper who had to be dug out of his bunker after it collapsed on him. According to initial reports, however, the 105 battery had been destroyed. Even if the fire did not spread to the 155 battery, its rate of fire and adjustment capabilities were too slow to provide support to units in contact. Using a secure net, Harrison called General Berry, who had also rushed to the scene in his command ship, and "requested the immediate reopening of Fire Base Gladiator, for the positioning of a 105 battery to support the troops on the ground in the Ripcord area. I asked that an engineer mine and booby trap element be dispatched to Camp Evans to join my recon platoon to check out Gladiator. I also requested [that] an infantry battalion and a 105 battery meet me in the air for insertion into and around Gladiator that afternoon."

General Berry placed the 1-501st Infantry under Harrison's operational control from the 2d Brigade for the reopening of Gladiator, which sat on a small, bald hilltop in the low ground seven klicks northeast of Ripcord. Past problems aside, Berry was impressed with the way Harrison and Lucas handled the crisis, writing home that he had monitored Lucas's command net "during the whole burning, smoking, exploding mess and heard calm, cool, and collected professionals doing their job in a business-like manner."

Chaplain Fox, who went from bunker to bunker after the fires had been brought under control, talking with the troops and taking their measure, recalled that "nothing ever fell apart. Things got crazy there for a while, and we had to reorganize a lot of things, but nobody lost their head. Everyone was still holding up well."

Initial reports of the destruction of the howitzer battery were not exaggerated: All six 105mm guns had been put out of commission. They were just scrap metal. Nothing was left of two or three but tubes lying on the ground, the wheels and carriages having burned away. Until a decision was made about flying in replacement guns, Michaud and Wintermute ended up as artillery spotters on the perimeter, and their cannoneers were used to beef up the infantry positions or were integrated into the 155 crews of A/2-11th FA.

As troops reestablished their positions, some of the hot shells that had been tossed all over the area continued to cook off, randomly, unnervingly, and the enemy continued to drop in mortar salvos. There was a heavy, twenty-round barrage of 120mm fire at 6 P.M., which wounded several GIs and killed Pfc. Burke H. Miller of A/2-11th FA. The enemy also doused the hill with CS. "It was terrible because all of our equipment and personal gear had been destroyed in the fire, including our protective masks," noted Captain Michaud. "As soon as the gas clears, you're okay, but when you're sucking that stuff down in your lungs, you get violently ill, you puke, and the tears run together at the point of your chin. . . ."

Elements from the 1-501st were at that time securing Gladiator. As the infantry began digging in, six CH-47s, with a howitzer and its basic load of ammunition sling-loaded beneath each, began moving a 105 battery, B/2-320th FA, commanded by Capt. Charles R. Brooks, from Tomahawk to Gladiator. It was dusk by the time the entire battery was on site, and the cannoneers laid their guns and prepared their ammunition in the light of an orbiting flareship. The crews worked fast. It took less than forty minutes from the arrival of the first gun before the battery fired a registration salvo of WP shells in the low ground below Gladiator. "There were no land lines hooked up yet," recalled Frank Parko, "so one of the lieutenants stood on top of an ammo crate and shouted out 'Battery adjust,' followed by the deflection and elevation to Ripcord, then, 'Round, HE. Fuse, quick.' Next, he shouted out the number of rounds we were to fire, and that's when everyone's jaws hit the ground because it was two hundred rounds per gun. That was the whole basic load. The last thing he shouted was, 'Target—known mortar positions and enemy troop concentrations.' "

The cannoneers peeled off their shirts in the muggy heat and, firing without respite, sent two hundred, then three hundred, then four hundred rounds per gun flashing into the night, additional ammo being brought in by Chinook. "Everybody knew everybody else's job, and everybody pitched in," recalled Parko. "We all did a little of everything—loading, firing, hauling ammo, cutting charges, putting in fuses." The battery's ammo section had a flatbed Mechanical Mule, which it used to haul shells from the helipad at the edge of the jungle to the howitzers at the top of the hill. The mule couldn't keep up with the demand. "There were two or three guys on each gun. Everyone else was busting open ammo crates and humping ammo up from the helipad," noted Parko. "We'd heft the rounds on our shoulders, hump 'em up, drop 'em off, then go back for more. There were so many empty canisters and expended brass piled up, we were tripping over the stuff. We were hauling ammo and bustin' caps like bats out of hell all night long."

Colonel Harrison spent the night on Ripcord, helping Lucas and his staff arrange for and coordinate the supporting fires, the flareships, and the resupply effort that continued in the dark as ammunition of all types was collected from other division firebases and sling-loaded up to Ripcord by Chinook. The pilots, all volunteers, delivered the ammo under fire, the constant counterbattery fire and the night-flying Marine Intruders suppressing most but not all of the enemy mortar crews in the black hills around Ripcord.

The expected ground attack did not develop. During a quiet interlude in the ops center, one of Lucas's staff officers admonished him for rushing to the scene of the burning Chinook. "Look, sir," he said, "there's only so many chances you can take."

"Nobody's indispensable," Lucas replied. "We can get new captains out to the companies in no time flat. If I get killed, there will be a new battalion commander out here within four hours."

"Sir," the staff officer blurted, "let's not talk about that."

"Look, that's just one of the facts of life around here."

That Lucas was a man of great personal courage is indisputable; his competence as a commander is a matter of much controversy, however, one of the darker enigmas of Ripcord. "Lucas meant well, but common sense did not always prevail," said Fred Spaulding, who thought Lucas too reckless with not only his life but the lives of his troops. "He would move units into areas and send helicopters into LZs without adequate prep fires," according to Spaulding. "There were a lot of pilots who refused to fly for him. Those scout pilots had brass balls, but, shit, Lucas could be totally irrational. I was in the air almost every day during the battle, looking for targets and helping coordinate our fire support from a LOH. There were numerous instances in which I'd have to call a check-fire because Lucas's chopper had suddenly gotten in the way. I'd tell him, 'Clear the area, you're holding up progress here.' "

Lieutenant Anderson of the division pathfinders recalled that when a new three-man pathfinder team was sent to Ripcord, the team that rotated off "described the battle as a total fuck-up being run by some hopeless lieutenant colonel." The CH-47 crash was not the only issue. "Our guys also said that Lucas gave them a direct order to have helicopters fly along certain routes so that they would elicit ground fire and help him pinpoint enemy positions," noted Anderson. "There were numerous anecdotes like that, and lots of passionate anger in the pathfinder platoon about Lucas. The animosity was so intense that we gave serious consideration to seeing what we could do to get Lucas court-martialled."[2]

The last word about Lucas should come from those who worked closely with him in the TOC on Ripcord. The colonel's operations section was a tight, sharp little group, including as it did Bill Williams as S3 and Charlie Lieb as S3 Air, with two low-key, highly respected ex-platoon leaders, 1st Lt. Gary L. Watrous and 1st Lt. Henry J. Bialosuknia, assigned as the assistant S3s. To these men Lucas was a cool professional who did a remarkable job in the face of an overwhelming enemy force and a puzzling lack of support from above. "Lieutenant Colonel Lucas was the finest damned battalion commander I'd ever served under, bar none," Williams would write. "He was a fighting soldier. My only problem with Lieutenant Colonel Lucas was that he ran too slow; when we were moving around the firebase and there was incoming, he kind of jogged. At times like that, I wanted to pick it up a bit."

Gary Watrous's impressions are especially valuable. Having joined the army at eighteen and graduated from OCS with no college, he was leading a rifle platoon in Vietnam shortly before he turned twenty. Watrous was so good that Lucas's predecessor had selected him to run the battalion reconnaissance platoon; out of respect and affection, the recon troops, many of them older than Watrous, called their platoon leader Teenager. Watrous thought Lucas a bit too spit 'n polish but noted that "Lucas treated the junior officers on his staff very well and respected our opinions. We had a lot of field experience which he didn't have. Lucas was a leader and a fighter. He imparted the feeling that anything could be done. It was rare to see him in a down moment no matter how bad things were. He kept everybody in the right frame of mind. I thought he was a very caring, compassionate individual, too. It broke his heart, every casualty, every fatality. . . ."

Lieutenant Edwards would have agreed, recalling the day that Lucas visited the engineer area by himself after a helicopter had lowered a prefabricated wooden bunker into an entrenchment. The entrenchment was not deep enough, however, and most of the bunker remained aboveground. Lucas motioned Edwards over as he sat down on some sandbags. "Young man," Lucas said softly, almost wearily, "I really don't want to write your mother a letter saying that you died on this hill. That bunker may seem solid to you, but it's not solid enough and it sticks out of the ground so much we might as well paint a big bull's-eye on it." Edwards had his engineers cover the exposed bunker with several layers of sandbags, reflecting later that Lucas's tone and manner "made it apparent that he really cared about my welfare, that he wasn't just a senior officer telling a junior lieutenant about field fortifications. It was in vogue at the time for high-ranking infantry officers to look mean and angry, but Lucas was not of that school. In fact, there seemed to be a gentleness about him that was really a little disarming. It occurs to me that I never saw him smile. There was a perpetual hint of weariness, maybe sadness, in his face."

General Berry visited the firebase the morning after the Chinook crash. "Getting into Ripcord by then was like playing a shell game," said John Fox, the general's pilot. There were four helipads. The pathfinders, or Black Hats, did not communicate by radio with approaching aircraft on the assumption that the enemy was monitoring their frequency. "Instead, you'd make your approach," explained Fox, "and at the last possible moment a Black Hat would pop out of a foxhole and wave you towards the pad that had been cleared for landing. As soon as you landed, everyone got off the aircraft immediately and you departed immediately because there was probably an incoming mortar round headed for that pad."

Berry spent an hour on Ripcord. "It was good for me to talk with the soldiers there," Berry wrote home. "Their calmness and matter-of-factness reassured me and built my confidence." Berry described how he squatted beside a young GI who was sitting on the ground in the 155 area, cleaning the breechblock of one of the howitzers: "I stuck out my hand and said, 'I'm General Berry. What's your name?' He looked up disbelievingly, stuck out his oily hand, shook hands, and exclaimed, 'Jesus, what's a general doing here? I thought you'd be back at a headquarters or some shit like that.' "

When it came time to pick Berry back up, Fox played the same shell game with the Black Hats. "When I landed," Fox recalled, "General Berry and the division sergeant major came running out of a foxhole with the general's aide right behind them, and nobody stepped into the aircraft—they all dove in belly first. . . ."

Captain Andrew Breland choppered in that same morning, July 19, with a three-man team from the 287th Explosive Ordnance Disposal (EOD) Detachment, USARV, out of Phu Bai. Two members of the detachment had actually been dispatched to Ripcord the day before, only a few hours after the Chinook had crashed into the ammunition supply point. "They were totally unprepared for what they found," noted SSgt. Robert J. Lynch; between the incoming mortar fire and exploding artillery ammunition, "it was impossible to do any work. From what they described after they flew back to Phu Bai late that evening, this was going to be an EOD nightmare, the big one you hoped never happened. . . ."

Sergeant Lynch's narrative continued:

> The door gunner on our Huey pointed towards Ripcord. We could see smoke and small fires. The burned-out Chinook was still smoldering. We off-loaded the Huey as fast as we could and reported to the TOC. We were briefed, then escorted to the top of the firebase. The area was just strewn with ordnance . . . hand grenades . . . 40mm shells in the armed condition . . . High Explosive rounds . . . White Phosphorus rounds . . . Bomblets from a type of artillery shell called Improved Conventional Munitions, better known as Firecrackers, were also scattered in the rubble. If you accidentally stepped on one of the golfball-sized bomblets, it was designed to spring about six feet into the air before detonating. This was an extremely dangerous situation.
>
> We started stacking the ordnance in shell craters and detonating the piles with C4. We used everything we had brought with us. More was flown in from Camp Evans. I don't remember how many cases we used, but at one point, Camp Evans ran out and started sending TNT blocks until they could get more C4. The heat was terrible as we went about our work. By noontime, it was unbearable. Even the ground was hot from all the fires. I was new in-country, and my arms were almost purple to go with the terrible heat rash developing under my arms and between my legs. The lack of drinking water made it worse. I've never been so thirsty. All the water bladders on the base were nearly empty. To get any water at all, several guys would jump up and down on a bladder. If you were lucky, a few mouthfuls would come out.

The demolition work was carried out under fire. Lynch had a chunk of skin torn away under his right knee by mortar shrapnel his first day on Ripcord. When the EOD team returned the following day, having choppered to Phu Bai for the night, he took additional shrapnel in his left leg. "Later that second afternoon," he wrote, "a mortar round went off not far from me, and the blast knocked me through a razor-wire barrier, resulting in multiple cuts."

Lynch described the ongoing give-and-take of fire:

> Shell craters were everywhere, which proved handy during the mortar attacks. There seemed to be another salvo every twenty minutes. There was almost constant sniper fire, too; occasionally, you would hear one zip by your head.
>
> The grunts on the perimeter were spotting for the 81s, and they frequently pointed out enemy soldiers moving on the ridges around us. The Quad-50s would rake the hillsides whenever someone reported movement or smoke from a mortar tube. Pink Teams were buzzing the ridges, the LOHs flying at treetop level, trying to draw ground fire, the Cobras rolling in if the enemy shot at the scouts, just tearing up the area with rockets, miniguns, and automatic grenades. We also had a ringside seat to numerous air strikes. The Phantoms would come out of nowhere, dive, and release their payload of snake-eye bombs, retarding fins popping out so that the bombs seemed to float down into their targets. None of it suppressed the enemy for long. I gained a lot of respect for the NVA. They were just as determined as us, I was learning. . . .

The ordnance team was assisted by a small M450 bulldozer that had been lifted in after the Chinook crash from the 326th Engineer Battalion headquarters at Camp Eagle. Because the bulldozer was a regular magnet for enemy fire, three crewmen took turns using it to push the debris and unexploded ordnance and destroyed 105s over the side of the mountain, clearing the battery area for replacement guns. All three were later awarded Silver Stars, Lynch recalling in particular "a black GI who refused to leave the bulldozer no matter how heavy the sniper fire and incoming mortar fire."

Lieutenant Edwards's platoon sergeant, SSgt. Ronald L. Henn, a big, cheerful Regular Army NCO with red cheeks and a good ol' boy smile, a fellow Kentuckian, removed by hand those shells that the bulldozer could not reach, earning a Bronze Star. There were dozens of them, blown into corners and tight spaces between bunkers. Some of the shells were cracked and leaking gunpowder, and all were so hot that you had to wear gloves to handle them. "Any one of them could have gone off at any moment," noted Edwards, "but Henn went about picking them up and carrying them to the disposal area for hours. He had a helmet and flak jacket on, in addition to his asbestos gloves. Of course, had a 105 round cooked off while he was carrying it, nothing would have been found of him or his 'protective' gear, but it was the principle of the thing."

Frank Parko volunteered to join one of the working parties sent by the 2-320th FA to help with the cleanup. "Ripcord to me was like a long, long Mad Minute," Parko later wrote. He elaborated:

> We were told to pair up and help where we could. I teamed up with my buddy Dennis Murphy. During the day, we helped clear debris, humped supplies off the helipads, ran ammo down to the infantry positions on the perimeter, things like that. There was movement all around the hill, and snipers among the boulders of a rock outcropping about five hundred meters off one of the helipads. When we saw muzzle flashes, Murphy and me'd pop right back with our M16s. Everybody would. We didn't get much sleep at night. One night, we helped man the 155s. Another night, we were part of a human chain passing rounds from the mortar section's ammo bunker down to the crews in the 81 pits, running into the bunker when incoming came crashing in. We finally joined the 81 crews. They were pumping off hundreds of rounds that night, HE and Illum. . . .

Parko encountered an angry grunt one of those nights who informed him that he'd caught a Vietnamese scout shining a flashlight and calling to the NVA. "If you see a Kit Carson shining a flashlight out there," the grunt intoned, "shoot the sonofabitch."

Lucas finally had all the Kit Carsons on the firebase confined to a bunker, basically putting them under house arrest. "They were yelling to the enemy on the other side of the wire," recalled Sp4 William W. Heath of HHC/2-506th, "and there was some misunderstanding as to whether they were trying to give themselves up or trying to provide information to the NVA."

Through it all, the casualties continued to pile up. Captain Williams and Captain Lieb were hit on July 19 when the NVA, as they always did when the officers on the base gathered for the evening briefing, dropped a mortar round on the VIP pad in front of the TOC. "You could almost set your watch by that round," noted Captain Harris. The battalion surgeon recalled that there were a dozen or so officers lounging against the TOC's blast wall, waiting for the briefing to begin, when Williams, concerned about the target they presented, ushered them inside: "Hey, maybe we better get our ass out of here because they're gonna drop one in pretty soon."

Captain Williams was the last man through the doorway and thus took the full brunt of the round that exploded on the VIP pad. His injuries were massive. In addition to a ruptured eardrum and several dozen flesh wounds in his back and buttocks, his left lung was punctured and collapsed, the back of his skull was crushed, and the right side of his jaw was shattered, the lower portion blown off. "Williams was laying on his back about halfway down the stairs, blood just pouring out of a wound in his throat. His jugular vein had been cut by the piece of shrapnel that broke his jaw," recounted Harris, who scrambled to the unconscious Williams and stuck his fingers into the throat wound. "It was a torrential hemorrhage," Harris continued, "but after a few minutes, it seemed to stop. I stuffed some gauze sponges in there, and that's when he came to." Williams was out of his head, screaming and yelling as several officers, including Lieb—who had been splattered with shrapnel through his flak jacket badly enough to be medevacked—held onto him to ensure that he didn't reopen his neck wound as they talked him down. Alerted that a medevac was on the way, a litter team gingerly moved Williams up the steps. Someone told him that it would be a long time before he rejoined the battalion, and Williams, barely able to breathe, barely able to talk, grunted his response: "Fuck you."

Lieutenant Edwards was called to the rear the next morning, July 20. In his absence, two of his men—Sp4 Durl G. Calhoun and Sp4 Dennis F. Fisher—were killed by a barrage of 120s when they were caught in the open, helping to clean up the mess on top of the hill. Calhoun could have gone home to Leesville, Louisiana, almost two months earlier but had instead extended his tour. He was a veteran of the engineer advance party that had CA'd onto Ripcord during the April Fools' Day Assault. "That alone established him as 'hardcore,'" noted Edwards, "but he had also participated in several other missions that involved heavy combat, so he was a legend in his own time around the company, one of those guys who had 'seen some real shit.'

"It was great to have Calhoun in the platoon," Edwards continued. "He was quiet, dependable, and worked like a Trojan. Physically, he was young, tanned, and thin with lady-killer looks. I never got to know him well, but like everyone else, I admired him. He usually had a slightly amused look when I talked with him. I think he wanted to let me know that he was not overly impressed with this lieutenant's budding combat experiences. When Calhoun got killed, there was more disbelief than anger. It reminded me of when they finally killed Paul Newman in *Cool Hand Luke*."

Morale began to unravel. The troops, unable to comprehend why division did not either pile on or pull them out, became gripped with a certain numb despair, a feeling that they had been abandoned to their fate. "I don't think the mortars are ever going to stop coming in," Edwards wrote in his journal after returning to Ripcord. There were grunts who basically flipped out under the onslaught, taking bets on whether they could survive walking from one bunker to the next amid the incoming, whistling, hands in their pockets. Other grunts never left their bunkers. "It was terrible picking people for the working parties that had to go topside," Sergeant Rubsam reported.

"You could hardly look 'em in the face. We spaced it out as reasonably as we could so a guy didn't have to go up top every day."

People were physically and emotionally frazzled not only from the dangerous and exhausting working parties but from trying to stay awake half the night on watch, the perimeter positions having been reduced to two men each because of the heavy casualties. Sometimes guys just ran out of steam. Chip Collins and his best friend, Al Riddle, tough troopers both, jumped into a bunker during one particularly heavy barrage, abandoning whatever task they'd been assigned to that day. They were soon confronted by a furious captain whom they did not know. "What do you fuckers think you're doing in here?" the captain barked. "We've got things to do up on top of the hill. You get your asses up there." Neither man budged, not even when the captain said that he was giving them a direct order. "We just laughed at him," recalled Collins, "which elicited a threat of court-martial. We laughed that off, too, and he just sort of disappeared."

Replacement guns were not flown in as planned. The chances were too great that one of the Chinooks trying to place new 105s on site would be brought down, either by the .51s or the 82s and 120s. It was not uncommon for resupply CH-47s to pull away from Ripcord with shrapnel damage despite the fact that they barely slowed down to unhook their sling loads. "[W]e're taking 75–80 rounds a day and they're deadly accurate," Lieutenant Edwards wrote on July 21. "[M]edevacs are constantly in + out with the wounded. . . . A ground attack is sure to follow, as the whole hill is all but wiped out + no supplies can get in. Really feel low . . ."

The casualties continued to pile up. Edwards himself received a number of cuts and scrapes when a direct hit caved in part of the roof of the bunker he was in. The engineer platoon sergeant, the indomitable, always-smiling Sergeant Henn, was wounded badly enough to be medevacked on July 21 when he and Edwards were running working parties on different parts of the hill. Edwards raced to a small bunker near him when the explosions started. "At least one other trooper was wedged in there with me," he recounted; when the incoming let up, "Henn came barrel-assing in, telling everyone to clear out as he hit the door on all fours. His lower leg was a bloody mess, but he was lucid—and seriously pissed. For the first time ever, he wasn't very keen on showing proper military courtesy. Luckily, Henn had caught frags from a CS round rather than an HE round. Had it been HE, it is doubtful that Henn would have survived as close as the round landed to him."

Sniper fire was received that same morning from the south side of the base, and Al Riddle of Bravo Three began returning it with a ground-mounted .50-caliber machine gun. The enemy put the gun out of action within moments, dropping a single 82mm mortar shell just behind the position, almost a direct hit. "Unfortunately, there were five or six guys from the platoon clusterfucked around Al, watching him fire, seeing if they could help," recalled Chip Collins, one of many who rushed to help when word went out that they had casualties. The scene was devastating. "All I saw was a mass of bodies, and we began pulling them out of the position," Collins wrote. Private First Class Francis E. Maune had been killed instantly, and five others were wounded, including Pfc. Larry J. "Mac" McDowell, who would die of his injuries after being medevacked. Riddle was at the bottom of the pile, one of the wounded; though dazed and peppered with shrapnel, he had been spared death or serious injury by his flak jacket and the men around him who had absorbed most of the blast. As Collins helped him to cover, Riddle kept repeating, "Those fuckin' gooks. . . . Those fuckin' gooks. . . ."

Specialist Fourth Class Roberto C. Flores of Bravo Two was also killed on July 21, felled while on a working party. Flores, a draftee, had a wife and baby waiting for him in Brownsville, Texas. Rubsam, who counted Flores as one of his best friends, described him as smart, upbeat, a completely dependable soldier. That was what got him killed. "Most of us would go whenever we were called upon, but some guys eventually said ain't no way," recalled Collins. Between those who were medevacked to safety and those who simply faded into the woodwork, the most dangerous assignments were falling disproportionately on men like Flores. "Roberto came over to my position the very morning he was killed," noted Rubsam, "and complained to me that the new lieutenant running Bravo Two was always picking him for details and working parties. He was depressed about being out there on top of the hill day after day. Roberto was very well liked in the whole company, and it really hurt when we found out that he was KIA."

Flores was killed toward dusk when the enemy dropped a heavy salvo of 82s into the 155 area from the reverse slope of Hill 805, hoping to catch those troops moving howitzer ammunition that had just been sling-loaded onto the battery helipad by a fast-moving Chinook. The salvo did just that, wounding seven men and killing Flores and Sp4 David E. Johnson of A/2-11th FA.

The salvo also killed Lieutenant Kalsu, the big, popular pro-football player serving as acting commander of Battery A. Kalsu had been standing with pathfinder Nick Fotias at the top of the stairs leading down into his FDC. "It was foolish to be in the open like that," admitted Fotias; the problem was that the enemy gunners were "clobbering us with a round of CS and then three HE in that pattern, just constantly. It got to the point after a while," explained Fotias, "that you didn't even wear your gas mask because it was so sweltering hot you couldn't breathe with the darn thing on. You'd rather breathe the CS than suffocate in your mask. I guess you just had to decide which was the lesser of two evils. It was so hot down in the bunkers anyway, you sometimes gave up the safety of being inside one just to get a breath of anything close to fresh air."

Lieutenant Kalsu had been telling Fotias that his wife, pregnant with their second child, was due to deliver that very day when an 82 suddenly slammed in about five feet from the entranceway to the FDC. Fotias was blown down to the bottom of the stairs and Kalsu crashed atop him, big and heavy. Fotias, stunned from the blast, rolled Kalsu off him when he came back to reality. The lieutenant had been killed instantly, a shrapnel hole above his left eye. "I put my hand up there and tried to stop the blood," Fotias recalled, "and then I realized I was holding a piece of his brain in my hand. . . ."

The death of the gregarious Kalsu sent a shock wave across Ripcord. "Even Colonel Lucas gasped a little bit when he heard," noted Harris. Bob Kalsu, the only professional athlete killed in the Vietnam War, was sorely missed by the men in his battery, as was the dead cannoneer, David Johnson. "One was a highly educated white professional athlete," said Alfred Martin, a section chief, "the other a poor colored kid from Humnoke, Arkansas, who didn't have shit goin' for him. Kalsu and Johnson had nothing in common except their size and their hearts. They were both giants, and they were both two of the nicest guys you'd ever want to meet.

"They were together all the time," Martin continued. "Everything was a competition to 'em. Them 155 rounds we carried, they weighed ninety-seven pounds apiece. They carried three, one across each shoulder, which we all did, but then they'd have a third laid across the back of their necks, supported by the other two. That's three hundred pounds. They'd hump three rounds at a time off the helipad as long as they could, just to see who'd say uncle first. . . ."

Lieutenant Edwards felt himself sliding into a hopeless funk. "Every time a chopper approached, the entire hill headed for cover because we knew that incoming was on the way," he wrote. "Cobras would be circling and artillery fire smashing into the adjacent hills, but nothing could stop the incoming. We felt helpless, at the mercy of the enemy. Sustained incoming has to be one of the worst tortures ever inflicted on a soldier. There is an element of humiliation involved, too—you just have to sit and take it."

As men were methodically wounded and killed by an enemy who seemed immune to the allies' overwhelming fire superiority, Edwards felt "vulnerable, humiliated, sickened, angry. When the bastards gassed us, it just added to the humiliation of it all. It's impossible to look macho in one of those anteater gas masks. We all looked like dorks, and felt that way, too."

Edwards finally succumbed to the numb resignation of combat fatigue. "I can remember saying to myself, I'm gonna die on this damn hill. It was an awful, apathetic feeling. Finally, near the end, the passivity bordered on indifference to death. Maybe there was no other way to cope with what was happening day in, day out, more incoming every day, almost constant, more body bags stacking up to be evacuated. Who next? Who cares? Here it comes again. . . ."

PART SEVEN

The Storm

We were just dust in the wind out there.

—Pfc. Walter M. Jurinen
Company D, 1st Battalion, 506th Infantry
101st Airborne Division

CHAPTER 22

Behind Enemy Lines

Captain Hawkins was sitting against his ruck like the other men in the column along the ridge—a rest halt had just been called—when he heard someone crunching through the leaves that covered the jungle floor. Coming to instant, nerve-tingling alert, he spotted the approaching North Vietnamese. There were two that he could see, one leading, the other a few paces behind, passing between the trees twenty feet away as they hiked up the side of the ridge at an angle. They were traveling light, no helmets, no packs—they wore fatigues and web gear and had fresh, close-cropped haircuts—and, unaware of the silent column above them, their AK-50s were slung over their shoulders. They were the first enemy soldiers Hawkins had seen face-to-face in five months of combat, and he froze at the sight of them. He realized that no one else had noticed the enemy, that no one was going to shoot them before they crested the ridge and were among them, but his body would not respond. A tremendous weight bore down on his shoulders and he could not breathe. He could not call out. His arms would not lift his M16.

Hawkins's heart was pounding. C'mon, boy, he thought, cursing himself, don't freeze on me now. You can do it. React.

He did. The lead weight evaporated and adrenaline flooded his system as he leveled his M16 on the lead enemy soldier from the hip, buttstock clamped under his arm. Hawkins cut the man down with a quick three-round burst to the chest—*tang-tang-tang*—then, shifting slightly, did the same to the second NVA. *Tang-tang-tang.*

Hawkins rolled to his knees, pumping more rounds into the bodies. Fearing he had killed merely the point team of a larger enemy force, he dug a grenade out of an ammo pouch, pulled the pin, cocked his arm, and tried to lob the grenade through the tree branches above him. The frag hit one and bounced back, landing between him and one of his radiomen. Hawkins shouted a warning and they frantically low-crawled away from the grenade, the radioman springing to action after it exploded, thinking it had been an enemy satchel charge as he sprayed the brush with his M16. Others joined in, but Hawkins, regaining his composure, realized that there were no other enemy in the area and bellowed, "Cease fire. Cease fire."

Lieutenant Widjeskog made a sweep of the area, then joined Hawkins, who remarked that he had basically been preparing for such a moment since entering West Point. "All that training really paid off," he exulted. "I did exactly as I was supposed to."

Everything had been going Hawkins's way since he had magically called in the air strike on the ammo cache six days earlier as Company A moved off Hill 805. The company spent that night below 805, moved onto the southeastern end of the ridge running down from Ripcord the next day, then dropped off the ridge the day after that, July 15, its stated mission to find enemy graves—higher command apparently wanted something to show for all the munitions being expended in defense of the firebase—its unstated mission to screen the southern approach to Ripcord. By late afternoon, Hawkins was moving onto a subhill, a klick down from the firebase, which had appeared a good NDP site but atop which were discovered two fresh enemy bunkers. Ominously, there was a pile of fresh feces beside one of the bunkers. It was too late to move to another location, so Company A dug in where it was. "Sometime in the wee hours of the morning, around three or four A.M.," Hawkins wrote, "I woke up with an uncanny feeling that we were going to be hit." Hawkins and his radiomen "went around to quietly wake up the platoon leaders"; the company "rucked up as silently as possible and moved out into the dead of night. I didn't know where we were going, just downhill, away from that NDP." An hour later, at which time the company was half a klick from the knoll and the sky was turning a twilight gray, "we heard a mortar being fired, and moments later, heard and felt the crash of the rounds impacting on our former NDP. The enemy fired fifteen to twenty rounds, enough to cause a lot of havoc had we still been there. Eerie. There were a bunch of guys in Alpha Company who were starting to wonder what sort of crystal ball their Charlie Oscar was using."

The predawn move allowed Hawkins to slip under the enemy's radar screen, so to speak, and numerous NVA positions were discovered on the side of the ridge during the next few days. There were mortar and machine-gun pits, sleeping bunkers, hospital bunkers, even an underground kitchen. The grunts paused long enough at each position to blast it with a plastic jug of crystallized CS wrapped with det cord, thus impregnating the earthen walls with tear-gas powder and rendering the position unfit for human habitation. Company A had never operated with such stealth. "We were really scared and we stayed real quiet," explained Lieutenant Widjeskog. The grunts felt themselves on enemy ground, vulnerable at any moment to ambush. Gunfire seemed to echo continuously through the jungle as other units made contact, and the CH-47 that was shot down on Ripcord seemed to throw in doubt which side was winning. Widjeskog's platoon, Alpha Two, was close enough to hear the muffled report of the .51 that nailed the Chinook and to watch it crash and burn, setting off a chain reaction of explosions. "Pieces of shrapnel could be heard hitting the trees between us and the firebase," wrote Widjeskog. "The explosions seemed to go on forever, a haze of black smoke filling the sky. We were certain that many had been killed up on Ripcord."

The tension built to the point that the sergeant in charge of the squad whose turn it was to lead Alpha Two at that particular time had to inform Widjeskog that he couldn't get anyone to walk point. Widjeskog didn't think he could persuade anyone to walk point by force of personality, having little standing with his grunts—in their eyes, he was just another green lieutenant—and he didn't want to give anyone a direct order to do so. Those men who disobeyed a direct order would be packed to the rear on the next resupply slick to await court-martial, an option that Widjeskog knew would appeal to the more uptight grunts in the squad. He also rejected as unfair the idea of putting a different squad in the lead. "Okay," he finally said, "if you guys won't do it, I'll do it. I don't care. I'll walk point."

Lieutenant Widjeskog had proceeded about two hundred meters down a trail when the squad leader came up to tell him that he had found somebody to take the point. "Afterwards," noted Widjeskog, "I heard that no one wanted me getting killed on point because none of the sergeants wanted the responsibility of taking command of the platoon. That kind of problem did not occur again."

Lucas instructed Hawkins to begin pushing southeast as of July 19 toward the narrow valley pinched between the southwestern base of Hill 805 and the major ridgeline knifing east from Coc Muen Mountain. That same morning, the 155s on Ripcord fired a six-gun salvo uncomfortably close to Alpha Two. Hawkins received an agitated call from Widjeskog to get the firing stopped, which he did by immediately contacting the TOC. Hawkins then demanded to talk with the S3. Captain Williams got on the horn—this was his last day on the firebase before being wounded—but made a throwaway comment to minimize the incident upon learning there had been no casualties. "Listen, friend," Hawkins barked, "this is my AO and anyone fires into it, I'm going to know beforehand. You got that?"

Williams got a bit huffy, so Hawkins, wanting to be seen by his men as a commander who took care of his troops, proceeded to lay down the law: "I have just had six one-five-five rounds nearly hit one of my platoons. I didn't call for fire. I don't know where it came from and I don't give a shit. If it happens again, I am going to personally RIF up to the TOC and de-nut you. Do you roger?"

That was the end of it. Williams told Hawkins not to worry, he would make sure things stayed under control. Widjeskog's men had been shaken by the friendly fire. To bolster their morale, Hawkins decided to move his CP, then with Alpha Three, the half klick to Alpha Two. Meanwhile, Hawkins instructed Lieutenant Pahissa of Alpha One to take control of Alpha Three, which was commanded by a less-than-aggressive E5. Pahissa was then to lead the descent into the valley—the eager academy graduate sounded pleased when so informed—and find a good company-sized NDP.

Charlie Oscar's presence did not have the desired effect on Alpha Two. There were eight men in the command group: Hawkins; his three RTOs; the FO and his RTO; the senior medic; and Sfc. Pham Van Long, the ARVN interpreter attached to Company A. "There was so much activity because of the radiomen and all the things the CP had to do," noted Widjeskog, "that I was immediately getting complaints from my men that these guys were too noisy and were sure to get us into trouble. We could hardly wait till the CP joined another platoon and left us quietly alone in the jungle."

Hawkins's group was still with Alpha Two late that afternoon when Widjeskog called a rest halt, having just realized to his dismay that he was going to have to turn the whole show around, because he had taken the wrong ridge to reach the overnight position being secured by Pahissa. It was at that moment that Hawkins, waiting for the column to proceed, shot the two unwary North Vietnamese. Hawkins recalled that upon moving on to the overnight position, which was atop a knoll on a ridge that descended southeast into the valley, Bill Pahissa and his platoon sergeant, Gerald Singleton, "offered a mock round of applause for the kills. I waved it off."

Hawkins had taken a small brass cigarette lighter as a souvenir from the first man he shot, from the other a belt with the prized red-star buckle. "It's your kill, captain," a grunt had said. "You get first pick." The lead enemy soldier had a wallet in which were tucked a piece of notebook paper, a letter, postage stamps, photographs of what were presumed to be his wife and child, plus a few folded-up pages from an American skin magazine. The company interpreter examined the material, which identified the NVA with the wallet as a sergeant named Van Thai, his companion a Private Thuan, both reconnaissance personnel from "K3 Company, D9 Battalion." The sergeant had partially healed wounds in his back and legs, and the notebook paper—a supply request he'd been dispatched to carry from his company commander to some higher headquarters—indicated that he was on light duty after having been hit by ARA shrapnel during the night attacks on Hill 805. As recorded in the battalion journal, the letter had been written by the sergeant to an older brother in Bac Thai, North Vietnam, and in it he "complained about lack of uniforms, medicine, and food."

Hawkins had his own worries. There was obviously a large enemy force encircling Ripcord, but "if there were so many NVA in the area," he later wrote, "why was Lucas sending a lone company into a valley, vulnerable from all around, to suffer what so many enemy might throw at it?" Lucas had told Hawkins when talking to him on the secure net that, given the extent of the entrenchments on Hill 1000 and the fact that the firebase was taking 120mm fire—the enemy did not usually employ their heaviest mortar until they had invested an area in at least regimental strength—"he thought we might be up against a regiment, maybe two regiments. But it came across as only speculation. The truth is that we simply didn't know what we were really up against at that particular time." Hawkins had no choice but to take the mission at face value, which meant that he was to "look for the enemy and kill him; find his bunkers and supply caches and destroy them. What I was being asked to do wasn't a heck of a lot different from the search and clear patrols we'd been doing since I joined the battalion. The big difference was that I would keep the platoons within mutually supporting distance of each other. Our platoons usually operated rather independently in order to cover all the territory we had."

Lieutenant Colonel Lucas had been running out of options when he sent Hawkins into the valley. Not one to reveal doubts to subordinates, Lucas, outwardly positive, could not have but felt abandoned when he took stock of the situation that morning; his firebase was half demolished, the incoming was relentless, and the division reserve had been withdrawn, nullifying any hopes of securing Hill 1000. Lucas had basically been left to fight alone with his battered battalion—actually, those two companies not tied down on firebase security—plus an attached company, D/1-506th, commanded by Capt. Donald R. Workman, which had been inserted onto Triple Hill upon the departure of the Geronimo Battalion.

Division was counting on firepower to disperse the enemy on Hill 1000. Lucas hoped to deny the enemy their other major stronghold, Hill 805, with the ground forces available to him; thus did Lucas send Hawkins into the valley southwest of 805 and make plans to assault D/1-506th the following day onto a ridge fifteen hundred meters northeast of Hill 805. Chuck Hawkins and Don Workman had been classmates at West Point. "Don's company and mine were going to link up, and then work our way up the backside of 805, rooting out the enemy," wrote Hawkins, who was somewhat dubious about the enterprise, given what the NVA in the area had been able to muster against D/2-501st when it had held Hill 805.

Many grunts were convinced that Hawkins had volunteered them for the mission into the valley. It seemed a suicidal venture, and Hawkins had to call in a medevac on the morning of July 20 for a GI who had shot himself in the foot with his M16. "He says it was an accident, but it's sure a good way to get out of the field," a skeptical medic remarked to Hawkins after treating the GI.

Captain Workman and D/1-506th, meanwhile, CA'd into a hot LZ two and a half kilometers away on the other side of Hill 805. Hawkins's luck still held as Alpha One—continuing southeast down the ridge from the overnight position after the medevac, followed in column by Alpha Two, then Alpha Three—reached the heart of the valley without incident, whereupon it made the most important intelligence coup of the entire battle for Firebase Ripcord.

It was 2:25 P.M. when Hawkins received the urgent radio call from Lieutenant Pahissa: "I think you better come down here."

Hawkins asked Pahissa what he had. "High-speed trail and commo wire—and it isn't ours," Pahissa answered. "We're rigging a wiretap and we'd like the company interpreter to listen."

Alpha One, nine hundred meters from the overnight position, had just discovered a major enemy trail, three to four feet wide, at the southwestern base of Hill 805, a klick down from the top. Several feet to one side of the trail, running parallel to it in the thick underbrush, was a black phone line that had been "laid on the ground or over trees and bushes as it was spooled out," noted Hawkins, who quietly moved to the scene with his interpreter and two RTOs. "Pahissa and Singleton were excited and delighted at their success at finding and tapping the wire. . . ."

"How'd you tap the wire," Hawkins asked Pahissa.

"Earplug from a Sony transistor radio—one of the men had it."

For reasons of noise discipline, troops in Company A weren't supposed to have transistor radios in the field, "but at that point it was a serendipitous violation of my policy," mused Hawkins. "Pahissa already had his Kit Carson listening in and making notes; he then cut the cord of a PRC25 handset and spliced that into the commo wire so Sergeant Long, my interpreter, could listen, too."

The line was extremely active. Long wrote in a notepad as fast as he could, with the radio handset squeezed between his ear and shoulder. It appeared, said the enthused, grinning ARVN NCO, that the phone line ran between a mortar unit firing on Ripcord from the reverse slope of Hill 805 and an enemy division headquarters somewhere to the southwest in the direction of Hill 902.

Hawkins passed intell directly to Lucas and General Berry, who was overhead, monitoring A/2-506th's activities and D/1-506th's ongoing engagement from his C&C. Company A also encountered the enemy several times as the day wore on. The first contact involved an ambush that Alpha Two had established between Alpha One, which was deployed in defensive positions around the wiretap, and Alpha Three, which had backtracked up the ridge to secure the high ground. The ambush was on a bluff a hundred feet above a fast-moving, boulder-strewn stream running between the lower edge of the ridge and the base of Hill 805, overlooking a spot that seemed readily accessible to enemy soldiers who might need to refill their canteens. Hawkins moved to the scene when Pfc. Alan R. Miller, one of the ambushers, opened fire on a water detail that did indeed appear at the stream. Miller had time for only a quick burst before the enemy disappeared back into the jungle. "I think I winged one in the foot," Miller said with a chagrined look.

Hawkins was talking with Widjeskog when several more M16 shots rang out from the bluff, followed by a blast from an M79. Miller, who packed both weapons, had just ambushed another water detail. Hawkins was stunned that the enemy would return to a spot where they had taken fire but surmised—and this spoke to a great number of enemy in the area—that the second water detail had been dispatched by an entirely different NVA unit on Hill 805.

Hawkins hustled up to Miller's position to find a dead NVA spread-eagled on a flat rock down below at the edge of the stream. "Good shooting," Hawkins exclaimed; in response, Miller, short, chunky, and tough, one of the few who wanted to fight in a unit full of draftees—he had dropped out of college to enlist and had wangled his way into an infantry unit after being assigned as a clerk because of his education—"just looked up at me," wrote Hawkins, "and smiled the biggest shit-eating grin I can remember. . . ."

Hawkins returned to the wiretap, and Long reported that, in addition to the location of the enemy division headquarters, they had also determined the center of mass of four major subordinate units—regiments, according to Long—on the high ground north, south, east, and west of Ripcord. There had been discussion of a mass assault on the firebase that night, but apparently no final decision had been reached, because reinforcements expected that day had failed to arrive. The Kit Carson eavesdropping with the earplug was visibly shaken, but Long, delighted at the trick they were playing on the enemy, beamed as he told Hawkins, "Beaucoup NVA. . . . Full division. . . . F-5 Division. . . . many men."

The dual taps had lowered the transmission signal, and Long presently informed Hawkins that a repair team was being sent out to inspect the line. The jig's up, thought Hawkins. It was, but it wasn't. The enemy soldiers on the radio, even if they suspected that the line had been tapped—and it appeared that they were responding matter-of-factly to what they thought was a technical problem—knew neither the location nor the size of the force that had entered their valley. The situation was ripe for another ambush. To confuse the enemy, Pahissa suggested they fire up the linemen with the AKs recovered from the two sappers Hawkins had shot. Hawkins agreed. Pahissa took one of the captured weapons and joined those grunts covering the trail as it ran into their perimeter from the direction of the enemy headquarters, while a Sergeant Ross did likewise with the other AK-50 on the side of the perimeter facing Hill 805.

The linemen came down the trail in Ross's direction. Ross shot the lead NVA in the chest at close range, but the man bounced back up and darted into the brush even as a machine gunner cut loose in his direction and other grunts frantically opened fire with M16s.

Pahissa, rushing over, asked Frank Marshall where the NVA had gone. "He went down right there," Marshall said, pointing to the trail, "then went through those little bushes over there."

"Go ahead," Pahissa said, his blood up. "We'll follow you."

"No, you won't," Marshall blurted to the brand-new platoon leader. "You're crazy. I ain't goin' in there first—I got the '79."

Pahissa darted on to one of the riflemen, and a small group took off in hot pursuit of the wounded NVA. They followed a heavy blood trail down to the stream, but the man had disappeared.

It was time to get out. Hawkins moved northwest with Alpha Two to rejoin Alpha Three, leaving Pahissa and Alpha One, as Hawkins later wrote, to "hang around the wire-tap a bit longer to see what developed, and to give me time to get up the slope so the whole company wouldn't be clustered together. . . ."

It took the enemy about an hour to organize a response to the ambush of their linemen. Pahissa briefly engaged the NVA as they approached, then ripped out fifty feet of telephone line and moved out to follow the rest of the company up the ridge. Pahissa, wearing one rucksack and dragging another, was really huffing and puffing by the time he reached Hawkins. Seeing the extra ruck, Hawkins thought Pahissa had lost a man, but it turned out that the platoon leader had relieved one of his troopers of his rucksack so the man would be unencumbered as he covered the withdrawal.

Hawkins had Lieutenant Olson, his forward observer, call fire down on the wiretap area as Company A moved several hundred meters west of the trail leading back to its previous overnight position to establish a new NDP. "I didn't want to be found too easily," noted Hawkins. Berry and Lucas had been full of praise as Hawkins relayed information to them from the wiretap, and as things settled down that night, Hawkins recalled that he was "pleased, excited, and feeling very proud of Alpha Company."

Hawkins thought it was time to get out of the valley. Lucas, however, wanted him to come up with a prisoner the next day to confirm the intelligence from the wiretap. Hawkins's impression was that the new mission had come down from division. "The concern, apparently, was that the enemy may have suspected the wiretap and sent false information to mislead us," noted Hawkins. "I doubted that, but could not say in so many words why. If the order to get a prisoner had originated with division, that means there was [a] strong feeling in higher headquarters not to believe how many enemy we were up against, even at that late date. . . ."

CHAPTER 23

Wrong Place, Wrong Time

The men disembarking from the first slick into the landing zone included 2d Lt. Randall Thompson, 1st Platoon leader in D/1-506th. Thompson's group dashed to the south side of the man-made clearing, grabbing positions to provide suppressive fire for the next helicopter in the five-ship lift bearing Delta One. "When we reached cover," recalled Sp4 Richard E. Drury, the platoon leader's radioman, "we realized that there was a communications wire running from one side of the landing zone to the other, as well as bunkers all around the edge of the LZ. I looked at Thompson, and he looked at me—we knew that this was not going to be good."

It wasn't. Thompson popped red smoke on the landing zone—it sat in a saddle between two knolls at the south end of a ridge, the terrain falling away to the east and west—as AK-47 fire greeted the second Huey. Approaching from the east, it deposited its troops, then banked away to the south at full throttle. The others followed in turn, door gunners blasting back as green tracers zipped past. As each Huey flared over the clearing, nose up, tail down, the grunts on board leaped from the skids and scrambled for the brushy cover from which Thompson's group, reinforced with each new load, sent wave upon wave of M16 and M60 fire into the jungle below the LZ.

Captain Workman—the highly respected company commander was known to all by his call sign, Ranger—went in with Delta One. The slicks circled back to Triple Hill to pick up 1st Lt. John H. Smith's platoon, Delta Two, which was to secure the north side of the LZ. The platoon sergeant's slick took multiple hits as it came in. Forced to break off, it sputtered its way to Camp Evans, the shaken grunts on board eventually going back in aboard another Huey.

Leaving Thompson, Captain Workman had joined Smith on the north side of the clearing by the time SSgt. John W. Fraser, the shake 'n bake platoon leader of Delta Three, hit the LZ. Workman stepped from the trees to wave Fraser over. The enemy fire evaporated as the last slick departed, and Workman, exultant that the entire company had made it in unscathed, greeted Fraser with, "We're still eighty-four fighting bastards—no one's hurt yet."

Workman radioed his first sergeant at Camp Evans: "Put in for Air Medals for all my cherries—we just hit a hot one."

Ranger's cherries included Lieutenants Smith and Thompson, Sergeant Fraser being the only combat-experienced platoon leader in Company D. Getting organized, Workman instructed Thompson to secure the knoll to the south—it was a hundred meters to the top by way of an enemy trail that ran along the spine of the ridge, bisecting the landing zone—while Smith secured the larger knoll to the north, also a hundred meters from the saddle. The ridge came to an end at the south knoll. From the north knoll, it cut eight hundred meters northwest to the top of a small mountain. The dominant terrain feature in the area—Hill 805, which was the reason the company had been inserted—lay to the west. The western base of the landing-zone ridge met the eastern base of 805 in a shallow valley. It was sixteen hundred meters from the LZ to the top of Hill 805.

Lieutenant Smith was preparing to move out when three enemy soldiers suddenly sauntered into the perimeter, having come down the trail from the north knoll. They were still at sling arms, and before they could react, one of Smith's veterans, Sgt. Bobby M. Rosas, shouted a warning—"Dinks"—as he leveled his machine gun on the startled NVA. Rosas, standing, firing from the hip, cut them down where they stood, blazing away without pause until he had expended the entire 150-round belt in the M60.

With the enemy soldiers reduced to a clump of bloody rags on the trail, Rosas shouted triumphantly to Workman, "Ranger, I got three."

"Good," Workman yelled back. "Cut their dicks off."

Ranger was not serious, but his exhortation, met with shouts and cheers, summed up the grim satisfaction of the moment. "It boggles my mind that those guys simply walked into our perimeter," Smith later wrote. "I guess they thought that since this was their backyard, they could walk around oblivious to their surroundings. . . ."

There was contact moments later on Lieutenant Thompson's side of the clearing when one of his new guys, Pfc. James G. McCoy, ammo bearer for the gun team covering the trail, spotted an NVA trotting downhill toward the LZ. Only the man's bush hat was visible over the brush. "Do we have any friendlies up there?" McCoy called out in a panic. "There's someone running down the trail."

Private First Class Brian Redfern, a veteran, immediately jumped on the M60 and opened fire, shouting at McCoy to "Feed me." Most of the platoon joined in, blindly shredding jungle. McCoy noticed that a fellow cherry, Tommy Smith, had ceased firing. Thinking he'd run out of ammo, McCoy tossed him some M16 magazines. Smith did not pick them up but simply stared up the trail in shock, eyes popped wide open. When the firing petered out, McCoy asked Smith why he had stopped shooting. "My gun jammed," Smith gasped. "That gook was so close I could have shook hands with him."

Lieutenant Smith took the north knoll with Sgt. Terry W. Handley's squad. They advanced cautiously, pausing while Ranger worked their front with ARA, then swept the crest on line, spraying the brush with M16 fire. Thompson, meanwhile, secured the south knoll—both knolls had freshly dug enemy positions on them—without incident. The plan was to spend the rest of the day running RIFs, then for Workman, Fraser, and Smith to NDP on the north knoll and Thompson the south knoll. Most of the grunts, thinking the battle over, "just sat around talking with each other," wrote McCoy. "I occasionally glanced down the trail I was supposed to be watching. It seemed like no one else was paying any attention, and I remember being amazed that they could relax so soon. . . ."

The battle had actually only just begun. McCoy turned to take another look down the trail and realized that there was an enemy soldier lying there. "Too scared to yell, I reached down and picked up my M16," he wrote; the man raised up as McCoy sighted in, so that the cherry found himself "looking at a gook that was now looking at me." McCoy fired a burst, and the NVA dropped flat, seemingly killed instantly. The shot was the signal for everyone to begin blasting the jungle again. Redfern sent several bursts down the trail, then stood up and while McCoy watched, amazed at his cool, pulled the pin and released the spoon on a fragmentation grenade, then let it cook off for a second or two in his hand before throwing it, getting an airburst. The firing quickly died down. McCoy recalled that the guys from his platoon "came over to me and patted my now-shaking self on the back in a moment of congratulations for what appeared to be my first kill. For the first time I actually felt like I was one of the guys, but little did they know the turmoil I felt inside for killing another person." McCoy's platoon was shortly to be shot to pieces, however, and "the dead and wounded Americans I would see erased any remorse I may have felt at that moment. . . ."

One platoon took heavy casualties that day, the rest of the company even more casualties the next. It could have been worse. Captain Workman, three weeks to go on his tour, was due to be rotated to the rear. His successor had already been selected. The new captain was a good man but mild mannered and inexperienced. "I must admit," wrote Lieutenant Smith, "that I'm glad Ranger was still in command when we stepped in it at Ripcord. . . ."

Don Workman—strong, outgoing, a natural leader—was seven and his sister three when their parents divorced and they went to live on their maternal grandparents' farm near Springfield, Missouri. He was thirteen when they rejoined their mother, who was back on her feet financially by then, settling finally in Kirkwood, a quiet suburb of St. Louis. Working days, going to college at night, Workman joined the army at nineteen to get the GI Bill. Two years later, he was at West Point with the Class of '68.

Lieutenant Workman, airborne and ranger qualified, arrived in Vietnam in August 1969. He led a rifle platoon and the battalion recon platoon for eight months before getting D/1-506th on April 14, 1970, his twenty-seventh birthday. He was still a lieutenant at the time; he was that good. "Ranger was very professional, very competent," noted a squad leader. Workman was crisp, autocratic, and supremely confident, fond of Hav-a-Tampa Jewels, a small cigar with a wooden tip. He was also approachable, the kind of officer who could enjoy having a beer with his men in boisterous circumstances, the familiarity breeding anything but contempt. "Everybody loved him," said the squad leader. "He was a big brother to everybody in Delta Company."

The grunts had originally learned to put their faith in Lieutenant Workman after Company D CA'd into the Maureen AO on May 5. The mission involved numerous contacts and heavy losses. There was a devastating sapper attack on Delta Two—the action in which Kenneth Kays won the Medal of Honor—and the ambush death of Delta One's point man, followed by the platoon leader's enraged and fatal one-man charge on the next enemy bunker they encountered. To add to the company's troubles, an errant U. S. 155 shell killed one GI and wounded five. Smith and Thompson joined Company D when it came in for stand-down at the end of the month; they were replacements for the two lieutenants killed during the mission. "The battalion exec told us that he was assigning us to the best company commander in the 101st," recalled Smith. "He further stated that Workman would one day be Chief of Staff of the Army."

Following the stand-down, during which Workman was promoted to captain, Company D spent an uneventful week in the bush, then a month on Firebase Kathryn, getting reorganized and absorbing replacements. "I was immediately taken with Ranger," wrote Smith, a sharp, personable country boy from the Tennessee Tech ROTC program who intended to stay in the army. "Ranger was the consummate professional, calm and detached, firm but fair, accepting of no nonsense. He expected my best, but was also readily available with guidance. I felt like I was learning from the master.

"Ranger was aggressive," Smith continued, "believing the best defense is a good offense. At the same time, he did not believe in taking unnecessary chances. He told me that he had two rules for his platoon leaders: never lie to him, and never send troops forward without first paving the way with prep fires. You can buy more ammunition, he said, but you can't buy a soldier's life back."[1]

Captain Workman did not mesh as well with Lieutenant Thompson as he did with Lieutenant Smith. Randy Thompson, a draftee graduate of officer candidate school, jump school, ranger school, and jungle school, knew how to run a platoon. Cocky, profane, and irreverent, he knew how to win the loyalty of his grunts. "Randy was one of the guys," said Sgt. Robert J. "Jerry" Wise, a veteran squad leader in Delta One. "His people would have died for him because he always took care of them." Thompson was also headstrong, independent, and disdainful of authority, the consequence perhaps of a bitter relationship with his hard-nosed father, a colonel in the air force. "Randy was a little more laid back than Ranger wanted," noted Lieutenant Smith. If Thompson thought an order unwise—and he was especially unimpressed when Workman's successor began running night RIFs—"he'd wink at me," explained Wise, "and we'd RTO the whole thing, reporting the patrol's progress by radio without actually moving an inch out of our NDP. Randy was like that even before Ripcord."

Lieutenant Thompson lost two men when a case of grenades in their foxhole exploded during a Mad Minute on Kathryn. The cause of the blast was never determined. Several possibilities were discussed—someone on top of the hill accidentally lobbed a frag into the hole, a sapper had wiggled in close with an RPG—but when a 105 round in the artillery section was subsequently found to have been booby-trapped, fingers were pointed at a certain untrusted Kit Carson scout. "They had to escort him on a helicopter and fly him off the firebase," noted Wise, "or he would have died right there."

Workman did not approve of Thompson's emotional response to his first KIAs; the platoon leader bitterly recalled that Ranger took him aside and "told me I cared too much about my people."

Thompson did not think his superiors cared enough; it was one of the reasons he joined the Vietnam Veterans Against the War chapter at the University of Arkansas. He would later contend that Workman withheld information about the odds that Company D would be facing when inserted into the Ripcord AO. According to Thompson, Workman led him to believe that the company was conducting a routine CA. "My recollection of our operations order was that most of the Vietnamese had left," said Thompson, "and that we were to look for graves. It was well known [by higher command] how many Vietnamese were there. It's always offended me [that we were not properly briefed at the platoon level]."

Why would Workman mislead Thompson? "Maybe," offered one of Thompson's troops, "they figured a bunch of us wouldn't go if we knew what was waiting for us." That explanation is charitable. Thompson's account has convinced many that higher command, with Workman's collusion, deliberately dropped Company D into an enemy base camp—"right in the gook's chow line"—to cover the evacuation of Ripcord. "Nobody was expected to come out of there alive," contends one furious survivor. "We were a diversion."

"Ranger failed us," says Jerry Wise. "He didn't tell us what we needed to know because if we'd understood the threat, we might not have gone out on RIFs, you know what I'm saying? If we did go, we would have moved slower, we wouldn't have gone as far. We also suspect Ranger volunteered us to make his resume for major look better—that's the perception we have now."

Workman cannot be held to blame for the disaster that befell his command. Division simply did not begin to appreciate the magnitude of the enemy buildup until Hawkins's wiretap, by which time Workman had already CA'd into the hot LZ. Likewise, the bunker complexes in the area had been unknown to division intelligence. Workman could not have been acting as a decoy in any event, the decision to evacuate Ripcord being made only after and in part because of D/1-506th's heavy contact east of Hill 805.

It is also unlikely that Captain Workman deceived his troops about the mission. According to Smith, Workman called his platoon leaders into his hootch after the company moved to Camp Evans on July 17 to prepare for the move into the Ripcord AO. Breaking out a map, Ranger identified Coc A Bo, a mountain southeast of Ripcord, as a known "NVA haven" and stated flatly that the company would make contact during the mission, enjoining Fraser, Smith, and Thompson to "get your cherries ready for combat." There might have been some discussion of searching for enemy graves that distracted Thompson, but "the mission statement I remember," Smith later wrote, "was to conduct RIFs to establish contact with whatever enemy forces were in the area. Everyone in the brigade knew that Ripcord was crawling with dinks. The battle had been going on for nearly three weeks and was part of our daily briefings all during that time."[2]

The company spent the night at Camp Evans. "We had one hellacious party," recalled Sp4 Steve W. DeRoque. "Lot of beer, lot of steaks. After the fact, it almost seemed like the Last Supper."

Company D CA'd onto Triple Hill on July 18. Lieutenant Thompson's medic, Pfc. Ronald J. Kuntz—the name, a pseudonym, will reappear—"came down with 'heat stroke' almost immediately," noted Lieutenant Smith. "Ranger didn't buy that for a minute; he could stay on the LZ or come with the rest of us, but there would be no medevac. Kuntz quickly recovered."

It was indeed hotter than Hades as the grunts spent that day and the next sweating up and down the ridges between Triple Hill and Hill 1000. They walked, spooked, through the residue of the reserve battalion's actions—bloody bandages, empty drip bags, web gear, a torn jungle boot—but they encountered no NVA. That might have led Lieutenant Thompson to his erroneous conclusion that the mission was routine, the enemy having withdrawn; why else would D/1-506th alone have been sent to replace the entire 2-501st?

On the other hand, it should have been obvious as the

enemy relentlessly shelled Ripcord that Company D would eventually run into at least a few NVA. When it happened, Ranger's grunts fared badly. The problem was not that they had been misled but that the company was so heavy with replacements. "Everything changed after Maureen," remembered Sp4 K. C. James, one of the veterans. "Really, I had, too. I wasn't going to make no friends with nobody in case they got killed." James's observations about morale were trenchant. "Webster defines morale as the mental and emotional condition—enthusiasm, confidence, or loyalty—of an individual or group with regard to the function at hand," he wrote. "Under that definition, morale was good; we all worked together and trusted each other. We all wanted to get back to The World, but not many days went by that we didn't find something to laugh about. Webster also defines morale as the level of individual psychological well-being based on such factors as a sense of purpose and confidence in the future. A sense of purpose? We would take a hill, then go off and leave it. Confidence in the future? The future for us was the next hour. Psychological well-being? Give me a break. . . ."

Having secured the south knoll, Lieutenant Thompson presently instructed Sergeant Wise to run a patrol down the slope to the south. Specialist Fourth Class Eloy R. Valle, the point man, had gone about a hundred meters and was crossing a small clearing under the canopy when his diminutive slack man, Pfc. Patrick T. "Little Bit" DeWulf, suddenly yelled, "I see one." Wise, third in line, hit the dirt and, along with Valle, opened fire into the thick brush ahead even as he shouted at the wide-eyed DeWulf to "shoot, shoot." Snapping out of it, DeWulf cut loose with his M16. Wise began lobbing grenades. Surprised that the enemy did not fade away but kept up their fire, Wise reckoned that they were ensconced in bunkers. It was time to break contact and call in the Cobras. "We got caught in the open," recalled Wise. "We got out on our hands and knees, got back to where we had some cover behind some trees, and moved back up to the platoon position. They let us go."

Captain Workman, informed of the situation by radio, chastised Thompson, telling him that Wise should have held his ground while the platoon leader brought the rest of Delta One forward to reinforce the action. "Ranger wants another RIF," Thompson told Wise. Moving out again, Valle took a different route to the contact area, circling in from the right. Coming across another clearing—it was about seventy-five feet across, carpeted with scrub brush—he cautiously started across, followed by DeWulf. Instead of maintaining a fifteen-foot interval behind his point team, Wise instinctively let Valle and DeWulf get almost all the way across the clearing before he started into the open, followed by Sgt. Paul Mueller, the assistant squad leader acting as Wise's RTO.

The rest of the patrol had yet to enter the clearing as Valle reached the far side. Unable to see the camouflaged bunker in the heavy underbrush, he was only a few feet from it when the NVA inside squeezed a burst of AK-47 fire into the quiet Mexican American from Rio Grande City, Texas. "Valle was dead before he knew what was happening," recounted Wise. "I actually saw the muzzle flash. Valle just kind of leaned over and collapsed."

DeWulf, horrified—Valle and tough, cocky Little Bit had joined the company together almost three months earlier and were best friends—turned, screaming to Wise, "They got Valle."

In the next instant, DeWulf was stitched by the AK-47. "It had to be the same shooter," noted Wise. "He shot Valle, then just turned on DeWulf and gave him the other half of the clip."

It was 5:30 P.M. on July 20. Wise scuttled into some deep brush, trying to disappear, losing track of Mueller as the assistant squad leader scrambled behind a tree and blindly fired back. Wise unlimbered several grenades from the prone position, then something suddenly exploded beside him. His glasses went flying as he was peppered with shrapnel in the face and shoulder. Unable to see beyond the tip of his nose and with his sense of direction gone, he frantically crawled out of the kill zone, hoping he wasn't rushing right toward the enemy bunker in his confusion. He instead came across his grenadier, Pfc. John C. Knott, an eighteen-year-old kid who had been fifth in line behind Mueller and was now hunkered by himself behind a tree, having become separated from the rest of the squad. Wise, who hurried past, continuing his half-blind retreat, was, it was later determined, the last person to see Knott alive—except the North Vietnamese.

Lieutenant Thompson had already started down with another squad as the enemy began mortaring the south knoll, but Wise missed them as he clambered uphill to the NDP. Jim McCoy was stunned by the look of terror and anguish on Wise's face as he screamed, "Little Bit and Valle are dead."

As Wise's squad pulled back, the enemy darted to where Valle and DeWulf lay, probably already dead, and to Knott, who had been left behind in the confusion, apparently wounded. When his body was recovered, it reportedly sported the bandage from his first-aid pouch. McCoy later wrote that those up in the NDP "heard screaming, followed by bursts of AK-47 fire, then a faint, muffled scream and another short burst. The NVA were finishing off Valle, DeWulf, and Knott. I carry in my head those final screams to this day, and I'm sure for the rest of my days on this earth. . . ."

Lieutenant Thompson had left Sgt. Elger Sneed, his young but combat-hardened country-boy platoon sergeant, to hold the south knoll in his absence. Meeting Wise as he entered the perimeter, Sneed exclaimed that he was bleeding. Wise, aware only then that he'd been hit, removed his shirt. "Any big wounds?"

"Naw, I don't see anything," said Sneed. "Just blood."

More firing erupted as Thompson's force collided with the NVA. Sneed, meaning to bring additional troops to help the lieutenant, looked Wise in the eyes: "Can you lead me down there?"

Glasses gone, the world a fog around him, Wise needed everything he had in him to lead Sneed back down the hill. They found Lieutenant Thompson sitting beside a trail, a medic bandaging his forearm, the platoon leader having been knocked out of the action with a grenade. The relief force suffered other casualties, including Pfc. Dale V. Tauer, who, badly wounded and blasted down the slope by an explosion, was rescued at great risk by his buddy Pfc. Randy L. Benck. Private First Class Bill G. Browning, one of the cherries, was killed, apparently by the same RPG that wounded Tauer. "Browning was my RTO," recalled Sergeant Sneed. "When we were starting downhill, Browning threw off the radio and moved ahead, saying I could carry my own radio, he was going to get Valle and DeWulf. That was the last I ever saw of him."

Sneed got several men on line and pushed forward, blasting the jungle, covering the movement of the wounded back to the NDP. Mueller was firing from behind a log when Sneed dropped beside him, blood running down his forehead from a shrapnel wound; his steel pot had been blown off. Sneed was lugging the radio with which he was in contact with the Cobras that had just arrived. "We popped smoke, and they started firing rockets and miniguns, just tearin' the jungle up," recalled Mueller. "Sneed kept working the ARA in closer and closer until we had shrapnel flying overhead."

Workman sent a squad under Sergeant Fraser to assist in recovering the casualties, but as Sneed attempted to move forward while moving the Cobra fire back out, his people and Fraser's came under heavy fire from the North Vietnamese. The decision was made to break contact. Having moved down the hill, Brian Redfern, assisted by Jim McCoy, put his M60 into action to cover the withdrawal to the NDP. When purple smoke blossomed behind them, Redfern, thinking they were inadvertently being marked for the Cobras, shouted to McCoy, "Let's get the hell outta here."

After catching up with the rest back atop the knoll, Redfern—one of the few, thought McCoy, to keep his cool during the short, intense action—spat, "Hey, thanks for leaving us the fuck behind."

Captain Workman had previously dispatched Lieutenant Smith and a squad from Delta Two to secure the LZ. It was getting dark by the time the first medevac arrived. When a trooper stepped into the clearing to guide in the medevac with a strobe, Smith "looked up and saw Lieutenant Thompson walking very unsteadily out of the woods towards the chopper. The bright white bandage around his arm really got my attention. I was struck, too, by his dazed demeanor. He just seemed very unsteady at the moment." Smith asked his friend if he was okay. Thompson said that he was, incorrectly brushing off his injuries as minor. "He was obviously troubled by something else," noted Smith. "I didn't know until someone else told me that four of Randy's troops were missing. . . ."

Thompson, Sneed, and Wise were medevacked together, depriving Delta One of its platoon leader and its two most experienced NCOs. Two wounded grunts went out on the next medevac. Machine-gun teams, meanwhile, laid down into the jungle an uninterrupted sheet of fire, under which several volunteers crawled, hoping to recover the bodies of Valle, DeWulf, Knott, and Browning. It was too dark, and the effort was unsuccessful.

Workman told Smith to return to the north knoll with his security squad and Delta One. "The remaining members of the platoon were quite shaken and jittery, very demoralized," wrote Smith. The group followed the trail running uphill from the saddle, the way lit by flares. It was too late for the Delta One grunts to dig in, and the rest of the company had already found the soil too rocky and choked with too many big roots from the trees covering the knoll to do more than scrape out shallow depressions. The perimeter was basically a ring of troops tucked behind trees, concealed by thick brush, claymores facing out. Illumination was fired all night over the knoll from Granite. "We had listening posts out to our front and rear a short ways," wrote Smith, "and about midnight, the post to the north started reporting movement. Oh shit. This report was repeated several times, and I assumed we were being located for an attack. The LPs wanted to come in, but Ranger refused their repeated requests. I was brand new to combat and had to rely on his instincts, but gut feeling was that we were about to be hit, and I sympathized with the LPs." There was no attack, however, "and as strange as it might seem," noted Smith, "sleep came easy for those not on guard duty because we were all so exhausted."

The company was getting ready to move out the next morning to recover its missing men when Lieutenant Smith heard a muffled popping—three thumps in rapid succession—from the low ground to the southwest. Captain Workman also heard the mortar tube and was already calling in an azimuth and estimated position for counterbattery fire as Smith shouted to the troops to get in their foxholes, such as they were. He was amazed that many of the men, having heard nothing themselves, simply stared at him in disbelief as they sat eating a C-ration breakfast. The first three rounds exploded on the LZ. Smith heard two more thumps, his shouts growing more urgent as those rounds exploded halfway up the north knoll. With that, everyone began scrambling for whatever cover was to be found before the enemy adjusted the next salvo right on top of them.

Smith and his platoon sergeant darted along the perimeter to make sure their guys had their heads down. Seeing that they all did, the two literally dove toward the large roots of a tall tree as the third salvo whistled in. Fragments from the first shell to explode on the hilltop caught Smith in the lower back—he felt a sudden, clublike impact, then burning—and he burrowed his head and shoulders into the roots. He was convinced as explosions erupted all around that he was going to lose his legs and his testicles, that there was no way he was going to survive such a firestorm. "It seemed the rounds would never stop," recalled Smith, shocked by the intensity of the fire; he had been under the impression that the enemy, being poorly supplied, "would drop a few mortar rounds on you, then cease fire to conserve ammo. These guys obviously didn't know they needed to save their rounds, they just kept firing and firing after finding the range to our position." Each salvo took half a minute to land. "There is no scarier feeling in the world than waiting for indirect fire to impact," wrote Smith. "My stomach still tightens when I think of it. As I came to my senses, I began to hear cries of pain from all around the perimeter. We were taking casualties."

Captain Workman and his RTOs squeezed into a narrow, enemy-sized zigzag trench atop the knoll and shouted at nearby troops to cover the vital radios with logs as they directed 8-inch fire on the enemy mortars from Rakkasan. The salvos kept coming. Lucas's battalion journal records that the shelling began at 7:12 A.M. on July 21 and that within a few minutes an incredible eighty 82mm rounds had been sent crashing into D/1-506th's NDP from positions nine hundred meters away at the southeast base of Hill 805.

Those few minutes were excruciating. "Everyone was hysterical," wrote Jim McCoy, who, having no cover—others had scurried into the enemy spiderholes on the hilltop—lay curled up in a ball, his rucksack protecting his back. The grunt at the prone position beside McCoy suddenly screamed that he was hit. McCoy saw a hole in the man's arm, but he had no sooner bandaged it than "he started yelling that his foot was also hit. I looked down and saw a bloody hole in the side of his boot, but I didn't have another bandage. . . ."

Walt Jurinen, one of the replacements in Delta Two, had rushed to Ranger's trench when the thumps started—it seemed the safest place on the hill—but Workman had barked at him to get back to his position on the perimeter. Jurinen was thus at the prone position beside the platoon medic, Pfc. Robert B. Hays, another cherry, when the first on-target volley splattered both of them with fragments. Jurinen took it in both legs, Hays in the groin area. Sergeant Handley, a veteran squad leader in Delta Two, happened upon Jurinen and Hays as he checked positions between volleys. Hays, a sensitive, devoutly religious conscientious objector, did not appear badly hurt, but he was terrified, almost delirious with fear. "I'm gonna die," he mumbled. "I'm gonna die, I'm gonna die. . . ."

Handley tried to calm him down. "Doc, you are wounded, that's correct, but it doesn't look too bad. You're gonna be okay."

It did no good. Hays kept repeating that he was gonna die, and when the next salvo slammed in—Handley was hit in the calf and buttocks—Hays shut his eyes and slipped into shock. Responding to Handley's shouts, two other medics, Pfc. Richard Finley and Pfc. Barry K. Marchese, rushed over; they spent several minutes giving Hays mouth-to-mouth, but he never regained consciousness, leaving his comrades to wonder whether he died of shock or internal bleeding. Marchese must have been beside himself; only moments before, he had lost another man, Pfc. Peter P. Huk, also a replacement, who gasped his last breath even as Marchese taped a piece of plastic over his sucking chest wound.

Private First Class Frank L. Asher, yet another replacement, was also killed by the incoming fire, his body blasted down the side of the hill. Asher and Huk were so new—less than a week with the company, in fact—that Richard Drury did not know which of the two it was whose death he witnessed; Drury had already been wounded himself when "I saw a fellow soldier jump up, yelling, 'I can't take it anymore,' and the next mortar round killed him. . . ."

Acting before the entire company was flogged to death on the little hilltop, Captain Workman stood up, shouting to his troops to move down to the LZ. "By that time," recalled Smith, "the damned dinks had dropped a few CS rounds in. We abandoned the hill in gas masks, taking our wounded with us and dragging the body of Doc Hays along in a litter made by folding a poncho around two poles."

Private First Class George T. Pourchot, a radioman from the company command group, remained behind—although he had been wounded in the head—to cover the move, spraying the jungle with his M16. The mortar fire petered out as the company moved downhill, but the troops were on the verge of panic. Everything seemed to be spinning out of control. "I don't think we're gonna fuckin' get outta here," Jurinen found himself blurting to the grunt who'd dived behind a log with him when one of the last mortar shells crashed in. Mueller caught a glimpse of one trooper dragging his rucksack and M16 along in one hand, his other arm hanging limp and bloody at his side. Jim McCoy saw his buddy Pfc. John E. Millard limping toward him, wounded in both legs, calling, "I'm hit, I'm hit." McCoy forced himself to wait for Millard and, throwing an arm around his waist, began helping him down the hill. Millard had a radio strapped to his rucksack frame. It had been badly damaged by shrapnel. "Get that thing off," McCoy shouted.

"No way, it saved my life," Millard shouted back. McCoy got Millard to the bottom of the knoll, then went back to help a young black soldier who was holding a large bandage against the side of his face, the ties having come undone. The kid let go of the bandage when McCoy reached him. "I could see that part of his cheek was missing, exposing shattered teeth and gum," McCoy wrote. "I tried not to let him see the sickened look on my face when I tried to put the dangling bandage back.

I was unable to reattach the bandage, and simply placed it back against his face, then put his hand to it, and told him he would have to hold it in place. I know it must have hurt him badly to hold it in place. I felt terrible that I was unable to help him. . ."

Workman organized a hasty defensive perimeter at the base of the knoll on the north side of the landing zone, realizing as he helped place people in position that he had only forty able-bodied soldiers left, three having been killed during the shelling, another thirty wounded. Workman put Sergeant Handley in charge of the medevacs, ordering the wounded squad leader, one of their best, to evacuate himself on the last Huey. The seriously wounded included Sergeant Fraser of Delta Three, who had been hit in both legs at the beginning of the barrage. Workman sought out Lieutenant Smith, the only platoon leader still on his feet, to ask him how badly he had been hurt. "I'm okay," Smith said. He was in some discomfort, but a medic had already assured him—Smith had been afraid to look at the wound himself—that there was only a small hole in his lower back. Workman wanted to be sure. "Can you stand the pain?" he asked. "If you can't, I'll send you in, but if you can, I really need you—you're the only officer I have left."

Smith assured Workman that he could count on him. Others felt the same way. Ron Kuntz did not; while Handley and medics Finley and Marchese, the latter one of the walking wounded himself, busily treated the numerous casualties, Kuntz—the medic who had earlier come down with "heat stroke"—sat on the trail, mouth agape, hands shaking. "What's the matter with you, Doc?" Workman asked. Kuntz's reply: "I've got shell shock, sir."

The perimeter had no sooner been established than Workman dispatched a five-man patrol to recover a machine gun left behind during the hectic withdrawal. Reaching the abandoned position, the patrol presently came face-to-face with several enemy soldiers who had just crested the knoll from the opposite direction. The NVA disappeared into the brush when fired upon, and the patrol quickly scooped up the lost M60 and hustled back down to the LZ.

The enemy soon followed. There were numerous short, intense firefights throughout the morning as the enemy attacked in small groups from various directions, always fading back in the face of heavy return fire, always returning after a lull. Company D took no serious casualties, but it was, in effect, surrounded, and neither the M16 and M60 fire of the troops, which became almost constant after the first few attacks, nor the numerous Cobras that Workman brought in gave more than momentary pause to the North Vietnamese. Lieutenant Smith was confident that the company could hold its own, but, shocked as he had been by the intensity of the mortar barrage, he was dismayed that the enemy seemed to hold the initiative throughout the ongoing battle. "We were in the middle of an NVA stronghold," he wrote, "under attack from all sides by an enemy that was better trained and organized than I'd ever been led to believe from my own training and the war stories I had heard. They had their shit together. They'd had our number, in fact, from the moment we touched down on that same LZ the day before."

Many of the walking wounded joined the defense of the perimeter. Steve DeRoque of Delta Two had been badly wounded in his legs and stomach; the second-tour veteran nevertheless took over for a machine gunner whose hands were a bloody mass of shrapnel wounds. "We fired that M60 until the barrel went red," he recalled, "then switched barrels, and continued to rock and roll."

Medevacs had been requested. The first to arrive, at approximately 8:20 A.M., was flown by 1st Lt. Laurence Rosen from Eagle Dust-Off, the all-volunteer Air Ambulance Platoon, 326th Medical Battalion. Sergeant Handley, aided by a group that included Finley, Marchese, and Bobby Rosas—another of the walking wounded—rushed out of the trees to meet the medevac as it flared to land, carrying the company's six most serious casualties in ponchos. Rosen's own medic, Sp4 Brent R. Law, jumped out to help load the wounded, and the Huey quickly departed, having taken no direct fire thanks to the infantrymen blazing away on the perimeter and the Cobras slicing low around the LZ.

First Lieutenant Allen Schwartz arrived at the controls of a second medevac as the first pulled out, and he circled out of range of ground fire while Rosen provided a sitrep by radio and a recommended approach and egress route while speeding for Camp Evans. Handley's team emerged again from its cover as Schwartz landed and loaded two litter cases—Steve DeRoque and Sgt. Michael Thomas, a squad leader in Delta Two—as soon as the skids of the medevac touched earth. Six walking wounded clambered aboard next. Schwartz's crew chief gave him clearance to take off as Handley's team withdrew, but Schwartz had lifted up only a few feet when the Plexiglas windshield suddenly shattered in a hail of automatic-weapons fire. The aircraft immediately lost lift and crashed straight back down; it began to shake violently a moment later, a rocket having blown off the tail boom. "The dink who fired the RPG was up in a tree," noted Smith. "Someone saw him as he fired, so while he was successful in his mission to bring down a helicopter, he also paid the ultimate price."[3]

Unsure what had happened, Lieutenant Schwartz tried to hold the helicopter steady and get it shut down even as those casualties not strapped in went bouncing out the open doors. The Huey vibrated backward all the while toward the slope on the east side of the LZ. "Get out," Schwartz screamed to his copilot, who was physically launched out of his seat upon unhooking his seat belt and opening his door. The same thing happened to Schwartz; unfortunately, he had not yet managed to shut off the engine when he went flying. He landed hard, tumbled, and ran a short distance to get away from the out-of-control aircraft, then he hit the dirt, trying to keep low until he figured out what was going on and what he should do. He totally lost track of the other crewmen. Luckily, there were two grunts dug in at the edge of the landing zone, one of whom called Schwartz over while the other crawled to a new position to make room for the stranded and terrified pilot. "I didn't know I'd been injured until the grunt in the foxhole asked me what had happened to me and pointed to my face," Schwartz later wrote. "I wiped my gloved hand across my mouth and it was immediately saturated with blood; at some point, I must have gotten slammed into some component of the aircraft, and my lower teeth had penetrated right through the skin between my chin and lower lip."

Most of the wounded were able to rush back to Handley's position, Jurinen and DeRoque running painlessly on bloody legs, numb with adrenaline. Mike Thomas, however, was able to exit the aircraft only after it came to a stop at the edge of the LZ. Thomas, unarmed and unable to walk, joined another wounded grunt who'd also gotten separated from the rest and who had no magazine in the M16 he'd come up with, only the single round in the chamber. Together they crawled into a little furrow on the east slope about twenty feet below the Huey. "The main blade was still pumping," said Thomas. "There were gooks in the debris farther down the slope, trying to shoot the bird and blow up the fuel tanks. White tracers were going right over our heads."

Captain Workman shouted encouragement to his men as they kept up their fire, shouted at them to get their heads down whenever he brought in another Cobra. "Ranger's language was quite colorful, and I'm sure the pilots loved performing for him," wrote Smith. "The rocket explosions would literally lift us off the ground, and we often had shrapnel landing around us. . . ."

It was then and there that Lieutenant Smith learned his final lesson about fighting the NVA: "It takes somebody that's either crazy or extremely dedicated to stand up and shoot at a Cobra gunship that's bearing down right at you, but those suckers would do it with an AK-47. They were incredibly brave. . . ."

Lieutenant Rosen was dismayed upon returning to see that the main rotors on the wrecked medevac were still pumping away, the engine revving up to an explosive level. Upon touching down, Rosen's medic, Brent Law, hauled Lieutenant Schwartz aboard by his survival vest—the downed pilot had made a break from his foxhole when Rosen flared to land—then raced across the landing zone, climbed aboard the vibrating Huey, and shut it down by hitting the fuel cutoff switch. Law dashed back in time to help Handley's team load the last of nine wounded aboard his own medevac. One of them was

Mike Thomas, who ended up wedged between pilot and copilot on the overloaded Huey. "It seemed to take forever," Rosen wrote, "but, in reality, we were airborne again in less than two minutes, kissing the treetops with our skids on our way out."

There had been no enemy fire. It took Lieutenant Rosen thirty minutes to reach base camp, unload the wounded, and return at top speed to the embattled, smoke-shrouded LZ. Warrant Officer Douglas J. Rupert, the copilot, made the landing; he was flying left seat, in training as an aircraft commander. The suppressive fire from the grunts and gunships again kept the enemy at bay as Handley's team loaded five wounded men on the Huey. The rest of Schwartz's crew also clambered aboard, one of the airmen having exclaimed when he saw the helicopter approaching, "That's it, I'm aviation, I'm not a grunt. I'm getting my ass outta here."

Ron Kuntz was of the same mind. The medic who had previously tried to get out with heat stroke, then shell shock, was now at Sergeant Handley's elbow, literally begging to be medevacked: "I need to get out on the next bird—I'm really sick."

"No way," Handley said. "You're one of the only medics we have left. I don't care how sick you are, you just can't leave."

Kuntz, in an absolute panic, wouldn't let up, and Handley finally agreed to call Captain Workman: "I've got a man here who says he's physically ill and needs to be medevacked."

"What's the story?" Workman asked.

"It's Doc Kuntz," said Handley. "We can't afford to let him go. He's not wounded, he's not that sick, and we need him out here."

"I agree," Workman said. "If he's not wounded, he stays."

"Ranger said you can't go," Handley told Kuntz.

"I want to talk to Ranger," Kuntz implored, but Handley had had enough. "The answer's no," he snapped. "You're stayin'."

Doc Kuntz was actually beyond helping the wounded, so consumed was he with fear, but he was not an entirely unsympathetic character. Kuntz had served six months with the 199th Light Infantry Brigade before being transferred to the 101st two months before Ripcord. Having already earned his combat medic's badge, he was assigned to the relative safety of the 1-506th battalion aid station. Kuntz, however, was a necklace-draped pothead, his attitude—and the fact that he helped malingerers find medical reasons to stay in the rear—his ticket to a disciplinary transfer back to the bush. He joined Company D only the day before its assault into the Ripcord AO. Kuntz felt that he had been screwed. "But you've got to work with the cards that are dealt you," as Handley put it. "Kuntz didn't."

Kuntz wasn't the only one getting freaked out. During one of the lulls in the ground attacks, Captain Workman had dispatched a second small patrol to the north knoll to ensure that no one had been left behind. One member of the patrol happened upon the body of Frank Asher, already bloating in the heat, sprawled some thirty meters below the top of the hill. The man rolled Asher over, retrieved his wallet, and brought the dead man's ID card to Workman. Sergeant Mueller of Delta One was instructed to organize a squad-sized element to recover the KIA. "The thought of going back up that hill sent shivers up my spine and they had to call my name two times when I was selected to join the squad," wrote Jim McCoy. The advance up the trail could not have been more cautious. When the point man spotted movement, Mueller spread out his jittery troops on line and reconned the area to their front by fire. The enemy did not respond, but Mueller, sensing an ambush, nevertheless radioed Workman, trying to beg off the mission, arguing that "it's just some equipment up there, and a guy who's already dead."

"You're not in contact," Workman answered unsympathetically. "Now, move up, secure the area, and drag back that KIA."

"No fuckin' way," Mueller blurted. After a moment of stony silence on the radio, Workman told him to fall back to the LZ.

As the ground attack continued, many grunts thought it was only a matter of time before they would be overrun. They were especially demoralized when they overheard the normally unflappable Ranger, apparently in an argument with Lucas, bark on the radio: "What are you trying to do, get us all killed out here?"

During one of the attacks, Lieutenant Smith's young platoon sergeant, Sgt. Gilbert C. Rossetter—a seasoned veteran who had just turned twenty the day before—was checking positions when he looked up and saw an NVA lean from behind a tree to throw a satchel charge at two men in a nearby foxhole. Rossetter immediately opened fire, so close to the enemy soldier that he could see the expression on the man's face change as he was hit, then scooped up the satchel charge to throw it back. It exploded just as he got rid of it. Lieutenant Smith turned at the sound of the blast. Rossetter was just standing there, an odd look on his face. "Gib, are you okay?" Smith asked. Rossetter, not answering, continued to stare out toward the enemy. "The explosion had dazed and deafened him," recounted Smith, "but had not physically damaged anything except the ammo vest he was wearing. I told Rossetter to sit down, that he was truly ineffective at that point and needed to stay out of harm's way until we could get him to the rear."

Moments later, several grunts shouted that a "dink" with an RPD machine gun had darted behind a large tree only fifteen feet outside the perimeter. Specialist Fourth Class James E. Fowler, a big, soft-spoken black GI who performed magnificently throughout the battle, engaged the enemy gunner with his M60, covering Smith and several others as they popped up to lob grenades at the RPD.

In the middle of this minibattle, dazed Sergeant Rossetter strode past Smith, heading straight for the RPD as he mumbled to himself about taking care of that "goddamned machine gun."

Smith had no choice but to stand up to stop Rossetter. Leading him back to cover, Smith instructed one of his men to keep Gib there even if he had to sit on him. The enemy machine gunner was silenced, meanwhile—one of eight NVA known to be killed by Company D and its supporting ARA during the fight on the LZ.

At about 9:40 A.M., a slick from the 158th Aviation Battalion darted in and quickly unloaded ammo and picked up casualties, including wounded platoon leader John Fraser, amid an eruption of AK fire and RPGs. As the chopper was lifting off, one rocket hit the tail boom but failed to explode.

"The tail shaft of the rocket was sticking out of the tail boom," remembered Richard Drury, the wounded radioman. "I stared at it all the way back, thinking the rocket would go off at any moment, but it never did, thank God."

Lieutenant Rosen was less than ten minutes behind the slick, the interior of his medevac splattered with blood from the first three trips, the mood of his crew somber. "We all knew that the repeated use of the same approach and departure routes to the same landing site was practically suicidal," noted Rosen. "We all knew that we had already pressed our luck beyond our wildest hopes." Given the resupply slick's narrow escape, Rosen felt obligated to ask his crew if they were willing to go in again, but everyone on board—Rupert, Law, Sp5 Donito C. Deocales, the crew chief, and the new medic whom Law was training, Sp4 James L. Wieler—agreed that "we would keep going in until there were either no more wounded or we were shot down," as Rosen later wrote. "We were all of one mind. . . ."

Rosen dropped into a two-foot hover over the LZ. All the other wounded having previously been evacuated, Handley, Rosas, and Marchese sprinted for the medevac to finally get out themselves. Only Rosas, however, had gotten aboard—in the lead, he literally dove into the cabin on Rosen's side—when an enemy soldier stood up from the debris at the west edge of the landing zone and opened fire with his AK-47 directly into the left front of the Huey. Bullets exploded through the windshield. With Rupert screaming that he was hit, Rosen pulled back on the stick, lifted up, then banked hard to the right to escape the fire, wheeling all the way around to exit the clearing the way they had come in. Law, also hit, started to fall out, but Wieler caught him and pulled him back inside the Huey.

Rosen sped for the aid station, Doug Rupert in agony beside him, his smoldering left arm blown almost completely off above the elbow. Deocales and Wieler, meanwhile, were urgently attending to Brent Law; the bullet that had blasted through Rupert's arm had shattered against the copilot's armored seat, a fragment of it catching Law just below the edge of his "chicken plate," the body armor worn by aircrews. There was little that Deocales and Wieler could do, for the bullet fragment had ruptured Law's liver, and he bled to death almost instantly on the floor of the Huey.

In the chaos, no one on the medevac was aware of a drama involving their helicopter that left those watching from the ground absolutely dumbfounded. Handley and Marchese had been a few steps from the medevac when the shooting started and the helicopter pulled up. As they threw themselves to the ground to avoid being clipped by the tail rotor, Ron Kuntz darted past—unknown to Handley, the panicked medic had dashed out with them—and, reaching up with both hands, managed to grab the right skid just before the medevac wheeled around. Handley thought Kuntz was deserting. It is entirely possible, however, that with the wounded evacuated, Workman had given Kuntz permission to get on the last medevac.

"At first, Kuntz had both his arms and legs wrapped around the skid," recounted Handley, who watched with almost surrealistic detachment, everything seeming to stop around him, as "the helicopter went into a dive down the side of the ridge. The wind was blasting Kuntz so strongly that his legs came loose, and he was just hanging on with his hands. The helicopter started pulling up at that point, going full throttle, and that's when Kuntz was blown off the skid. The helicopter must have been several hundred feet up and going in excess of a hundred miles an hour when he lost his grip. I watched him fall. He just went straight down into the jungle, almost as if in slow motion. There was no way he could have survived. . . ."

During Workman's battle, Hawkins and A/2-506th, tasked with securing a prisoner to confirm the wiretap intelligence, continued to pass unnoticed among the enemy on the other side of Hill 805. Alpha Three led the move back into the valley, its point team, moving down a trail, shortly encountering two NVA coming up the trail. The point team fired them up, dropping one and sending the other scurrying into the brush, a blood trail in his wake that was followed without result. The enemy soldier who was sprawled on the trail was still breathing despite a cracked skull that was leaking brains. "He ain't gonna make it," Doc Draper, the platoon medic, reported to Hawkins on the radio. "He's as good as dead."

"You sure we can't take him prisoner?"

"No, sir," answered Draper. "He's dyin'."

"Okay, put him out of his misery," said Hawkins, who heard, a few seconds later, the report of a single M16 shot in the jungle.

Company A continued to the bluff where the water party had been ambushed the day before. The body on the rock was gone. Still empty-handed, the company started west to grab some high ground and set up a new NDP. To make sure they weren't being followed, Hawkins had Lieutenant Widjeskog, who was bringing up the rear, drop off a two-man OP a hundred meters short of the NDP.

In short order, one of the men at the observation post, Sp4 Robert M. Journell, opened fire on two NVA, wounding one—who left a blood trail—and killing the other. "The guy's head just exploded like a watermelon," Journell told Hawkins. The dead NVA—the grunts booby-trapped his body with a frag—had broken cigarettes, sugar packets, and tins of peanut butter on him, having apparently scrounged through the company's previous NDP. More importantly, there was a note on the body; translated by Long, the company interpreter, it identified the dead man as a sergeant named Son and explained that he was part of a recon team tasked with finding the best approach through Ripcord's defenses in preparation for a two-battalion assault. There was also a French-made topographical map on which the sergeant had made notes in Vietnamese and drawn arrows outlining the planned attack on Ripcord. Bingo, Hawkins thought, we don't need a prisoner anymore. If Hawkins was gratified with his company's latest intelligence coup, he was also becoming increasingly nervous. "We had killed numerous enemy soldiers," he noted, "but too many had also escaped during those encounters for me to feel safe. We were pushing our luck."

The pressure on Workman would undoubtedly have gotten worse if not for Captain Rollison and D/2-506th, which Lucas inserted atop Hill 605, the small mountain eight hundred meters northwest by way of the connecting ridge from D/1-506th's LZ. Rollison's orders were to move down the ridge as quickly as possible and link up with Workman. Rollison led the assault with Lieutenant Flaherty's Delta Three, the only one of his platoons still commanded by an officer—Jim McCall had recently left to take over the battalion headquarters company—and went in himself on the first Huey. The time was 10 A.M.

Despite the gunship prep, the lead slick took fire from the left side of the LZ. "We deassed that helicopter right quick," said Rollison, who, along with radioman Rick Rearick, "went running for this big blob of green on the right side of the landing zone that I thought was a bush. We dived into it, but it wasn't a bush, it was a camouflage net, and we slid through it into an enemy gun position." The .51 was mounted atop an earthen pole in the center of the ring-shaped position. Its crew was unable to fire, it was later discovered, because the weapon's firing pin was broken. The men were escaping into a tunnel even as Rollison and Rearick crashed through the camouflage netting. "I saw the ass end of the last guy as he went into the tunnel," recounted Rollison. "I pitched a frag in there after him, let it go off, then rolled back, stuffed my shotgun in the opening, and pumped off three or four shells. With all the dust, I couldn't tell if I hit anyone or not. It appeared that the tunnel led into a fairly large bunker where I assume the gunners kept their ammo and took shelter whenever we hit 'em with artillery and air strikes."

Lieutenant Flaherty's platoon secured the landing zone after a quick firefight, losing two men wounded. Rollison excitedly called Flaherty over and pointed out something incredible about the captured .51-caliber machine gun. Not only was it in an ideal position to fire on CH-47s approaching Ripcord from the lowlands, but the enemy had gone so far as to cut a V-shaped notch in the trees at the top of a ridge situated between the gun position and Ripcord, three klicks to the southwest. "The notch appeared to be about ten feet across and five or six feet down," recalled Flaherty. "All they had to do was just aim at the notch, and they'd be putting .51 fire right on Ripcord, which was visible in the distance through the notch. Amazing."

Rollison put Flaherty's platoon on point as Company D

started down the ridge, passing numerous enemy bunkers along the way and losing two more people to a booby trap. One was the amiable company coward, Pat Dooley, who sat along the trail, half his foot blown off, feeling no pain—the medics treating him had given him morphine—as he smoked a cigarette, smiling, happy to have been maimed if it meant getting out of Vietnam alive.

Glad to see Dooley go, radioman Bruce McCorkle crouched beside him for a moment on his way down the ridge. "Hey, sorry you're hurt, guy—can I have your pound cake and peaches?"

Rollison's column found the bodies of Asher and Huk and brought them along, suspended from bamboo poles by their hands and feet like slain deer. Company D also passed a dead NVA. "He was just lying on the side of the trail, kind of smiling like corpses do when their face muscles tighten up," noted McCorkle. "He had a gold-capped tooth, and looked well-fed, almost plump, and well-equipped, too, right down to a belt buckle with a big red star on it."

Shouts echoed through the jungle to ensure that there would be no friendly fire as one company of uptight grunts neared the other before Rollison linked up with Workman at 12:20 P.M. "So you're a ranger, too," Workman said, noting the tab on Rollison's shoulder.

"You just ain't a bullshittin'," Rollison replied.

To further reinforce the situation, Lucas inserted Captain Lamb and C/2-506th onto Hill 605 from Firebase O'Reilly—the captured machine gun was evacuated shortly thereafter—then landed himself to talk with Rollison and Workman. Lucas evidently thought he had enough forces on the ground at that point to push the enemy off the ridge, prelude to recovering D/1-506th's missing KIAs. "Ranger told us to dig in deep," recalled Lieutenant Smith. "We would be spending the night, which I couldn't believe."

Captain Workman couldn't believe it either. Jim McCoy has a vivid memory of Workman telling Lucas, "If we get hit again, it's going to be every man for himself." Workman was apparently trying to impress upon Lucas that his company was no longer combat effective and needed to be extracted, "but the effect that Ranger's comment had on the few of us who remained was devastating," wrote McCoy. "Any hope of getting out of there was now lost. That's the one thing that I could never forgive Ranger for. . . ."

Rollison's first move after linking up with Workman was to secure the south side of the landing zone. The ground attacks had fizzled out, but Workman warned Rollison that there was a mortar to the southwest, the time in flight to his position about thirty-five seconds. Wanting to test that, Rollison, stepping into the open, "waved and made obscene gestures in the direction of the enemy, and, *bonk-bonk,* two rounds hit the bottom of the tube. I ran back inside the tree line, and the rounds lit right in the middle of the landing zone, and, sure enough, it was about thirty-five seconds or so."

With that, Rollison sent his men across the landing zone two at a time. "Whenever we sent two guys running across, you'd hear the enemy fire another salvo," recalled McCorkle, amazed that Workman's "glassy-eyed troops were to the point where they wouldn't take extreme measures to seek cover when we had incoming on the way. They seemed catatonic. They would just duck down a little, like, well, if it hits me it hits me. Running across an open LZ with eighty pounds on your back, knowing mortar rounds were coming in, was a real fun feat, but we all made it. We immediately began digging in. . . ."

Rollison, taking control of the operation at that point, brought in arty and 81mm fire on the suspected enemy mortar positions. But when a medevac tried to evacuate the last of Workman's wounded and those who had arrived with Rollison—six altogether—it was driven away by AK-47 fire from the southwest. After Rollison brought in the ARA, a second medevac was able to touch down on the LZ.

Sergeant Handley was slated for the medevac, but out of loyalty to Workman, he said, "I'm okay, and I'm willing to stay out here."

"We don't want infection to set in," Workman replied, insisting that Handley needed to go and praising his coordination of the earlier medevacs. "I really appreciate the job you did."

The medevac was completed at 2:48 P.M. Lucas informed Rollison and Workman shortly thereafter that they were to be extracted. Lucas might have originally thought to stay and fight it out, but General Berry had recommended to Colonel Harrison—battalion, brigade, and acting division commander were all overhead in their command ships—that withdrawal might be a wiser course of action. "Priority is to get the 1-506th out of trouble," Berry radioed Harrison, according to the brigade log. "Number two, get everyone out of the area before dark. We're on their ground," Berry added, referring to the enemy. "They have all the advantage."

Harrison concurred. To subdue the enemy before the lift ships arrived, he had tear-gas missions run along the western side of the ridgeline—the CS canisters were jettisoned from low-flying slicks—while air strikes went in on the suspected mortar positions on 805. "When the F-4s screamed in," said Pfc. Merle Delagrange of D/1-506th, "they'd tell us to hit the deck, and when the jets pulled out, there'd be jagged, white-hot pieces of shrapnel sticking in the trees."

Flaherty and a team of grunts pushed the downed medevac completely off the landing zone to clear the way, then Rollison and Workman passed the word to lay down suppressive fire as slicks from the 158th arrived to extract D/1-506th. It was now approximately 4 P.M. Workman's people had already been organized into four-man helo teams, everyone loaded down with weapons and equipment from the casualties. Seeing the first slick approach from the east, Lieutenant Smith and another of the men who had been selected to go out first moved into the landing zone so that they would be able to clamber aboard the left side of the Huey while the other two men in the group, running to meet the helicopter from the tree line, simultaneously climbed aboard from the right, thus minimizing the ground time on the LZ. "As the bird touched down and we ran to board," recalled Smith, "I saw a black trooper hauling ass towards it from the trees wearing an enemy pith helmet and carrying an AK. I'll bet some Vietnamese forward observer did a double take on that one. Since there were known enemy positions to the west, the bird hovered backwards after loading up.

As we backed out and turned around, the second bird touched down, and as we headed rearward, we saw the next helicopter in line pass us on our left as it approached the LZ. . . ."

The first two slicks landed and departed without incident. The third drew fire. Jim McCoy was supposed to go out on the fourth but was so afraid that he didn't leave the cover of the tree line and start toward the slick until Workman, shouting at him to get moving, ran over and gave him a solid shove from behind. "As the chopper landed, we dived in and tried to find anything to hold onto as it lifted off," wrote McCoy. The fourth slick also came under fire. As the door gunners blazed back, "I just kept my head down and prayed as hard as I could. A few moments later I felt a hard slap on my back, and looked up to see our Kit Carson Scout smiling at me. We had made it out alive. We all sat up and began cheering."

The door gunner beside McCoy grabbed his arm and, pointing back toward the landing zone, shouted over the roar of the engine and rotors, "The bird behind us didn't make it out."

The cheering stopped. As it transpired, Captain Workman, weapon in one hand, a radio in the other, had just reached the fifth slick with his two RTOs when it was hit by AK-47 fire and began swaying from side to side where it sat on the LZ. The door gunner motioned the grunts to get back. Unable to hear the fire over the rotors, they hesitated and were only just starting to move back when the Huey flipped onto its side. The main rotor caught Workman in his right shoulder, instantly slicing him in half at a downward angle across his chest. No one could believe what they had seen. One moment, Workman was turning to dash back to cover; the next, the rotor was striking earth in a blast of dust, flinging Workman's head and shoulders under the helicopter as it came to rest on its side, his rucksack tumbling end over end through the air, his headless, armless body crashing into the dirt in a welter of blood.

Workman was posthumously awarded the Silver Star, which he deserved for all that had come before. His death, however, was controversial. Two loads of Workman's battered troops were still on the ground when their commander, the last officer among them, attempted to make good his own escape. Under the circumstances, there were those who thought he should have waited to depart on the last lift ship. The fact that Workman was at the very end of his last mission after eleven months in combat probably explains why he did not. Blair Case, who knew and admired Workman, was upset when he talked with Rollison after the operation. "Rollison spoke very critically of Workman and D/1-506th. He said that Workman's troops were 'completely beaten.' Rollison also said, 'If Workman hadn't been so eager to get on the helicopter, he would still be alive.' "

Lieutenant Flaherty dashed to the wrecked slick, crouched for a moment against the tail boom, then raised his head, only to find himself staring into the muzzle of a revolver aimed at his nose by the terrified pilot on the other side of the helicopter. The pilot had thought he was about to be overrun. "Put that fuckin' thing away before you hurt somebody," Flaherty snapped. The pilot indicated that his door gunner was pinned under the ship. Rollison was on the scene by then, and he used his knife to cut the cord to the door gunner's radio helmet, which was strangling the man as he lay pressed into the dirt, the weight of the helicopter on his chest.

"Whatever happens, don't let me burn, please don't let me burn," the door gunner implored, jet fuel running onto the ground around him.

Corporal Michael L. Mann and Sp4 Robert A. Gutzman of D/1-506th crawled to the slick with their entrenching tools; they tried to dig out the door gunner, but progress was slow. The longer it took, the more likely the door gunner would indeed be consumed in a fuel fire. Mann and Gutzman, along with Rollison and Flaherty, finally stood up in the middle of the firefight and rocked the tail boom up and down, allowing James Fowler to pull the gunner out from under the Huey. Flaherty hauled the radios from the helicopter and shot them up so the enemy could not use them. The door gunner, meanwhile, was dragged to cover. As the medics did what they could for him—it appeared he had some broken ribs, maybe internal injuries—the man moaned and screamed, his inconsolable keening so unnerving that one of the grunts finally barked, "Will somebody shut that guy up?"

The lift was canceled. Captain Rollison moved his people back to the north side of the LZ, then—there being only one way out at that point—got organized to march back up the ridge to Hill 605. Rollison expected a fight along the way and didn't want to devote men to litter teams to carry the bodies of Workman, Asher, Hays, and Huk. "I'll get all the live ones out of here," Rollison told Lucas by radio. "That's all I can do. I recommend leaving the KIAs."

Berry gave Lucas permission to leave the bodies, and Rollison moved out as dusk approached, his column burdened with much ammo and equipment from the casualties—much more was left behind—the pace set by the men hauling the injured door gunner in a poncho litter. The enemy did not oppose the trek up the ridge, thanks to the Cobras that continued to roll in.

The lift resumed once Rollison linked up with Lamb. "We had a lot of slicks coming in, just one right after the other," recalled Lieutenant Campbell. The last few members of D/1-506th went out first, followed by D/2-506th, and, finally, C/2-506th. "Those last few ships were coming into a pitch-black LZ," noted Campbell. "I had my strobe light out. It was hairy as shit."

After the extraction from Hill 605, A/2-506th was the only company still on the ground in the Ripcord AO. When setting up that night, Hawkins had "used a trick I had learned in ranger school to cover our tracks and throw off any recon scouts who might be watching us as we moved into our NDP. It's a simple but effective technique," he explained, "which involves setting up a fake NDP in the late afternoon, then making a night move past and a switchback into your real overnight position about five hundred meters past the decoy NDP. Prepositioned guides who have reconned the real position help put everyone in position." Having thus slipped into position in the dark, Hawkins noted that "we didn't dig in and were very quiet throughout the night." The only noise was the blast of the booby-trapped grenade that had been left under the body of the dead enemy recon sergeant. The enemy, it seemed, were out in the dark, trying to track down the element that had slipped into their valley. "It was that kind of thing," recalled Frank Marshall, "that had the whole company convinced that we had to get out of there. We weren't glory fighters. There were a couple guys in the outfit who wanted to fight, but most of us just wanted to get the hell out of that valley before the enemy caught up with us."

CHAPTER 24

Rethinking the Problem

General Berry wrote to his wife on July 20: "I had forgotten the physical manifestations of the responsibilities of combat command: constant butterflies in one's stomach; constantly thinking about what the enemy might be planning and doing; constantly wondering if you have done everything you ought to do for your men and unit . . . I think the load feels heavier because I am the interim commander . . . Good experience for the young general officer," he added with some irony. "When General Hennessey returns . . . I expect to have aged by several years. . . ."

Berry felt burdened not only by Ripcord but also by Operation Chicago Peak. He finally decided not only to postpone the offensive once again but also to scale back its objectives. He outlined his reasons in a letter written on the morning of July 21: "[T]he enemy is in strength [on Co Pung Mountain] and has many AA weapons; our artillery support is unlikely to be adequate to the need[,] especially in view of the action on-going around RIPCORD; and at this stage in the war, all U. S. offensive efforts must have an extremely high assurance of success and of low casualties. From the beginning, my professional instincts have suggested that our plan has called for us to take unacceptable risks without a high assurance of success. I have refrained from expressing those instincts because the operation has been on the books for several months and because of my being a newcomer to the division. Now that I personally must decide to launch the operation, I cannot, in good conscience, undertake the operation in light of the new information our intensive reconnaissance is bringing us . . . My judgment is that we'd lose too many aircraft and too many men. . . . Yesterday, for instance, we had 11 aircraft damaged by anti-aircraft fire while conducting low-level reconnaissance of the CHICAGO PEAK area. Most of the fire came from 12.7mm machine guns. Made in China. The area is lousy with AA guns and infantrymen who fire their small arms at our aircraft." Berry added wryly: "I must say that Jack Hennessey selected a great time for his leave. Hope he's enjoying it. . . ."

Berry noted in another letter to his wife that he was visited at division headquarters that afternoon by Maj. Gen. Donald Cowles, the MACV J3. "He stated that our division area is the most active in Vietnam and has been for some time," Berry wrote. "We have the most and toughest enemy and have been engaging in the heaviest fights. And taking the heaviest casualties. This concerns 'people up the line.' In the prevailing political atmosphere, General Cowles stated, we must hold our casualties to a minimum during [the] withdrawal of U. S. forces." Cowles also told Berry, as the latter paraphrased in his letter, that "the 101st [Airborne] Division's planned offensive [Chicago Peak] is the only operation on the books for this summer which has any hope of hitting the enemy where it will hurt him—where his supplies are stored in preparation for his own offensive after the wet season sets in and drastically curtails our flying."

Cowles also bore a message from Gen. William B. Rosson, acting MACV commander in the absence of General Abrams, who was recuperating in Japan from the gallbladder surgery he'd put off until the last U. S. troops had pulled out of Cambodia. "General Cowles stated that General Rosson's hopes for some kind of successful offensive this summer are pinned on us," Berry recounted in his letter, "but that we cannot afford to take 'unduly heavy' casualties. Meanwhile, our continued reconnaissance in the CHICAGO PEAK area finds more and more enemy there; and Ripcord's use as an effective artillery base in support of CHICAGO PEAK becomes highly questionable. Something of a dilemma here, isn't there[?]"

Colonel Harrison wanted division to pile on at Ripcord. The brigade commander would recall being "thrilled, excited" when the A/2-506th wiretap revealed not only the enormity of the North Vietnamese buildup but fixed the general location of the enemy units around the firebase. "[W]e finally had them bunched up and not going anywhere," Harrison later wrote. "I told my brigade staff to develop plans to destroy the four enemy regiments. The staff came up with a plan calling for six additional U. S. battalions. . . ."[1]

Conforming as it did to established doctrine about finding, fixing, and fighting the enemy, Harrison's plan would have been acted upon without hesitation earlier in the war. Berry, however, was reluctant to commit the requested forces to Ripcord; it was a battle that could be won, but at a price that would undoubtedly bring about the kind of congressional lambasting that the 101st's senior officers had endured in the wake of Hamburger Hill. Colonel Root appreciated the political situation better than fellow brigade commander Harrison. "I commiserated several times with Ben during the battle," recalled Root. "He was taking an awful beating, but showed the courage of a lion. It is revealing, I think, that I never considered that my own headquarters or resources from my brigade might be committed to Ripcord. I don't think division ever considered that possibility, either. Expanding a fight in terms of area or commitment of overwhelming force was not an option that came readily to mind in the climate of those days."

General Berry retired to his office late on July 21 to wrestle with the Ripcord question. It was true, as Berry jotted on a notepad, weighing the pros and cons of evacuation, that Operation Chicago Peak was "infeasible w/o Ripcord." That fact argued for holding the firebase. The dilemma was that to exacerbate political divisions in the United States and thus speed the withdrawals, the "NVA plan mil[itary] victory in Ripcord area." Meeting the enemy challenge would involve shifting such forces into the mountains around Ripcord as to seriously weaken the division's defense of the coastal plains, its primary mission, and the resulting battle would draw such adverse media and political attention as to jeopardize the entire Vietnamization program. In conclusion, Berry wrote:

Ripcord now a liability
a hostage
a potential NVA victory

Logic argued for immediate evacuation. The ethos of the division that Berry commanded did not. He was, he later wrote, "keenly aware of Bastogne" as he pondered what to do at Ripcord. He was also concerned with the effect that withdrawal would have on morale.

Rising before dawn the next morning, Berry typed a letter to his wife dated "0515 Wednesday 22 July 1970":

> We've now reached a point where we must question the continued use of RIPCORD. Is it worth the casualties for the purpose it is serving? If we decide "no," how do we get out of RIPCORD? If we vacate RIPCORD, then what do we do? Where will we place our artillery to support the attack we want to make into the NVA base camp and cache area?
>
> Today we must decide on a course of action that differs from what we are now doing. Now we are taking constant casualties on RIPCORD from incoming mortar rounds . . . We are taking constant casualties among the rifle companies operating in the mountains and jungles around RIPCORD trying to locate and destroy the enemy mortars and AA machine guns . . . Daily our artillery fire from RIPCORD grows less effective as enemy mortar rounds make it more difficult for the artillerymen to fire their howitzers. . . .
>
> There are plenty of NVA in those hills. Most of them are moving in from NVN [North Vietnam] via Laos. They are well equipped and supplied. The mountains seem loaded with 12.7mm AA machine guns. Yesterday, we had two more helicopters shot down in the same area where a rifle company [D/1-506th] was in a tough fight. The NVA want very badly to inflict a major defeat on US forces. . . .
>
> I'll be glad when I've decided what to do in the Ripcord

area and begin doing it. Dear God, help me to make the right decision.

Berry decided the issue upon finishing the letter, as described in a follow-up dispatch written later that day: "This morning I made the most difficult professional decision of my life: to get out of RIPCORD as quickly as possible. Easier said than done. . . ."

According to John Fox, the general's command-ship pilot, the decision to withdraw in the face of the enemy, however sensible, was to Berry a hateful thing that required the swallowing of much pride. "No soldier likes to bail out," as Berry himself later said. "It's not in my nature." Berry would write that his decision was "based on what I believed to be a costly, unjustifiable continuation of human casualties for no corresponding military advantage."

Berry flew to Camp Evans to speak in private with Colonel Harrison. "We're closing Ripcord," Berry announced without preamble. "What do you need in the way of support?"

Though the planning session that ensued was crisp and unemotional, Harrison was actually reeling in shock. "I was dumbfounded," the brigade commander later wrote. "It had never even occurred to me to consider a withdrawal, but I nevertheless made no plea or argument to change Berry's decision. I believe the thought went through my mind, yeah, you're probably right. . . ."

Colonel Harrison had spent the last five nights with Lucas on Ripcord, waiting for the ground attack that they were sure was to come and were confident they could destroy in the wire. "General Berry was able to see the battle from a more detached view," Harrison wrote. "I was too close. I was part of it. I was fighting right alongside Andre Lucas on Ripcord and in the air. I failed to step back from the immediate problem and think strategically." Had Ripcord been presented as a classroom problem at Benning or Leavenworth, Harrison concluded in retrospect, his decision "would have been the same as Berry's."

There are those convinced that Berry had been pushed to evacuate by higher command's subtle reminders about casualties and not so subtle restrictions on ammunition. As Berry would deny that, in fact, there had been any restrictions, so does he deny that his decision was influenced by anyone up the chain of command. "I, and I alone, made the decision to withdraw," Berry would write. "I never had the feeling that anyone from higher headquarters was trying to pressure me to decide one way or the other. If anything, there was an absence of guidance." Berry would recall "feeling pretty lonely" when trying to make his decision, and he "occasionally wished for clearer guidance from my superiors."

In the final analysis, though, said Berry, "I'm glad that they left me on my own," it being "within the best traditions of the Army that you leave the commander that is on the ground free to see things his own way and make his own decision—and then you support him from the next higher headquarters. That happened in our case. Once I made the decision, not a single commander above me did anything other than say, we think you made the right decision. There was no criticism, there was no second-guessing. That's how it should be. Such a decision is the ultimate responsibility of command, and relying on commanders to make their own decisions is one of the great strengths of the United States Army."

CHAPTER 25

Kill or Be Killed

Captain Thomas M. Austin was selected to replace Bob Kalsu as the acting commander of A/2-11th Artillery. Austin was not a seasoned combat officer; his normal assignments included serving as battalion intelligence officer, battalion club officer, and commander of the battalion's headquarters section. "I was a certified, card-carrying REMF," the short, chubby, redheaded Georgia boy would joke. "I was just sitting there fat, dumb, and happy at Camp Eagle."

More than willing to go where sent, Austin was nevertheless extremely apprehensive about taking over a firing battery in a place such as Ripcord and would recall "saying the prayer, Lord, please don't let me make a mistake that gets someone else killed."

After collecting a helmet, flak jacket, and duffel bag, Austin ran to the LOH that had been dispatched for him. "Where you goin'?" the pilot asked. "Ripcord," Austin shouted. With that, the pilot said, "Don't get in front—get in back—and if you want that duffel bag, it had better leave first."

It was dark by the time the LOH made it to Ripcord. Playing it safe, the pilot barely landed, balancing one skid at the extreme edge of one of the hillside pads, the rest of the aircraft suspended over space. "I threw the bag out, then dove out myself," recalled Austin. "When I looked back over my shoulder, all I could see was the light on the bottom of that Loach.

The pilot had literally turned that aircraft on its side and was rushing down the side of the mountain to build up airspeed to get the heck out of there."

The next day, July 22, was another bad day on Ripcord. "Everyone was in really sad shape about Kalsu," noted Austin, "but then things started happening again and nobody really had time to mourn."

When a resupply Huey landed on the POL pad, it was knocked out of commission by a mortar salvo that exploded directly in front of the aircraft, wounding the entire four-man crew. "We had those people in the aid station before they knew what was going on," noted Sergeant Rubsam of B/2-506th. "The whole platoon just materialized on the scene. They didn't think about themselves, they just saw what happened and took care of it. After all we'd been through, I was heartened that people would still respond like that."

Sergeant Diehl of D/2-506th was killed during the same incident, apparently while returning fire from the 81mm section. Diehl had been reassigned as a mortar crewman soon after his heroic performance on Hill 1000. "We were all happy for him because that was considered a REMF job," recalled Diehl's buddy Bruce McCorkle. Stan Diehl was zipped up in a body bag and laid on a stretcher, an unhappy reminder that there were no more safe jobs on Ripcord.

With the 105s eliminated, the enemy mortar crews concentrated their fire on Captain Austin's 155s. It got so bad that the cannoneers would fire a couple of rounds, then dart back into their bunkers before the enemy could reply with their 82s and 120s. One of the section chiefs, Sgt. Randal D. Burdette, ordered his men to stay under cover as he single-handedly manned their 155. Specialist Fourth Class Lanny W. Savoie, the senior battery medic, helped man the 155s when not treating the wounded, a task he performed without hesitation no matter how intense the incoming. "Doc Savoie was a very bright, engaging Frenchman from New Orleans," said Austin, "and the bravest man I have ever known."

Not all the casualties were from enemy fire. Late that day, the rotor wash from a Chinook blew several powder charges into a trash fire; the charges flew out of the fire as they exploded, igniting, in turn, the M79 rounds in the rucksacks on which they landed and wounding five GIs. The powder charges also started a fire in the 155 ammunition storage area. Sergeant Robert L. Seeman, a section chief, rushed to the scene; while two cannoneers—Sp4 Ronald D. Carpenter and Pfc. James H. Stroud, the latter burned and wounded—put out the blaze with fire extinguishers, Seeman picked up an activated 155 round, carried it to the edge of the firebase, and threw it down into the wire, where it exploded. Burdette, Savoie, Seeman, Carpenter, and Stroud were awarded Silver Stars.

"For all that was going on, I thought morale was pretty good," said Dennis Murphy, one of the cannoneers sent to Ripcord from Gladiator. "I was only there three days, but the guys who were there during the whole battle were one hell of a bunch of guys, very close-knit from what I could see. They did their jobs. Everybody seemed to be pulling for the same cause, and that was to get the hell off that mountain alive."

Lieutenant Colonel Lucas had informed Captain Hawkins by secure net that Company A was finally to be extracted from the valley southeast of Ripcord. In preparation for the move to the extraction point, security patrols moved out around the little hill that the company had moved onto ranger style after dark the evening before. "Nothing positive was seen, but we could actually smell the enemy," wrote Lieutenant Widjeskog. Others would also recall the same fish-saucy smell, but "since we had accumulated quite a bit of enemy equipment over the last three days," noted Widjeskog, "we thought the odor was from that, and not more North Vietnamese."

Hawkins planned to extract from an LZ on a ridge eight hundred meters northwest of his position, and he dispatched Lieutenant Pahissa and Alpha One southwest—the trail connecting the overnight position to the landing zone ran southwest before cutting northwest up the ridge—to secure a stream crossing below the NDP.

During the maneuver, Pahissa's second squad opened fire on the lead squad; the problem, according to Frank Marshall, was that the Kit Carson leading the second squad "took us off course, so that instead of linking up with the point squad from behind, we ended up to one side of them. We didn't expect anyone to be on our flank, so when we heard movement—the brush was so heavy we couldn't see anything—we opened fire. I think the Kit Carson was the first one to fire. The lead squad immediately started shooting back."

The intramural firefight died down as quickly as it had flared as men from both squads heard people shouting orders in English from the other side of the brush. "The Kit Carson ran away when we figured out that we'd been shooting at each other," recalled Marshall. "He just disappeared into the jungle." It remains unclear whether the scout—the same one who had tapped the enemy commo line with the earplug—had staged the whole event in order to escape or perhaps rejoin the NVA that he expected to overrun Company A, or whether he had honestly gotten lost but was afraid that his American buddies would not believe him and might prove it by accidentally shooting him. As Marshall said, "We never trusted those Kit Carsons."

Lucas presently contacted Hawkins again on the secure net and instructed him to move to the rocky hill immediately east of Ripcord for extraction. No reason was given, but Hawkins imagined that Black Spade wanted Company A to use the LZ on the rocky hill because, as he later wrote, "it was almost always safe to get in and out of, being masked from direct observation from many of the key features around Ripcord." Lucas probably also wanted Hawkins in a position to support Company B in case of ground attack on the firebase. To reach Lucas's LZ, however, required that Hawkins backtrack up the ridge he had originally taken into the valley, an unwise maneuver, he thought, considering the trouble that Company A's original passage had caused the enemy. "It also meant having to cover two-plus kilometers in a day," he noted. "It was certainly doable, but not without sacrificing security for speed."

Hawkins meant to object to the order, but his secure set went dead just as he said, "Wait, sir, I've got a better LZ in mind—"

Infuriated, Hawkins wrote out a brief message for Lucas, something along the lines of: Want to move to LZ grid 346182. Most secure for me. Your LZ tactically unsound. Please advise.

It took Hawkins and his radiomen ten minutes to encrypt the message letter for letter so that it could be sent over an unsecure net, by which time Lucas—unaware that Hawkins had a problem with his order—had departed the TOC, bound for a conference being organized at Camp Evans to plan the evacuation of Ripcord. "The radiomen in the operations center authenticated and acknowledged my message, but were unable to contact any battalion staff officers to resolve the dilemma," noted Hawkins. "I knew in my heart that, had Lucas been available, he'd have understood the logic of my position, but since neither he nor any staff officers were in the operations center, I had to choose between my instincts and the order of my commanding officer. With time slipping away, I made the decision to follow orders and march to the LZ east of Ripcord."

Hawkins pulled Pahissa's platoon back from the stream and put Widjeskog, who was to have brought up the rear, in the lead, the direction of march having been reversed from southwest to northeast. "They know we're here, and they've been following us," incredulous grunts muttered bitterly among themselves, "and now we're gonna turn around and walk right back into 'em?"

It was at least an hour after noon by the time the company was reorganized and ready to move. Lieutenant Widjeskog was fifth in his platoon's well-spaced, seventeen-man column, following a narrow trail through the jungle, when his point man scampered back less than 150 meters into the move to report that there were NVA setting up a mortar on the trail. "Why didn't you shoot?" Widjeskog blurted, but there was no time to argue. There was only time to inform his men, "Okay, if we got something up there, then we have to go up and get it."

The platoon pressed on, the tense silence broken when a rocket-propelled grenade suddenly shrieked into the tree beside the point man, blowing down the tree. It was 1:30 P.M. on July 22, 1970, and the single most costly engagement of the battle had just begun. Widjeskog's platoon dropped to its collective gut on the trail when the rocket exploded, but the platoon radioman was immediately shot in the leg as AK-47 and RPD fire began raking the column from the front and right flank.

Within moments, Widjeskog could hear rounds hitting the bottom of a nearby mortar tube, the shells arcing down not on his platoon but back uphill in the overnight position where Hawkins and his command group were standing ready to join Alpha Three when it moved down the trail behind Alpha Two, to be followed in turn by Lieutenant Pahissa and Alpha One.

Lieutenant Widjeskog helped drag his radioman back into the circle that his platoon had formed, the trail running down the center, as they returned fire, but he lost the RTO's rucksack and radio in the process. Widjeskog thus lost contact with Hawkins. It didn't matter. Captain Hawkins could not have helped Widjeskog at the moment, such was the pressure on his own position. "Mortar rounds were exploding everywhere," wrote Hawkins, who almost immediately caught a spray of speck-sized fragments in his upper back, neck, and shoulder. "Some exploded above us in the trees. Some dropped through the canopy and exploded among us, sending up geysers of earth." Men were shouting, screaming in pain. Casualties were heavy. Tear-gas shells were mixed in with the high explosive, and many grunts began scrambling down the north and west sides of the hill, away from the enemy, grabbing weapons but leaving rucksacks and ammo in their haste to get out from under the shelling. "Everybody just went in their own direction," said Frank Marshall, who was hit in the lower left leg as he tried to make good his own escape. "We became totally clusterfucked."

Hawkins took shelter behind a large hardwood tree. There was no one between his command group and the enemy assault force, which, having slipped in close during the mortar barrage, started up the east side of the hill the moment the last shell exploded. "Enemy soldiers started boiling out of the brush from as close as fifty meters," wrote Hawkins. "Whistles were shrilling. I could see some blue pith helmets among all the green ones, worn by leaders, I assume, for identification. They came at us in a massed attack, crouching low, running through the undergrowth, shouting and shooting. . . ."

Some of the onrushing enemy soldiers were killed or wounded as those troops still in position on the hilltop opened fire. The return fire lasted only moments, however. There were too many NVA. "CP. Rally point. North. Fifty meters," Hawkins shouted, indicating a small knoll where he hoped he could regroup as RPGs began exploding inside his embattled NDP. "Follow me."

Hawkins took off running, gear bouncing, and did not stop until he had reached the knoll, followed closely by his company and battalion RTOs. "I caught more shrapnel, in the leg this time, along the way," Hawkins would recount. "I also lost track of the rest of my CP."

Hawkins would learn only later that Lieutenant Olson, his forward observer, had been killed by an RPG, his left arm blown off. Hawkins's secure-set radio operator had been blinded by a satchel charge. Sergeant Long, his interpreter, had been shot and killed. Lieutenant Pahissa had also been cut down, shot in the head by an RPD machine gun at the onset of the assault. Sergeant Singleton had been killed as he rushed to Pahissa. Doc Draper was shot through the forehead while defending a wounded man as the enemy overran the hill and would later be found sprawled on his back, both arms flung straight out, an IV bag clutched in one hand, his .45 in the other.

"My stomach was churning with bile and the sounds of battle were raging all around," continued Hawkins. "Once we got our bearings, I forced myself to calm down and get on the radio to request gunships and tac air, thinking that wherever Olson was, he would be cranking up the arty and mortars. I think the enemy saw our antennas because we began taking more RPGs. We slid down the backside of the knoll as far as we could while still maintaining radio commo." A team of Cobras already airborne for another mission diverted to the scene within minutes, by which time Hawkins and a half-dozen stragglers had established a small perimeter on the knoll. Hawkins edged up to the top to direct the Cobras and, after shouting to his scattered men to get some idea of their location, brought the rockets in so close that "after one run, I noticed a pain in the area of my left shoulder, then smelled something burning. It was me. A rocket fragment had struck me, but without much force and was just lying on my back as it burned through my tee-shirt to my flesh. I flicked it away. . . ."

Frank Marshall was one of the stragglers with Hawkins. The grenadier had initially linked up with two guys from Alpha Three, but the enemy had opened fire on them from the top of the hill, killing or wounding the Alpha Three GIs and sending Marshall scrambling.

"First Platoon, where are you?" Marshall screamed.

In response, his buddy Ron Janezic shouted, "Over here."

Marshall started toward Janezic, only to come under direct fire from the direction of his buddy. "Don't fire. It's me, it's me."

"It wasn't us. There's a gook in between us."

Marshall darted to Pfc. Danny J. Fries, medic for Alpha One, who lay nearby, screaming for help. As Marshall later wrote in his journal, the medic's "ass was half blown off." Marshall was just bending down to help Fries when "a satchel charge was thrown down on us," he wrote, "hitting him in the back as he laid there[,] blowing up and knocking me down the hill. I was blinded for a few seconds and my ears were ringing." Fries was killed. Regaining his senses, Marshall finally found refuge with Hawkins. "In a few minutes," he noted, "I was fine except for some facial burns. . . ."

Lieutenant Olson's radioman, Sp4 Floyd Alexander, was trying to assist the blinded secure-set operator when the enemy overran the position. Alexander covered the man with his body and, playing dead, watched through half-closed eyes as the NVA walked up to the dead and wounded GIs on the hilltop and shot each in the head. When an enemy soldier stopped before him, Alexander knew that his time had come. The radioman's head was down, so he could see only the man's sandals. But after giving Alexander a vicious kick to the forehead, which elicited no response, the NVA moved on without using his AK-47. Alexander and the secure-set operator continued to play dead among the enemy for the remainder of the battle. They survived. Ten others on the hill did not: Olson and Long from the CP; Pahissa, Singleton, Fries, Sp4 Donald J. Severson, and Pfc. Robert J. Brown from Alpha One; plus Doc Draper, Pfc. John M. Babich, and Pfc. Virgil M. Bixby from Alpha Three.

Specialist Fourth Class Rick T. Isom of Alpha Three recalled that when the enemy took the top of the hill, "they immediately started firing and throwing satchel charges in the direction we had gone. They also used the grenades attached to our abandoned rucksacks." Isom had taken cover by himself in a tangle of thick brush not far from the top of the hill, close enough to "hear some of the NVA yelling orders as they directed their men into positions around the hilltop. I could see that the enemy soldiers had pith helmets, pressed fatigues, and AK-47s. I did not dare move." One of the enemy soldiers, a young boy, took up a security position only ten meters uphill from Isom. "He acted as though he was scared to death," Isom later wrote. "He kept peeking around the side of a big tree he was hiding behind. I knew I would be in trouble if he spotted me, so I sighted in and blew the top of his head off the next time he showed his face." Having exposed his position, Isom jumped up and dashed down the hill, shouting "Currahee, Currahee," so he wouldn't be shot by his own guys, even as "a satchel charge went past, its fuse sizzling. It exploded away from me. Several grenades also came down the hill at me, and some nearby enemy soldiers were firing, but the vegetation was too thick for them to really draw a bead. I was finally able to hook up with ten or twelve other GIs."

Spared a mortar barrage, Lieutenant Widjeskog and Alpha Two fared better than the other platoons, though they too faced a considerable number of NVA. When the main assault went past Widjeskog's right flank as he faced down the trail—the knoll on which Hawkins regrouped was to the left—a secondary force maneuvered behind Widjeskog, so that the point platoon, already out of radio commo with the rest of the company, now found itself physically cut off as well. Widjeskog kept his head throughout the crisis, proving himself in the heat of battle to grunts who had previously been skeptical of their soft-spoken, highly educated L. T.

The troops themselves fought like natural-born killers. The platoon sergeant, Sgt. John W. Brown, who had been bringing up the rear, was shot in the face before he could join the perimeter that Widjeskog had formed up ahead, the bullet tearing through his right cheek and out his left, shattering teeth and part of his jawbone. Brown could not raise his head without choking on his own blood. The enemy thought to overrun the rear of the platoon, but the three men with Brown—his radioman, the pugnacious Al Miller, and a brand-new E6 named Whitecotton—cut them down as fast as they charged down the trail, shooting at least ten before the rest darted for cover and began sniping at the little group from behind trees. The radioman was wounded, but he kept shooting. The left shoulder of Whitecotton's shirt was blown off and his arm was burned by a satchel charge, which did not prevent him from lobbing grenades while Miller provided cover fire. Whitecotton threw every frag that the four of them had, killing and wounding so many enemy soldiers that there was a lull in their fire. Miller and Whitecotton, accompanied by the radioman, took advantage of the lull to drag Brown down the trail to rejoin Widjeskog. By that time, Miller, his own weapon having been shot out of his hands, was carrying an AK-50 that he had secured from a dead North Vietnamese.

Widjeskog had hoped to use Brown's radio to regain contact with Hawkins, but the platoon sergeant's wounded radioman had lost his ruck. "We had a third radio, but it was not working and we had planned to send it back for repairs on the next resupply chopper," noted Widjeskog, who set his own wounded radioman to getting that radio up and operational. "The radioman broke it down and went through the parts, trying to figure out what the problem was, even as the rest of us continued to return fire."

Widjeskog's medic, Pfc. Martin J. Glennon, a skinny, bespectacled, decidedly naive, and extremely religious kid, had frozen up at the start of the fight. He pulled himself together when he saw Brown. Glennon saved the platoon sergeant's life, expertly administering blood filler and a transfusion of dextrose, then keeping Brown out of shock, consoling and encouraging him whenever he started to fade. Widjeskog, meanwhile, made a head count. Brown and the platoon RTO were seriously wounded, and one man, Sp4 Thomas R. Schultz, was missing. One of the grunts told Widjeskog that Schultz had lost his glasses in the opening volley. They had sought cover together, but several satchel charges had exploded around them. When the smoke cleared, Schultz was gone, apparently having decided to make a run for what he mistook to be the safety of the hilltop NDP. Widjeskog didn't think he'd make it. Schultz's body was, in fact, subsequently discovered sprawled in the jungle between his platoon and the rest of the company. "Schultz was from the squad that had refused to walk point the week before," noted Widjeskog. "Everybody was nervous, but Schultz more so than anybody else. He had even approached his squad leader about getting out of the field. Maybe he was getting premonitions that he was going to be killed. Sometimes those kinds of things are self-fulfilling, I think."

There were peaks and lulls in the action as Widjeskog's grunts, at the prone position and facing outward, visibility no better than five meters, fired short, controlled bursts whenever they took fire or saw or heard something in the thick brush ahead of them. Widjeskog kept control of the action from the center of the platoon—he was the only man on the trail, the only one up on his knees—darting over to whoever had last fired to ask what they had. More than one grunt reported that he'd been able to square an enemy soldier in his sights and had actually seen the man go down.

The enemy suddenly released a shower of grenades and satchel charges, most of which fell short or flew from one side of the trail to the other, missing Widjeskog's men altogether. Rushing the perimeter from all sides behind a crescendo of AK-47 fire, the enemy ran into a matching crescendo of M16 and M60 fire. It took five intense minutes, the air under the canopy growing hazy with smoke, to beat back the attack, during which time a grenade went off to Widjeskog's left, peppering his arm and shoulder and thigh. A big fragment from the same grenade smashed into the right cheek of the machine gunner beside him, Sp4 Anthony J. Galindo, a tough, stolid Mexican American from Texas. With his right eye swelled shut, Galindo switched to his left hand as he continued to fire his M60.

Robert Journell was screaming bloody murder as he sprayed the brush flat in front of him, his M16 on automatic. Journell was cut down as he fired, and Doc Glennon, superficially wounded himself in the temple, could do little more than ease the man's pain with morphine, for he was bleeding internally.

It took Journell forty-five minutes to die. "His life left him right in front of us all," recalled a horrified Glennon. "He was kicking until the end."

Widjeskog saw a muzzle flash about thirty feet away on the left flank, where the terrain fell away. Sergeant Whitecotton saw it, too. "There's a guy shooting from behind that tree," he shouted to Widjeskog. "Give me some cover fire while I throw a grenade."

Widjeskog came to his knees and, shouldering his M16, squeezed off single shots in rapid succession, keeping the enemy soldier pinned while Whitecotton let his frag cook off before throwing it so the NVA wouldn't have time to grab it and throw it back. The grenade exploded as it landed, eliminating the enemy soldier but also wounding Widjeskog; his lips were parted in a grimace as he fired his last shot before ducking when a piece of shrapnel shattered his upper left incisor and skidded up into his gum. He felt the impact, but the pain was masked by adrenaline, however bad the blood running from his mouth looked to the grunt who pointed it out to him. Whitecotton shouted for more frags. Doc Glennon dug a baseball grenade out of his pocket and, without thinking, pulled the pin before handing it to Whitecotton. Realizing what he'd done, he blurted to Whitecotton that the grenade was armed. "He immediately threw it," recalled Glennon. "It rolled down the hill and exploded. None of our guys were hurt, thank God."

Amid the continuing fire, it dawned on Widjeskog that they were eventually going to be overrun. "We weren't going to get out of there alive," he recalled. "That realization actually seemed to calm me. I figured we might not make it, but we would fight to the end." The situation improved somewhat when the platoon radioman managed to bring their third radio back to life about ninety minutes into the battle, and Widjeskog was finally able to regain contact with Hawkins. "We learned that the enemy had taken the hill, and that the company had been split into three or four groups, but that they were holding their own at that time," wrote Widjeskog. "Hawkins had thought us dead, but when I informed him that the enemy appeared to be coming from an area east of the hill not more than a hundred meters from my position, he was better able to direct the gunships and artillery he was already bringing in on the North Vietnamese."

Captain Hawkins would recall that "when the Cobras first appeared overhead and I heard the pilots on the radio, I stopped being frightened." The Cobras halted the enemy assault, allowing an increasingly confident Hawkins to get his act together. When tac air was made available, "that's when I got angry, and started to fight the battle the way I wanted, not the way the enemy commander wanted. At that point, it was him and me, his will against mine. He had thrown his best punch and we were still standing. Now I set out to destroy him."

Hawkins orchestrated the fire support to simultaneously hit the enemy with 81s, arty, and ARA, even as a forward air controller, Maj. "Skip" Little, USAF, whom Hawkins knew from the battalion stand-down, fired white-phosphorus rockets along the enemy's likely routes of reinforcement to guide the F-4s in the placement of their napalm and 250-pound high-drag bombs. "We worked Phantoms up and down the enemy lines all afternoon," wrote Hawkins. "Trouble was that Skip wasn't authorized to drop ordnance any closer than five hundred meters from friendly troops. We were in deep trouble, though, so he fudged the danger-close margin down to three hundred meters. Still not good enough. Most of the NVA were fifty to a hundred and fifty meters away, and sometimes closer, and a mortar was still throwing rounds at us from just on the far side of our old NDP."

Several times, a trooper near Hawkins caught his attention and shouted over the din, "Charlie Oscar, we got to do something."

The man was right. The only way to regain the high ground was by frontal assault. Hawkins and his group started up the north side of the knoll at that point. Sergeant John W. Kreckel of Alpha One provided suppressive fire from the draw west of the knoll where he had pulled a half-dozen able-bodied stragglers together and to which he had already dragged several wounded men under heavy fire. The assault group ran into some of that same fire. The near miss of an RPG left Hawkins with a piece of shrapnel lodged in his cheekbone. Sergeant Ross was grazed in the mouth by an RPD round. "I heard Ross swear when the bullet kissed his lips," recalled Hawkins. "We both low-crawled backward to get out of the line of fire. . . ."

Frank Marshall caught a piece of shrapnel in the right arm between the shoulder and elbow. Feeling nothing—he was literally numb with fear—he was shocked when he put his hand over the injury and his middle finger went into a hole that was nearly bone deep. Having no time to worry about it, Marshall threw down his M79, ineffective as it was in the thick brush, and picked up an abandoned M16. With the attack stopped, Captain Hawkins was sitting, talking on the radio, when an enemy soldier popped into view on the hilltop. "Wait one," he said into the handset and, putting it down, reached for his M16. "The NVA was standing full up with an RPG launcher on his shoulder," Hawkins wrote later. "He was either aiming at us, or was trying to acquire us in his sights. I got a good sight picture while still sitting, and squeezed the trigger. I was aiming for him dead center in his chest, but the round went six inches high and blew through his neck. His head snapped back, the launcher dropped like a weight, and he went down flat on his back. . . ."

Hawkins resumed the assault. Sergeant Kreckel's group moved up the west side of the hill, Pfc. Buster G. Harrison of Alpha Three laying down heavy cover fire with his M60. Specialist Fourth Class Lowell T. Webster, the de facto leader of Alpha One, led another dozen grunts uphill from the north, followed closely by Hawkins and his RTOs. The troops leapfrogged forward, tree to tree, in the face of AKs and RPDs and RPGs. Hawkins demanded that Little put a strike on the enemy mortar, regulations be damned. "We're dying down here," he shouted. Although the FAC did not answer, the very next Phantom came in lower and closer than the others, one high-drag bomb hitting the top of the hill in the jet's earsplitting wake, the other landing directly in the vicinity of the mortar position to the east. The first bomb failed to explode, but the one that went in on the mortar "filled the sky with black smoke that blocked the sun for a short while," noted a stunned Widjeskog, whose hunkered-down platoon was a scant hundred meters from ground zero. "Dirt and tree limbs fell all around us. After the smoke cleared, we could suddenly see deep into the jungle, many of the trees having been cut down to eight inches in height. That single bomb effectively ended the enemy threat to my position."

Enemy soldiers could be heard screaming in the wake of the explosion. As their fire lulled, Kreckel and Webster—shrapnel having slashed just overhead as they neared the top of hill, their men gagging on smoke and gas from the bomb blast—were able to reach the NDP. The grunts could see enemy soldiers dragging their wounded away, and Hawkins wrote that his men "shot some of the NVA in the back as they ran. Enemy dead and our own dead, our equipment and theirs, were scattered together all over the hilltop."

The enemy retreat was covered by an RPD gunner firing from the northeast edge of the hilltop. Seeing a grunt walking unawares into the gunner's field of fire, Sergeant Kreckel rushed over and pushed him down just as the RPD opened fire on the GI. Kreckel took the burst meant for the other man and, shot in the head, died some minutes later on the hilltop, several of his buddies gathered around him, doing what they could to comfort him. Kreckel was posthumously awarded the Distinguished Service Cross.

The attack stalled even as the enemy broke contact, few of the grunts willing to push on to secure the far side of the hill. Being a squad leader, Rick Isom decided he had no choice but to set the example. Isom had no sooner reached the forward edge of the hill, however, than an NVA spotted his silhouette against the dusk sky as he moved between the denuded trees and squeezed off two shots from his AK-47. One round grazed Isom under the arm, the other took him in the chest, knocking him down. Isom knew he was in trouble. Not only was the enemy soldier who shot him only twenty to thirty meters away, but one of their supporting gunships was, as previously directed, rolling in on a rocket run. Barely able to breathe for his injuries, Isom was unable to move to take cover, "and when the rockets came ripping through the trees above me, I received shrapnel wounds in the hip and back, one piece hitting me in the spine and paralyzing me from the waist down. . . ."

Isom saw a young black grunt hiding behind a downed tree.

"I told him to go and find my friend Buster Harrison and bring him back to help me," recounted Isom, who was drowning in his own blood, air and blood bubbling from his sucking chest wound. "The kid didn't move. He was frozen with fear. I emphasized to him over and over that I was going to die if he didn't go get Buster, and he finally crawled off across the hilltop to find Buster. . . ."

Buster Harrison cautiously moved forward with the black grunt. No one else would go with them. Seeing where Isom was sprawled, Harrison crawled toward him, covered by the other GI. "Rick, can you move?" Harrison whispered as he approached Isom.

Isom, his voice weak, said that he could not, so Harrison rolled him onto his side, grabbed him under his arms, and, dragging him back out of the line of fire, began hollering for a medic.

Captain Hawkins, meanwhile, had just joined Webster at the top of the hill when the enemy fired a last RPG at them, marked as they were by the company commander's RTOs. Instead of being blown to bits, Hawkins and Webster and the battalion radioman were merely wounded, the rocket hitting a tree limb on its way in so that it exploded in front of them instead of at their feet. The effect was bad enough. Hawkins took a piece of shrapnel full in the throat, the impact knocking him down onto his rear end with such force as to leave him gasping for breath. Hawkins thought he was mortally injured but realized as he grabbed the radio to pass command to Widjeskog that he could still breathe and that he was actually barely bleeding. The shrapnel had zipped through his windpipe and out the left side of his neck, missing his spine and jugular vein. The injury did leave Hawkins rasping a bit, however, as he redirected their fire support onto the path of the retreating North Vietnamese.

Widjeskog had a clear view through the shattered jungle at one enemy soldier who tried to dash away, his arm straight down at his side, toting an RPD by its carrying handle, the weapon parallel to the ground. Up on his knees, Widjeskog was the only one in the platoon who could see the man—everyone else was at the prone position—and, realizing that, he opened fire with his M16. Widjeskog squeezed off single shots, his target frantically darting left-right-left-right as bullets smacked into the trees and leaves to either side of his head and shoulders. Widjeskog fired without aiming, so overly excited that he emptied the magazine without result, even as he thought to himself between shots *I . . . got . . . to . . . draw . . . a . . . bead.* The enemy soldier cut hard to his right, disappearing into some deep brush. Widjeskog called in a Cobra on the spot. "We all got down as the gunship fired its rockets," he wrote. Whitecotton, however, raised his head to watch and "a rocket fragment bounced towards us and hit him on the nose," continued Widjeskog. "He later said that he just couldn't take his eyes off the fragment even as it was about to hit him. It bloodied his nose and slowed him down as we moved back up the trail to rejoin the rest of the company. . . ."

The battle had lasted five hours. The company slowly regrouped on the hilltop as night fell, some of the wounded staggering into the perimeter on their own power, others being dragged in by the light of the illum popping overhead. The rucksacks strewn across the hill were checked for ammo, grenades, and water, which everyone desperately needed, as Hawkins called a wall of artillery fire around what was left of his company. "We were all exhausted, but we dug in as well as we could and set up fields of fire," noted Lieutenant Widjeskog. "We were certain we were going to be hit again."

Doc Glennon and the only other surviving medic, Sp4 Ian Hailstones—the senior company medic had been hit twice—used up all their bandages, albumen, and morphine, such were the casualties. Thirteen men had been killed and fifty-one wounded, fifteen so badly that they would have qualified as urgent medevacs had there been time and manpower to clear a landing zone. Rick Isom was one of them. Buster Harrison, who was to spend the night helping with the wounded, put a poncho over Isom and one of the medics, allowing the medic to turn on a flashlight as he sealed Isom's sucking chest wound. "He told me to lay with the wound down," Isom later wrote. "That helped a lot, at least it didn't feel like I was drowning anymore. The medic, of course, couldn't do anything for my spinal injury, and not only did I grow progressively weak through the night from loss of blood, but I also became very sick because my bladder was paralyzed and urine was backing up in my system. I was awake all night and pretty much on my own, but the thought that I would be going home helped me hang on."

Captain Hawkins had only twenty men who could still move and fight, and all but six of them were wounded to some degree. There simply were not enough troops left to form a perimeter large enough to encompass all the casualties. "I elected to leave the seriously wounded outside the perimeter on one side," Hawkins wrote. "It was the toughest decision of my life, but the men understood. We placed the wounded in small groups of twos and threes between tree roots and anywhere else they'd have some cover and a chance of surviving another attack. Some were in agony, some in shock, but most could still hold a weapon and even if they couldn't walk without assistance were ready to fight if need be. The guys on the perimeter who had wounded to their front knew where they were and fires were arranged accordingly."

Those grunts who thought that Hawkins had volunteered to go into the valley would forever hold him to blame for the disaster. Those who thought that Hawkins had only been following orders saw it differently. "You did a good job, sir," one grunt said to Hawkins as he checked positions that night. "Without you, we'd all be dead."

Everyone was traumatized, joking and crying in the same breath but otherwise hanging tough. Hawkins was particularly impressed with an immobilized grunt who was propped up against a tree, rifle across his lap, ammo within reach. "Let 'em come back," the kid muttered to Hawkins. "We'll whip the shit out of 'em again."

At some point during the night, the metal rings from the mortar illumination rounds being fired from Ripcord began crashing through the trees and smacking here and there on the hilltop. Hawkins shifted the fire, but not before he heard someone on the perimeter let out a cry as one of the rings crashed into his position. Hawkins went over to find Glennon treating Al Miller, who had blood streaming down the side of his face.

"All day I've fought," Miller shouted at Hawkins, "and I don't get a scratch, and now our own guys are doing it to us." Exhausted and exasperated, Miller trailed off in midsentence, "I'm gonna go up there and . . ."

"You just sit tight," Hawkins said as Miller settled down. "I've got the fire shifted. It won't happen again."

Lucas got Hawkins on the horn around nine or ten that night. "Raffles Four-three, this is Black Spade," Lucas said. "We're going to evacuate tomorrow. Deal Four-three"—Rollison—"will be inserted to assist you." Hawkins rogered the message, then Lucas asked, "What's your status? How are your men?"

The casualty count that Hawkins gave was far greater than what he had earlier reported. Lucas's composure cracked as the numbers sank in; he was troubled by the thought that, had Hawkins moved northwest as he had wanted instead of northeast as Lucas had ordered—the battalion commander had found Hawkins's message waiting for him when he returned to the firebase—he might have avoided the enemy attack. "Chuck, I'm so sorry," Lucas sobbed into the radio, his voice breaking. "I'm so goddamned sorry."

"It's okay," Hawkins stammered. "We'll be fine. Currahee, sir."

"Roger," Lucas said, his voice steady again. "Currahee. Out."

Figuring that the enemy knew where they were anyway, Hawkins secured a strobe light to a pole and placed it in the center of his perimeter, a reference point for the Cobras that took turns orbiting the hill all night in case of attack. The gunships were eventually joined by a flareship. Hawkins spent the night outside the perimeter with his medics, going from casualty to casualty, until about four in the morning, when one of his radiomen realized that he was becoming incoherent and led him back into the perimeter, firmly telling him to lie down and get some rest. "I passed out and slept till first light," Hawkins would recount. "When I opened my eyes, I was staring into the face of a dead North Vietnamese. . . ."

CHAPTER 26

The Evacuation

Although looking gaunt and fatigued, Lieutenant Colonel Lucas continued to project an attitude of energy and confidence that last night on Ripcord. His staff had been startled when he'd returned from Camp Evans to announce that division had decided to evacuate the firebase. Whatever Lucas's own views, he put the best face possible on the situation, enthusiastically explaining that once the firebase was evacuated, the NVA who had massed in the area to destroy Ripcord would themselves be destroyed by waves of B-52s. "We got 'em right where we want 'em," Lucas exclaimed. "He was almost snickering," recalled Gary Watrous. "He wasn't the least bit depressed about pulling out. He felt like we'd done our job. We'd pulled several thousand NVA in around us, and now he couldn't wait to start blowing them to pieces with Arc Lights."

The withdrawal was to begin at dawn. Fortified by much coffee, Lucas and what remained of his staff stayed up most of the night getting organized. "There was no time to debate or ruminate on the decision to evacuate," said Watrous. "We were all too busy."

Major Kenneth P. Tanner also participated in the planning session, having been assigned from the division G3 shop only the day before to take over as Lucas's S3. "Tanner was a tall, cheerful, red-headed infantryman just bursting with enthusiasm for his assignment to a line battalion," said Herb

Koenigsbauer, who spent several hours with Tanner in the division mess facility at Camp Eagle, bringing him up to speed on how the battalion operated. Tanner then flew to Camp Evans, "and from what I understand," noted Koenigsbauer, "he dropped his bags in the hootch the exec and operations officer shared in the battalion rear area, and without even unpacking, immediately caught a chopper out to Ripcord."

Captain Vazquez, the battalion supply officer, came forward that evening, as did Lieutenant Caballero from the pathfinders and a liaison officer from the 159th Aviation Battalion. The three assisted Lucas in surveying the base and determining how many CH-47 sorties would be required to lift out all the equipment on site. As riggers from DISCOM prepared the loads, Austin's 155 crews hastily expended the approximately thirteen hundred rounds in the battery's ammunition supply point so the howitzers themselves could be readied for extraction. The evacuation of personnel actually began that night with Michaud's cannoneers and Edwards's engineers. The rest of the troops on base were to be evacuated after the equipment move in the morning. Manifests were drawn up and each man was assigned a number indicating the order in which he was to board the Hueys.

Vazquez returned to Camp Evans, meanwhile, to represent Lucas as the air-movement and suppressive-fire plans were finalized at brigade. The division's air cavalry squadron and aerial-rocket artillery battalion stood ready to support the evacuation, and a massive amount of artillery and tac air had also been lined up. "The mood in the brigade TOC was nevertheless one of gloom and dread," noted Blair Case. "I think most of us expected the evacuation to be a complete disaster."

The mood was the same on the firebase. Captain Harris had been superficially wounded in the buttocks that evening while helping load a litter patient aboard a Huey that was itself damaged by the mortar salvo that hit the landing pad. Presently, the battalion surgeon filled two canteens, secured as many magazines as he could carry in addition to his medical gear, then carefully cleaned and polished ammunition and loaded it into the magazines so his M16 wouldn't jam should he need to use it. "I wanted to make sure that I'd be ready if the evacuation choppers couldn't get in," recalled Harris, "and we were forced to walk off the hill and fight our way out of the area. I was a little disappointed that we didn't get a little help out there instead of being ordered to evacuate. You kind of hate to feel that you're being pushed around.

"On the other hand," he continued, "it might not have been worth it to take a lot more casualties to hang onto Ripcord. That's what all my medics were saying—it just wasn't worth it. The position was completely untenable. The way the enemy mortar and antiaircraft positions were multiplying around us, in another day or two we wouldn't have been able to get our casualties out of there anymore."

Having grabbed maybe two hours of sleep, Lieutenant Colonel Lucas was up again at 4:30 A.M. The battalion commander spent an hour checking to make sure that all loads were rigged and that his subordinates understood the evacuation plan, then he departed Ripcord in the C&C dispatched for him from Evans, accompanied by Ray Williams, his arty LNO. Lucas and Williams coordinated prep fires in the predawn gloom on and around a knoll one klick southeast of Ripcord and one klick northwest of Hawkins's position, into which Rollison and Company D were to be inserted so as to move to the aid of Company A. Lucas had tried to assault Rollison onto the knoll the night before, but brushfires started by the air strikes supporting Hawkins had spread to the landing zone atop the knoll and the lift ships had been forced to return Company D to Camp Evans.

The idea of a night CA and a night march through jungle teeming with enemy had struck Rollison's troops as ill conceived at best, foolhardy at worst, and they'd been relieved when the mission was aborted. "There was a somber attitude that night," said Bruce McCorkle. "We were all very grateful we didn't go, but we all realized that there were men dying out there. They needed help."

General Berry and Colonel Harrison arrived on station some thirty minutes after Lucas went airborne. Settling into orbits successively higher than the battalion commander's, Berry maintained an overwatch position while Harrison, this being an operation planned by brigade and under brigade control, assisted Lucas in coordinating the suppressive fires that began smashing at that point into all the hills around Ripcord. The battlefield had been divided so that artillery fire—and every tube that could range on the area was firing—could be directed onto certain targets, even as Cobras rocketed others. Harrison's chemical officer, flying low in a Huey, smothered still more known and suspected enemy firing positions under choking blankets of tactical CS.

As the prep fires went in, the seventeen slicks that were to insert D/2-506th approached in a long, staggered trail from the east, the sun on the horizon behind them. The Hueys were followed by the fourteen CH-47s that were to pull the equipment off Ripcord. "The pilots had been briefed to maintain radio silence so the enemy wouldn't be able to figure out the game plan," said Lieutenant Fox, pilot of Berry's C&C. "There was no conversation, and no enemy fire, but you could feel the tension as the aircraft neared Ripcord."

The lead ship was flown by Capt. Randolph W. House of C/158th Aviation Battalion. The infantrymen on board included Rollison himself. Although dawn was breaking, it was still dark, especially under the canopy, when the CA began at 6:25 A.M. to coincide with the first air strike of the morning. The landing zone, a particularly small one, was hemmed in on all sides by tall trees, requiring House to hover straight down, his blades barely clearing the jungle. The enemy opened fire on the aircraft as it made its slow descent, and in the confusion the crew chief accidentally cleared House into a denuded, limbless tree on the right side of the Huey. There was a ferocious jolt as one of the main rotors whacked into the tree, followed by an onimous vibration that left House wondering if the blade was going to come loose as he pressed on to unload Rollison's group on the LZ. Talking with Rollison after the operation, House "got the feeling that if I had tried to pull out after hitting that tree, he would have pointed his M16 at me and demanded that I land. That's how intense everyone felt about rescuing Alpha Company."

The next sixteen slicks hovered down the mine shaft in their turn, door gunners blazing in the face of AK fire from nearby enemy soldiers and .51 fire from Hill 805. Lucas, controlling the insertion from his command ship, which was itself the target of some of the .51 fire, helped direct the Cobras escorting House's flight onto the gun position, then brought in the F-4s. Rollison, meanwhile, had his troops fire a Mad Minute into the jungle around the LZ, then took a compass reading and, to avoid the ambushes likely to be waiting on the trails, struck out cross-country in a straight line toward Company A. The pace was brisk. Relying on speed for security, Rollison's column brushed through the enemy, ignoring those who could be heard moving in the jungle on either flank and barely pausing to return fire when the tail-end platoon was engaged. "We ain't got time to fuck with these people," Rollison had informed his platoon leaders. "Just leave 'em alone and keep moving." Hawkins could hear the muffled reports of gunfire as Company D neared Company A's little last-stand position. "We'd made it through the night only because the enemy hadn't come back to finish the job," recalled Hawkins, who knew that he and his troops would not survive the day by themselves but "didn't believe that Rollie would actually make it to us. Lucas had informed me that radio intercepts indicated that we'd been hit by a full battalion the day before. I figured Rollie would run into part of that force or maybe another battalion entirely and get bogged down in another terrible fight."

The equipment move began before the combat assault ended. The mission made little sense from an aviation perspective. Lieutenant Fox thought it would have been wiser to simply destroy the equipment and howitzers on the base rather than risk another disastrous CH-47 crash. "My thought at the time was to hell with the howitzers," said Fox. "We'll buy you a new howitzer. Let's get the troops out. I couldn't believe we were going to attempt to pull howitzers out of a position surrounded by mortars and antiaircraft guns. Chinooks are big targets. You could hardly miss one while it sat in a hover, waiting for the riggers to get the load hooked up underneath. It was really dumb to send in the Chinooks."

The decision to extract the 155s—and, if possible, even the ruined 105s—was Berry's. It was a matter of unit pride. Berry was also concerned, as he wrote home, that abandoning artillery would cast the evacuation as a "bugout" to the troops and the media. He hoped by recovering the howitzers "to preclude the 'spiking the guns' reporting that seems to appeal to young newsmen."

Directed into position by Lieutenant Caballero's pathfinders, the first CH-47 pulled out the first 155mm howitzer at 6:32 A.M. There was no enemy fire. The next five Chinooks, however, made their approaches through .51 fire and extracted the five remaining 155s amid incoming mortar salvos. Two crewmen were wounded, and three of the Chinooks were grounded due to battle damage after reaching Camp Evans with the 155s. Dennis Murphy watched in amazement as one of the riggers "hung onto the airlift straps after getting them hooked up instead of jumping off the 155, and went straight up in the air and got out of there under the Chinook."

It took half an hour to extract the howitzers. Lucas broke station then to refuel, radioing the TOC before he departed to ask if any particular assistance was required; the casual reply from one of the radiomen, Sgt. Jon E. Penfold, heartened all those senior officers who were listening: "No sweat, sir, we'll get out of this shit."

The equipment move continued, the Chinooks forming a daisy chain—pick up a load, take it to the rear, get back in line—between Ripcord and Evans. Eight more CH-47s received battle damage in the process, and at 7:35 A.M. one from B/159th was shot down while attempting to extract one of the engineer bulldozers. The Chinook took hits from the .51 firing from Hill 805 and rotated completely around—a wisp of smoke coming from a bullet hole in one of the port engines—before the pilot regained control and crash-landed in the 105 area. The crew quickly scrambled out and headed for cover. Ten minutes later, the last of twenty-four loads—radar, bulldozers, ammunition, conexes filled with supplies and communications equipment—was picked up by the last Chinook.

Captain Alton J. Caldwell, the 2-319th FA's supply officer, had been inserted onto the base that morning with three enlisted men, rigging equipment for six howitzers, and a rucksack full of thermite grenades. Caldwell's mission—and he was visibly unenthused about being sent into a firestorm over what was essentially scrap metal—was to extract Battery B's 105s or, should that prove impossible, disable them with the thermites. The Chinook that crashed into the battery area, sending Caldwell's people rushing into a covered firing position, would have obstructed any attempts to lift out the 105s, so Caldwell passed out the thermites at that point.

The procedure to disable a howitzer involved closing the breech and sliding a thermite—they looked like smoke grenades and produced a tremendous amount of heat—down the tube so as to fuse the breech shut. One of the 105s was so badly damaged, however, that Caldwell could not get the breech closed all the way, and when one of his men popped a thermite down the tube, it fell to the ground through the partially opened breech. Caldwell kicked the thermite under the howitzer. Seeing the burning thermite, Major Tanner started hollering at Caldwell to stop, concerned that the thermites would ignite fumes from the crashed Chinook. Fuel from the disabled aircraft had, in fact, begun running downhill into the TOC, and Tanner was in the process of setting up a new command post in the adjacent 155 FDC. According to various after-action reports, the 105s were put out of commission with thermites. Caldwell would recall, however, that the pin had been pulled on only that single thermite that hit the ground before Tanner ordered him to cease and desist. "I guess I kind of failed in my mission," Caldwell later said. Not that it really mattered, he added, because "the frames and sights had been twisted and melted down in the original ammo fire, and the tubes had probably been affected by the heat, too. I doubt it would have been safe to fire them even if we had recovered them."

Lucas dashed into his battalion headquarters while his command ship was being refueled at Camp Evans to ask Major Davis, the battalion exec, if Major Koenigsbauer's efficiency report had been typed up yet. It had, and Lucas quickly signed it before heading back to Ripcord, thus ensuring that no matter what might happen to him during the evacuation, Koenigsbauer's service to the battalion would be officially recognized. Koenigsbauer, informed of the incident by Davis, would marvel at the professional loyalty of "a commander so concerned for the men who worked for him as to do something like that in the middle of an event as hectic and stressful as the withdrawal from Ripcord."

Back on station as of 7:40 A.M., Lucas continued calling in fire as Berry and Harrison also departed to refuel their command ships at Camp Evans. The staff officers with Berry had brought thermoses of coffee with them, along with a breakfast of C-rations. "I knew better than to drink coffee on a helicopter. There's no place to get rid of it afterwards," recalled Fox, who watched amused as "all those ashen-faced majors and lieutenant colonels piled out both sides of the helicopter as soon as we landed to refuel and hosed down the area."

Lucas, Harrison, and Berry were stacked up over Ripcord again when slicks from the 101st and 158th Aviation Battalions began pulling the troops off as of about 8:30 A.M. "The beginning of the evacuation was a nightmare," recalled WO1 Kenneth L. Mayberry of C/158th. "Flights of ten were orbiting everywhere you looked over the flats in the Firebase Jack area just below the mountains. Mass confusion reigned. The air mission commander's radios were breaking up and he had trouble communicating with us."

Captain House, at the controls of a replacement aircraft, finally broke off from his flight and took over as air mission commander. "In short order, House turned mass confusion into an orderly evacuation," noted Mayberry. House used a well-known landmark—a spectacular waterfall three kilometers northeast of Ripcord—as the final checkpoint from Evans to Ripcord. He directed the slicks in from the falls three at a time, a tactic that minimized the number of lift ships exposed to enemy fire at any one time and maximized the number of gunships available to cover them. Arriving three at a time, the slicks landed on the various helipads where pathfinders were stationed, wearing glow vests and using hand and arm signals to guide the Hueys. Many pilots were forced to abort their approaches at the last moment because of incoming mortar fire. Realizing that the base was being shut down when they saw the howitzers lifted off, the enemy mortar crews had begun using at a furious rate the ammunition they had stockpiled for the siege. The incoming was so intense that "the troops finally stopped getting on the aircraft that did make it in," recounted House. "They didn't want to leave their cover. Our aircraft were going in empty and coming out empty. They could only sit on those pads for a matter of seconds, then they had to take off whether anyone got on board or not because of the heavy fire."

After making a futile touchdown of his own to confirm what his pilots were reporting, House called Lucas: "Nobody's getting on. I can't keep sending birds in through this fire if nobody gets on 'em."

The radio in Lucas's command ship malfunctioned at that critical moment—it was now 8:45 A.M.—cutting off communications with Major Tanner on Ripcord. Lucas had originally planned to land at the end of the operation so as to ensure that everyone had been extracted before going out with the last load of troops. Presently, though, he contacted Harrison: "The air mission commander says the troops aren't getting on the aircraft. I've lost commo with the firebase, so I'm going to go in and take charge on the ground."

Mortar fire forced Lucas's pilot to turn away when he attempted to land on the VIP pad. After several other harrowing approaches, the pilot was finally able to set down for an instant on the POL pad at the other end of Ripcord. The enemy dropped a salvo on the pad even as the command ship banked away, sending Captain Williams—the arty LNO had disembarked with Lucas—diving into the closest foxhole. Striding on through the fire, Lucas shortly encountered Cpl. Michael L. Renner of A/2-11th FA, who was huddled in a vacated mortar position with several other GIs. In a scene that blew Renner's mind, Lucas stood at the edge of the position, suited up in helmet and flak jacket, his fatigues clean and pressed, his boots glistening, casually ignoring the incoming fire as he asked the young cannoneer where the infantry command group was located. "Up the hill, sir," Renner shouted, indicating the 155 FDC. "You're doing a good job, son," Lucas said, throwing Renner an encouraging salute as he continued on. "Airborne all the way."

Hoping to set an example, Lucas, having moved around the

base to take stock of the situation and do what he could to encourage the troops, stood in the open on the path cutting between the mess bunker and the front of the 155 FDC on its way to the VIP pad. Major Tanner joined him, as did, briefly, Lieutenant Bialosuknia—responsible for the airlift, he was gratified to report that the troops had begun boarding the lift ships again—and Lieutenant "Teenager" Watrous, who, a radio strapped to his back, had been calling in air strikes through the FAC orbiting Ripcord. Much of the enemy fire was coming from a 120mm mortar on Hill 805. The position was marked by the tall plume of smoke that burst through the vegetation around it each time the crew dropped a round down the tube. Though pinpointed, the position was so deep and narrow that neither the F-4s nor Cobras had been able to score the direct hit required to knock it out. Captain Caldwell watched one Cobra roll in on the mortar, minigun blazing. "The top of the hill seemed to come alive with thousands of tiny, dusty explosions," he wrote. "It was somewhat like large drops of water striking the calm surface of a pond. The fire completely covered the top of the hill, and might have been effective had the pilot not come in from the north, as it appeared the mortar was sheltered in a gully that ran east to west. Less than ten minutes after the Cobra banked away, a Phantom came on station. The pilot had the correct angle, approaching from the southwest, but the two high-drag bombs he released completely missed the little hilltop, going right over the enemy and into the valley beyond. The explosions were incredibly loud. The concussion actually shook the firebase. . . ."

Lucas, who could see the smoke himself as the mortarmen put an almost continuous stream of rounds in the air, instructed Watrous to, "Go get the sons of bitches."

Watrous intended to, but before he moved out, he urged Lucas and Tanner to take cover inside the FDC. "Sir," he said to Lucas, "there's nothing for you to do out here except get killed."

Lucas shrugged as if to indicate that such were the risks of command, but he was seriously wounded only minutes later—at about 9:15 A.M. on July 23, 1970—when a 120mm round exploded three feet from him, apparently fired by the invulnerable mortar on Hill 805. The round exploded with such force that Captain Williams and the battalion radiomen, positioned behind the blast wall protecting the entrance to the FDC, were hurled, stunned, across the floor of the bunker. Captain Harris, the battalion surgeon, immediately rushed out of the FDC to see if there were any casualties. Two men, obviously dead, lay twisted on the ground, killed instantly judging by their massive injuries. One of them was Major Tanner. The other was Pfc. Gus Allen, a black trooper who had ended up on the firebase some days earlier on his way to rejoin A/2-506th from the rear. Allen happened to have been moving past Lucas and Tanner on the path the moment the shell landed. Lucas lay on his back, unconscious, mouth agape, legs mangled but barely bleeding—the mortar shrapnel, white hot, had cauterized the wounds—his face so aged by fatigue and shock that Harris did not even recognize the battalion commander as he grabbed him by the shoulders of his flak jacket to drag him inside the FDC. "I got him inside, and, boy, it wasn't five seconds later that four more rounds went off right outside," said Harris, who was awarded his second Silver Star for the rescue. "There were several other people in that artillery bunker, and we just looked at each other. It had been a close call."

Harris didn't realize whom he had saved until he unzipped Lucas's flak jacket and spotted the crossed rifles and black oak leaf on the battalion commander's collar. Harris got an IV going and began administering albumen. There was not much else he could do for Lucas. The colonel had been protected from the waist up by his flak jacket, but his legs were so shattered that bandages would have been useless. Half of one kneecap was blown away, the tibia popped out of the socket. "Lucas's injuries were horrible," said Harris. "There were bones sticking out, and he had shrapnel wounds all the way up into his buttocks on one side. It was obvious that both his legs would have to be amputated once he was medevacked. . . ."

Lucas came awake in about ten minutes and asked what had happened. "You got the shit knocked out of you, sir," said Harris.

Lucas squeezed his testicles and, relieved to find them intact, joked, "My wife wouldn't want anything to happen to them."

Captain Benjamin F. Peters, four days in command of B/2-506th on the perimeter, had been called to the 155 FDC, and Lucas handed him his blood-splattered map. "Well, Ben, looks like you got it."

"Yes, sir, I think I can handle it."

"I know you can," Lucas said.

Captain House, who much admired Lucas, went in to evacuate him—a single Huey escorted by four blazing Cobras. Lucas was loaded aboard the slick on a stretcher, but as quickly as House got the battalion commander to the aid station at Camp Evans, it was too late. Lucas had apparently gone into shock during the flight. Harris was later informed that "Lucas took one last breath as the medics unloaded him from the chopper, then died there on the pad."

Lieutenant Colonel Walker, commander of the 2-319th FA, was over Ripcord in his own C&C; when Black Spade's death was reported on the command net, "I felt a great personal loss," recalled Walker. "I was deeply moved. I thought Andre Lucas was a super guy and was pleased to call him a friend. That he was a superb commander was exemplified by the way he died. . . ."

There was no time to mourn. "I was in front of the operations center, calling in air strikes again when I got the word about Lucas," said Lieutenant Watrous. "I can remember feeling horrible—and then snapping out of it in a matter of moments because the task at hand was so serious. I just went back to calling in air strikes to shut those mortars down so other people wouldn't get hurt. . . ."

Lieutenant Fox recalled that when Berry relayed the news of Lucas's death, the general was "simple, direct, very military, but also very compassionate. General Berry actually sounded sickened, but the mission went on. That's the way it was. The mission continues."

Harris was also sickened, not only by Lucas's death but also by the loss of Major Tanner, who would be posthumously decorated with a Silver Star. "I only met him the evening before we evacuated," noted Harris. "It was already dark out. Fifteen hours later, he was dead. It hurt because he was one of my friends. Every man on that hill was my friend. There's a certain bond you establish under stress, and it existed between me and Major Tanner even though we really didn't know each other at all. He's still one of my friends. It's the kind of thing you can't understand unless you've gone through an experience like Ripcord. . . ."

There were those who did not mourn. Captain Wilcox, banished from the battalion, was one of the duty officers in the brigade TOC at Camp Evans during the evacuation of Ripcord. "When it came in over the radio that Lucas had been killed," recalled Wilcox, "there was this hush that fell over the room and a lot of standing around being somber. I wondered why we didn't get hushed when some private got blown away. I was still a little pissed at that point, too, about Lucas and Hill 1000, and I remember I spoke up rather loudly, and said, 'Well, listen, I've discussed losing people with Colonel Lucas, and he thinks casualties are all just in the game.' No one said anything, and we all just slowly got back to work."

The slicks came in low and fast along a ridge that led from the falls to the firebase, running a gauntlet of ground fire. Gunships flanked the slicks, and jets flashed over them, homing in on their targets. The battlefield was obscured with clouds of smoke from friendly and enemy fire, which the slicks flew through before finally flaring to land amid green tracers and dusty explosions on Ripcord. Watching from his orbit, Captain House was moved to remark to his copilot, "Damn, this looks like *Twelve O'Clock High.*"

The evacuation was chaotic yet organized. Flight corridors had been established so that lift ships approaching the firebase would collide neither with those flying back along the ridge with troops aboard, nor the scouts and gunships ranging the battlefield looking for targets of opportunity, nor the slicks running tear-gas missions, nor the jets dropping bombs and napalm on enemy firing positions. The aircraft involved also had to avoid the trajectories of the artillery fire pounding the high ground from other firebases.

House was in radio contact with Lieutenant Bialosuknia, who, positioned at the entranceway to the ops center, controlled the evacuation of the support troops packed in the TOC. The troops went out five at a time, mostly from the VIP pad. Three would rush to the landing slick from the command bunker, two others from foxholes on the other side of the pad into which they had moved at Bialosuknia's direction to await the Huey. Bialosuknia also directed troops to the log pad in the vacated 105 area just above the TOC.

Captain Austin, meanwhile, was in a dugout adjacent to the log pad in the 155 area, in radio contact with his fire direction officer, a lieutenant, who was in a bunker with most of the battery personnel; each time Austin got five troops out on a slick, he would have the fire direction officer send five more running to his dugout to await the next Huey. House was playing the old shell game by then, such was the fire, sending the lift ships in one at a time so the pathfinders could wave each approaching pilot to the pad that was taking the least amount of fire at that moment. Once the troops had clambered aboard, the pilot would pick up to a hover, back past the edge of the base, make a pedal turn, then dive down the northeast side of the hill to avoid the enemy fire—which was mostly coming in from the west and southeast—and the next inbound Huey. "You got out of there right on the deck," noted House. "People literally had tree limbs stuck in their skids when they landed at Camp Evans."

No lift ships were shot down on the firebase. At least four were badly damaged by mortar shrapnel, however, including one piloted by Ken Mayberry of C/158th, who described the incident at length:

> I had begun my flare when another mortar round landed between my aircraft and the five troops I could see to my front, waiting to board. There was a puff of smoke and dust, and they were knocked flat like bowling pins. At the same instant, my aircraft was splattered with shrapnel, and it felt like someone had stuck a burning hot poker into my left leg. Someone yelled over the intercom to "go around"—to abort the mission and get back in line—but when I saw those guys

go down, I felt responsible, and knew I couldn't leave them there. I said we had to get the wounded first, and set down.

When the skids hit the ground, my crew chief, Sp5 John T. Ackerman, and my door gunner, Sp4 Wayne E. Wasilk, jumped from the aircraft and ran forward to get to the wounded, an act of tremendous courage given the machine-gun and mortar fire impacting all around. . . .

I don't know how long it took them to carry and drag the wounded on board, but it seemed like forever. More than one aircraft making its final approach to the pad I was sitting on had to make a go-around, and Captain House was calling to ask what my situation was. I couldn't answer. I just stared straight ahead at the scene before me. Everything was happening in slow motion. I was afraid if I moved I'd break the spell and the next mortar round would kill us all. . . .

Finally, all the wounded were loaded and Ackerman yelled, "All clear." The spell was snapped and I pulled pitch.

As I made my call, "Chalk 1 is coming out," my throat was so dry from fear that I didn't even recognize my own voice.

I began to relax on the way back and watched my instruments to detect anything amiss. I knew we'd taken some hits, but didn't know the extent of the damage. Another aircraft from our company, piloted by WO1 David J. Wolfe, flew all around us so his crew chief could check us over visually. He didn't see any major damage, but thought he detected some smoke, so Wolfe escorted me all the way back to Charlie Med at Camp Evans in case the engine quit.

I called ahead, and there were medics waiting on the pad with stretchers for the wounded when we landed. One of the doctors stuck his head through my window to ask if we were okay. I told him we were fine. It was rather comical as he looked at the holes in the aircraft and down at my chin bubble, which also had a shrapnel hole in it, and asked me, "Are you sure you're okay?" My leg stung, but it wasn't a big deal. I would have been embarrassed to go into Charlie Med where the really seriously wounded guys were, so I pulled pitch and flew over to Phoenix Nest, our company area at Camp Evans. I parked outside the hangar so maintenance

> could check me out. Maintenance took one look and Red-X'd my aircraft. We had over forty shrapnel holes and had sustained structural damage. Maintenance was preparing for a long day of battle damage, and didn't want to give me one of their replacement aircraft, but I eventually got one and got back in the air near the end of the evacuation. . . .

The airmanship displayed during the evacuation was phenomenal. More than one gunship pilot flew directly between a descending lift ship and the .51 firing on it, for example, drawing the fire away from the slick even while attempting to silence the gun crew with miniguns and rockets. Every pilot involved in the evacuation save one was later awarded a Distinguished Flying Cross, every crew chief and door gunner an Air Medal for Valor.

The exception was a young, relatively new warrant in House's company who, forced to break off his attempted landing on Ripcord, did not rejoin those lift ships circling the flats but instead headed for Camp Evans. House thought the warrant had been injured or needed to refuel, but "later learned that he had cracked. As I understand it, he climbed out of his aircraft in shock after he landed and just walked into his quarters. He was a good kid, and was absolutely ashamed when I talked to him after the mission. He got it together, as I recall, and started flying again after Ripcord."

Frank Parko of the 2-320th FA described his escape:

> There were beaucoup people in the TOC. We were all crunched together, standing room only. An officer with a PRC25 radio [Lieutenant Bialosuknia] was at the doorway, calling out names from a list as the choppers came in. Somebody had a transistor radio off to one side, and the Rascals came on in the middle of all this with, "It's a Beautiful Morning." Everybody in the bunker started laughing and snickering, "You should be here."
>
> When my group was called up to the door, the officer with the PRC25 said, "You know where the 155 pits are? Go down this road, get in the 155 pits, and the slick will be right there."

He tapped us on our backs—"Go!"—and we hauled ass down the road to the 155 area. I was wearing my flak jacket, and had my helmet in one hand and my M16 in the other. Mortar rounds were coming in, and there were some zings going by, so I figured we were getting sniped at, too.

We got down to the empty 155 pits—and there was nothing there—no chopper—and we kind of just looked at each other and headed for cover—and all of a sudden the chopper dropped straight in from out of nowhere. The pilot must have come right up the side of the firebase. He hovered about two feet off the ground, and we all ran to climb aboard. One of the guys was having trouble getting in, so me and another guy who had our feet on the skid just grabbed him by the seat of his pants, threw him in, and piled in right behind him.

We were on the floor of the chopper, holding on to each other and the webbing of the seats as the pilot lifted off and put the pedal to the metal. We were flying over the valley below the firebase when we started taking fire, and the pilot banked hard to the right to avoid it—and everybody said, "Holy shit, look at that," because [of] the way we were tipped, we were looking straight down at fifteen or twenty NVA. They were hauling a 120 mortar. Three of them had the tube over their shoulders like a log. The rest of them were ammo bearers with mortar shells strapped to their backs. They were going down the side of a hill, like they were changing positions or something. Most of them were shooting up at us with their AK-47s. We swept right over them. . . .

Under fire from the debris below the wire, the grunts of Company B—who were to hold the perimeter until the support troops had been evacuated, then follow them out—lobbed grenades and LAWs in return, and burned out the barrels of their M60s. Captain Peters himself secured an abandoned machine gun at one point and returned fire on an enemy position marked by dust and a muzzle flash. "I picked up some little shrapnel wounds in my left hand and arm," recalled Peters, who would be awarded the Silver Star. "It was just a little sting. I didn't pay attention to it in the heat of the moment, and only later realized that I was bleeding. . . ."

The mortar fire continued throughout. Lieutenant Wallace was checking the line with his radioman, Don Colbert, when he came across one of his troops, Sp4 Andre L. Rice, sprawled out, one leg blown off, the stump cauterized. "Don't move, we'll get somebody here in a minute," said Wallace. Rice nodded. Wallace saw Chris Hinman, the company's two-tour, hard-to-control veteran, at the top of the hill, working out with an M60. "Hinman was a cocky kid," recalled Wallace. "I think he actually enjoyed running around with the bullets whizzing. I hollered that Rice was down, and Hinman got a stretcher team together ASAP."

There were so many casualties that Lieutenant Caballero's pathfinders exposed themselves not only to guide in aircraft but to load wounded aboard the evacuation Hueys. Caballero had three men on the base with him, to include his section sergeant, SSgt. Samuel Williams, a black Regular Army NCO, and two enlisted pathfinders, Cpl. Jimmy D. Howton and Pfc. William H. Kohr. At one point, Caballero and Williams came across several wounded GIs clumped together below Impact Rock. It looked as though they had been abandoned in the chaos—the nearest positions were empty, as if the troops in them had bolted for better cover—and Williams immediately began piggybacking the casualties up the hill one at a time, impervious to the incoming. "Williams was a section sergeant extraordinaire," noted Caballero. Williams, in civilian life a boxer from down south, went by the call sign Prizefighter. "He was incredibly ripped, incredibly strong," recalled pathfinder Mike Anderson. "His lips had been split, his nose crushed, and his eyebrows cut up so many times prizefighting that he was permanently scarred. A kinder soul you'd never find, though."

Williams was coming up the hill after rescuing the wounded when a mortar shell exploded directly behind him, shattering one arm and blowing a huge chunk of muscle out of the back of one of his thighs. Lieutenant Caballero jammed a towel in the thigh wound to stop the bleeding, secured a tourniquet, and packed Williams out on the next Huey. Caballero was wounded himself—superficially, in his arms and legs and hands—shortly thereafter as he continued directing aircraft in. It did not slow him down. Sergeant Rubsam of Company B helped Caballero "drive some people out of the mortar pits and onto the slicks. They were incoherent, just at the end of their rope, I suspect." In contrast, noted Rubsam, "Caballero was doing one hell of a job, man, and loving it, too. He was totally in charge, totally up to the task at hand. That's what he'd been trained for, and now he was doing it. He was completely in his element. He was just reveling in it."[1]

Captain Austin was spun around and knocked down by a mortar round while evacuating his cannoneers, catching a spray of fragments in his hip and his right armpit through the armhole of his flak jacket. It hurt so much that Austin thought he was dying, but after Doc Savoie pulled him into a bunker to attend to his injuries, he discovered that he had suffered little more than bad skin abrasions. Able to continue, Austin got all his people evacuated, then—having checked the battery area to ensure that no one had been left behind—went to report to the command group at the 155 FDC.

There were two sergeants standing at the entrance. Austin was exchanging greetings with them as he approached when he was suddenly sent flying by an explosion just behind and below him on the side of the hill leading to the FDC. He had no sooner landed than someone grabbed him by the back of his shirt, shouting, "C'mon, get up, get up, we gotta get outta here." Austin gasped that he couldn't move his legs—his right calf was shredded and the Achilles tendon in his left leg was completely blown away—then passed out. When he regained consciousness, he was on a stretcher being hustled toward a slick that was flaring to land. The litter team was moving so fast that they slammed the hefty Austin into the side of the Huey when they went to load him aboard. Trying again, they bounced him onto the cargo floor. Another litter case came sliding in next to Austin. With that, the pilot pulled pitch and banked away, thus ending Austin's forty-hour career as a combat officer after having lived the good life at Camp Eagle. For his valor, the self-confessed REMF would be awarded a Silver Star.

Lieutenant Watrous had been dusted by the debris of several near misses before he was finally put out of action by a shell that went over his head and landed behind him as he ran toward a perimeter position to call in yet another air strike on yet another target. Actually, Watrous had been putting tac air on the same set of positions on a revolving basis. "I would call in strikes on a mortar or machine gun that was firing on the choppers," he recalled. "The fire would cease, and I'd run to the other side of the base to start calling in strikes on the targets over there—and all of a sudden the enemy would be active again in the position I'd just silenced. It seemed like the fire was coming from everywhere. . . ."

The shell that landed behind Watrous knocked him unconscious. He came awake on his back, his legs bent under him. His helmet, flak jacket, and the radio on his back had absorbed most of the fragments from the waist up—the radio was demolished—but he realized after pulling his legs out from under him that he was badly hurt from the waist down. He was in excruciating pain, both legs riddled, blood flowing from a gaping hole behind his right knee. He ripped a ragged strip from his shirt to tie off the wound, then, unable to move, lay there in the open, praying he wouldn't be hit again. Watrous realized that a couple of terrified troops whom he recognized as new guys were looking at him from a nearby foxhole. "Get the hell out here and get me," he bellowed over and over, and finally they did, hastily dragging him to the TOC. Bialosuknia himself grabbed one stretcher handle as a litter team rushed his friend to the next slick that came in. "I was only a couple weeks away from rotating home," recalled Watrous, "and I was seriously worried that I wouldn't get out of there because the landing pads were completely zeroed in. I don't even know if we took any fire on the way out. I was so relieved to be on that helicopter and flying out of there that I don't remember much about the flight. . . ."

Captain Rollison's people had previously worked the area through which Company D now moved, but once-familiar terrain became unrecognizable—all craters, tattered brush, and splintered trees—as the relief column neared Company A. Rollison, on the horn with Hawkins, asked that Company A make some noise that he could guide in on. Hawkins fired three shots from his M16. Rollison asked him to fire three more shots some time later, which Hawkins did, then three more yet again. "Just follow the bodies," Hawkins said, skittish that his signal shots might also draw the enemy to his position.

There was indeed a string of enemy bodies—sixty-one by official count—and abandoned enemy equipment strewn in the blown-down jungle that led directly to Company A. Rollison was about fifty meters from linking up with Hawkins when he heard a transmission over the battalion net to the effect that the battalion operations officer had been killed and the battalion commander wounded and medevacked. Rollison's radiomen, Bruce McCorkle and Rick Rearick, looked at him, astonished. "Don't open your mouth, don't say a word," Rollison snapped, concerned about the effect it would have on the troops if they thought that effective command and control had been lost. "You didn't hear that. You didn't hear nothin' and you don't know nothin'."

Rollison didn't even tell Hawkins about Black Spade when he reached Company A's position at about 9:25 A.M. Rollison would be awarded his second Silver Star for making it to Hawkins. "I was never so glad to see anyone in my life," Hawkins later wrote, "as I was when Rollison strode—yes, strode—into our perimeter. . . ."

The survivors of Company A felt the same way. "I had chills when I saw Delta Company coming through the bushes," recalled thrice-wounded Frank Marshall. "They immediately started giving us food and water and chocolate bars and stuff. It was fantastic. I was absolutely scared shitless until they got there. . . ."

Chuck Hawkins, wounded five times, a dressing mottled with dried blood around his throat, stood up to greet Rollison: "When Black Spade told me it was you, I knew you'd get here."

"How many effectives you got?" Rollison asked.

"Maybe twenty who can still fight."

"Okay, then they'll provide security for us while we blow an LZ," Rollison said matter-of-factly. "This is lieutenant's work, Hawk. You an' me are going to have a cup of coffee."

The coffee was brewed up field style. Rollison, trying to get

Hawkins to relax, made note of his throat wound as they began sipping, and he joked, "Dang, Hawk, y'all bleedin' in the coffee."

Loosening up, Hawkins—also to be awarded the Silver Star—provided Rollison and his RTOs a glib account of the battle. Rollison, in turn, told Hawkins about having rescued Workman's company two days earlier: "Your classmate's dead, Hawk. . . ."

In contrast to Workman's benumbed troops, the Company A grunts "were still pretty alert," noted McCorkle. "They looked like they'd been in a dogfight, but they were still with it. It was obvious that they had fought hard, and fought bravely. I felt humbled. . . ."

The enemy lobbed a few mortar rounds toward the hilltop as the landing zone was being blown, but all fell short of the perimeter. In the event of a major attack on Hawkins and Rollison, General Berry had an entire battalion, Chuck Shay's 2d of the 502d, standing ready to combat-assault into the area from the main pad at Camp Eagle.

Enough trees had been blown down by 10:00 A.M. to allow a medevac to make a dangerous descent and hover low enough over jagged stumps for Hawkins's ten most serious casualties to be loaded aboard, including Rick Isom and Sp4 Harvey R. Neal of Alpha Three, who had suffered some eighteen hours with a stomach wound only to expire after making it to the evac hospital.

The work continued. By the time Lieutenant Flaherty, in charge of clearing the landing zone, had blown down almost all the trees required to allow a Huey to safely land, he reported to Rollison that he was almost out of C4. "Get out your LAWs and knock down those remaining trees," replied Rollison. Flaherty did just that. "I fired probably twenty LAWs," the platoon leader recalled. "They'd blow a nice little hole in the trunk. You'd pack it with plastic explosives and you could knock down a good-sized tree with less than a pound of C4. Normally," he explained, "you'd daisy-chain the explosives around the trunk, and it'd take ten or twelve pounds to do the job. The only problem with firing so many LAWs was that I couldn't hear a thing in my right ear for something like two weeks afterwards. I've still got a sixty percent hearing loss in that ear. That was the least of my concerns at the time, though. We were working fast. We had no idea what the hell was going on, but from the bits and pieces we were catching on the radio, it sounded like the world was coming to an end up on Ripcord. . . ."

With Lucas dead, Colonel Harrison instructed his operations officer, Major King, to take command of Ripcord. King was near the end of his tour and, doubting under the circumstances that he would survive his eleventh-hour return to combat, his knees were shaking as one of the desk sergeants helped him strap and buckle on his helmet, web gear, and flak jacket in the TOC. Calming down, King met the LOH that landed for him on the brigade pad. It was piloted by a brigade scout pilot, WO1 Steven M. Wandland, who had been pulled off an artillery-spotting mission over Ripcord. King climbed in the back. Captain Spaulding, the S3 Air, having been instructed by Harrison to take control of the extraction of Hawkins and Rollison, climbed into the seat beside Wandland. Ripcord was obscured by so much smoke and dust when Wandland arrived that Spaulding was forced to lean out of the aircraft and clear him to the ground with hand signals. "When we touched down, Jim King hopped off with a case of grenades we had thrown on board," recalled Spaulding. "It was so heavy it just about yanked his arm off and knocked him flat. I think that saved him because two or three mortar rounds hit right there just as we were lifting off. . . ."

King got on the ground at about 10:45 A.M. The evacuation was half over at that point, Lieutenant Bialosuknia having departed, as planned, with the last load of support troops—he would be awarded the Silver Star for his part in the evacuation—turning over to Lieutenant Wallace responsibility for extracting Company B.

The fire was so intense when King took over—it was officially estimated that six hundred to a thousand mortar rounds pounded the firebase during the evacuation—that he closed Ripcord to all air traffic as of 11:05 A.M. Gunships and tac air were able to operate more freely with the sky clear of lift ships. Amid the onslaught, there were numerous aerial sightings—fleeting because of the smoke blowing across the battlefield—of NVA moving up the side of Ripcord. They were coming uphill from the north and south in squads and platoons. Most were still five hundred meters or more from the perimeter, but tactical CS was dropped on a mortar that had begun lobbing rounds into the base from only two hundred meters away. The enemy was attempting to "hug" the perimeter, a classic NVA tactic to get out from under U. S. firepower, and position themselves to breach the wire when the opportunity presented itself. "There was hardly any vegetation left on the upper slopes," noted Captain House, the air mission commander. "There was just red clay and stumps and logs and debris. The enemy was in amongst that stuff. We'd roll F4s in on 'em with snake 'n nape, or Cobras, depending how close they were to the perimeter. . . ."

Major King had House resume the extraction, then shut it down again at 11:45 A.M. when Lieutenant Caballero—having just sent out his two remaining pathfinders with all the secure communications equipment on the base—advised that it was too dangerous to continue landing aircraft on the log pad in the 105 area. The Chinook that had crashed nearby was ablaze, the fuel cells ruptured by the direct hit of a mortar round. The fire had spread to the TOC, too, preventing the recovery of the radios and 81mm mortars left there by the mortar platoon when it was extracted. The twenty-five men still on the ground moved at that point to the lower tier of the firebase and set up around Impact Rock.

Major King was there, along with Captain Peters and Captain Williams, Lieutenant Caballero, Lieutenant Wallace and his radioman, Don Colbert, plus Chip Collins, Phil Tolson, who had multiple shrapnel wounds, and Chris Hinman, who had powder burns on the side of his face and a peppering of fragments in his arm and leg. A .51 round had blown up the ammo box that Hinman was feeding from as he fired cover for the slicks with his M60. The enemy was using tear gas, and clouds of the stuff drifted across the base, even as black smoke boiled from the burning Chinook. More smoke curled up from the TOC and the refueling point, which had also been set afire by the incoming, and from brushfires started in the perimeter wire by the claymores and phougas barrels that the grunts had detonated before pulling back from their fighting positions. Caballero began bringing slicks in on the POL pad, long intervals between each as the way was prepared with still more tac air and ARA. The slicks came through the smoke and banked away at top speed, door gunners firing into the smoking, burning mess below the whole time. "After I left there were 8 men left," Colbert wrote home. "Man I was scared. There were Gooks coming up the hill when I left. They were trying to shoot our chopper down. We had to leave our rucks up there plus a lot of weapons, etc. . . ."

Chip Collins went out next on the second-to-last Huey. "As we left that place, the whole goddamn bird lit up," he recalled. To prevent accidents, grunts weren't supposed to fire from helicopters, "but it was a spontaneous reaction. Everybody was firing indiscriminately at anything and everything."

The last slick departed at 12:14 P.M. It is unclear who was on board. The citations to Major King's Silver Star and Phil Tolson's Bronze Star credit them with being on the last helicopter off Ripcord. Personnel listening to the evacuation in the brigade TOC would confirm that King was the last man to get aboard that last Huey. Tolson recalls, however, that the only other passenger was a grunt, not an officer. Captain Williams, the arty LNO, remembers that there were actually six passengers and King was not one of them.

Williams described the final moments of the evacuation this way:

> By the time we were down to the last few loads, there were enemy soldiers coming up into the 105 battery area on the other side of Ripcord. I could see them with my binoculars. They were rummaging around, looking for whatever they could find. They didn't seem to be in any big hurry to get over to our side of the base, and they basically laid low after some of the infantrymen took them under fire with M60s.
>
> I was the last person to leave that firebase. They tried to get me to go on an earlier chopper, but I refused. Somebody

had to stay and coordinate the fires. I found a place where I could see everything, and called in fire until the last Huey arrived. There was a lieutenant from the infantry company [Wallace], myself, and four enlisted men on that last chopper out. He touched down, we jumped on—and we were gone in a flash, Cobras laying down fire all around us. . . .

General Berry was informed after the evacuation that Caballero was, in fact, the last man on the last slick. Caballero would concur: "Steve Wallace and I were the last two guys off that hill."

It is the vague memory of Lieutenant Wallace, however, that he went out on the last Huey not with Caballero, but with Peters:

I was pretty scared as the last of us waited to get out, but the situation wasn't overly tense. We knew they'd get us. We had good pilots. They weren't going to leave us behind. I was on what I thought was the last ship out. I thought Captain Peters was on that ship, too, but I'm not positive after so many years. What I do remember is that when I climbed aboard, I had about as much equipment as I could carry, including ammo bandoliers and rucksacks, plus my weapon and an M14 and an M60 I saw laying there. I grabbed 'em up and took 'em with me. I wasn't going to leave 'em for the NVA.

Peters tends to concur with Wallace's description of the end of the evacuation. To quote Captain Peters:

After the second-to-last helicopter got out, myself and another individual were the only people left on Ripcord. I cannot definitively remember who that other individual was. I remember that he was wearing a radio. It might have been my RTO, but I think it was probably Lieutenant Wallace. He was wearing a radio by that point, and he was the kind of officer who would have insisted on being the last to leave.

Whoever it was, we went around to all the fighting positions on the base to make sure we weren't leaving anyone.

We were hollering, "Is anyone still here, is anyone still here?" but no one answered. There was absolutely nothing going on when we called the last helicopter in—no incoming, no nothing. When the two of us disembarked at the Currahee Pad back at Camp Evans, there had been enough of a lull between our helicopter and the second-to-last helicopter that the guys thought we had been left behind. I remember there was a group of people going from helicopter to helicopter, trying to get one of the pilots to take them back to get us. . . .

Though not mentioned in any official accounts, two people—one dead, one alive—had inadvertently been left behind in the confusion of the evacuation. The dead man was Sergeant Diehl, the mortarman killed the day before; his body-bagged remains had been overlooked as they lay on a stretcher at the entrance to the TOC.

The live one was the young Kit Carson attached to the 1st Platoon of B/2-506th. The scout's GI handler, who spoke Vietnamese, had been medevacked some days earlier with a head wound. Friendless, unable to communicate with the troops being evacuated, the scout had taken refuge in a bunker, emerging only when everything went ominously quiet, the enemy shelling having petered out about the time the last Huey departed Ripcord. Luckily, a Pink Team went in to look the base over at that point; popping yellow smoke to get the Loach pilot's attention, the scout frantically waved and pointed at the Screaming Eagle patch on his shoulder so as not to be mistaken for an NVA. Harrison went down to confirm the sighting—"Roger, that's one of our boys," the brigade commander announced, thinking the man was a GI—and a request went out over the radio for a volunteer to pick up the individual. In response, CW2 Leslie R. Rush, an artillery spotter with A/377th FA, landed his LOH, and the scout scrambled aboard. Not sure who he had, Rush told his door gunner to keep an eye on the man as they headed for Camp Evans. One of the desk sergeants in the brigade TOC described the scout's escape in a letter home: "A LOH Pilot with Genitalia the size of basketballs went down to pick him up. When he gets down there he finds it[']s a Kit Carson Scout [instead of a GI] . . . He goes and picks him up[,] not knowing whether he is a VC in US fatigues or really a good guy. The Major [King] sez there would be one less Kit Carson Scout before I'd take a risk like that. . . ."

With the firebase cleared, all that remained was to evacuate Hawkins and Rollison. The effort was to be coordinated by Captain Spaulding, who, riding in the left seat of Wandland's unarmed LOH, had been buzzing around the area at treetop level since dropping off King on Ripcord, searching for those enemy positions in range to fire on the approaching and departing slicks when the extraction began. Spaulding leaned out to pitch smoke grenades directly into the positions they found. Spaulding ran out of smokes before he ran out of targets, at which point Wandland began marking them for their supporting gunships and jet fighters by hovering directly over the NVA. The scout ship took several hits in the process and, while hovering between two hills looking for more targets, was almost blown out of the sky by an RPG. "I looked out my window," recalled Spaulding, "and there were three little dudes scurrying on the side of the hill about fifty yards away. I could see 'em because most of the vegetation had been blown away. One jumped up with an RPG launcher and fired that sucker, and it looked like a damn football was coming right at us."

Spaulding screamed a warning to Wandland, who immediately pulled back on his stick so that instead of hitting the aircraft directly, the RPG skimmed underneath, creasing the aluminum—the body of the warhead touched the aircraft, the detonator in the nose did not—before exploding against the opposite hillside, showering Wandland with dirt and debris through his window. "I was so scared," Spaulding said, "it felt as though somebody had slammed me in the chest with a sledgehammer. I could barely catch my breath. That bird should not have flown—we saw the crease and realized the stabilizer bar was barely hanging on when we shut down on the brigade pad—but we managed to make it back to Camp Evans."

Spaulding and Wandland immediately went airborne again in another LOH. More targets were marked, more hits received. The AK rounds did little damage, but the aircraft finally came under .51 fire from underneath, "and, hell, each hit would move the Loach up five or six inches," recounted Spaulding. "All the warning lights started flashing, and we lost hydraulics. The aircraft wouldn't go forward. Wandland had to fly sideways all the way back to the brigade pad. He shut it down and we frantically unstrapped our seat belts and unplugged our radio helmets, and ran like hell to get away from the thing in case it exploded." Instead of exploding, Spaulding noted, "the whole damn aircraft started wobbling and shaking on the pad, and the tail boom came apart from the main body. . . ."

Spaulding and Wandland were back up in a third LOH when the extraction of Hawkins and Rollison began at 1 P.M. It took half an hour to get Company A out, House's slicks having to once again hover straight down a 150-foot mine shaft that had been blown in the jungle. Until all the dead had been evacuated, the aircraft load for each slick was two body bags and four troops. Rollison's people were to follow Hawkins out, but the extraction of Company D had no sooner begun than three Hueys took hits in rapid succession from a .51 caliber that began firing from a distance of a hundred meters and enemy soldiers who had moved in as close as thirty-five meters on the north side of the LZ. Spaulding and Wandland went back into action, taking more hits as they marked targets for the Cobras, which splintered the trees all around Company D. The enemy fire petered out as the extraction continued. Spaulding and Wandland would both be decorated with the Silver Star. "I expected their LOH to be shot down at any moment," recalled Blair Case, who observed the action from Harrison's C&C. "It seems like a miracle that they survived. In my mind, Spaulding and Wandland are the real heroes of the evacuation of Ripcord."

Captain Rollison went out on the third-to-last ship, turning over the last two loads to Lieutenant Flaherty, who said to his platoon sergeant, George Strasburg, as the next Huey hovered into the LZ: "Go ahead, George, I'll go on the last ship."

"No, L. T., you go," said Strasburg. "I'll get the last load out."

Flaherty climbed aboard the second-to-last slick, and

Sergeant Strasburg and the last few grunts followed him on the last Huey. The evacuation was thus completed at 2:07 P.M., arty being called shortly on the friendly and enemy equipment piled up on the LZ.

Major Davis and other members of the battalion staff greeted Peters, Hawkins, and Rollison as they touched down in their turn on the Currahee pad. It was a mob scene on the pad, troops cheering as each new load came in, first sergeants hugging company commanders and slapping platoon leaders on the back. The men were delirious with relief.

It all came crashing down for Rollison, though, when informed that Lucas had died of his injuries. "Rollison loved Colonel Lucas," said Flaherty. "He was absolutely devastated by the news of his death. He came up to me when I landed, and said, 'The Spade is dead,' and broke down right there on the pad. He cried and cried and cried. We all cried. . . ."

Once all the troops were out, it was open season on the enemy. Unable to keep track of the call signs of all the jet fighters stacked up over the area, Spaulding finally announced over the radio: "It's like a barber shop, guys—everybody get a number and get in line. You know who you are. When I say 'Next,' you pop on the line and tell me what ordnance you got and I'll tell you where to put it."

The aircraft rolled in one after the other. "Okay, Sortie Six," said Spaulding, "you'll take care of that .51 we've got marked with purple smoke on the south slope of Hill 805."

The pilot rogered that and rolled in. "Sortie Seven," Spaulding continued, "once you see Sortie Six's hit, move a couple hundred meters to the east—and just let 'em fly."

"Any specific target?" the pilot asked.

"Hell, they're all over down there. Don't worry about it. Wherever you put your bombs, you're gonna hit somebody."

Most of the jets dropped two bombs at a time. One pilot reported that he did not have enough fuel to make repeated passes. "Well, just drop the whole damn load at once," said Spaulding, who would recall "watching something like twenty-six bombs flying towards the target as the jet pulled out of its dive. The whole damn side of the mountain erupted, and I thought, take that, you little shits."

By the time Berry and Harrison broke station after nine hours in the air, Ripcord itself was being bombed. "The last view I had of Ripcord," noted Case, "was of jets streaking toward it and geysers of debris erupting from the top of the base as the bombs exploded. . . ."

Major Little directed the air strikes on the firebase from his little Bird Dog, assisted by Lieutenant McCall, who had gone airborne with the FAC because Little had specific orders to destroy the TOC and McCall knew the exact layout of Ripcord. There was some concern at division that certain sensitive items that should have been evacuated or destroyed might have been left behind in the operations center. "To make sure the enemy didn't secure any such items, "we put marking rockets right into the TOC door," noted McCall. After the operations center had been bombed, Little and McCall marked other key targets for destruction, including the howitzers on top of the firebase. Little would pull up to make way for the jets, "then we'd come back down after each strike to do a bomb damage assessment and make sure the bombs had landed where we wanted them," explained McCall. "It was like a roller-coaster ride. One thing that confused us was that we could see footprints in the dust that had settled across the firebase from the air strikes. We were getting right down on the deck, and could see footprints going from one position to another inside the perimeter. We called back to confirm that there were no friendlies still on the ground, and were told that everyone had been accounted for and to continue the mission." It was McCall's impression that the enemy, having breached the perimeter wire, was hiding in the bunkers that had just been evacuated. "I think every time we rolled in hot, they would take cover, so we never actually saw anybody. But there was definitely evidence that somebody was running around up there, and more than one. . . ."

Epilogue

General Berry conducted an awards ceremony two days after the evacuation, presenting Silver Stars to Colonel Harrison and a dozen officers and men from the 2-506th Infantry. Pinning the medal to Harrison's pocket, Berry called the evacuation "the most brilliantly planned and executed airmobile operation of the war."

Concerned about morale, Berry spent considerable time talking with men from the 2-501st and 2-506th Infantry. Berry did his best to present the battle as a victory. The 155mm battery on the firebase had been able to inflict such damage on the enemy's supply lines, said Berry, that the NVA had been forced to move an entire division into the area to neutralize Ripcord. By concentrating around a fixed point, the enemy had exposed himself to massed firepower and had suffered heavy casualties. Though division had been restrained by political considerations from bringing in the ground forces that would have been required to push the enemy back, the 2-506th had bravely held out as long as possible in order to maximize the enemy's losses before being evacuated from Ripcord. In conclusion, Berry assured the troops that operations were even then being planned to strike into the supply areas of the enemy units that had besieged Ripcord.

Many officers were impressed with the concern that Berry showed during his visits. The grunts were not of the same mind. "We had a formation where Berry tried to give the troops a pep talk," recalled Chaplain Fox of the 2-506th Infantry. "The troops didn't receive him very well. There was a lot of anger from the troops at that time."

As the grunts saw it, they had been used as bait, then left hanging when the enemy closed around Ripcord. "Nobody had a clear perception of the big picture," said Fox, "but the one thing many people were angry about was that they didn't feel that we had gotten the support from higher-higher that we should have." In response, numerous troops threatened to refuse to return to the field as the battalion got organized for its next operation. Fox had "a lot of conversations with guys, trying to keep them out of court. It took some work, but most did go back out with their units. All most of them had needed was a little time to get it back together."

During one of Berry's visits, he discussed with Harrison the subject of a posthumous award for Lucas. Harrison suggested the Distinguished Service Cross. "Berry asked if I didn't think Lucas was more deserving of the Medal of Honor," wrote Harrison. "I said yes, but wasn't sure we could make that kind of case." Lucas had not been involved in any action that in itself merited the nation's highest award for valor. "Berry nevertheless said he wanted to make the effort," noted Harrison, "and would base the recommendation on Lucas's sustained gallantry over an extended period." Berry wrote home at that time, "Over the entire 23 day spasm of Ripcord that I observed, Lucas was magnificent. He was utterly and courageously devoted to his mission and his men. I don't know why he wasn't killed much earlier. Medal of Honor recommendations take a long time to go all the way, but I believe this one will make it."

It did. Lucas became the only infantry officer above the rank of captain and one of only two battalion commanders—the other was an artillery officer—to be awarded the Medal of Honor during the Vietnam War.

The award was a matter of considerable controversy, best summed up by a squad leader who remarked that "Lucas's handling of the battle was a fiasco. He got his people in bad situations and didn't know what to do. It was the kind of situation where if he had lived, he probably would have been brought up on charges, but since he got killed, he ended up with the Medal of Honor."

Hawkins and Rollison thought that Lucas richly deserved the Medal of Honor. Herb Koenigsbauer agreed, writing that the criticism of Lucas was "rooted in frustration with an unpopular war and an assessment of tactics by junior persons who did not have the information required to arrive at such stinging conclusions about Lucas." Harrison believed that Berry, in seeking the Medal of Honor for Lucas, meant to do more than recognize his courage; Berry also meant the award to be a "tribute to all the soldiers involved in Ripcord," wrote Harrison, "a way to let the world know that something big and important had happened there."

Something big indeed had happened at Ripcord. The Screaming Eagles had lost 74 KIA and more than 400 WIA during the fighting of July 1–23, 1970. Military spokesmen released to the press the figure of 61 U. S. KIA, making the losses appear smaller than they actually were while also avoiding a scandal by failing to note the 13 MIAs who remained on and around Firebase Ripcord.

Enemy losses are unknown. The 101st did not inflate body counts. The approximately 125 NVA kills that appear in the journals of the units involved in the siege reflect only those physically counted by the Screaming Eagles. The communists undoubtedly lost many more men, given the sheer weight of the firepower employed during the battle and in the week after the evacuation as likely routes of withdrawal from the area were subjected to a relentless round-robin of artillery fire, air strikes, and Arc Lights. Berry told the troops during his visits that "a conservative estimate of the number of NVA killed is over 500."

Operation Chicago Peak finally commenced on July 25 when Chuck Shay's 2d of the 502d opened FSB Maureen east of Co Pung Mountain while under the operational control of the 1st Brigade, 101st Airborne. After artillery had been airlifted to Maureen, elements of the 1st ARVN Infantry Division combat-assaulted onto Co Pung on July 30. After some initial resistance, the enemy faded away, choosing not to defend Co Pung by direct action but by launching a diversionary offensive against FSB O'Reilly. The offensive was initiated on August 6 by the 6th NVA Regiment. The other regiment that had participated in the Ripcord siege, the 803d, was not involved in the O'Reilly action, having withdrawn into the mountains to refit due to the casualties it had suffered at Ripcord.

General Hennessey, back from his leave, terminated Chicago Peak on August 12 to allow the ARVN to concentrate on defending O'Reilly. Thus between Ripcord and O'Reilly did the communists blunt the big summer offensive. One division-level report referred to Chicago Peak as a "moderate success," noting that the "operation netted 97 enemy killed and 32 enemy weapons captured; however, no major cache sites or logistical facilities were discovered."

Harrison, meanwhile, was anxious to return to the Ripcord area to recover his MIAs. There seemed no point in risking troops to search for the C/2-506th GI lost on Hill 902, or the two bodies from D/2-506th left on Hill 1000. All three men had apparently been blown to bits during the battle. Harrison instead combat-assaulted his brigade recon platoon into the area of D/1-506th's fight on August 3, the surrounding high ground having been secured by Livingston's 2-501st Infantry. The body of the medic who had tried to escape on a helicopter skid was never found. The other eight MIAs from D/1-506th were zipped into body bags and evacuated aboard Harrison's C&C Huey. "The odor was overwhelming," wrote Harrison. "We had difficulty flying and not throwing up."

Because of bad weather, three weeks passed before Harrison was able to launch a "body-snatch" mission to recover the remains of the D/2-506th mortarman left behind during the evacuation of Ripcord. The firebase was by then unrecognizable, having been turned upside down by air strikes. After Livingston's battalion again secured various strategic points in the area, a LOH from the brigade aviation platoon, covered by a team of gunships, touched down on Ripcord on the morning of August 27. The mortarman's body bag was loaded aboard, but the LOH took fire on takeoff and burst into flames upon crash-landing back on Ripcord. An element from B/2-501st marched to Ripcord and secured the crash site long enough for another helicopter to dart in to recover the body and the crew of the LOH. The aerorifle platoon from B/2-17th Cav landed on Ripcord the next day to prepare the LOH for extraction. That accomplished, the 2-501st Infantry was withdrawn on August 29.

Colonel Harrison, meanwhile, had launched a major operation that was connected emotionally if not physically with Ripcord. The operation began when Chuck Shay's 2d of the 502d was placed under 3d Brigade control and inserted on August 13 into landing zones around FSB Barnett, a U. S.–ARVN position overlooking the Khe Ta Laou river valley from a mountaintop fourteen kilometers northwest of FSB O'Reilly in Quang Tri Province. Division intelligence had determined that the narrow valley and the hills rising along it were honeycombed with bunker complexes that served as way stations for enemy troops and supplies moving across the border from Laos. The jungle-covered hills also sheltered a high-level NVA command group suspected to have orchestrated the siege of Ripcord before turning its attention to FSB O'Reilly.

Shay's battalion was in contact from the moment it hit the ground in the Barnett AO. On the second day of the operation, A/2-502d found a hilltop dotted with 150 bunkers and fighting positions; a typewriter and mimeograph machine uncovered in one of the bunkers identified the complex as a North Vietnamese CP.

On the third day, August 15, B/2-502d had a contact west of Barnett in which an enemy soldier was killed and a bamboo bridge spanning a mountain stream was destroyed by ARA. Shay reinforced Company B with a platoon from D/2-502d. The enemy mortared the combined force after sundown, then launched repeated ground attacks against it from midnight to dawn on August 16. The combined force lost one dead and seventeen wounded. The enemy left thirty-four bodies around the NDP.

Shay combat-assaulted C/2-502d that morning into a hot LZ half a klick west of Company B. One enemy soldier was killed, another captured. Pushing out from its embattled position, Company B found a nearby bunker complex guarded by an enemy soldier who lay dead beside his RPD thanks to the prep fires. Commo wire ran into the jungle from the complex.

Surgical equipment and bloody bandages were found in a bunker that had been used as an aid station; a pair of binoculars and a map were discovered amid the rice, rucksacks, and ammunition in the other bunkers. The map was whisked to brigade, then forwarded to division intelligence.

Shay requested that the map be returned, unsatisfied with what division had been able to glean from it. "We initially didn't read the map too well ourselves," said Shay; unlike U. S. maps, which were divided into one-kilometer grids, the enemy's French-made map had two-kilometer grids. "Harrison got the map back for me," said Shay, "and in my flying around, I finally picked up a physical point—the intersection of two streams—that I was able to identify on both my map and the enemy map." As various way stations were marked on the enemy map, "we just went from there," noted Shay, "and were very successful in rooting out the NVA."

On the sixth day of the operation, Company B seized another bunker complex, then followed the commo wire snaking from it to a four-lane trail. Company B spotted an NVA unit moving up a partially denuded hill the next morning, August 19, and called in tac air and ARA before launching a ground assault. One enemy soldier was captured and twenty-five were killed in the battle; a plethora of weapons and equipment was policed up, including a field radio and an 82mm mortar. The action had been nose to nose. The lead platoon had been nearing the top of the hill when the NVA had begun firing AK-47s and throwing grenades from a cluster of bunkers that had survived the air strikes. Private First Class Frank R. Fratellenico crawled close enough to the nearest bunker to toss fragmentation grenades through the firing port, killing the five enemy soldiers inside. Fratellenico was advancing on the next bunker when he caught an RPD burst in his chest; knocked to the ground, he dropped the grenade whose pin he had just pulled, but reached out, grabbed it, and pulled it in under his chest before it could explode and injure his fellow GIs. Killed by the blast, Fratellenico was posthumously awarded the Medal of Honor.

Eight enemy soldiers were killed when Companies A and D established numerous ambushes around Hill 848, a major terrain feature two klicks south of FSB Barnett. The 2-502d

Infantry suffered five KIA and sixty-four WIA during the Barnett operation, but it took two prisoners and, in combination with its supporting arms, killed eighty-four NVA before being extracted on August 30.

Although the Barnett operation did considerable damage to the enemy, the pressure nevertheless continued to mount against O'Reilly as the communists reinforced the 6th NVA Regiment with the 9th and 29th. While the base itself was subjected to 82mm and 120mm mortar fire, the ARVN units operating in the area came under repeated ground attack. Approximately forty ARVN were killed, as was an Australian advisor. The enemy's casualties were far worse thanks to the 2-17th Cavalry, the 4-77th Aerial Rocket Artillery, and the U. S. Air Force, which provided such overwhelming fire support to the ARVN as to turn the hills around O'Reilly into a North Vietnamese killing ground. The ARVN claimed to have found nearly five hundred enemy bodies before the approaching monsoon necessitated the evacuation of FSB O'Reilly on October 7.

Though the success of the Barnett operation had not been total, it had been satisfying. "The Barnett operation was basically a continuation of the Ripcord battle under terms that were more favorable to us," noted Shay. "The decision to withdraw from Ripcord had been the right move. Harrison had gotten a tiger by the tail during the siege, though, and he didn't let go. He was a bloodhound. He kept his eye on the intelligence picture until he thought he had found the headquarters element responsible for the siege. We had a good intelligence briefing before we went into the Barnett area, and Harrison was relentless in ensuring that we received timely intelligence during the operation itself." The results spoke for themselves. Shay would remark that "Ben Harrison can rest in peace knowing that we made the enemy headquarters that had controlled the siege pay dearly for Ripcord."

The relationship between Berry and Harrison, already tense, became increasingly strained in the weeks following the evacuation of Ripcord. Berry was actually dissatisfied with the performance of all three brigade commanders, writing home that "they are all failing the real test of effectively using their supporting fires in combat."

If Berry found all the brigade commanders wanting, he focused his ire most severely on Harrison, given that the 3d Brigade's area of operations was the most active and thus the most critical sector in the entire 101st AO. "Berry critically questioned everything that I and my staff did," noted Harrison. "He picked on my briefers, apparently trying to trip them up. He told me that my standards were too low and that I tolerated incompetence on my staff."

Berry took Harrison aside after one briefing. "You're not mean enough to be a brigade commander," he said.

"I'm tough," Harrison replied in his defense, "but I never expect to be mean."

While still serving as the acting division commander, Berry dispatched Brig. Gen. Olin E. Smith, assistant division commander for support, to Camp Evans with instructions to closely inspect the base, for which Harrison had responsibility, as well as the rear areas of all the 3d Brigade units stationed there. Before reporting back to Berry, Smith told Harrison that he had uncovered nothing significant. "Watch yourself, though," Smith said. "General Berry is after you." Smith assured Harrison, "You have nothing to worry about from me. I'm just like Allstate," he said, cupping his hands together in a parody of the insurance company's advertisement. "Your career is in good hands." Smith then opened his hands, exclaiming to an unamused Harrison, "Oops!"

Berry informed Harrison shortly after Hennessey's return that he had requested that the general relieve him of command. Berry handed Harrison a copy of a letter he had prepared for Hennessey on the subject, along with a draft efficiency report. "Berry criticized me in the draft for tolerating a weak staff," recalled Harrison. "He stated further that I had extensive aviation experience, but was lacking infantry experience and was poor at fire-support coordination. All the numerical ratings were at the bottom or next to the bottom."

Shocked and depressed, Harrison lay awake in his quarters

that night until three in the morning. Harrison was able to get to sleep only after destroying the letter and draft efficiency report, thinking that no purpose would be served by dwelling on them. Harrison respected Berry's combat record but thought that the general had come to a wrongheaded conclusion about his own abilities. "I concluded that I was doing a very good job as a brigade commander," he wrote, "and that I should simply go on doing my job and not spend any more time worrying about getting fired."

General Hennessey visited Harrison the next morning. "Do you know that Sid Berry wants me to relieve you?" Hennessey asked.

"Yes, sir, he told me in person and in writing."

"I'm not going to relieve you," Hennessey said, "but you've got a problem. I have confidence in you. Berry doesn't. I'm not going to change his mind. That's your problem. You'll have to do it."

Harrison had plenty of opportunity to do so as Berry continued to visit the 3d Brigade every day for what Harrison referred to as "my daily ass-chewing." Berry began to ease off a bit near the end of Harrison's command tour, at which point Hennessey told Harrison, "Ben, I think Sid is comfortable with you now. He has never said he was wrong, and I don't think he ever will, but you are doing okay."

Harrison turned his brigade over to Dave Grange in December and was reassigned as senior advisor, 1st ARVN Infantry Division.

Harrison worked with Berry again at Khe Sanh during Operation Lam Son 719. Their relationship became much improved at that time, Berry expressing admiration for the job that Harrison was doing not only with his counterpart but also as de facto senior advisor for the ARVN Airborne Division and I Corps Forward. Berry's own performance during the ill-fated incursion was one of the war's great examples of general-officer leadership; by exposing himself daily to heavy antiaircraft fire over Laos and working tirelessly to coordinate activities between various U. S. and ARVN commands, Berry was able to impose a semblance of control over an operation badly mismanaged otherwise by I Corps, XXIV Corps, and MACV.

That a rapprochement was possible between Berry and Harrison had not seemed likely when Harrison left the Screaming Eagles. Hennessey had given Harrison top marks in his efficiency report, recommending him for promotion to general officer. He also noted: "Colonel Harrison had the most demanding command tour of any brigade commander in this Division for the past six months. He did a great job. He spent more time on the ground with his platoons and companies than anyone else. He had less [*sic*] problems in the rear areas than anyone else. I would have kept him in command for a full year were it not for the fact that he had been previously selected to become the senior advisor to the 1st ARVN [Infantry] Division—a job I hold more important, at this time, to the 101st Airborne Division and the United States Army."

Berry, on the other hand, described Harrison as a middle-of-the-road officer who, barely competent when he took command, had gradually grown into the job. Berry added insult to the injury of his efficiency report during the change-of-command ceremony in which the brigade guidon was passed from Harrison to Grange. Battalion and brigade commanders in Vietnam customarily received the Legion of Merit at the end of their command tours, in addition to an almost routine "package" of valor awards. Berry, however, presented only a single decoration to Harrison during the change-of-command ceremony. It was not a Legion of Merit. Nor was it a Bronze Star. To save face, even commanders who had been relieved for cause were usually presented with one or the other on their way out the door. For his six months of combat command, Harrison instead received the Army Commendation Medal (ARCOM), the lowest award then available and one normally reserved for junior enlisted men. "I was flabbergasted," recalled Harrison. "No one from division had informed me before the ceremony that I would be receiving an ARCOM. There should have been some explanation or discussion. To me, the medal was a cheap shot."

* * *

Before assuming command from Harrison, Colonel Grange went on leave to Hong Kong. While there, he and his wife visited a department store operated by the Chinese communist government that sold antiques from the mainland. Grange had expected the red banners and communist slogans with which the store was decorated. He had not expected to be confronted with a lavish window display devoted to the Battle for Firebase Ripcord. The display featured a series of photographs taken by enemy cameramen of the destroyed howitzers atop the base, as well as shots of abandoned, bombed-out Ripcord itself. The accompanying text described how the imperialist aggressors had been put to flight at Ripcord by the People's Army of Vietnam. "It was interesting," said Grange, "but it also rankled the hell out of me to see that."

Most participants in the battle would come to view Berry's decision as both militarily and politically sound. To credit Berry with making the right decision, however, is by implication to cast doubt on the original plan to open Ripcord. "The decision to evacuate," wrote Chris Straub, "confirms my view that from the start the 101st's push into the Ripcord AO was not in consonance with what the U. S. was trying to accomplish in Vietnam in 1970."

Chuck Hawkins would write that he didn't understand "why we didn't use the advantage of our airmobility to keep the enemy off balance. We could have choppered into Ripcord, built a base, waited for signs of enemy activity, then choppered over to the next mountain to continue harassing their lines of communication with artillery fire. Can you imagine the effort the bad guys put into preparing for the Ripcord siege? What if they had to do that all over again in order to ring the next mountaintop we occupied?"

Ripcord's establishment as a hardened, semipermanent bastion in enemy territory implies, as was speculated at the time, that division wanted to draw the NVA into a showdown. That division would want to do so perplexed Straub. "The people down in Saigon were biting their nails every night, wondering who was going to get involved in the next Hamburger Hill," he reflected. "So why the mix-up? Why did the 101st commit itself to a grandiose operation out on the edge of the A Shau

Valley, an area that was obviously home to a lot of NVA, if the division leadership was aware that once they'd taken a certain number of casualties, they'd have to pull out because of pressure from MACV and USARV?"

Herb Koenigsbauer would be unable to talk about Ripcord without becoming emotional. Lucas and Koenigsbauer had both been under the impression that division was committed to a major battle when it tasked the Currahees with opening Ripcord. "It never occurred to me that the will did not exist to engage the enemy and destroy him once the battle was joined," said Koenigsbauer. "Lucas and I made repeated requests that division commit additional forces to the action. We had fixed a sizable enemy force around Ripcord. We were at the peak of good weather for using our helicopters and air support. There were no other significant actions in the division to divert resources away from Ripcord. If division was going to react, we said, now was the time. The opportunity was there to hurt the enemy, but higher command was not prepared to follow through and do what was required to win the battle, and I must admit to a certain sense of disillusionment that after all the sacrifices that had been made to take and hold Ripcord, we just turned around and gave it back to the North Vietnamese."

Koenigsbauer's analysis of the battle continued in writing: "I cannot reconcile in my mind that the chain of command could not foresee the impact the opening of Ripcord would have on the NVA. The potential for a major enemy response must have been realized at the highest levels. If the political climate was so clear to the people above battalion and brigade that evacuation was the only viable option when the enemy massed around the firebase, it makes no sense that the battalion was ever committed to taking Ripcord. There had been no change in the political situation from the time we were ordered to take Ripcord and the time we were ordered to evacuate. To write Ripcord off made clear to those of us fighting the war that there was no national commitment to fight and win. I respect General Berry as a professional soldier, and hindsight tells us that his assessment of the situation was absolutely correct. The evacuation saved U. S. lives, but it was also one more step towards our tactical, operational, and strategic defeat in Vietnam."

* * *

In the months that followed the evacuation, General Berry would have his command-ship pilot, John Fox, circle the demolished base whenever their flights from one firebase to another took them through the area. Berry would stare down at the battlefield with sulfurous eyes, studying the cratered brown lump that had been Ripcord and the scarred hilltops around it. "He might have been evaluating the battle in professional terms," recalled Fox, "but what I really think he was doing was grieving. You could tell that he was in pain over what had happened. It weighed on his mind for a long time that we'd had to pull out of Ripcord. He wouldn't say anything as he looked out the helicopter window, and, finally, he would just give me a quick hand signal to continue on."

Appendices

Appendix A

Killed in Action, Battle for Firebase Ripcord, Thua Thien Province, Republic of Vietnam

July 2, 1970
Capt. Thomas T. Hewitt (C/2-506th)
Sgt. Thomas H. Herndon (C/2-506th)
Sgt. Lee N. Lenz (C/2-506th)
Sp4 Roger D. Sumrall (C/2-506th)
Sp4 Robert P. Radcliffe, Jr. (C/2-506th)
Sp4 Robert W. Zoller II (C/2-506th)
Pfc. Richard J. Conrardy (C/2-506th)
Pfc. Stephen J. Harber (C/2-506th)*
July 3, 1970
Pfc. Robert S. Utecht (B/2-506th)
July 4, 1970
1st Lt. William L. Sullivan (C/2-501st)
Pfc. Carl L. Mickens (C/2-501st)
Pfc. William C. Ray (58th Scout Dog Plt, 101st AbnDiv)
Pfc. Jimmie L. Robinson (C/2-501st)
Pfc. Gary D. Thaden (C/2-501st)

*Killed in action/body not recovered (KIA/BNR)

July 5, 1970

Sp4 Michael K. Waymire (C/2-501st)

July 7, 1970

Sp4 Lewis Howard, Jr. (D/2-506th)*
Sp4 Gerald L. Risinger (C/2-506th)
Pfc. Charles E. Beals (D/2-506th)*
Pfc. Michael J. Grimm (D/2-506th)

July 8, 1970

Sp4 James E. Hupp (C/2-506th)
Pfc. Rickey L. Scott (C/2-506th)

July 9, 1970

Sp4 Terry E. Williams (E/2-501st)

July 10, 1970

Sp4 Fredrick C. Raymond (A/2-11th FA)
Pfc. Patrick J. Bohan (Pathfinder Plt, 101st AbnDiv)
Pfc. Victor L. De Foor (B/2-506th)
Pfc. Larry J. Plett (B/2-319th FA) (DOW† July 20, 1970)

July 14, 1970

1st Lt. Terry A. Palm (D/2-501st)
SSgt. James T. Hembree, Jr. (D/2-501st)
Sgt. William E. Jones (D/2-501st)
Sp4 Paul G. Guimond (D/2-501st)
Sp4 Dennis W. Huffine (B/2-501st)
Sp4 John L. Keister (D/2-501st)
Pfc. Keith E. Utter (D/2-501st)

July 15, 1970

Sp4 Gary L. Schneider (D/2-501st)

July 16, 1970

Pfc. Richard R. Timmons (A/2-501st)

July 17, 1970

Sp4 David R. Beyl (D/2-501st) (DOW July 18, 1970)
Sp4 Wilfred W. Warner (D/2-501st) (DOW July 23, 1970)

*Killed in action/body not recovered (KIA/BNR)
†Died of wounds.

July 18, 1970
Sp4 Michael A. Walker (A/159th AvnBn)
Sp4 William D. Rollason (E/2-501st)
Pfc. Burke H. Miller (A/2-11th FA)

July 20, 1970
Sp4 Durl G. Calhoun (B/326th EngBn)
Sp4 Dennis F. Fisher (B/326th EngBn)
Sp4 Eloy R. Valle (D/1-506th)
Pfc. Bill G. Browning (D/1-506th)
Pfc. Patrick T. DeWulf (D/1-506th)
Pfc. John C. Knott (D/1-506th)

July 21, 1970
Capt. Donald R. Workman (D/1-506th)
1st Lt. James R. Kalsu (A/2-11th FA)
Sp4 Roberto C. Flores (B/2-506th)
Sp4 David E. Johnson (A/2-11th FA)
Sp4 Brent R. Law (Air Ambulance Plt, HHC/326th MedBn)
Pfc. Frank L. Asher (D/1-506th)
Pfc. Robert B. Hays (D/1-506th)
Pfc. Peter P. Huk (D/1-506th)
Pfc. Francis E. Maune (B/2-506th)
Pfc. Larry J. McDowell (B/2-506th) (DOW July 27, 1970)
Pfc. Ronald J. Kuntz (D/1-506th)* (pseudonym)

July 22, 1970
1st Lt. William A. Pahissa (A/2-506th)
2d Lt. Steven A. Olson (A/2-506th)
Sfc. Pham Van Long (ARVN Interpreter, A/2-506th)
SSgt. Gerald B. Singleton (A/2-506th)
Sgt. Stanley G. Diehl (D/2-506th)
Sgt. John W. Kreckel (A/2-506th)
Sp4 Mark G. Draper (A/2-506th)
Sp4 Harvey R. Neal (A/2-506th) (DOW July 27, 1970)
Sp4 Robert M. Journell III (A/2-506th)
Sp4 Thomas R. Schultz (A/2-506th)
Sp4 Donald J. Severson (A/2-506th)
Pfc. John M. Babich (A/2-506th)
Pfc. Virgil M. Bixby (A/2-506th)
Pfc. Robert J. Brown (A/2-506th)
Pfc. Danny J. Fries (A/2-506th)

July 23, 1970

Lt. Col. Andre C. Lucas (HHC/2-506th)
Maj. Kenneth P. Tanner (HHC/2-506th)
Pfc. Gus Allen (A/2-506th)

Appendix B

Veterans of Firebase Ripcord

101st Airborne Division

Major General Wright retired with three stars and **Major General Hennessey** with four. **Brigadier General Berry** commanded the 101st at Fort Campbell after getting his second star and was appointed Superintendent of the U. S. Military Academy after getting his third. His upward trajectory did not survive the cheating scandal that embarrassed West Point during his watch or his own opposition to the integration of women into the corps of cadets; instead of becoming Chief of Staff, he retired with three stars after commanding a corps in Germany. He now lives with his wife in Arlington, Virginia. **Lieutenant Colonel Dyke** retired with three stars and is now a business executive in McLean, Virginia. **Lieutenant Colonel Young** was killed in a commercial airline crash after the war. **Lieutenant Fox** retired a major with twenty-six years of enlisted, warrant, and commissioned service and lives with his wife in Atlanta, Texas.

3d Brigade, 101st Airborne Division

Colonel Bradley retired with his wife to St. Petersburg, Florida, where he embarked on a successful career in commercial real estate. **Colonel Harrison** retired with two stars and lives with his wife in Belton, Texas. **Major Turner** retired as a colonel to Williamsburg, Virginia. **Captain Spaulding** had nine years enlisted and five years commissioned service when he was offered the choice of converting to E8 or facing the infamous reduction in force in 1972; he chose to get out and went on full-time duty with the National Guard and reserves before being recalled to active duty. He retired as a lieutenant colonel in 1987 and now lives with his wife in Indianapolis, Indiana. **Lieutenant Case** is now editor of an official military publication *(Air Defense Artillery Magazine)* and lives in El Paso, Texas.

2d Battalion, 506th Infantry

Lieutenant Colonel Lucas was buried at Arlington National Cemetery, his headstone bearing an engraved facsimile of his Medal of Honor. **Major Koenigsbauer** retired as a colonel and lives with his wife in Colchester, Vermont. **Captain Fox** is still with the woman he married before the war. The father of one, he is a Baptist minister in Aurora, Colorado. **Captain Harris** lives with his wife and three children and is a surgeon in Worthington, Minnesota. **Captain Lieb** left the service a major with two graduate degrees and is now a business executive in Green Bay, Wisconsin. **Captain Ray Williams** was caught in the 1972 reduction in force and is now a supervisor with the U. S. Postal Service; he lives with his wife in Washington, West Virginia. **Lieutenant Bialosuknia** was married before the war; still married and the father of three, he is an account executive with IBM and lives in Salt Point, New York. **Lieutenant Edwards** went to medical school after the war and was a surgeon at Walter Reed Army Hospital before retiring a colonel; he is now a staff surgeon at the University of Florida. **Lieutenant Watrous** was medically discharged and wears a brace on his right leg because of his wounds; married and the father of one during the war, he is still married, is now the father of two, and works in a small bank in his hometown of Groton, New York. **Jon Penfold**, the father of two grown sons, is a high-school teacher and wrestling coach and lives with his wife in Greeley, Colorado. **Danny Thompson** has a 100 percent service-connected disability; now divorced and retired from his job as a vehicle supervisor with a lumber company, he lives in Weymouth, Massachusetts.

Company A, 2-506th Infantry

Captain Hawkins and his first wife divorced and he left active-duty service after the war; retired from the reserves as a major, he now travels extensively as an international defense and military operations analyst and lives with his second wife in northern Virginia. **Lieutenant Noll** returned to teaching after the war and married his high-school sweetheart; they have five children, two adopted children, and a Vietnamese foster child. A colonel in the reserves, he commanded a psychological warfare battalion in Operation Desert Storm. He lives in Forrest Lake, Minnesota. **Lieutenant Widjeskog** is a wildlife biologist with the New Jersey Division of Fish, Game, and Wildlife. The father of two grown children, he lives with his wife in Rosenhayn, New Jersey. **Martin Glennon** is an insurance agent and lay minister; he lives with his wife and eight children in Valparaiso, Indiana. **Rick Isom** is confined to a wheelchair because of his wounds, and his marriage broke up under the physical and emotional strain. Eventually coming to terms with his new life, he completed his college education, competed internationally with the U. S. Disabled Ski Team, and is now remarried and working for the U. S. Forest Service doing community development work; he lives in Austin, Colorado. **Frank Marshall**, a real-estate agent, lives in Bensalem, Pennsylvania.

Company B, 2-506th Infantry

Captain Peters returned to the enlisted ranks thanks to the 1972 reduction in force, retired as an E6 after twenty years of enlisted and commissioned service (he was later advanced to captain on the retirement rolls, his highest-held rank), and is now a supervisor with the U. S. Postal Service; he lives with his wife in Lynn Haven, Florida. **Captain Bill Williams** spent nine months in hospitals having his jaw rebuilt after being medevacked from Ripcord; he was medically retired as a major a year later, diagnosed with migraines and psychomotor epilepsy as a result of his crushed skull. He married after the war and is the father of two children, who both followed him into the army; he lives with his wife in Lake George, Colorado. **Lieutenant Wallace** extended his tour to serve with the Special Forces, only to be seriously wounded in December 1970; medically retired, he went back to school and is now a lawyer in Chesterfield, South Carolina. **Don Colbert** married shortly after the war and is now the father of four; he is a self-employed flooring mechanic living in Troy, Missouri. **Chip Collins** was divorced twice after the war; he got a degree in social work and has worked as a coal miner, social worker, and human-rights advocate with the Department of Mental Health. He now lives in Birchleaf, Virginia. **Bob Judd** married and divorced after the war; a worker at a jet-engine casting factory since the war, he lives with his second wife in a rural area outside Twin Lake, Michigan. **Tom Rubsam** and his wife own a painting and decorating center in his hometown of Newton, Illinois. **Phil Tolson** earned a business degree after the war. He married his high-school sweetheart and is now the father of two, holds a middle-management position with a book-distribution company, and lives in Clarks Summit, Pennsylvania.

Company C, 2-506th Infantry

Captain Wilcox left the service at the end of his five-year West Point obligation and worked as a large system marketing representative for IBM in New York City for four years before leaving to attend graduate school; he spent the next several years as a veterans activist in Seattle and San Francisco as he processed through a case of post-traumatic stress disorder (PTSD). He has been a real-estate broker since 1987 and lives with his wife in Saugatuck, Michigan. **Lieutenant Campbell** returned to law school after the war and, now the father of two grown children and a lawyer in the oil and gas business, lives with his wife in Shreveport, Louisiana. **Paul Burkey** owns the auto-body shop where he worked before the war; he lives with his wife and daughter in New Middleton, Ohio. **Frank Bort** is a child-welfare specialist with the Department of Children and Family Services in Chicago, Illinois. **Jerry Cafferty** married his fiancée after the war; they have three children, and he works for the post office in New Haven, Connecticut. **Steve Manthei** was divorced after the war and lost his job at General Motors because of PTSD; pulled out of his downward slide by his daughter and his second wife, the father of two is now a security supervisor and lives in Janesville, Wisconsin. **Rodney Moore** married his girlfriend after the war; a letter carrier, he lives with his wife and five children in Clarksburg,

Massachusetts. **Jerry Moyer** got a job with the phone company after the war; he and his wife, whom he married before the war, live in Springfield, Missouri. **Mike Mueller** was married and divorced after the war; a full-time member of the Alaska National Guard, he was medically retired as an E6 in 1985 because of spinal cancer. Now disabled, he lives in Wasilla, Alaska. **Bob Smoker**, married and the father of four, is the associate pastor of his church and a tool-and-die maker in Red Lion, Pennsylvania. **Gary Steele** works for the U. S. Bureau of Engraving and lives with his wife and two daughters in Upper Marlboro, Maryland. **Mike Womack** got married and divorced after the war; he is now the chief of police of Forsyth, Missouri.

Company D, 2-506th Infantry

Captain Rollison retired as a lieutenant colonel; married and the father of two grown children, he is a safety engineer in Eagle River, Alaska. **Lieutenant Flaherty** resigned his commission in 1982 (he was then a major) when his daughter came down with melanoma and his family needed more of his time than a military career allowed him to give; he now owns and operates a lens-manufacturing business and lives with his wife and three children in Norwood, Massachusetts. **Lieutenant McCall** left the active-duty army in 1971 at his wife's insistence and returned to college to finish his degree; he commanded an engineer battalion before retiring from the National Guard as a lieutenant colonel and is now a narcotics intelligence agent with the Louisiana State Police. **Bruce McCorkle** earned a marketing degree after the war; now a sales manager with a publishing company, he lives with his wife and two children in Hudson, Ohio. **Gary Radford**, married and the father of two, is a truck driver in Pittsburgh, Pennsylvania; ever loyal to his troops, he flew to Ripcord in 1996 aboard a Soviet-built Mi-17 helicopter flown by a Vietnamese pilot, then hiked with a U. S. MIA recovery team to Hill 1000, where he buried the copper MIA bracelets bearing the names of Charles Beals and Lewis Howard. **George Strasburg,** divorced after the war, went back to school and, now remarried with two children, is director of quality control for a manufacturing company; he lives in Dexter, Michigan.

Company E, 2-506th Infantry

Robert Granberry, married three times, is a helicopter mechanic at the Marine air base at Cherry Point, North Carolina. **John Mihalko**, a warehouse worker, lives with his wife and two children in Lakewood, Colorado. **John Schnarr** completed his degree in marketing after the war and, now a regional sales manager for a mining equipment and construction machinery company, lives with his wife and two sons in Evansville, Indiana.

2d Battalion, 501st Infantry

Lieutenant Colonel Livingston retired a colonel and, now a widower, lives in Florence, South Carolina. **Captain Goates** was medically discharged with an 80 percent disability due to his wounds; married before the war, he is the father of three grown children, owns a construction business, and, having earned Master of Divinity and Doctor of Ministry degrees from Southwestern Baptist Theological Seminary, is pastor of a small church in Fort Worth, Texas. **Captain Straub** retired a lieutenant colonel; married after the war, he is now the father of three and chief of staff for Sen. Bob Kerrey (D-NE). **Lieutenant Arndt** retired a major with twenty years of enlisted and commissioned service; now a computer engineer, he lives with his wife in Orem, Utah. **Lieutenant Potter**, who retired from the reserves as a lieutenant colonel, works as a civilian in the USAF Materiel Command; married after the war and the father of three grown children, he lives with his wife in Warner Robins, Georgia. **Lieutenant Kwiecien** divorced after the war; now a freelancer in the computer industry, he lives with his second wife in Manitou Springs, Colorado. **Lieutenant Selvaggi** operates two health clubs and lives with his wife and two daughters in Easton, Connecticut. **Dennis Belt** never fully recovered from his wounds and finally retired with a 50 percent VA disability from his job as a machinist; divorced, he lives with his sister in Rodeo, California. **Ray Blackman**, a tool-and-die maker, lives with his wife and four sons in Valparaiso, Nebraska. **Gary Fowler** is a sales rep for an industrial-pipe manufacturer and lives with his wife and children in Irmo, South Carolina. **Rod Soubers** returned to college after the war and, now an archivist with the National Archives and Records Administration, lives in Alexandria, Virginia.

Company D, 1-506th Infantry

Lieutenant Smith left the service in 1972, primarily to please his wife; they later divorced. Now remarried, he is office manager for a brick-manufacturing company in Stanton, Kentucky. **Lieutenant Thompson** fought forest fires after the war with the forest service in Arizona and was working for the park service in the Grand Canyon when he was killed by a falling boulder in 1996. **Merle Delagrange**, married before the war and the father of four boys, is a construction worker in St. Joe, Indiana. **Steve DeRoque** retired an E6; the divorced father of one, he is a truck driver and lives in Lafayette, Indiana. **Richard Drury**, also a truck driver, lives with his wife in Wayland, Michigan. **John Fraser** is a nonsworn officer in the Commercial Vehicle Enforcement Unit of the Maine State Police; he has a daughter in college and lives with his wife in Augusta, Maine. **Terry Handley** is a partner in an injection-molding company and a manufacturer's rep for a molding shop; divorced after the war, he lives with his second wife and children in Ada, Michigan. **K. C. James** works for DuPont Chemical in Nederland, Texas. **Walt Jurinen** is a forest ranger and lives with his wife and daughter in Munising, Michigan. **Jim McCoy** is a patrolman with the California Highway Patrol. **Gib Rossetter**, married and the father of two, is an orthopedic physician assistant in North Platte, Nebraska. **Elger Sneed** returned to his job in a manufacturing plant after the war and lives with his wife and two sons in Goshen, Ohio. **Jerry Wise**, married before the war, recently divorced, and the father of one, is the postmaster in Richland, Missouri.

Division Artillery

Lieutenant Colonel Walker, now a business executive, lives with his wife in Colorado Springs, Colorado. **Captain**

Austin was medically retired from the army in 1971 due to the wounds he received on Ripcord; he now works for the Defense Contract Audit Agency and lives with his wife and two daughters in Atlanta, Georgia. **Captain Caldwell** was divorced after the war and left the army due to the 1972 reduction in force; remarried, he owns five apartment complexes in Lawton, Oklahoma. **Captain Michaud** retired a colonel and lives with his wife in Saint Agatha, Maine. **Lieutenant Wintermute** married his fiancée after the war; a retired lieutenant colonel and the father of three, he is now a bank executive in Las Vegas, Nevada. **Alfred Martin** is a truck driver and lives with his wife and two sons in Beaver Falls, Pennsylvania. **Dennis Murphy** works for Caterpillar, Inc., and lives with his wife in Newark, Illinois. **Frank Parko** went through two marriages while working through his PTSD; now employed by a tool and engineering company, he lives with his third wife in St. Louis, Missouri.

Division Aviation

Captain House extended his tour six months after a year of combat flying to command a rifle company (C/2-506th) and was twice wounded on the DMZ during Operation Lam Son 719; he commanded a brigade of the 1st Cavalry Division during Operation Desert Storm (earning a Silver Star) and is presently a lieutenant general on active duty. **Lieutenant Anderson** retired from the reserves as a lieutenant colonel; now the head of human resources for a worldwide manufacturing company, he lives with his wife in Wausau, Wisconsin. **Lieutenant Caballero** retired as a lieutenant colonel and lives with his wife and son in Anderson, California. **Lieutenant Rosen** is now a doctor and lives with his wife in San Antonio, Texas. **Lieutenant Schwartz** retired a major and, now the owner and manager of a llama farm, lives with his wife in Rochester, Washington. WO1 **Barrowcliff** is an equipment specialist in the research division of an electronics company and lives with his wife in Vancouver, Washington. WO1 **Mayberry** flew with the National Guard until retiring due to multiple sclerosis; he lives with his wife and two children in York, Nebraska. **Tom Chase** is a senior quality engineer for an aerospace company and lives with his wife and children in Brunswick, Ohio. **Chuck Holmen** works for the railroad and lives with his wife and two children in Eau Claire, Wisconsin. **Terry Stanger** now works in New York City selling Russian aluminum in North America and lives with his wife and son in Griffith, Indiana.

Other

Chris Jensen finished college after the war and is now a reporter with *The Plain Dealer* in Lakewood, Ohio. **Bob Lynch** retired a master sergeant and went on to earn his bachelor's, master's, and doctorate degrees; he is a mechanical engineering technician with the U. S. Army Research Laboratory in Adelphi, Maryland. The father of three, he lives with his wife in Hanover, Maryland.

Note: Though only a few were willing to admit to it in print, many of the veterans on these pages were affected or are still affected to some degree by the symptoms associated with PTSD. The great majority have been able to get on with life regardless. A small number have yet to come to terms with their experiences in Vietnam. It is also worth noting that more than a few of these veterans agreed only reluctantly to talk to me about Ripcord; the majority of veterans to whom I wrote never responded to my request to be interviewed.

Notes

Chapter 3

1. Troops from the 1-506th and 2-506th were called Currahees. A Cherokee word meaning "stand alone," Currahee had been the official nickname of the 506th Parachute Infantry Regiment, 101st Airborne Division, during World War II.

2. Captain Charles R. Lieb, the battalion air operations officer (S3 Air), led the relief force that helicoptered from Ripcord to Hill 902 at first light on July 2, 1970. The mission was personal for Lieb, a former platoon leader in C/2-506th; when one of the SSI team members subsequently "told us that they had known the attack was coming, several of us got quite upset," recalled the husky West Point football player. "We had some discussions with them about the need for immediate information at the local level. After that, they began bending the rules and telling us quite a bit more about what they were reporting back through their channels."

Chapter 4

1. The lieutenant eventually recovered enough to get on the radio with Lucas and Koenigsbauer in the TOC on Ripcord. "The information he could pass to us was limited, but just by whispering over the radio, the FO was endangering his life by giving his position away," recalled Koenigsbauer. Credited with taking command of the company and directing a counterattack,

the FO was subsequently awarded the Silver Star. The citation was fraudulent. "Talking on the radio was a brave act," wrote Koenigsbauer, "but both Lucas and I failed when we tried to motivate the lieutenant to action. We wanted him to adjust the supporting fires and to show some leadership and coordinate a defense. In response, he would repeat that he was injured—I believe he had lost a finger and had minor shrapnel wounds—and that he was unable to move without being killed."

Chapter 6

1. Major Law, Captain Williams, and Lieutenant Darling were all awarded Silver Stars for the April Fools' Day Assault. Darling was subsequently killed when the log bird taking him from Ripcord to Camp Evans was shot down on May 18, 1970.

2. If that was not the plan, then the 101st was simply and reflexively going after the enemy where it would hurt him most when it targeted Ripcord and Co Pung Mountain, however overreaching the plan seems in light of Vietnamization. Interestingly, when the NVA besieged the ARVN at FSB O'Reilly in August 1970, an impolitic division staff officer wrote in an after-action report that "since the massing of enemy forces presented numerous targets which were vulnerable to allied fire support systems, the decision was made to maintain the fire base and exploit the massed enemy."

Chapter 7

1. Colonel Bradley had seemed a natural for general officer. To the dismay of his staff, the best brigade commander in the division instead retired shortly after his Vietnam tour, such was the damning effect of the fitness report he received from General Hennessey in the aftermath of the attack on FSB Henderson.

2. Unable to cope with what he had gone through, Kays turned to drugs, was committed to his state mental institution, and committed suicide in 1991.

Chapter 8

1. Following the battle for Dong Ap Bia, Zais was promoted to lieutenant general and given command of XXIV Corps in

Da Nang. Zais repeatedly postponed Operation Chicago Peak as too risky; the operation had still not been launched when Zais turned over his command to Lt. Gen. James W. Sutherland in June 1970.

Chapter 9

1. The award was presented nonetheless, given the bureaucratic efficiency of the battalion personnel officer who saw Lucas's name in the battalion surgeon's log. Lucas was visibly embarrassed when Colonel Harrison, the brigade commander, pinned the Purple Heart on him at FSB Ripcord.

2. For the record, Livingston had no problem with Goates. It should also be noted that Goates was wounded in action four times, once during his tour as an ARVN advisor, again during a mortar attack at FSB Granite on May 1, 1970, while serving as Livingston's S2, and twice more as CO of A/2-501st. In addition to the injury he suffered on July 7, Goates was seriously wounded on August 27, 1970, when, armed with only a pistol, he pursued an enemy soldier he had spotted, only to be shot with an AK-47 from a concealed position under a berm. Goates was awarded the Silver Star for his one-man charge, but the gunshot wound was so serious that it resulted in a medical retirement, prematurely ending his career in the U. S. Army.

Chapter 12

1. Gary Radford, unable to forgive himself for not bringing back all of his men, alive or dead, never felt that he deserved the Bronze Star he was awarded for Hill 1000. "There were a lot of brave guys up there," he reflected. "I didn't do anything more than what a platoon sergeant was supposed to do, and not even that."

2. What happened to Beals and Howard tormented Radford for years. "In 1988, I finally got up enough courage to look the families up," he said. He was especially anxious to talk with the family of his friend Lewis Howard. "Because of the racial thing, I wanted them to know that he was with people that cared, that he wasn't just left out there because he was black and most of us were white."

Chapter 16

1. The dead man was the younger brother of future film star Chuck Norris.

Chapter 19

1. The enemy's effective antiaircraft fire had an intimidating effect, as noted by Lieutenant Case, who spent a week as an aerial observer with a scout detachment before being tapped to serve as the acting brigade arty LNO. "On my first day as an aerial observer," wrote Case, "I was picked up from a landing pad at Camp Evans, and we circled Ripcord for most of the morning. About midday, we returned to Evans, where I switched helicopters and circled Ripcord most of the afternoon. I could not coax the pilot of either LOH down to altitudes where I might have actually spotted the mortar and antiaircraft emplacements we were supposedly looking for. They both flew at such high altitudes to avoid the antiaircraft fire and stay out of the way of fast-movers on bombing runs that we practically needed oxygen masks. On the second day, I wore a field jacket to keep from freezing to death. I had previously thought of the scout pilots as suicidal maniacs with huge death wishes, and was surprised, and secretly relieved, that they refused to fly at treetop level. I know this doesn't square with the heroism displayed by pilots during medevac and extraction missions during the Ripcord battle, but perhaps that is because there was a greater sense of urgency during such missions. As it was, there was so much ordnance hitting the ridges around Ripcord, and the sky was so full of fighter-bombers, that we felt as inconsequential as a gnat in our LOH."

Chapter 20

1. When correspondent Arthur Hadley visited the 101st in the fall of 1970, a battalion commander produced an index card from his pocket and handed it to him with the comment, "These are what guide my life." On the card was typed the exact number of M16, M60, and 40mm rounds, plus claymore mines and 81mm shells, that the colonel's battalion was allowed to fire each month, in addition to the amount of artillery fire it was allowed to request. "The colonel carries on another

card the number of hours each day he can fly the various helicopters assigned to him," wrote Hadley. "This limitation, called the blade-hour limitation and used throughout Vietnam, is the most rigid cost-control tool of the war. This year, helicopters will fly roughly one-sixth the hours they did last year. . . . U. S. participation is not just winding down. It is flooding toward the close. . . ."

Chapter 21

1. Every crewman in B/2-319th Field Artillery was awarded a BSMv or an ARCOMv, that is, the Bronze Star or the Army Commendation Medal for Valor. At least one man, Sgt. Robert L. Dunner, won the Silver Star: "When a round impacted in the parapet of Sergeant Dunner's position and wounded three members of his section, he carried the wounded men to a sheltered area to await medical assistance. Maneuvering back to his gun, he single-handedly delivered an intense volume of suppressive fire which was instrumental in destroying two enemy positions."

2. First Lieutenant Gabino J. "Joe" Caballero was platoon leader of the pathfinder teams rotating on and off FSB Ripcord; he recalled that the colonel commanding the 101st Aviation Group "tried to pin the donkey's tail on the team that was up there for the CH47 that was shot down on July 18th. I'm a mustanger, so I wasn't about to roll over. I still had that NCO blood in me. I told my boss, the aviation group operations officer, that he'd better go to the group commander and tell him that I demanded an Article 32 investigation, the whole nine yards, before they tried to pin any tail on my people. My pathfinders had nothing to do with controlling that aircraft. Lucas was the one who diverted that CH47 to the artillery ASP. The next thing I knew, the heat was off. The crash was just written off as a 'Combat Loss.' "

Chapter 23

1. Private First Class John Chamless offered not only a different perspective on Workman but also an insight into the doubts that many of the troops had about the cause they served. He wrote of his conversation with SSgt. Michael Saunders on

the eve of the man's DEROS out of Vietnam: ". . . I shared a foxhole with Mike as we stood bunker guard at the basecamp one night. He surprised me. 'I don't plan to stay in the United States,' he said. 'I'm going back to finish school, but then I intend to get a job in a country like Sweden. I can't see raising children and then letting them be placed in a situation like this. The country has gone crazy.' This wasn't a radical speaking. Mike was . . . drafted and sent to Vietnam as a private. He was promoted until he attained the rank of staff sergeant[,] then was offered a field commission. He turned the commision down because becoming an officer would mean spending an additional year in the army. 'Even Ranger scares me,' he confided. 'He is concerned with protecting his troops, but he also loves to kill. Haven't you ever noticed him talking about how he loves to kill gooks? He doesn't consider them human. I can't stay in a country that fosters that. . . .' "

2. Captain Workman might very well have volunteered for the mission, although his doing so would have been superfluous. When the 1-506th was instructed to detach a company to the 2-506th, it was only logical to send Company D: It was commanded by the most experienced company commander in the battalion and, after a month's refitting on Kathryn, was in better shape than the other companies for heavy combat. Smith noted that "Ranger was getting a little antsy to get our company off the firebase and back into the jungle. He was afraid we were losing our sharpness."

3. The NVA wanted to bring down a helicopter to block the LZ and trap D/1-506th. That the helicopter happened to be an unarmed medevac, noted Handley, "just meant that they had a big red cross to use as a bull's-eye."

Chapter 24

1. Although the A/2-506th interpreter did report that there was one mortar and three infantry regiments in the area, much of this force, if the intelligence from the wiretap was indeed accurate, must have been held in reserve during the battle, perhaps in anticipation of a massive ground attack on Ripcord. There had otherwise been no big-unit engagements around Ripcord; even the actions at Hill 805 and Hill 1000 had in-

volved enemy platoons and companies, not massed battalions and regiments. At the time of the wiretap, other available intelligence indicated that U. S. units in the Ripcord AO had been actively engaged by two NVA infantry battalions supported by a mortar battalion and transportation battalion; these elements were controlled and reinforced by the two regimental headquarters, each the size of an extra infantry battalion, that had also moved into the area, the 6th in the vicinity of Hill 902, the 803d on Hill 975. The regimental headquarters were controlled in turn, according to the wiretap, by the headquarters of the F-5 Division, which was believed to be located somewhere around Hill 902 or Coc Muen Mountain.

When Harrison was awarded the Silver Star, he was cited for fighting his brigade against six enemy battalions at Ripcord. Enemy units being smaller than their U. S. counterparts, an estimated 2,300 NVA had participated in the battle, according to a recommendation that the 101st prepared for a Valorous Unit Award. Perhaps because such a figure does not adequately convey the advantages the enemy enjoyed—the cover and concealment provided by the terrain and bunker complexes virtually immune to artillery and air strikes—Berry and Harrison have tended to cite the wiretap intelligence without qualification when discussing enemy troop strength at Ripcord. That the enemy had brought a division to the battle became an accepted fact among Ripcord veterans when Berry stated at a reunion, "There were for sure three, and probably four regiments. . . . So let's say there were nine to twelve thousand [enemy soldiers besieging Ripcord]."

Chapter 26

1. The four pathfinders who controlled the evacuation—Caballero, Williams, Howton, and Kohr—were all awarded Silver Stars. The article on General Berry in *Life* magazine included a photograph of the acting division commander decorating Williams in his hospital bed at the 85th Evac, Phu Bai.

Bibliography

Sources

I have wanted to write about what happened at Ripcord since first learning of the battle in 1984 while researching *Into Laos,* a book about Operation Lam Son 719. I held off because of two related works in progress, one a memoir by Chuck Hawkins, the other a historical analysis of the battle by James Fairhall, Ph.D., a former infantryman in the 101st, 1970–71. Family and financial responsibilities prevented Hawkins and Fairhall from finishing their works in a timely fashion. I had few such responsibilities of my own at the time, and Hawkins, who had helped me with *Into Laos,* finally encouraged me to go ahead and write my own account of Ripcord in 1996. For his part, Fairhall graciously provided me access to his files; of particular value were a series of interviews he had conducted with veterans of D/2-501st.

I started doing my own interviews in early 1997, starting with members of the Ripcord Association, a veterans group that publishes a newsletter *(Ripcord Report)* and organizes yearly reunions. The first *Ripcord Report* was put together by Chip Collins in 1983; at that time, Collins had only three other Ripcord vets on his mailing list. By 1999, the organization had almost four hundred members.

Hawkins succeeded Collins as editor of *Ripcord Report* in 1990. Veterans of the battle previously unaware of the Ripcord

Association can join by writing Fred Spaulding at 7702 White Dove Drive, Indianapolis, Indiana 46256-1750.

In addition to the assistance provided by Hawkins and Fairhall, I received an invaluable boost from Stan Sirmans, a retired navy officer and Vietnam veteran, who tied together many loose ends for me at the National Archives as I was finishing the manuscript in 1999. Because Sirmans lives near the archives and I do not, he poured over unit journals to help solve the mystery of when and how the body left behind on Ripcord during the evacuation was recovered. Sirmans also searched out friendly-fire incident reports and, most incredibly, culled through thousands upon thousands of award citations in the 101st's general-orders files, finding and photocopying approximately five hundred that were related to Ripcord. Thanks to the various white-pages services on the Internet, those citations led me to many Ripcord heroes who were not on the Ripcord Association mailing list.

I have never encountered a Vietnam battle as dramatic, tragic, convoluted, and bewildering as Ripcord; in retrospect, I'm glad that I was forced to wait more than a decade to write about it. It was only through the books I wrote in the interim that I acquired the literary seasoning needed to even attempt to do justice to the Ripcord story.

Books

Atkinson, Rick. *The Long Gray Line: The American Journey of West Point's Class of 1966.* Boston: Houghton Mifflin Company, 1989.

Del Vecchio, John M. *The 13th Valley.* New York: Bantam Books, 1982.

Hauser, Lt. Col. William L. *America's Army in Crisis: A Study in Civil-Military Relations.* Baltimore: The John Hopkins University Press, 1973.

Palmer, Laura. *Shrapnel in the Heart: Letters and Remembrances from the Vietnam Veterans Memorial.* New York: Random House, 1987.

Zaffiri, Samuel. *Hamburger Hill: May 11–20, 1969.* Novato, Calif.: Presidio Press, 1988.

Periodicals

Chamless, John. "Vietnam Was Never in the Past." *The Dallas Morning News,* March 15, 1996, 6J.

Coffey, Raymond R. "Story of GI Retreat a 'Classic Cover-Up.'" *Chicago Daily News,* July 25–26, 1970, 2.

Collins, Chip. "The April Fools." *Ripcord Report,* May 1986, no page numbers.

———. "From Ripcord to Recon." *Ripcord Report,* June 1990, 9–15.

———. "Shag." *Ripcord Report,* January 1986, no page numbers.

Harrison, Maj. Gen. Benjamin F., Ret. "The Fire Base Ripcord Siege as Seen by the Brigade Commander." *Ripcord Report,* November 1994, 1, 6–7.

Hawkins, Charles F. "Hell Night at Henderson." *VFW Magazine,* April 1996, 36–38.

———. "Rendezvous at Ripcord." *VFW Magazine,* June–July 1996, 24–27.

———. "Ripcord: A Charlie Oscar's View." *Ripcord Report,* August 1990, 10–15.

Hirst, Don. "The Battle of Ripcord." *The Overseas Weekly-Pacific Edition,* August 29, 1970, 6.

Lapham, Lewis H. "Case Study of an Army Star." *Life,* September 25, 1970, 54–68.

Linden, Eugene. "Fragging and Other Withdrawal Symptoms: The Demoralization of an Army." *Saturday Review,* January 8, 1972, 12–17, 55.

Mihalko, John. "Back to the Mountains." *Ripcord Report,* July 1988, 5–9.

———. "Chops." *Ripcord Report,* September 1987, 16–19.

———. "Eagle Beach." *Ripcord Report,* January 1988, 8–13.

———. "The Ides of March." *Ripcord Report,* October 1987, 8–10.

———. "Into the Maelstrom." *Ripcord Report,* December 1987, 23–28.

———. "Massacre." *Ripcord Report,* January 1987, 4–5.

———. "Metamorphosis." *Ripcord Report,* March 1988, 11–14.

———. "Retrospective." *Ripcord Report,* December 1985, no page numbers.
———. "Retrospective." *Ripcord Report,* June 1986, no page numbers.
Mihalko, John, and Lt. Col. Jerry D. Rodgers. "Eagle Dustoff Remembered." *Ripcord Report,* September 1988, 9–16.
Rendezvous with Destiny (quarterly magazine of the 101st Airborne Division, Vietnam), 1969–71.
Saar, John. "You Can't Just Hand Out Orders: A Company Commander in Vietnam Confronts the New-Style Draftees." *Life,* October 23, 1970, 30–37.
Self, Sp5 Charles C. "The Last Few Hours at FSB Ripcord." *Pacific Stars & Stripes,* date unknown.
———. "Misplaced Bomb Saves Embattled Troopers." *Pacific Stars & Stripes,* date unknown.
Warsh, David. "The Evans Nine." *Newsweek,* June 29, 1970, 50.

Documents

The official history of the Battle for Firebase Ripcord, like that of all the U. S. Army's battles in Vietnam, resides in the manila file folders stored by the ton at the National Archives branch at College Park, Maryland; one of the staff archivists, Mr. Clifford L. Snyder, was instrumental in finding the relevant documents.

"Combat Operations After Action Report, Operation TEXAS STAR, 1 April 1970–5 September 1970 (U)" (prepared by the 101st Airborne Division).
"Daily Staff Journal or Duty Officer's Log: S2/3 Section[,] 1-327 Inf." May and June 1970.
"Daily Staff Journal or Duty Officer's Log: S2/3 Section[,] HQ[,] 2-502 Inf[,] 1st Bde[,] 101st Abn Div (Ambl)." July and August 1970.
"Daily Staff Journal or Duty Officer's Log: S2/S3, 3d Bde, 101st Abn Div." April, May, June, July, and August 1970.
"Daily Staff Journal or Duty Officer's Log: 2/17 Cav, 101st Abn Div." July, August, and September 1970.
"Daily Staff Journal or Duty Officer's Log: TOC[,] 2d Bn

(Ambl)[,] 506th Inf." February, March, April, May, June, and July 1970.

"DEPARTMENT OF THE ARMY, Headquarters[,] 2d Battalion (Airmobile)[,] 506th Infantry, APO San Francisco 96383, AVDG-CC-C, 15 August 1970: Extraction from FSB RIPCORD, 23 July 1970."

"DEPARTMENT OF THE ARMY, Headquarters, 3d Brigade, 101st Airborne Division (Airmobile), APO San Francisco 96383: Combat After Action Interview Report (U), 22 May 1970" (regarding the May 6, 1970, attack on FSB Henderson).

"HEADQUARTERS 101ST AIRBORNE DIVISION (AIRMOBILE), Office of the Chief of Staff: After Action Report, FS/OB [Fire Support/Observation Base] Ripcord (U), 1 September 1970."

"HEADQUARTERS 101ST AIRBORNE DIVISION (AIRMOBILE), Office of the Commanding General: Senior Officer's Debriefing Report, 15 January 1971" (prepared by Maj. Gen. John J. Hennessey).

"MACJ3-06[,] 18 July 1970[,] SUBJECT: Artillery Ammunition Expenditures (U)" (message from USARV to XXIV Corps, I Field Force Vietnam, and II Field Force Vietnam).

"Operational Report—Lessons Learned, 101st Airborne Division (Airmobile) Period Ending 30 April 1970, RCS CSFOR-65 (R2) (U)."

"Operational Report—Lessons Learned, 101st Airborne Division (Airmobile) Period Ending 31 July 1970, RCS CSFOR-65 (R2) (U)."

"Operational Report—Lessons Learned, 101st Airborne Division (Airmobile), Period Ending 31 October 1970, RCS CSFOR-65 (R2) (U)."

"Report of Inquiry Concerning Alleged Simple Assault, Possible Racial Tension in the 1st Battalion (Airmobile), 501st Infantry, T[h]ua Thien Province, RVN APO 96383[,] 26 September 1970" (prepared by the Inspector General, 101st Airborne Division).

"Unit History, March, 71" (prepared by Capt. Charles F. Hawkins, S1, 2-506th Infantry).

Untitled award recommendation files, with witness statements and proposed citations, prepared by the 101st Airborne Division for Lt. Col. Andre C. Lucas (Medal of Honor), Lt Col. Charles J. Shay (Distinguished Flying Cross), Maj James E. King (Silver Star and Distinguished Flying Cross) Capt. David F. Rich (Distinguished Service Cross), Sgt. John W. Kreckel (Distinguished Service Cross), Sp4 Brent R. Law (Silver Star), Pfc. Frank R. Fratellenico (Medal of Honor), and the 101st Aviation Group (Valorous Unit Award).

Untitled friendly-fire investigation files, with witness statements and disciplinary recommendations, prepared by the 101st Airborne Division regarding the cases of D/2-506th (strafed by C/2-17th Cav, April 8, 1970); D/1-506th (shelled by A/2-11th FA, May 19, 1970); D/1-327th (hit by air strike, June 7, 1970); A/2-501st (fired on by element from same unit, July 5, 1970); and A/2-501st (strafed by C/4-77th ARA, July 14, 1970).

Untitled missing-in-action investigation files, with witness statements, prepared by the 101st Airborne Division, regarding the cases of Sp4 Lewis Howard (D/2-506th; MIA, July 7, 1970) and Pfc. Ronald J. Kuntz (pseudonym) (D/1-506th; MIA, July 21, 1970).

Interviews

Most interviews were conducted by letter and phone, a handful in person. Quotes from the interviews were often edited for clarity and conciseness; everyone involved had the opportunity to review the book manuscript for accuracy before publication. The following veterans, divided by unit, participated in the interviews:

USARV and 101st Airborne Division: Gen. Paul F Gorman (Ret.), Gen. William B. Rosson (Ret.), Lt. Gen. Sidney B. Berry (Ret.), Lt. Gen. Charles W. Dyke (Ret.), Lt Gen. David E. Grange (Ret.), Lt. Gen. John M. Wright (Ret.) Col. Charles A. Hoenstine (Ret.), Col. Charles J. Shay (Ret.) Col. Walter H. Root (Ret.), Maj. John R. Fox (Ret.), ex-Sgt James T. Bannon, ex-Sgt. Robert Hageman.

3d Brigade, 101st Airborne Division: Maj. Gen. Benjamin L. Harrison (Ret.), Col. William J. Bradley (Ret.), Col. Rober

A. Turner (Ret.), Lt. Col. Fredrick L. Spaulding (Ret.), ex–1st Lt. William B. Case, ex-CW2 Steven M. Wandland, Sgt. Maj. Lloyd J. Rahlf (Ret.), ex-Sp4 Gary D. Jestes.

2d Battalion, 501st Infantry: Col. Otis W. Livingston (Ret.), Lt. Col. Christopher C. Straub (Ret.), Lt. Col. James M. Potter, USAR (Ret.), Maj. Victor E. Arndt (Ret.), ex-Capt. Donald R. Goates, ex-Capt. James W. Kwiecien, ex–1st Lt. Ralph L. Selvaggi, 1st Sgt. John T. Schuelke (Ret.), ex-Sgt. Raymond H. Blackman, ex-Sgt. James A. Plenderleith, ex-Sp4 Dennis W. Belt, ex-Sp4 Gary L. Fowler, ex-Sp4 Clement A. Neiderer, ex-Sp4 Richard R. Soubers.

1st Battalion, 506th Infantry: Maj. Gen. Bobby B. Porter (Ret.), ex-Capt. John H. Smith, SSgt. Steve W. DeRoque (Ret.), ex-SSgt. John W. Fraser, ex-Sgt. Terry W. Handley, ex-Sgt. Paul Mueller, ex-Sgt. Gilbert Rossetter, ex-Sgt. Elger Sneed, ex-Sgt. Michael Thomas, ex-Sgt. Robert J. Wise, ex-Sp5 Richard Daniels, ex-Sp4 Roger L. Black, ex-Sp4 John Chamless, ex-Sp4 Merle Delagrange, ex-Sp4 Richard P. Doyle, ex-Sp4 Richard E. Drury, ex-Sp4 Richard Finley, ex-Sp4 Kay C. James, ex-Sp4 Walter M. Jurinen, ex-Sp4 James G. McCoy.

2d Battalion, 506th Infantry: Col. Herbert E. Koenigsbauer (Ret.), Col. James P. Noll, USAR, Lt. Col. Leroy Fox, USAR (Ret.), Lt. Col. James R. McCall, USAR (Ret.), Lt. Col. Rembert G. Rollison (Ret.), Maj. Charles F. Hawkins, USAR (Ret.), Maj. William J. Williams (Ret.), ex-Maj. John A. Flaherty, ex-Maj. Charles R. Lieb, Capt. Benjamin F. Peters (Ret.), ex-Capt. James D. Harris, ex-Capt. Raymond A. Williams, ex-Capt. Jeffrey D. Wilcox, ex–1st Lt. Henry J. Bialosuknia, ex–1st Lt. James H. Campbell, ex–1st Lt. Stephen C. Wallace, ex–1st Lt. Gary L. Watrous, ex–1st Lt. Lee E. Widjeskog, CW3 Wayne L. Hoesing (Ret.), Cmd. Sgt. Maj. James A. Williamson (Ret.), SSgt. Michael K. Mueller, Alaska National Guard (Ret.), ex-SSgt. Paul E. Burkey, ex-SSgt. Gary A. Radford, ex-SSgt. Thomas E. Rubsam, ex-SSgt. George K. Strasburg, ex-SSgt. Raymond M. Womack, ex-Sgt. Lin L. Bashford, ex-Sgt. Frank Bort, ex-Sgt. Robert O. Granberry, ex-Sgt. Keith L. Harold, ex-Sgt. Robert L. Judd, ex-Sgt. Bruce W. McCorkle, ex-Sgt. Rodney G. Moore, ex-Sgt. Jerry D. Moyer, ex-Sgt. Jon E. Penfold, ex-Sgt. Frederick Rearick, ex-Sgt.

Robert C. Smoker, ex-Sgt. Daniel C. Thompson, ex-Sgt. Thomas P. Tolson, ex-Sp4 Gerald A. Cafferty, ex-Sp4 Donald E. Colbert, ex-Sp4 Rodger D. Collins, ex-Sp4 Christopher Garrett, ex-Sp4 Martin J. Glennon, ex-Sp4 William W. Heath, ex-Sp4 Rick T. Isom, ex-Sp4 Richard G. Ives, ex-Sp4 Patrick E. McCloskey, ex-Sp4 Stephen L. Manthei, ex-Sp4 Frank W. Marshall, ex-Sp4 John Mihalko, ex-Sp4 James D. Neff, ex-Sp4 John A. Schnarr, ex-Sp4 Gary A. Steele.

Division Artillery: Col. Philip L. Michaud (Ret.), Lt. Col. Sheldon C. Wintermute (Ret.), Lt. Col. William A. Walker (Ret.), ex-Capt. Thomas M. Austin, ex-Capt. Alton J. Caldwell, ex-Sgt. Marc L. Aronson, ex-Sgt. Daniel F. Esposito, ex-Sgt. Alfred L. Martin, ex-Sgt. Frank J. Parko, ex-Sp4 George D. Murphy, ex-Sp4 Norman L. Simmons, ex-Pfc. John P. Jones.

Division Aviation: Lt. Gen. Randolph House, Col. Jerry D. Rodgers (Ret.), Lt. Col. Michael D. Anderson, USAR (Ret.), Lt. Col. Gabino J. Caballero (Ret.), Lt. Col. Michael S. Lancaster (Ret.), Lt. Col. Ronald W. Rankin (Ret.), Maj. Allen Schwartz (Ret.), ex–1st Lt. Laurence Rosen, ex-CW2 Robert A. Barrowcliff, ex-CW2 Kenneth L. Mayberry, ex-CW2 Leslie R. Rush, ex-CW2 Rich Walker, ex-SSgt. Terry A. Stanger, ex-Sp5 Thomas J. Chase, ex-Sp4 H. Charles Berger, ex-Sp4 Nicholas A. Fotias, ex-Sp4 Charles L. Holmen.

Other Units: Col. Fred H. Edwards (Ret.), Col. Steven R. Rader (Ret.); MSgt. Robert J. Lynch (Ret.), ex-Sp5 Charles C. Self, ex-Sp5 Christopher W. Jensen, ex-Sp5 Gregory L. Kiekintveld, ex-Sp4 Ted McCormick, ex-Sp4 Michael Kelley.

Family Members: Mrs. Laurence J. Law (widow of Col. Laurence J. Law, (Ret.), who died of natural causes in 1996); Mrs. Karin J. Loke (sister of Capt. Donald R. Workman, killed at Ripcord); Mrs. Agnes M. Kohr (mother of Pfc. William H. Kohr, who was killed in an auto accident in 1979); Mrs. Madeleine M. Lucas (widow of Lt. Col. Andre C. Lucas, killed at Ripcord); Cmdr. John W. Palm, USN (Ret.) (father of 1st Lt. Terry A. Palm, killed at Ripcord, and author of an invaluable and heart-wrenching document, "Return to Ripcord-805," prepared in 1976 based on his interviews with veterans of D/2-501st).

Index

Look for this remarkable memoir of small-unit leadership and the coming of age of a young soldier in Vietnam

PLATOON LEADER

A Memoir of Command in Combat

by James R. McDonough

"Using a lean style and a sense of pacing drawn from the tautest of novels, McDonough has produced a gripping account of first command. . . . Rather than present a potpourri of combat yarns . . . McDonough has focused a seasoned storyteller's eye on the details, people, and incidents that best communicate a visceral feel of command under fire. . . . For the author's honesty and literary craftsmanship, *Platoon Leader* seems destined to be read for a long time be second lieutenants trying to prepare for the future, veterans trying to remember the past, and civilians trying to understand what the profession of arms is all about."

—*Army Times*

P.O. 0005158353 202